HERB
GARDNER
THE COLLECTED PLAYS

HERB GARDNER

THE COLLECTED PLAYS

AND THE SCREENPLAY

WHO IS HARRY KELLERMAN AND WHY IS HE SAYING THOSE TERRIBLE THINGS ABOUT ME?

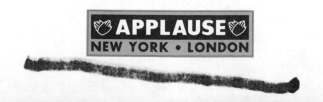
APPLAUSE
NEW YORK • LONDON

An APPLAUSE Original

HERB GARDNER: THE COLLECTED PLAYS and the screenplay
Who Is Harry Kellerman and Why Is He Saying Those Terrible Things About Me?

© 2000 Herb Gardner

Library of Congress Cataloging-in-Publication Data

Library of Congress Card Number: 00-100721

British Library Cataloging-in-Publication Data

A catalogue record for this book is available from the British Library.

Applause Books	Combined Book Services
1841 Broadway # 1100	Units I/K Paddock Wood Distribution Centre
New York, NY 10023	Paddock Wood, Tonbridge Kent TN12 6UU
Phone (212) 765-7880	Phone (44) 01892 837171
Fax: (212) 765-7875	Fax (44) 01892 837272

Printed in Canada

For My Friend, Shel

C O N T E N T S

PLAYS

SCREENPLAY

INTRODUCTION

IN this dream I always have I am sitting on the stage of the old Morosco Theatre wearing a tuxedo, writing the third act of a play. Unfortunately, it is the opening night of the play I'm writing, and the opening night audience is filing into the theatre. They come down the aisles and take their seats; I hear the familiar and expectant buzz of well-wishers and killers. I scratch away with dried-out felt-tipped pen on loose-leaf paper on a trembling card table, around me the crisp opening night air of Bar Mitzvah and execution. I wave to them. I offer a comforting smile. I am cordial; they are restless. I keep writing. I hold my free hand up from time to time as though to say "please wait, I'll be ready soon." The stage is littered with props, parts of costumes and pieces of sets. I look around for clues: there is a trampoline and a piece of a train, the outside motor of a forties icebox is strangely new and polished, a school desk and a U-Boat periscope, an abandoned sneaker lies on a witness stand, a five-string banjo and a Dodgers' cap, a battered phone booth; twenty-two clocks, all of them with a different time and all of them wrong, a straw hat, a derby, a steel safe with a doily and a bowl of flowers on it, the cabin of a ferris wheel, a rotting B.L.T. and a rocking chair. The objects stand in some order, ready for use. As always, I'm sure there is a pattern to this debris, and as always I don't know what it is. In the wings an ancient stage hand sits with half a pastrami sandwich, dozing; he awakens briefly, smiles at me, offers a wink of recognition and whispers the word "shmuck." He is my muse. He whispers the word again; I tell him that I am a playwright. There is always a confusion between us on this issue. Actors and actresses of various ages and in various shapes and sizes wait in positions around the stage, in doorways, at the top of stairways, one is behind the wheel of a taxi and another is mumbling under a trapdoor at my feet. "Please wait," I say, "I'll be ready soon." In the back of the theatre a white-haired man is speaking calmly into a walkie-talkie, arranging a lawsuit. He is the producer. "Please wait," I shout to him, "I'll be ready soon." I hold onto the card table and we shake together. I look down at the manuscript; it is entitled "Please Wait." I feel a strange mixture of terror and comfort, I am in that familiar, anxious place: a theatre. I am where I have always wanted to be, wondering what I will do there. A barefoot tap dancer with marvelous plans, a hopeful amnesiac waiting to remember. The conspiracy is clear and the dream is complete; the players, the playgoers and the playwright wait for the play.

THE editor of this volume, a hopeful and kindly fellow, has been waiting for this introduction for two months. I have offered him a series of deadlines, lies, promises and apologies which we have both decided to believe. How do I explain that I write plays, that I speak in the voices of other people because I don't know my own; that I write in the second person because I don't know the first; that I have been writing plays most of my adult life waiting to become both an adult and a playwright, and that it takes me so many years to write anything that I am forced to refer to myself during these periods as a playwrote? I have tried to write this introduction at desks, in taxis, on long plane rides; I have worked on it at thirty-thousand feet and in bathtubs; I have spoken it into tape-recorders and the ears of friends and loved ones. There are several problems: I can't seem to invent the character who says the lines; I am writing words that won't be spoken aloud and in a strange language, English — my first, last, and only language; and, most importantly, I cannot offer an explanation for why I wrote these plays because there is none. Playwriting is an irrational act. It is the Las Vegas of art forms, and the odds are terrible. A curious trade in which optimism, like any three-year-old's, is based on a lack of information, and integrity is based on the fact that by the time you decide to sell your soul no devil is interested. Your days are spent making up things that no one ever said to be spoken by people who do not exist for an audience that may not come. The most personal thoughts, arrived at in terrible privacy, are interpreted by strangers for a group of other strangers. The fear that no one will put your plays on is quickly replaced by the fear that someone will. It's hard to live with yourself and even harder for people to live with you: how do you ask a Kamikaze Pilot if his work is going well? The word "Playwright" looks terrible on passports, leases, and credit applications; and even worse in newspaper articles alternately titled "Where Did These Playwrights Go?" and "Why Don't These Playwrights Go Away?," usually appearing in what the New York Times whimsically refers to as The Leisure Section. The most difficult problem, of course, is that I love it.

God help me, I love it. Because it's alive. And because the theatre is alive, exactly what is terrible is wonderful, the gamble, the odds. There is no ceiling on the night and no floor either; there is a chance each time the curtain goes up of glory and disaster, the actors and the audience will take each other somewhere, neither knows where for sure. Alive, one time only, that night. It's alive, has been alive for a few thousand years, and is alive tonight, this afternoon. An audience knows it's the last place they can still be heard, they know the actors can hear them, they make a difference; it's not a movie projector and they are not at home with talking furniture, it's custom work. Why do playwrights, why do we outsiders and oddballs who so fear misunderstanding use a medium where we are most likely to be misunderstood? Because when this most private of enterprises goes public, and is responded to, we are not alone. Home is where you can tell your secrets. In a theatre, the ones in the dark and the ones under the lights need each other. For a few hours all of us, the audience, the actors, the writer, we are all a little more real together than we ever were apart. That's the ticket; and that's what the ticket's for.

Some words of advice about reading these plays. Sometimes I'm out in the street and I think of a character or a scene; on the way upstairs to my desk I lose fifty percent. While translating these captionless pictures into intelligible language I lose another twenty-five. A good actor can put back the seventy-five percent I lost on the way to my desk. So I ask you, for whatever might be good in these plays, read them like good actors; because a play on paper is only a code book, signals, notes for emotions, vague road maps for countries in constant border dispute, and nothing without you. Also, of course, none of these plays is finished; but please wait, I'll be ready soon.

— HERB GARDNER
NEW YORK CITY
JAN 2000

Plays

A THOUSAND CLOWNS

Sheldon Secunda

Sheldon Secunda

Top, Jason Robards and Sandy Dennis
Above, Barry Gordon, Robards and Dennis

A THOUSAND CLOWNS

The Palace Bar and Grill was right next door to the Hudson Theatre Stage Door on West 45th Street. It was a fast two-step from the drama of the theatre to the real drama of a watering hole for theatricals. Naturally, I found it whilst acting in a Lillian Hellman drama at the Hudson and, fortunately, a young dramatist named Herb Gardner found me there one night after a performance. We had never met before but nevertheless he entrusted me with his first play *A Thousand Clowns*. Of all the wonderful plays in this collection of his plays I feel it is his masterpiece. That feeling is not because I was in it for a year and also made a movie of it but because it is a real human comedy of poignancy and laughter with all of humanity's foibles and eccentricities. Sadly, it is also about the capturing of a free spirit which is a type of rara avis not seen about very often these days. But it is also about the love and understanding between a child and his parent figure and a chance for the child to "see all the wild possibilities, all the glorious maybes there are; and to know the subtle, sneaky, important reason why he was born a human being and not a chair." There is a great depth of love and understanding for all in this play. There are great life lessons to learn daily which I find myself still doing and oh, the laughter! For Herb Gardner to have written this play in his early twenties is a miracle which he has given to us all. He has gone on to write other miraculous plays and anyone reading this volume will come away blessed many times over. I have been blessed doing the play which enabled me to have a long and loving relationship with Herb for the last thirty-seven years. I'm twice blessed!

Which brings us back to the Palace Bar and Grill. Until it closed a few years ago, I went there often as a sort of a memorial to Herb and the play and all of the special and wonderful actors who became our family: Sandy Dennis, Barry Gordon, A. Larry Haines, Billy Daniels, Gene Saks and Murray Burns. I also went there just in case Herb came by with another masterpiece.

— JASON ROBARDS
Southport, Connecticut

A Thousand Clowns was first presented by Fred Coe and Arthur Cantor at the Eugene O'Neill Theatre, New York City, April 5, 1962, with the following cast:

(In order of appearance)

NICK BURNS . . . . .Barry Gordon

MURRAY BURNS . . . . .Jason Robards, Jr.

ALBERT AMUNDSON . . . . . . .William Daniels

SANDRA MARKOWITZ . . . . . .Sandy Dennis

ARNOLD BURNS . . . . .A. Larry Haines

LEO HERMAN . . . . .Gene Saks

Directed by Fred Coe
Scenery designed and lighted by George Jenkins
Costumes by Ruth Morley

ACT I:

Murray Burns' apartment, Manhattan, eight-thirty in the morning, early April, 1962.

ACT II

Scene 1: Murray Burns' apartment, eight o'clock the following morning.

Scene 2: Arnold Burns' office, later that afternoon.

Scene 3: Murray Burns' apartment, early that evening.

ACT III

Murray Burns' apartment, half an hour later.

ACT ONE

In complete darkness, before the curtain goes up, we hear the voice of CHUCKLES THE CHIPMUNK.

CHUCKLES' VOICE   *(Intimately, softly)*   Goshes and gollygoods, Kidderoonies; now what're all us Chippermunkies gonna play first this fine mornin'?

CHORUS OF KIDS   Gonna play Chuckle-Chip Dancing.

CHUCKLES' VOICE   And with who?

CHORUS OF KIDS   With you!

CHUCKLES' VOICE   *(Louder)*   And who is me?

CHORUS OF KIDS   *(Screaming)*   Chuckles the Chippermunkie! Rayyyyyyyyyy.

(The curtain goes up on this last screaming syllable, revealing MURRAY BURNS' *one room apartment. The voices of* CHUCKLES *and the* KIDS *continue but are now coming from an ancient table-model TV set at Left. The set is facing away from the audience and is being watched by* NICHOLAS BURNS, *a twelve-year-old who wears glasses. The apartment is on the second floor of a brownstone on the lower west side of Manhattan. It consists of one, large, high-ceilinged room in which borrowed furniture rambles in no meaningful arrangement, some gaudy, some impractical, no matching pieces. It is obvious from* MURRAY BURNS' *apartment that he is a collector, though it is not entirely clear just what he is a collector of. All about the room, on the floor, on the coffee-table, on dresser-tops, is* MURRAY'S *collection: eighteen broken radios, some with interesting cathedral-style cabinets; over two dozen elaborately disabled clocks of different sizes, some of them on the wall; parts of eight victrolas, mostly cabinets; a variety of hats including a Prussian helmet and a Deerstalker; a pirate pistol, a bugle, a megaphone, stacks of magazines and books; also several eagles, including one with its wings spread in flight at the top of the bed's very tall, ornately shelved headboard. It is somehow, though, a very comfortable-looking apartment. There is an alcove at Left, with a small bed, a child's desk and some bookshelves. This is* NICK'S *part of the place and it is very neat, ordered, organized, seeming almost to have nothing to do with the main room. There is a bathroom door at Left below the small alcove. Right of the alcove are three large windows and a built-in window seat. A closed venetian blind covers all three windows. Center Stage is a large comfortable rumpled bed and above it an elaborate wooden headboard running up the wall almost to the ceiling.*

The headboard is loaded with clocks, radios, various knick-knacks and two lamps. Up Center is the entrance door to the apartment. To the Left of the door are two large office-style filing cabinets in which MUR-RAY keeps some of his clothes and to the Right of the door is a bureau covered with clocks and other knick-knacks on which MURRAY'S vast array of hats are hung. Down right is the kitchen door and next to it a desk buried under papers, etc., and built-in bookshelves stuffed with a jumble of books, lamps, clocks and nonsense. There is a closet next to the desk. Beside the bed is an armless wicker chair loaded with maga-zines and a telephone. A Morris chair and an armless swivel chair on casters are on either side of a small table at Right, and there is a brightly colored beach chair in front of the windows.

AT RISE: It is eight-thirty on a Monday morning; it is rather dark, the only real light is a scattered haze from the television set. The CHORUS OF KIDS are now singing the Chuckles Song. NICK watches expressionlessly)

CHORUS OF KIDS: *(Singing)*

> "Who's whitcha at—eight-thirty
> Whose face is so—so dirty
> Who's sparky—who's spunky
> Chip, Chip, Chip, Chip—Chippermunkie."

NICK   *(Quietly)* Oh, this is terrible. This is rotten.

CHORUS OF KIDS

> "Who's always good—for funnin'
> Whose Scooter Bike—keeps runnin'"

(MURRAY enters from the kitchen carrying a cup of coffee; he is in his mid-thirties. He is wearing shorts and an undershirt and is not quite awake yet)

MURRAY   *(Walking across to bed)* Get those kids outa here. *(Sits on bed)* Nick, what'd I tell you about bringing your friends in here this early in the morning?

NICK   It's not my friends; it's the TV.

MURRAY   Play with your friends outside. Get those kids out of here. *(NICK turns set off. MURRAY looks over at front door, waves at it and shouts)* Good. And none of you kids come back here till this after-noon.

NICK   It wasn't my friends. It was Chuckles the Chipmunk.

MURRAY   *(Sleepily)* That's very comforting.

NICK   *(Brings cigarettes to* MURRAY*)* Boy, it's a terrible program now. It was a much better show when you were writing it.

MURRAY   When Sandburg and Faulkner quit, I quit. What kind of a day is it outside?

NICK   *(Going to kitchen)* It's a Monday.

MURRAY   I mean warm or cold or sunny is what I mean.

NICK   I haven't been outside yet.

MURRAY   *(He pulls the blind up revealing the window; there is no change whatever in the lighting, the room stays dark. They are windows with no view other than the gray blank wall of the building a few feet opposite)* Ah, light. *(He leans out of the window, cranes his head around to look up at the sky)* Can't see a thing. Not a thing. *(Pulls his head back in)* No matter what time of day or what season, we got a permanent fixture out there; twilight in February.

NICK   *(Bringing coffee-pot out of kitchen and filling* MURRAY'S *cup)* You better call the weather record like always.

MURRAY   One morning I'll wake up and that damn building'll have fallen down into Seventh Avenue so I can see the weather. *(Picks up phone, dialing)* Using a machine to call up another machine. I do not enjoy the company of ghosts. *(Into phone)* Hello, Weather-Lady! Well, I'm just fine, and how is your nasal little self this morning? What's the weather? Uh-huh. That high? And the wind, which way does the wind blow this morning? Ah, good. Uh-huh, all the way to East Point and Block Island. Humidity? Very decent. And tonight, what about—? Bundle up? Absolutely. Thanks. Whoops—there you go again. You simply *must* learn not to repeat yourself. I keep telling you every morning that once is enough. You'll never learn. *(Hangs up)* Women seldom sense when they have become boring. *(Goes to window again, leans out, raises his voice, shouting out of the window)* Neighbors; I have an announcement for you. I have *never seen* such a collection of dirty windows. Now I want to see you all out there on the fire-escape with your "Mr. Clean" bottles, and let's snap it up—

NICK   Gee, Murray, you gotta shout like that every morning?

MURRAY   Clears my head. *(After glancing about the clock-filled room)* What time is it?

NICK   It's eight-forty. *(Picks up tarnished brass flagpole fixture from end-table)* Another eagle?

MURRAY   Can't have too many eagles. Eight-forty—what're you doing here? Why aren't you in school?

NICK   It's a holiday. It's Irving R. Feldman's birthday, like you said.

MURRAY   Irving R. Feldman's birthday is my own personal national holiday. I did not open it up for the public. He is proprietor of perhaps the most distinguished kosher delicatessen in this neighborhood and as such I hold the day of his birth in reverence.

NICK   You said you weren't going to look for work today because it was Irving R. Feldman's birthday, so I figured I would celebrate too, a little.

MURRAY   Don't kid *me*, Nick, you know you're supposed to be in school. I thought you *liked* that damn genius' school—why the hell—

NICK   Well, I figured I'd better stay home today till you got up. (*Hesitantly*) There's something I gotta discuss with you. See, because it's this special school for big brains they watch you and take notes and make reports and smile at you a lot. And there's this psychologist who talks to you every week, each kid separately. He's the biggest smiler they got up there.

MURRAY   Because you got brains they figure you're nuts.

NICK   Anyway, we had Show and Tell Time in Mrs. Zimmerman's class on Monday; and each kid in the class is supposed to tell about some trip he took and show pictures. Well, y'remember when I made you take me with you to the El Bambino Club over on Fifty-Second?

MURRAY   Nick—you showed and you told.

NICK   Well, it turned out they're very square up at the Revere School. And sometimes in class, when we have our Wednesday-Free-Association-Talk-Period, I sometimes quote you on different opinions—

MURRAY   That wasn't a good idea.

NICK   Well, I didn't know they were such nervous people there. Murray, they're very nervous there. And then there was this composition I wrote in Creative Writing about the advantages of Unemployment Insurance.

MURRAY   Why did you write about that?

NICK   It was just on my mind. Then once they got my record out they started to notice what they call "Significant Data." Turns out they've been keeping this file on me for a long time, and checking with that Child Welfare place; same place you got those letters from.

MURRAY I never answer letters from large organizations.

NICK So, Murray—when they come over here, I figure we'd better—

MURRAY When they come *over* here?

NICK Yeah, this Child Welfare crowd, they want to take a look at our environment here.

MURRAY Oh, that's charming. Why didn't you tell me about this before, Nick?

NICK Well, y'know, the past coupla nights we couldn't get together.

MURRAY That was unavoidable. You know when I have a lot of work you stay up at Mrs. Myers.

NICK (*Pointing at dresser*) Murray; your work forgot her gloves last night.

MURRAY That's very bright.

NICK Anyway, for this Child Welfare crowd, I figure we better set up some kind of story before they get here.

MURRAY You make it sound like a vice raid.

NICK I mean, for one thing, you don't even have a job right now.

MURRAY Look, you want me to put up some kind of front when they get here? O.K., I will. Don't worry, kid. I'll snow 'em good.

NICK I thought maybe you could at least look in the papers for a job, this morning before they get here. So we could tell them about your possibilities.

MURRAY I look every day.

NICK Couldn't I just read you from the *Times* again like last week? While you get dressed?

MURRAY O.K., read me from the paper.

(*He starts to get dressed; his socks and shirt are "filed" in the file-cabinet*)

NICK And then, maybe, you'll take a shave?

MURRAY All right, all right.

NICK   *(Picking up "Times" from swivel chair)* This paper is three days old.

MURRAY   So what do you want me to do, bury it? Is it starting to rot or something? Read me from the paper.

NICK   But most of these jobs, somebody must have taken them. Look, I'll go down and get a newer—

MURRAY   We do *not* need a newer paper. All the really important jobs stay forever. Now start on the first page of Help-Wanted-Male and read me from the paper.

NICK   O.K. *(Puts on his glasses, reads aloud)* "Administ. Ex-Oppty; ninety dollars." What's that?

MURRAY   Administrative Assistant, excellent opportunity. Nothing. Keep reading.

NICK   But ninety dollars would be ninety dollars more than nothing. Nothing is what you make now.

MURRAY   Have you ever considered being the first twelve-year-old boy in space?

NICK   But, ninety dollars—

MURRAY   *You* go be an Administ Exoppty. They *need* men like you. Read further.

NICK   *(Reading from paper)* "Versatile Junior, traffic manager, industrial representative organization. One hundred to one hundred twenty-five dollars. Call Mr. Shiffman—"

MURRAY   *(Picks up cardboard from shirt collar and talks into it)* Hello, Mr. Shiffman? I read your name in the *New York Times*, so I know you must be real. My name is Mandrake the Magician. I am a versatile Junior and I would like to manage your traffic for you. You see, sir, it has long been my ambition to work in a pointless job, with no future and a cretin like you as my boss—

NICK   But, Murray, it says "One hundred and twenty-five dollars," that's a lot of—

MURRAY   Just read the ads. No editorial comment or personal recommendations. When I need your advice, I'll ask for it. Out of the mouths of babes comes drooling.

NICK   You said that last week. Murray, you don't want a job is the whole thing.

MURRAY Would you just concentrate on being a child. Because I find your imitation of an adult hopelessly inadequate.

NICK You want to be your own boss, but the trouble with that is you don't pay yourself anything. *(NICK decides that what he has just said is very funny. He laughs)* Hey—you don't pay yourself anything—that's a good line—I gotta remember that—

MURRAY That's what *you* said last week.

NICK Look, Murray. *(Puts paper down and stands up)* Can I speak to you man to man?

MURRAY That was cute about a year ago, buddy, but the line has got to go.

NICK *(He takes off his glasses)* Murray, I am upset. For me as an actual child the way you live in this house and we live is a dangerous thing for my later life when I become an actual person. An unemployed person like you are for so many months is bad for you as the person involved and is definitely bad for me who he lives with in the same house where the rent isn't paid for months sometimes. And I wish you would get a job, Murray. Please.

(MURRAY tries to control himself, but cannot hide his laughter; he sees that NICK is offended by this and tries to stop. NICK walks away from him, goes to his alcove)

MURRAY *(Goes to NICK in the alcove)* Kid, I know. I'm sorry. You're right. You are. This *is* terrible.

NICK You're not kidding.

MURRAY Nick.

NICK Yeah?

MURRAY Nick, y'know when I said I was looking for work last week? *(Somewhat ashamed)* Well, I went to the movies. Every day. In the afternoon.

NICK *Murray*, you mean you really—?

MURRAY Now don't give me any of that indignant crap. I happen to be admitting something to you, and it is bad enough I should have to discuss my adult problems with a grotesque cherub, without you giving me dirty looks on top of it. Swell crowd in the movies on a weekday working afternoon. Nobody sits next to anybody, everybody there figures that everybody else is a creep;

and *all* of them are right. *(Suddenly smiling, taking* NICK'S *arm)* Have you ever been to the top of the Empire State Building?

NICK   Yes. Six times. With you. In November.

MURRAY   Oh really? Have you ever been to the Statue of Liberty?

NICK   No.

MURRAY   Today is Irving R. Feldman's birthday. We will go to the top of the Statue of Liberty and watch the *Queen Elizabeth* come in, full of those tired, poor, huddled masses yearning to breathe free—

NICK   Murray, why did you go to the movies in the middle of the afternoon when you said you were looking for work?

MURRAY   There's a window right in her navel, we will look out and see—

NICK   What is it? Were you very tired, or what?

MURRAY   *(Sits down in his chair)* Well, see, last week I was going to check with Uncle Arnie and some of the other agents about writing for some of the new TV shows. I was on the subway, on my way there, and I got off at Forty-Second Street and went to the movies. *(Leans back in his chair, lights cigarette;* NICK *sits opposite him on the bed, listening interestedly)* There are eleven movie houses on that street, Nick. It is Movieland. It breathes that seductive, carpety, minty air of the inside of movie houses. Almost as irresistible for me as pastrami. Now, there is the big question as you approach the box-office, with the sun shining right down the middle of a working day, whether everybody going in is as embarrassed as you are. But once you are past the awkward stage, and have gotten your ticket torn by the old man inside, all doubts just go away. Because it is dark. And inside it is such a scene as to fracture the imagination of even a nut like yourself, Nick, because inside it is lovely and a little damp and nobody can see you, and the dialogue is falling like rain on a roof and you are sitting deep in front of a roaring, color, Cinemascope, stereophonic, nerve cooling, heart warming, spine softening, perfect happy ending picture show, and it is Peacefulville, U.S.A. There are men there with neat mustaches who have shaved, and shined their shoes and put on a tie even to come and sit alone in the movies. And there are nearsighted cute pink ladies who eat secret caramels; and very old men who sleep; and the *ushers;* buddy, you are not kidding *these* boys. They know you are not there because you are waiting for a train, or you are on a vacation, or you work a night job. They know you are there to *see* the *movie*. It is the business and the purpose of your day, and these boys give you their sneaky smile to show you that they know. *(Depressed by his own words, quietly, almost to himself)* Now the moral question for me here, is this: When one is faced with life in the bare-assed, job-hunting raw on the one hand, and eleven fifty-cent double-features on the other, what is the mature, sensible, and mentally healthy step to take?

(He is slumped in his chair now)

NICK   *(Seeing* MURRAY'S *depression, softly)* What's wrong, Murray?

MURRAY   *(Walks slowly to the window, leans against the wall, looks out; quietly)* I don't know. I'm not sure.

NICK   Hey, Murray, you all right . . . ? *(goes to* MURRAY, *touches his arm; then suddenly smiles)* Murray, let's go to the Statue of Liberty.

*(*MURRAY *turns, laughs in agreement and* NICK *starts for his jacket while* MURRAY *puts binoculars around his neck and starts putting on his coat. The doorbell rings.* NICK *looks at* MURRAY, *then goes to answer it.* NICK *is holding the front door only partway open, hesitating to let in two people we now see standing outside in the hallway. They are* ALBERT AMUNDSON *and* SANDRA MARKOWITZ. ALBERT, *graduate of N.Y.U.'s School of Social Work, is a middle-aged man of twenty-eight.* SANDRA, *though a pretty girl of twenty-five, wears clothes obviously more suited to a much older woman.* ALBERT *carries a small briefcase and* SANDRA *carries a manila file-envelope and a gigantic hand-bag)*

ALBERT   Hello, young man, I am Mr. Amundson, this is Miss Markowitz. We would like to speak to your uncle.

NICK   *(Still not opening the door all the way)* Well, I don't know if—

ALBERT   Isn't he in?

MURRAY   Hello.

ALBERT   How do you do, Mr. Burns? Miss Markowitz and I are a Social Service unit assigned to the New York Bureau of Child Welfare. We have been asked by the Bureau to—may we come in?

MURRAY   Certainly.

*(*NICK *opens the door all the way, letting them both into the main room)*

ALBERT   We, Miss Markowitz and I, have been asked by the B.C.W. to investigate and examine certain pupils of The Revere School. There is certain information which the school and the city would like to have, regarding young Nicholas.

MURRAY   Sit down, Miss Markowitz, please. Mr. Amundson. I'll just get rid of these things.

(MURRAY *takes pants, shirts, a bugle, a clock, a yo-yo, half-empty bag of peanuts and an ash tray off the Morris chair, and with one sweeping movement drops the whole thing on the bed. The two of them take seats around the coffee table:* SANDRA *in the swivel chair,* ALBERT *in the Morris chair,* NICK *standing nervously off to one side,* MURRAY *stands at the end of the bed)*

ALBERT   I'd like to explain just why we are here, Mr. Burns—

NICK   Would anybody like some coffee?

ALBERT   Why, thank you Nicholas. Miss Markowitz?

SANDRA   Yes, thank you.

NICK   *(Whispering to* MURRAY *on his way to the kitchen)* Watch it.

ALBERT   *(Smiling politely)* It might be best, Mr. Burns, for the child, if perhaps you sent him downstairs to play or something, while we have our discussion. Your case is—

MURRAY   Our "case." I had no idea we were a "case."

ALBERT   We do have a file on certain students at Revere.

MURRAY   So we're on file somewhere. Are we a great, big, fat file, or a li'l teeny file?

ALBERT   Due to the fact that you have chosen not to answer our letters and several of our phone calls, there are many areas in which the file is incomplete, several questions—Mr. Burns, it might be better if the child went outside—

MURRAY   You gonna talk dirty?

ALBERT   It would be more advisable for the child not to be present, since Miss Markowitz, who will be discussing the psychological area—that is, we will be discussing certain matters which—

NICK   *(From kitchen)* Cream and sugar for everybody?

ALBERT   *(To kitchen)* Yes, Nicholas. *(To* MURRAY *again)* Mr. Burns, it's going to be awkward, with the child present, to—

MURRAY   *(To* SANDRA) Miss Markowitz, may I know your first name?

SANDRA   Sandra.

MURRAY   And you are the psychologist part of this team, Sandy?

SANDRA   That's right, Mr. Burns.

MURRAY   *(To* ALBERT*)* And you, I take it, are the brawn of the outfit?

ALBERT   Perhaps I should explain, Mr. Burns, that the Social Service teams which serve Revere School are a carefully planned balance of Social Case Worker, such as myself, and Psychological Social Worker, such as Miss Markowitz, or, actually, *Dr.* Markowitz.

*(*NICK *enters from kitchen with four cups, gives one to* ALBERT, SANDRA, *and* MURRAY; *keeps one for himself)*

ALBERT   *(Continued)* Mr. Burns, it is not easy to define those elements, those influences and problems which go into the make-up of a young boy.

MURRAY   I thought it was just frogs and snails and puppy-dogs' tails.

ALBERT   *(Using once again, his polite smile)* I appreciate the informality with which you approach this meeting, Mr. Burns, but on the more serious side, if I may, Miss Markowitz and I have a few matters—

NICK   Is the coffee any good?

ALBERT   Yes, very good. Thank you, Nicholas.

SANDRA   Very nice, Nicholas. *(She sees the cup in* NICK'S *hand, speaks with professional interest)* Are you drinking coffee, Nicholas? Don't you think it would be better if—

NICK   No. Milk. I like to drink it from a cup.

MURRAY   *(To* SANDRA, *smiling)* Now aren't you ashamed of yourself?

ALBERT   *(Taking a rather large file out of his briefcase)* Now, to plunge right in here—

MURRAY   Sometimes I put his milk in a shot glass. Better for getting him to drink it than adding chocolate syrup.

SANDRA   *(Firmly)* Mr. Burns, Mr. Amundson and I have several cases to examine today, and we would appreciate a certain amount of cooperation—

MURRAY   *(To* NICK*)* East Bronx, Mosholu Parkway.

NICK   *(Looks at* SANDRA, *then to* MURRAY*)* With a couple of years in maybe Massachusetts.

MURRAY   No Massachusetts at all. Complete Bronx.

SANDRA   I don't understand what—

MURRAY   *(Sitting on beach chair)* Oh, excuse me. Nick and I are mere- ly testing our sense of voice and accent. Nick insists he's better at it than I am.

SANDRA   *(Smiling)* As a matter of fact, the Bronx is right, but it's Grand Concourse.

MURRAY   The Massachusetts thing, way off, right?

SANDRA   Actually I took my graduate work with a professor, a man with a very strong New England accent, who could very well've influenced my speech. Nick is quite right.

NICK   *(Proudly)* Thank you, lady.

SANDRA   You certainly have a fine ear for sound, Nick. Do you and your uncle play many of these sorts of games together?

NICK   Oh, yes. We play many wholesome and constructive-type games together.

MURRAY   You're a big phoney, Nick. Miss Markowitz has beautiful hazel eyes that have read many case histories and are ever watch- ful, and even clever little boys are not going to snow her. The lady is here for the facts.

ALBERT   Quite so, Mr. Burns. But facts alone cannot complete our examination. *(He takes out a pen, opens to a blank page in the file)* We wish to understand—

NICK   *(To SANDRA, showing off for her)* Jersey City, maybe Newark. And—a little bit of Chicago.

MURRAY   Uh-huh. Think you've hit it, Nick.

SANDRA   That's really quite remarkable. Albert—Mr. Amundson *is* from New Jersey, and he went to Chicago University for sever- al—

ALBERT   *(Firmly)* This is really quite beside the point, Sandra—

SANDRA   I just think it's quite remarkable, Albert, the boy's ability to—

ALBERT   *(Purposely interrupting her)* Suppose I just plunge right in here, before Dr. Markowitz begins her part of the interview—

(There is a noise at the front door and ARNOLD BURNS enters. He is carrying a medium-sized grocery-delivery carton filled with a variety

of fruit. He makes a rather incongruous delivery-boy in that he is in his early forties and dressed in expensively distinguished clothes, top-coat, and hat. He is MURRAY'S *older brother, and his agent. It is obvious in the way he enters and automatically sets the delivery-carton down on the desk that this is a daily ritual enacted at this same time every day and in the same manner.* MURRAY *does not even look up to greet him and* NICK *makes some casually mumbled greeting in his direction)*

ARNOLD   The honey-dew melon's in season again but not really ripe yet, so— *(He turns, sees that there are strangers there)* Oh, sorry. Didn't know you had company. *(Turns, goes to the door)* See you, Nick.

NICK   Yeah, see you, Uncle Arnie.

*(*ARNOLD *exits)*

ALBERT   *(Looking at the door)* There is somebody else living here with you?

MURRAY   No. That's just my brother Arnold. He brings fruit every morning on his way to the office. He's a fruit nut.

ALBERT   I see here in the file that our research team spoke to your brother; your agent, I believe. We also called the people at your last business address, N.B.C.—

MURRAY   *(Rising)* You really do a lot of that stuff, calling people, going into my personal   ?

ALBERT   You've refused for quite some time, Mr. Burns, to answer any of our regular inquiries. We understand that you have been unemployed at this point for nearly five months

NICK   *(To* ALBERT*)* He has an excellent opportunity to be an administrative assistant—

ALBERT   *(Pressing forward)* Other than your activities as free-lance script-writer, I understand that you wrote regularly for an N.B.C. program for several years—

MURRAY   I was chief writer for Leo Herman, better known as Chuckles the Chipmunk, friend of the young'uns, and seller of Chuckle-Chips the potato chips your friend Chuckles the Chipmunk chomps on and chuckles over.

ALBERT   And the circumstances under which you left the employ of—

MURRAY   I quit.

ALBERT   You felt that this was not the work you—

MURRAY   I felt that I was not reaching all the boys and girls out there in Televisionland. Actually it was not so much that I wasn't reaching the boys and girls, but the boys and girls were starting to reach *me*. Six months ago, a perfectly adult bartender asked me if I wanted an onion in my martini, and I said, "Gosh n' gollies, you betcha." I knew it was time to quit.

ALBERT   May I ask if this is a pattern, that is, in the past, has there been much shifting of position?

MURRAY   I *always* take an onion in my martini. This is a constant and unswerving—

(NICK, *concerned with* MURRAY'S *behavior, goes towards him in an attempt to quiet him down*)

SANDRA   (*Firmly, standing*) Mr. Burns. Perhaps you are not aware of just how serious your situation is. This entire matter is a subject of intense interest to the B.C.W. The circumstances of this child's environment—

ALBERT   Our investigation, Mr. Burns—

SANDRA   the danger of—

ALBERT   is the result of what the Bureau considers to be almost an emergency case.

NICK   He just likes to kid around, lady. But, see, we really got a great environment here—

MURRAY   (*To* NICK) Relax, kid. (*Goes toward them*) Look, people, I'm sorry. Let's get back to the questions.

ALBERT   Perhaps, Miss Markowitz, if you pursued your particular matters at this point.

SANDRA   Fine. Nick, suppose you and I have a little chat right here.

NICK   (*As he sits down next to her*) Fine. I was gonna suggest that myself.

SANDRA   Nick, I bet you love to come home when you've been out playing and you get tired. You say to yourself, "Gee, I'd like to go home now."

NICK   Sure. Right. And I'm happy here. Boy, if you think I'm happy now, you should see me when I'm *really* happy.

MURRAY (*To* SANDRA, *sympathetically*) He's on to you, honey. You're gonna have to be a lot foxier than that.

SANDRA And I'm sure that you and your uncle have a great deal of fun together.

NICK It's not *all* laughs.

SANDRA Oh, I'm sure there are times when the fun stops and you have nice talks and your uncle teaches you things, helps you to—

NICK I can do a great Peter Lorre imitation. Murray taught me.

ALBERT Nicky, what Miss Markowitz means—

NICK (*In the voice of Peter Lorre, a rather good imitation*) "You can't hang me . . . "

ALBERT is that you and your uncle must sometimes—

NICK "I didn't do it, I tell you; I am innocent . . . "

ALBERT No, Nicky, that's—

NICK "That's not my knife . . . "

ALBERT that's not what we meant—

NICK "It was all a mistake, I am innocent!"

ALBERT Nick—

NICK (*Screaming*) "I am innocent!!"

MURRAY (*Who has been beaming proudly*) What's the trouble? That happens to be a very good imitation.

ALBERT Perhaps; but we are trying to—

MURRAY Can *you* imitate Peter Lorre?

NICK (*Confidentially, to* SANDRA) I can do a pretty good James Cagney; I mean it's not fantastic like my Peter Lorre, but it—

ALBERT (*Raising his voice a bit, somewhat commanding*) Nicholas, please. Try to pay attention. Now if I may proceed to—

SANDRA (*Aside, to* ALBERT, *somewhat annoyed with him*) Albert, if you'll just let me handle this area. (*Then, to* NICK) Nick, let's talk about games, O.K.?

NICK O.K.

SANDRA Now, what kind of games do you like the best?

NICK Mostly I like educational games and things like that that Murray gets me to develop my natural inquiring mind.

SANDRA   I wonder, do you have any favorite games or toys you'd like to show me? Some plaything that is just the most favorite one of all?

NICK   I just now threw away my collection of *National Geographics* and other educational type magazines I had a whole collection of—

ALBERT   Nicky, Miss Markowitz is very interested in you and cares about you and everything. And if you brought out some of your favorite toys and playthings for her to see, I'm sure that she'd love them just as much as you do.

NICK   Well, there's Bubbles— (*Gets up to get it for them*)

MURRAY   I don't think you'd be interested in seeing Bubbles—

(NICK *goes to a cardboard carton on his bureau, opens it, and takes out a twenty-four-inch-high plastic statue of a bare-chested hula girl. The statue is in bright colors and has an electric switch at its pedestal.* NICK *places the girl-statue on the table between* ALBERT *and* SANDRA *and turns it on*)

NICK   Bubbles is what you'd call an electric statue.

(*The breasts of the statue light up and continue to blink on and off in rather spectacular fashion for the next part of the scene, first together and then one breast at a time.* ALBERT *looks at the statue, begins busily going through the file on his lap.* SANDRA *regards the statue scientifically, professionally*)

NICK   (*Continued*) It's got an electric battery timer in there that makes it go on and off like that.

SANDRA   Nick, is this your favorite toy?

NICK   Well, after a while it gets pretty boring. But it's a swell gimmick. There was another one in the store that was even better—

MURRAY   Anybody want orange juice or toast or anything?

SANDRA   Nick, tell me—do you like best the fact that the chest of the lady lights up?

NICK   Well, you got to admit, you don't see boobies like that every day. You want to see the effect when the lights are out? When the room is dark?

SANDRA   Tell me, Nick, is *that* what you like best about it, that you can be alone in the dark with it?

NICK Well, I don't know. But in the dark they really knock your eye out.

ALBERT *(With strenuous calm, blinking nervously at the blinking lights of the statue)* Perhaps, don't you think we ought to switch it off, turn off the . . .

SANDRA Nick, does Bubbles, does she in any way, does her face remind you at all of, oh, let me see, your mother, for example?

NICK *(Looks at the face of the statue for a moment)* No; I mean, it's just a doll, it's not a statue of anybody I know. I got it in this store downtown.

SANDRA Her chest, is that something which—?

NICK *(Smiling broadly)* It's *something* all right, isn't it?

SANDRA When you think of your mother, do you—?

NICK I don't think about her much.

SANDRA But when you *do* think of her, do you remember her face best, or her *hands*, or—?

NICK I remember she has this terrific laugh. The kind of laugh that when she laughs it makes you laugh too. Of course, she overdoes that a lot.

SANDRA I mean, physically, when you think of her, do you, well, when you see Bubbles, and Bubbles goes on and off like that—?

MURRAY Sandra, his mother's chest did not light up. Let's get that settled right now—mark it down in the file, Albert.

ALBERT *(Nervously, pointing at the blinking statue)* Nicky, I wonder if you would turn those off—I mean, turn *it* off, turn her off, unplug it—

(MURRAY turns the statue off, puts it back into the box)

SANDRA Nicky, when you bought this doll—

MURRAY Sandy, why don't I save you a lot of time? Nick is a fairly bright kid and he knows that girls are *not* boys. Other than that his interest in ladies is confined right now to ones that light up or don't light up.

NICK I mostly like to read books that are healthy, constructive, and extremely educational for a person.

MURRAY Don't push it, Nick. He does not have any unusual fixations, Sandy. He is no more abnormally interested in your bust than Mr. Amundson is.

ALBERT   Mr. Burns, it is not necessary to—

MURRAY   Of course, I might be wrong about that.

ALBERT   Our interest in that doll—

MURRAY   You really *are* interested in that doll, Albert.

ALBERT   Our interest—

NICK   *(To* ALBERT*)* I'll sell it to you for two dollars. That's fifty cents less than I paid for it.

(SANDRA *is unable to suppress her amusement and laughs happily)*

ALBERT   *(Quite annoyed with her)* Sandra, I fail to see—

SANDRA   *(Controlling herself again, but still smiling)* It's just that it was funny, Albert.

ALBERT   *(Taking command)* Suppose *I* pursue, then, the psychological part of—

SANDRA   *(Bristling at him)* Excuse me, Albert, I really do feel it would be better if *I* were to—

MURRAY   Albert, the lady was just laughing because something funny happened. That's actually the best thing to do under the circumstances.

ALBERT   Mr. Burns—

MURRAY   *(a genuine invitation)* How would you all like to go to the Statue of Liberty? I have it on good authority from the Weather Lady that today is a beautiful day.

ALBERT   Is it at all possible, Mr. Burns, for you to stick to the point?

MURRAY   Albert, I bet you'd make Sandy a lot happier if you took her off somewhere once in a while. Doesn't have to be the Statue of Liberty; actually any—

ALBERT   My relationship with Dr. Markowitz is of no—

MURRAY   Well, there's obviously some relationship. When Nick asked you if you'd have sugar in your coffee before, Albert, you answered for Sandy.

ALBERT   Mr. Burns, this entire interview has reached a point—

NICK   I'm going to get my educational books. I left them out on the street.

(He leaves the apartment, his exit unnoticed by the others)

ALBERT   This entire interview, Mr. Burns, has—

SANDRA   Mr. Burns, I—

ALBERT   Damn it, Sandra, don't interrupt me!

SANDRA   Albert, for goodness sakes, you—

ALBERT   *(Stands up)* Sandra, perhaps we— *(To* MURRAY*)* Would you excuse us for just a moment, Mr. Burns. I'd like to have a short conference with Sandra—Miss—*Dr.* Markowitz for a moment. *(She gets up,* ALBERT *and* SANDRA *walk over to the alcove where* MURRAY *cannot hear them.* MURRAY *starts to peer at them through his binoculars, until* ALBERT *turns and looks at him; he then goes to his desk and tinkers with a clock. Now alone with* SANDRA, ALBERT'S *manner changes somewhat. He speaks more softly and with more warmth, a departure from the stiff, professional manner which he uses in dealing with* MURRAY*)* Sandra, what are you *doing,* have we lost all control?

SANDRA   Are you seriously talking to *me* about control?

ALBERT   Dear, I told *you* and I told Dr. Malko. It's much too soon for you to go out on cases. You need another year in the office, behind the lines, I told both of you. You're simply *not* ready.

SANDRA   Really, Albert, you hardly let me get started. I was attempting to deal with the whole child.

ALBERT   Three months out of grad school and you want to go right into the front lines. Not advisable.

SANDRA   *(Whispering angrily)* Don't you think that this is rather stupid and unprofessional? Right here in front of him you decide to have a conference.

ALBERT   A necessity, I am supposedly the leader of our examining team—

SANDRA   Oh, *really*—

ALBERT   You get too *involved,* Sandra. Each case, you get much too emotionally involved. This is an exploratory visit, we are *scientists,* dear, you lose sight of the—

SANDRA   You make me sick, today, Albert. This is no way to approach this man's problem. We—

ALBERT   *(Sighing)* Oh, fine. That's just fine. Well—fine—

MURRAY *(At the other side of the room; through a megaphone)* How are we doing? *(Puts megaphone down, comes over to them in the alcove, sits between them; speaks sympathetically)* I personally don't feel that you're gonna work out your problems with each other, but I'm glad you came to me because I think I can help you. Al, Sandy is not going to respect you because you threaten her. Respect will have to come gradually, naturally, a maturing process—

ALBERT *(Approaching him)* Mr. Burns, the Board is thoroughly aware that Nicholas is not legally adopted. Consequently, they have, I assure you, the—

MURRAY *(Suddenly rising, angrily)* You don't assure me of *anything*, buddy, you make me damn nervous.

(Moves abruptly away towards kitchen)

ALBERT *(Sharply, solemnly)* Mr. Burns, according to the B.C.W., the child's continuance in your home is in serious and immediate doubt. (MURRAY *stops, the importance of* ALBERT'S *statement reaching him; silence for a moment.* ALBERT, *aware of the effect of his words, makes a genuine attempt now to speak warmly, understandingly)* Burns . . . aren't you at all willing to give some evidence in your favor for our report, some evidence to support your competency as a guardian?

(Silence again for a few moments. SANDRA *looks imploringly at* MUR-RAY. MURRAY *silent, thoughtful, for a few more moments, then—)*

MURRAY *(Softly)* O.K., Albert, O.K. . . . O.K. . . .

*(*MURRAY *returns to his Morris chair,* SANDRA *and* ALBERT *return to their original interview positions, once again opening their files, all reestablishing a formal atmosphere. Silence for a moment; then* MUR-RAY *proceeds, pleasantly)*

MURRAY Look, Folks, what's all the trouble? Nick is my nephew, he's staying with me for a while, he's visiting.

ALBERT How long has he been here?

MURRAY Seven years.

ALBERT Nicholas' father, where is he?

MURRAY That's not a *where* question, that's a *who* question.

ALBERT I don't quite—

MURRAY Nick's mother, she didn't quite either.

SANDRA She is still living?

MURRAY My sister is unquestionably alive.

SANDRA But her responsibility to the child—

MURRAY For five years she did everything she could for Nick—but get married. Now, that's not easy to understand since she used to get married to *everybody*. But, somehow, having Nick matured her, she felt a responsibility not to get married to just *any*body any more, so she didn't marry Nick's father, nor was she married at the time he was born. You might call Nick a bastard, or "little bastard," depending on how whimsical you feel at the time. (*Rises; a sweep of his hand*) I tell ya, we got a real Social Worker's paradise here, folks . . . My sister Elaine showed up here one day with two suitcases, a hat box, a blue parakeet, a dead gold fish, and a five-year-old child. Three days later she went downstairs to buy a pack of filter-tip cigarettes . . . (MURRAY *shrugs*) Six years later she returned for the suitcases and the hat box—the parakeet I had given away, the gold fish I had long since flushed down the toilet, and the five-year-old child had, with very little effort, become six years older. When Elaine returned for her luggage I reminded her of the child and the pack of filter-tip cigarettes and suggested that this was perhaps the longest running practical joke in modern history. She was accompanied by a tall chap with sunglasses who was born to be her fifth divorce and who tried to start a small conversation with me. At this point I slapped my sister, Fifth Divorce slugged me, Sister cried, stopped quite suddenly, and then proceeded to explain to me, briefly, her well-practiced theory on the meaning of life, a philosophy falling somewhere to the left of Whoopie. At which point, I remember, I started laughing, and then we all laughed and said "good-bye" like people at the end of a long party. That was almost a year ago. And I've still got Nick.

(SANDRA *is obviously sympathetic to this situation, emotionally involved in the story;* ALBERT *continues his cool professionalism, here and there jotting notes in the file*)

SANDRA But . . . but I'm sure she must have had *some* concern about Nicholas—about the child—

MURRAY His name is not Nicholas. I will admit that he has stayed with that name much longer than the others. No, actually he was "Bill" for almost eight months—

SANDRA I'm sure, on his birth certificate—

MURRAY Certainly an elusive document. Not having given him a last name, Elaine felt reticent about assigning him a first one. When Nick first came here this presented a real difficulty. Nick answered to nothing whatsoever. Even the parakeet recognized its own name. Nick only knew I was calling him when he was positive there was no one else in the room.

SANDRA   *(Very much emotionally involved in this now)* Well, how did you communicate with—?

MURRAY   I made a deal with him when he was six, up to which time he was known rather casually as "Chubby," that he could try out any name he wished, for however long he wished, until his thirteenth birthday, at which point he'd have to decide on a name he liked permanently. He went through a long period of dogs' names, when he was still little, "Rover" and "King" having a real vogue there for a while. For three months he referred to himself as "Big Sam," then there was Little Max, Snoopy, Chip, Rock, Rex, Mike, Marty, Lamont, Chevrolet, Wyatt, Yancy, Fred, Phil, Woodrow, Lefty, The Phantom . He received his library card last year under the name of Raphael Sabatini, his Cub Scout membership lists him as Dr. Morris Fishbein, and only last week a friend of his called asking if Toulouse could come over to his house for dinner. "Nick" seems to be the one that'll stick, though.

SANDRA   His mother, where—?

MURRAY   Elaine communicates with my brother and myself almost entirely by rumor. Well, I don't believe I've left anything out.

ALBERT   I was not aware that Nick was an O.W. child.

MURRAY   O.W.?

ALBERT   Out of wedlock.

MURRAY   For a moment I thought you meant Prisoner of War. I think it's that natural warmth of yours that leads me to misunderstand.

ALBERT   But as concerns the child— *(Looks around the room)* Where *is* the child?

SANDRA   You preferred not having him here anyway, Albert.

ALBERT   *(Sharply)* I am perfectly aware, Sandra, of what I *prefer* and what I do *not* prefer.

SANDRA   *(Sharply)* I don't care for that tone of voice at *all*, Albert.

ALBERT   *(Rises, begins to put on coat; calmly)* Sandra, I understand perfectly what has happened. We have allowed this man to disturb us and we have *both* gotten a bit upset. Now, I really do feel that it's time we got over to that family problem in Queens. It's there in your file, the Ledbetters, the introverted child. We've really given an unreasonable amount of time to this case. This interview, I'm afraid, Mr. Burns, has reached a point—

SANDRA   (*Attempting to sound authoritative*) Albert, I personally feel that it would not be advisable to leave this particular case, at this point.

ALBERT   Sandra, we have done here this morning all we—

SANDRA   I feel that we have not really given Mr. Burns a chance to—

ALBERT   Sandra, it's really time we left for Queens—

SANDRA   (*She hands* ALBERT *one of her two file envelopes*) Here's the Ledbetter file, I'm staying here.

ALBERT   (*Raising his voice a little*) Sandra.

SANDRA   I have decided to pursue this case.

ALBERT   (*Almost shouting*) Sandra, have we lost all professional control?

SANDRA   (*Angry, flustered*) You just—you just go yourself—to the Leadbellies—you go on to Queens.

ALBERT   (*Takes her by the arm, gently but firmly*) May I just talk to you for a moment?

(ALBERT *leads* SANDRA *over to the alcove, away from* MURRAY; MURRAY *takes the box of fruit from his desk, takes it into kitchen*)

ALBERT   (*Away from* MURRAY *now, he speaks softly, less stiffly, though still angry*) What *is* this, dear? What has happened to you today? What are you doing?

SANDRA   I'm doing what I think is right.

ALBERT   I know how you feel, Sandra, but there is no more we can do here.

SANDRA   (*Emotionally*) I just—I just don't understand your behavior when you're on a case. We're supposed to be of some help, he—

ALBERT   Of course I want to help. But don't forget that the child is the one who needs our protection, who needs . . .

SANDRA   Are you really going to leave that man here like that? You're not going to even try to help him or tell him what to do about the Board separating him from the child—I mean—just so cold—

ALBERT   (*Takes her hand*) Dear, you spent much too much time at that graduate school and not enough time in the field. That's your whole trouble. You've got to learn your job, Sandra—

SANDRA   Oh *really*, is that so? Albert Amundson, don't give me any of that nonsense!

ALBERT   Please, Sandra—dear, this is not the time or the place for—

SANDRA   (*Shouting*) Graduate school wouldn't have done *you* any harm, Albert, believe *me!* Oh, this is the most terrible thing— (*Very close to tears*) You mean . . . you're just going to leave? Do you know what you are? You're a . . . I don't know; but I'll think of something.

ALBERT   (*He walks away, leaving her in the alcove; goes into the main room*) Mr. Burns—

(*But* MURRAY *is not in the room*)

Mr. Burns?

(MURRAY *enters from the kitchen.* ALBERT *goes to him; retaining his control but just a bit shaken, as he picks up his briefcase, puts files away, preparing to leave*) Mr. Burns; you can assume at this point that Miss Markowitz is no longer involved with your case. The Board will be informed that she is no longer involved with this particular case. Her continuing here, to discuss your case—at this point—is entirely unofficial. You can dismiss any conference— that may resume after I leave—when I leave here, from your mind. And, regardless of what you think of me—

MURRAY   I think you're a dirty O.W.

(*Some of* SANDRA'S *file papers slip from her hand and fall to the floor*)

ALBERT   And—and do you know what *you* are? (*Readying himself to deliver a crushing insult to* MURRAY) Maladjusted!

(MURRAY *grabs his heart, struck by a mortal blow, leans against the wall behind him, slides down to the floor.* ALBERT *goes to door, opens it*)

ALBERT   Good afternoon, Mr. Burns. Good afternoon, Sandra.

(ALBERT *exits, closing door sharply behind him.* MURRAY *rises, turns toward* SANDRA *at other side of room, smiles pleasantly*)

SANDRA   (*She stands for a moment in the alcove; then begins to pick up the file papers she had dropped on the floor*) Mr. Burns . . . (*She is making a very strong attempt to control herself, but she is obviously on the verge of tears. She crosses to swivel chair, begins to collect files and purse to leave)* Mr. Burns, I must apologize to you. We . . . we have put you . . . you have been put at a disadvantage this morning. You have been involved in a personal problem that has nothing to do whatsoever with your particular case. It is entirely wrong for me to give you this impression of our . . . of our profession. *(She can no longer control herself, and becomes, suddenly, a sort of child. She stands quite still with her hands at her sides, and cries. It is not loud, hysterical crying, but intermittent and disorganized sobs, squeaks, whines, sniffles and assorted noises which punctuate her speech)* Do you know what? I just lost my job. This is awful. He's right, you know. I'm not suited to my work. I get too involved. That's what he said and he's right. *(Rummaging through purse for Kleenex)* Please don't look at me. Do you *have* to stand there? Please go away. Still, he didn't have to talk to me like that. This is the first *week* we've ever gone on cases together. I didn't think he'd behave that way. That was no way. Why don't I ever have any Kleenex? *(He gives her the closest thing at hand to blow her nose in, his undershirt from the bed)* Thank you. *(She sits on the bed)* Do you know that with even two fellowships it still cost me, I mean my parents mostly, it cost them seven thousand two hundred and forty-five dollars for me to go through school. I was the eighth youngest person to graduate in New York State last year and I can't stop crying. Maybe if I hurry, if I took a cab, I could still meet him in Queens.

MURRAY You can't. Queens is closed. It's closed for the season.

SANDRA Do you know what? *(Her crying lets up a bit)*

MURRAY What?

SANDRA *(With a new burst of sobs)* I hate the Ledbetters.

MURRAY Then I'm sure once I got to know them I'd hate them too.

SANDRA Mr. Burns, you don't understand, some of the cases I love and some of them I hate and that's all wrong for my work, but I can't help it. I hate Raymond Ledbetter and he's only nine years old.

MURRAY *(Pointing to the file-envelope on her lap)* You can't like everybody in your portfolio.

SANDRA But some of them I like too much and worry about them all day . . . *(She is making an attempt to control her tears)* It is an obvious conflict against all professional standards. I didn't like

Raymond Ledbetter so I tried to understand him, and now that I understand him I hate him.

MURRAY   Can I get you a cup of coffee?

SANDRA   *(She turns to* MURRAY *as if to answer him, but instead bursts into fresh tears)* He's gone to Queens and I'll never hear from him again. I wrote out what my married name would be after dinner last night on a paper napkin, Mrs. Albert Amundson, to see how it would look. *(*MURRAY *sits on the swivel-chair, near the bed)* We were going to get married. It was all planned; Mrs. Albert Amundson on a napkin. You have to understand Albert. He's really a very nice person when he's not on cases. He's a very intelligent man but last month I fell asleep twice while he was talking to me. I know him for so long. *(She tries once again to stop crying but the effort only increases her sobs)* Mr. Burns, don't look at me. Why don't you go away?

MURRAY   But I live here.

SANDRA   I would like everybody to go away.

MURRAY   *(Attempting to comfort her)* Can I get you a pastrami sandwich?

SANDRA   Oh, I don't know you and I'm crying right in front of you. Go away. *(Turning away again, still seated on the bed)* The minute I got out of school I wanted to go right back inside. *(With a great sob)* Albert is gone and I just lost my job.

MURRAY   *(He walks over to her)* Now, you're really going to have to stop crying, because I am going out of my mind.

SANDRA   I cry all the time and I laugh in the wrong places in the movies. I am unsuited to my profession and I can't do anything right, last night I burned an entire chicken and after seven years of school I can't work and I've got no place to go. An entire chicken.

MURRAY   If I do my Peter Lorre imitation, will you stop crying?

SANDRA   *(She pokes the file-envelope in her lap)* Look what I've done, I've cried on one of my files. The ink is running all over the Grumbacher twins . . .

MURRAY   *(In the voice of Peter Lorre, a decent imitation)* It was all a mistake, I didn't stab Mrs. Marmalade . . . it was my knife, but someone else did it, I tell you . . .

SANDRA   That's an awful imitation, Mr. Burns—

(She turns away from him and sobs into the bedclothes. He takes the Bubbles statue out of the box, places it on the floor near the bed, turns it on; it starts to blink on and off. Her face peeks out from where she has buried it in the bedclothes. She sees the blinking statue and puts her face back in the bedclothes, but we hear some giggles mixing with her sobs, now and then overtaking them, until she finally lifts her face out and we see that she is laughing)

MURRAY *(Smiling)* There. Progress. *(He turns off the statue)* Would you like a cup of coffee, or a pastrami sandwich or something?

SANDRA No, thank you.

(SANDRA begins to compose herself, she has stopped crying completely and is wiping her eyes with the undershirt he gave her. Then she begins to fold the undershirt neatly, smoothing it out into a nice little square on her lap)

SANDRA This is absolutely the most unprofessional experience I have ever had.

MURRAY People fall into two distinct categories, Miss Markowitz; people who like delicatessen, and people who don't like delicatessen. A man who is not touched by the earthy lyricism of hot pastrami, the pungent fantasy of corned-beef, pickles, frankfurters, the great lusty impertinence of good mustard—is a man of stone and without heart. Now, Albert is obviously not a lover of delicatessen and you are well rid of him.

SANDRA *(She is still sitting on the bed, her hands folded neatly in her lap on top of her files and his undershirt)* What am I going to do? This is an awful day.

MURRAY *(He sits on the swivel chair next to the bed)* Miss Markowitz, this is a beautiful day and I'll tell you why. My dear, you are really a jolly old girl and you are well rid of Albert. You have been given a rare opportunity to return the unused portion and have your money refunded.

SANDRA But . . . my work . . . what am I going to . . .

MURRAY You are a lover, Dr. Markowitz, you are a lover of things and people so you took up work where you could get at as many of them as possible, and it just turned out that there were too many of them and too much that moves you. Damn it, please be glad that it turned out you are not reasonable and sensible. Have all the gratitude you can, that you are capable of embarrassment and joy and are a marathon crier.

SANDRA   *(Looking directly at him)* There is a kind of relief that it's gone . . . the job, and even Albert. But I know what it is, it's just irresponsible . . . Oh, I don't have the vaguest idea who I am . . .

MURRAY   *(He takes her hand)* It's just there's all these Sandras running around who you never met before, and it's confusing at first, fantastic, like a Chinese fire-drill. But God-*damn*, isn't it great to find out how many Sandras there are? Like those little cars in the circus, this tiny red car comes out and putters around, suddenly its doors open and out come a thousand clowns, whooping and hollering and raising hell.

SANDRA   *(She lets go of his hand in order to pick up the undershirt in her lap)* What's this?

MURRAY   That's my undershirt. How's about going to the Empire State Building with me?

SANDRA   I'll have that coffee now.

MURRAY   You didn't answer my question. Would you like to visit the Empire State Building?

SANDRA   No, not really.

MURRAY   Well, then how about the zoo?

SANDRA   Not just now.

MURRAY   Well, then will you marry me?

SANDRA   What?

MURRAY   Just a bit of shock treatment there. I have found after long experience that it's the quickest way to get a woman's attention when her mind wanders. Always works.

SANDRA   Mr. Burns—

MURRAY   Now that you've cried you can't call me Mr. Burns. Same rule applies to laughing. My name is Murray.

SANDRA   Well, Murray, to sort of return to reality for a minute—

MURRAY   I will only go as a tourist.

SANDRA   Murray, you know, you're in trouble with the Child Welfare Board. They could really take Nick away. Murray, there's some things you could try to do . . . to make your case a little stronger . . .

MURRAY   Sandra, do you realize that you are not wearing your shoes?

SANDRA   *(She looks down at her bare feet)* Oh.

(The front door opens and NICK *bursts into the room, laden with books)*

NICK   Well, here I am with all my favorite books, *Fun In The Rain*, *The Young Railroader*, *Great Philosophers*, *Science For Youth*, a Spanish Dictionary. What I did was I left them out in the street when I was playing, and I went down to—

MURRAY   Nick, you just killed a month's allowance for nothing. Miss Markowitz isn't even on our case any more.

NICK   I shouldn't have left. You got angry and insulted everybody.

MURRAY   Don't worry about it, Nick; we'll work it out.

(He goes over to the closet for something)

NICK   *(Dropping his books regretfully on the chair)* Four dollars right out the window. *(To* SANDRA*)* Y'know, I really do read educational books and am encouraged in my home to think.

SANDRA   I'm sure that's true, Nicholas, but I'm not in a position to do you much official good any more.

NICK   We're in real trouble now, right? *(He turns to* MURRAY *who has taken two ukuleles from the closet and is coming toward* NICK*)* I figured it would happen; you got angry and picked on everybody.

MURRAY   *(As he hands the smaller ukulele to* NICK*)* Nick, we have a guest, a music lover, we've got to do our song. I am sure it will be requested.

NICK   *(Protesting, gesturing with his ukulele)* Murray, stop it . . . we . . . this is no time to sing songs, Murray . . .

MURRAY   *(Striking a downbeat on his ukulele)* Come on, where's your professional attitude?

*(*MURRAY *starts playing "Yes Sir, That's My Baby" on the ukulele, then sings the first line.* NICK *turns away at first, refusing to join him in the song, shaking his head solemnly at* MURRAY'S *behavior.* MURRAY *goes on with the second line of the song and* NICK *begins reluctantly picking out the melody on his ukulele, then* NICK *smiles in spite of himself and sings the third line along with* MURRAY.

They really go into the song now, singing and playing "Yes, Sir, That's My Baby," doing their routine for SANDRA. *She sits in front of them on the bed, smiling, enjoying their act.* NICK *is in the spirit of it now, having a good time. In the middle of the song* NICK *and* MURRAY *do a rather elaborate soft-shoe dance-step for a couple of lines, ukuleles held aloft. This is followed by some very fast and intricate two-part ukulele harmony on the last two lines of the song for a big finish.*

SANDRA *applauds.*

MURRAY *and* NICK, *singing and strumming ukes, go into a reprise of the song,* MURRAY *moving forward and sitting on the bed next to* SAN-DRA. NICK, *left apart from them now, does a line or two more of the song along with* MURRAY, *then gradually stops.* NICK *considers them both for a moment, as* MURRAY *goes on doing the song alone now for* SANDRA. NICK *nods to himself, circles around in front of them and, unnoticed by them, puts his uke down on the window-seat; goes to his alcove, gets school briefcase and pajamas from his bed.* MURRAY *is still playing the uke and singing the song to* SANDRA *as* NICK *goes past them on his way to the front door, carrying his stuff)*

NICK   *(Pleasantly, to* SANDRA*)* Nice to meet you, lady. I'll see you around.

MURRAY   *(Stops singing, turns to* NICK*)* Where you off to, Nick?

NICK   Gonna leave my stuff up at Mrs. Myers'. *(Opens the door)* I figure I'll be staying over there tonight.

(NICK *exits, waving a pleasant good-bye to* SANDRA. SANDRA *looks at the front door, puzzled; then she looks at* MURRAY *who resumes the song, singing and strumming the uke as . . .)*

THE CURTAIN FALLS

Above, Yves Montand and Didier Haudepin
Right, Jason Robards and Barry Gordon

Sheldon Secunda

Top, Barry Gordon, Jason Robards and Barbara Harris
Above, Gordon, William Daniels and Harris

ACT TWO

SCENE: MURRAY'S *apartment, eight* A.M. *the following morning.*

AT RISE: The phone is ringing loudly on the window seat. MURRAY *enters from bathroom with a toothbrush in his mouth, grabs a phone. The room is as it was at the end of Act I except that there is a six-foot high folding-screen placed around the bed, hiding it from view, and the shades are drawn again on the windows.*

MURRAY   *(Picks up phone and speaks immediately into it)* Is this some-body with good news or money? No? Good-bye. *(He hangs up. He pulls up the shade to see what kind of day it is outside. As usual the lighting of the room changes not at all with the shade up; as before, he sees nothing but the blank, grayish wall opposite)* Crap. *(With a sigh of resignation, he picks up the phone, dials, listens)* Hello, Weather Lady. I am fine, how are you? What is the weather? Uh-huh—uh-huh—uh-huh—very nice. Only a *chance* of showers? Well, what exactly does that—? Aw, there she goes again. *(He hangs up)* Chance of showers. *(Phone rings. He picks it up, speaks immediate-ly into it)* United States Weather Bureau forecast for New York City and vicinity: eight A.M. temperature, sixty-five degrees, somewhat cooler in the suburbs, cloudy later today with a chance of— *(The Caller hangs up; he stands, opens the window, leans out, raising his voice, shouting out the window)* This is your neighbor speaking! Something must be done about your garbage cans in the alley here. It is definitely second-rate garbage! By next week I want to see a better class of garbage, more empty champagne bottles and caviar cans! So let's snap it up and get on the *ball!*

*(*SANDRA'S *head appears at the top of the screen, like a puppet's head. She is staring blankly at* MURRAY. MURRAY *steps toward the screen, she continues to stare blankly at him. Her head suddenly disappears again behind the screen. The screen masks the entire bed and* SANDRA *from his view, and the view of audience. We hear a rustle of sheets and blankets from behind the screen, silence for a couple of seconds, and then* SANDRA'S *voice; only slightly tinged with sleep, impersonal, polite, and distant, one unintroduced party guest to another)*

SANDRA   Good morning.

MURRAY   Good morning.

SANDRA   How are you this morning?

MURRAY   I am fine this morning. How are you?

SANDRA   I am fine also. Do you have a bathrobe?

MURRAY   Yes, I have a bathrobe.

SANDRA   May I have your bathrobe, please?

MURRAY   I'll give you Nick's. It'll fit you better.

SANDRA   That seems like a good idea.

MURRAY   *(He takes* NICK'S *bathrobe from the hook in the alcove, tosses it over the top of the screen)* There you go.

SANDRA   Thank you. What time is it?

MURRAY   It is eight-fifteen and there is a chance of showers. Did you sleep well?

SANDRA   Yes. How long have you been up?

MURRAY   Little while.

SANDRA   Why didn't you wake me?

MURRAY   Because you were smiling. How does the bathrobe fit?

SANDRA   This bathrobe fits fine. Did you happen to see my clothes?

MURRAY   *(Starts for the bathroom)* They're in the bathroom. Shall I get them?

SANDRA   No, thank you. *(She suddenly pops out from behind the screen and races across the room into the kitchen at Right, slamming the kitchen door behind her. After a moment, we hear her voice from behind the door)* This isn't the bathroom. This is the kitchen.

(He goes to the bathroom, reaches in behind the door to get her clothes, brings them with him to the kitchen door. He knocks on the door)

MURRAY   Here are your clothes. Also toothpaste and toothbrush.

(The kitchen door opens slightly, her hand comes out. He puts the stuff in it, her hand goes back, the door closes again)

SANDRA   Thank you.

MURRAY   Sandy, is everything all right?

SANDRA   What?

MURRAY   I said, is everything all right?

SANDRA   Yes. I'm using the last of your toothpaste.

MURRAY   That's all right. There's soap by the sink.

SANDRA   I know. I found it.

MURRAY   That's good.

SANDRA   It was right by the sink.

MURRAY   *(Folding up screen from around bed)* Suppose we broaden this discussion to other matters . . .

SANDRA   I saw the soap when I came in.

(The door opens and ARNOLD BURNS *enters as he did before, carrying a grocery delivery carton filled with varieties of fruit. He sets it down on the desk)*

ARNOLD   'Morning, Murray.

MURRAY   *(Without turning to look at him)* 'Morning, Arnold.

ARNOLD   Murray, Chuckles called again yesterday. I told him I'd talk to you. And Jimmy Sloan is in from the coast; he's putting a new panel-show package together—

MURRAY   *(Sits on bed, begins to put on shoes and socks)* Arnold, you have many successful clients—

ARNOLD   Murray—

MURRAY   With all these successful people around, where are all of our new young failures going to come from?

ARNOLD   Murray, those people I saw here yesterday; they were from the Welfare Board, right? I tried to warn you—

MURRAY   Nothing to worry about.

ARNOLD   These Welfare people don't kid around.

MURRAY   Arnold, I don't mind you coming with fruit if you keep quiet, but you bring a word with every apple. Everything's fine. You'll be late for the office.

ARNOLD   *(After a moment)* Is Nick all right?

MURRAY   Fine.

ARNOLD   O.K., good-bye Murray.

MURRAY   Good-bye, Arnold. (ARNOLD *exits.* MURRAY *talks to the closed kitchen door again)* There's coffee still in the pot from last night, if you want to heat it up.

SANDRA   I already lit the flame.

MURRAY   Good. The cups are right over the sink. Will you be coming out soon?

SANDRA   I found the cups.

MURRAY   Do you think you will be coming out soon?

SANDRA   Yes, I think so. Cream and sugar in your coffee?

MURRAY   Yes, thank you.

SANDRA   Murray.

MURRAY   Yes.

SANDRA   I'm coming out now.

MURRAY   That's good.

SANDRA   I'm all finished in here so I'm coming out now.

MURRAY   That's very good.

>   (*The kitchen door opens.* SANDRA, *dressed neatly, comes out of the kitchen, carrying two cups of coffee and* NICK'S *bathrobe, neatly folded*)

SANDRA   (*Pausing at kitchen doorway, smiles politely*) Well, here I am. (*She goes to* MURRAY, *gives him a cup, sits on swivel chair. He sits on stool. She takes a sip of coffee, straightens her hair. She is quite reserved, though pleasant*) You know, yesterday was the first time I've ever been to the Statue of Liberty. It's funny how you can live in a city for so long and not visit one of its most fascinating sights.

MURRAY   That is funny. (*He sips his coffee*) This coffee isn't bad, for yesterday's coffee.

SANDRA   I think it's very good, for yesterday's coffee. (*Takes another sip*) What kind of coffee is it?

MURRAY   I believe it's Chase and Sanborn coffee.

SANDRA   "Good to the last drop," isn't that what they say?

MURRAY   I think that's Maxwell House.

SANDRA   Oh, yes. Maxwell House Coffee. "Good to the last drop."

MURRAY   It's Chase and Sanborn that used to have the ad about the ingredients: "Monizalles for mellowness" was one.

SANDRA   They used to sponsor Edgar Bergen and Charlie McCarthy on the radio.

MURRAY   Yes. You're right.

SANDRA   "Monizalles for mellowness." I remember. That's right. I have to leave now.

MURRAY   Oh?

SANDRA   Yes. I'll have to be on my way.

>   (*She stands, takes her handbag, puts on shoes, starts towards front door*)

MURRAY   (*Takes her file-envelope from the floor, hands it to her*) Don't forget your files.

SANDRA   Oh, yes. My files. *(She takes them from him, stands looking at him for a moment)* Well, good-bye.

MURRAY   Good-bye, Sandra.

SANDRA   Good-bye.

(She walks out of the apartment, and closes the door behind herself. Alone in the apartment now, MURRAY stands for a moment looking at the door. He then runs to the door and opens it—she has had her hand on the outside knob and is dragged into room as he does so)

MURRAY   *(Laughing, relieved)* You nut. I was ready to kill you.

SANDRA   *(Throws her arms around him, drops bag and files on floor)* What happened? You didn't say anything. I was waiting for you to say something. Why didn't you say something or kiss me or—?

MURRAY   I was waiting for *you,* for God's sake.

(He kisses her)

SANDRA   I didn't know *what* was going on. *(She kisses him, their arms around each other; he leans away from her for a moment to put his coffee cup on the table)* Don't let me go—

MURRAY   I was just putting my coffee cup down—

SANDRA   Don't let me go. *(He holds her tightly again)* Murray, I thought about it, and I probably love you.

MURRAY   That's very romantic. I probably love you too. You have very small feet. For a minute yesterday, it looked like you only had four toes, and I thought you were a freak. I woke up in the middle of the night and counted them. There are five.

SANDRA   I could have told you that.

MURRAY   *(He sits in swivel chair, she on his lap)* You knocked down maybe seven boxes of crackerjacks yesterday. You are twelve years old. You sleep with the blanket under your chin like a napkin. When you started to talk about the coffee before, I was going to throw you out the window except there'd be no place for you to land but the trash-can from the Chinese restaurant.

SANDRA   You mean that you live above a Chinese restaurant?

MURRAY   Yes. It's been closed for months, though.

SANDRA   Do you mean that you live above an abandoned Chinese restaurant?

MURRAY   Yes, I do.

SANDRA   That's wonderful. *(She kisses him; jumps up from his lap happily excited about what she has to say. Takes off her jacket, hangs it on the back of the Morris chair)* I didn't go to work this morning and I simply can't tell you how fantastic that makes me feel. I'm not going to do a *lot* of things any more. *(Pulls at the material of her blouse)* This blouse I'm wearing, my mother picked it out, everybody picks out things for me. She gets all her clothes directly from Louisa May Alcott. *(Picks up stool, changes its position in the room)* Well, we've all seen the last of this blouse anyway. Do you realize that I feel more at home here after twenty-four hours than I do in my parents' house after twenty-five years? Of course, we'll have to do something about curtains, we need color there, Murray—and I hope you didn't mind about the screen around the bed; I just think it gives such a nice, separate, bedroomy effect to that part of the room— *(Picks up her bag and files from floor where she dropped them and puts them in closet. She is moving in)* Oh, there's so many wonderful tricks you can try with a one-room apartment, really, if you're willing to use your imagination . . . *(He watches helplessly as she moves happily about the apartment judging it with a decorator's eye)* I don't care if it sounds silly, Murray, but I was projecting a personality identification with the Statue of Liberty yesterday—courageous and free and solid metal— *(She kisses him, then continues pacing happily)* I was here with you last night and I don't give a damn who knows it or what anybody thinks, and that goes for Dr. Malko, Albert, my mother, Aunt Blanche . . . Oh, I'm going to do so many things I've always wanted to do.

MURRAY   For example?

SANDRA   Well—I'm not sure right now. And that's marvelous too, I am thoroughly enjoying the idea that I don't know what I'm going to do next. *(Stops pacing)* Do you have an extra key?

MURRAY   A what?

SANDRA   An extra key. Altman's has this terrific curtain sale—

MURRAY   Oh, sure, a key—

SANDRA   I thought I would go and—

MURRAY   You know what, Sandy, I don't think I have one, an extra key . . .

(The doorbell rings. She flinches for a moment, but then smiles and stands firmly)

SANDRA   You'd better answer it, Murray.

MURRAY   Sandra, would you prefer to . . . ?

(He indicates the kitchen as a hiding place, but she stands right where she is, refusing to move)

SANDRA   I've got no reason to hide from anybody.

(MURRAY goes to the front door and opens it half-way but enough for us to see the visitor, ALBERT AMUNDSON. ALBERT cannot see beyond the door to where SANDRA is standing)

ALBERT   Good morning, Mr. Burns.

MURRAY   Albert, how-are-you?

(SANDRA, hearing ALBERT'S voice, races immediately into the closet, closing the door behind herself)

ALBERT   May I come in?

MURRAY   Sure.

(MURRAY opens the front door all the way, allowing ALBERT into the main room. MURRAY closes the door, then follows ALBERT into the room. MURRAY smiles to himself when he sees that SANDRA is not there and then glances at the closet door)

ALBERT   I called you twice this morning, Mr. Burns.

MURRAY   That was you.

ALBERT   That was me. Miss Markowitz did not show up in Queens yesterday.

MURRAY   So?

ALBERT   Her parents are quite upset. I am quite upset. Where is she?

MURRAY   She's hiding in the closet.

ALBERT   We're really all quite anxious to know where she is.

MURRAY   I'm not kidding. She's in the closet.

(ALBERT goes to the closet, opens the door, sees SANDRA, then closes the door. ALBERT comes back to MURRAY)

ALBERT   She *is* in the closet.

MURRAY   I wouldn't lie to you, Albert.

ALBERT   Why is she in the closet?

MURRAY   *(sits on the bed, putting on his other shoe)* I don't know. She's got this thing about closets.

ALBERT   That's a very silly thing for her to be in that closet.

MURRAY   Don't knock it till you've tried it. Now, what else can I do for you?

ALBERT   That's a difficult thing for me to believe. I mean, that she's right there in the closet. You are not a person, Mr. Burns, you are an experience.

MURRAY   *(Goes into the kitchen)* That's very nice, Albert, I'll have to remember that.

ALBERT   Actually, Dr. Markowitz is not the reason for my visit today. I came here in an official capacity.

MURRAY   *(From the kitchen)* You don't wear an official capacity well, Albert. Coffee?

ALBERT   No, thank you.

(MURRAY *brings the pot out, fills the two cups on the table; brings one of the cups of coffee to the closet and hands it through the partly open door; then returns to table, sits opposite* ALBERT)

MURRAY   What have you got on your mind, Albert?

ALBERT   *(Sits; begins hesitantly)* Burns, late yesterday afternoon the Child Welfare Board made a decision on your case. Their decision is based on three months of a thorough study; our interview yesterday is only a small part of that quite thorough . . . I want you to understand that I am not responsible, personally, for the decision they've reached. I—

MURRAY   Relax, Albert, I won't even hold you responsible for the shadow you're throwing on my rug.

ALBERT   For eleven months you have avoided contact with the Board, made a farce of their inquiries. You are not employed, show no inclination to gain employment, have absolutely no financial stability—

MURRAY   Look, Albert, there's—

ALBERT   Months of research by the Board and reports by the Revere School show a severe domestic instability, a libertine self-indulgence, a whole range of circumstances severely detrimental to the child's welfare—

MURRAY   Stop the tap-dancing for a second, Albert; what's going on, what—

ALBERT   It is the Board's decision that you are unfit to be the guardian of your nephew, and that action be taken this Friday to remove the child from this home and the deprivation you cause him.

MURRAY You mean they can really . . . *(Sips at his coffee, showing no emotion)* Who writes your material for ya—Charles Dickens?

ALBERT The Board is prepared to find a more stable, permanent home for your nephew, a family with whom he will live a more wholesome, normal—

MURRAY Look, Albert, there must be some kind of a hearing or something, where I'll have a chance to—

ALBERT *(Earnestly, making sure he understands)* Well, yes . . . you *will* have the opportunity Thursday to state your case to the Board. If there is some substantial change in your circumstances, some evidence they're not aware of; if you can demonstrate that you are a responsible member of society—

MURRAY It's Tuesday; what the hell am I supposed to do in two days, win the Nobel Peace Prize? They sent you here to tell me this?

ALBERT No, you were to be informed by the court. But in view of the confusion which took place here yesterday, for which I consider myself responsible, I felt it my duty to come here and explain . . .

MURRAY Buddy, you speak like you write everything down before you say it.

ALBERT Yes, I do speak that way, Mr. Burns. I wish that I spoke more spontaneously. I will always appear foolish in a conversation with a person of your imagination. Please understand, there is no vengeance in my activities here. I love my work, Mr. Burns. I believe that you are a danger to this child. I wish this were not true, because it is obvious that you have considerable affection for your nephew. It is in your face, this feeling. I admire you for your warmth, Mr. Burns, and for the affection the child feels for you. I admire this because I am one for whom children do not easily feel affection. I am not one of the warm people. But your feeling for the child does not mollify the genuinely dangerous emotional climate you have made for him. *(He moves towards MURRAY)* I wish you could understand this, I would so much rather you understood, could really hear what I have to say. For yours is, I believe, a distorted picture of this world.

MURRAY Then why don't you send *me* to a foster home?

ALBERT *(Sadly, regretfully)* I was right. You really can't listen to me. You are so sure of your sight. Your villains and heroes are all so terribly clear to you, and I am obviously one of the villains. *(Picks up his briefcase)* God save you from your vision, Mr. Burns. *(Goes to front door, opens it)* Good-bye.

(ALBERT *exits.* MURRAY *stands at window with coffee cup in hand, looking out at the gray, blank wall of the building opposite.* SANDRA *comes out of closet carrying her coffee cup;* MURRAY *does not look at her)*

SANDRA   *(Softly, sympathetically)* Murray . . .

MURRAY   Don't be nervous, lady, you're just at an awkward stage: Between closets. *(Quietly, calmly)* Look, if Nick has to leave, if he goes, he goes, and my life stays about the same. But it's no good for *him*, see, not for a couple of years, anyway. Right now he's still ashamed of being sharper than everybody else, he could easily turn into another peeled and boiled potato. Are you listening to me?

SANDRA   Yes, of course—

MURRAY   Well, make some kind of listening noise then, will you? Wink or nod your head or something.

SANDRA   But I'm—

MURRAY   *(Casually; gesturing with his coffee cup)* Tell you the truth, it's even a little better for me if he goes. I mean, he's a middle-aged kid. When I signed with the network he sat up all night figuring out the fringe benefits and the pension plan. And he started to make *lists* this year. Lists of everything; subway stops, underwear, what he's gonna do next week. If somebody doesn't watch out he'll start making lists of what he's gonna do next year and the next ten years. *(Angrily for a moment)* Hey, suppose they put him in with a whole family of list makers. I didn't spend six years with him so he should turn into a list maker. He'll learn to know everything before it happens, he'll learn to plan, he'll learn how to be one of the nice dead people. Are you listening?

SANDRA   Of course, I told you, Murray, I—

MURRAY   Then stamp your feet or mutter so I'll know you're there, huh? *(Still speaking quite calmly)* I want to be sure he knows when he's chickening out on himself. I want him to get to know exactly the special thing he is or else he won't notice it when it starts to go. I want him to stay awake and know who the phonies are, I want him to know how to holler and put up an argument, I want a little guts to show before I can let him go. I want to be sure he sees all the wild possibilities. I want him to know it's worth all the trouble just to give the world a little goosing when you get the chance. And I want him to know the subtle, sneaky, important reason why he was born a human being and not a chair. *(After a moment)* I will be very sorry to see him go. That kid was the best straight-man I ever had. He is a laugher, and laughers are rare. I mean, you tell that kid something funny—not just any piece of corn, but something funny, and he'll give you your money's worth. It's not just funny jokes he reads, or I tell him, that he laughs at. Not just set-up funny stuff. He sees street jokes, he has the good eye, he sees subway farce and crosstown-bus humor and all the cartoons that people make by being alive. He has a good eye. And I don't want him to leave until I'm certain he'll never be ashamed of it. *(Still quite calmly)* And in addition to that . . . besides that . . . *(Sharply, shouting loudly)* Sandy, I don't want him to go. I like having him around here. What should I do, Sandy? Help me out. *(Suddenly slumps forward in his chair, covers his face with his hands)* I like when he reads me from the Want-Ads.

SANDRA *(Comes over to him, takes his hands)* Murray, don't worry, we'll do something. I know the Board, their procedure; there's things you can do—

MURRAY *(Quietly, thoughtfully)* What I'll do is I'll buy a new suit. The first thing is to get a dignified suit.

SANDRA If you could get some kind of a job, get your brother to help you.

MURRAY Right. Right.

SANDRA Is there something you can get in a hurry?

MURRAY Sure, one of those summer suits with the ready-made cuffs—

SANDRA No, I mean a job. If we could just bring some proof of employment to the hearing, Murray, show them how anxious you are to change. We'll show them you want to be reliable.

MURRAY *(brightening)* Yeah, *reliable*— *(Rising, going across the room to the phone)* Sandy, we will put on a God-damned *show* for them. Spectacular reliability; a reliability *parade*; bands, floats, every-thing. *(Dialing)* Sandy, go to the files and pick me out a tie that is quiet but at the same time projects a mood of inner strength. *(Into phone)* Arnold Burns' office please.

SANDRA *(On her way to the file cabinet)* One quiet tie with a mood of inner strength.

MURRAY *(Into phone)* Hello, Margo? It's Murray. Oh. Well, when Arnie comes in here's what you do. First you tell him to sit down.

Then you tell him I want to get a job. When he has recovered sufficiently from that shock, tell him— (SANDRA *comes to him with a tie*) Excuse me a second, Margo. (*Looks at tie*) Yes, quiet but with strength. (SANDRA *laughs*) Keep that laugh. I'll need it later. (*Into phone*) Margo, tell him I'm going downtown to pick up a new suit for myself and a beautiful pineapple for him, call him back in about an hour, O.K.? Thanks, Margo. (*Puts phone down, goes to get his jacket*)

SANDRA   Can I come with you? I'd love to buy a suit with you.

MURRAY   (*Moving quickly up to front door*) Better not, Sandy. Gotta move fast, you wait here . . . (*He stops, comes back towards her, then takes something from his pocket*) Here's a key for ya . . .

SANDRA   Thank you . . .

MURRAY   Look, don't go away, huh?

SANDRA   I won't. (*She kisses him*)

MURRAY   (*Goes to front door*) Say "Good Luck."

SANDRA   Good Luck.

MURRAY   Now say "You are a magnificent human being."

SANDRA   You are a magnificent human being.

MURRAY   (*As he exits*) I *thought* you'd notice.

(*She stands in the doorway now and watches him go; we begin to hear the sound of an oncoming Subway Train, quietly at first and then building to a clattering roar as the Lights Fade down on* SANDRA *waving to the offstage* MURRAY *and continuing into the Blackout. In the darkness the sound of the train is soon overtaken by the even more powerful roar of Mid-Town Rush Hour Traffic, a grinding, screaming War: sirens wailing and whooping like wounded animals, desperate honking, groaning buses, screeching trucks and shouting competitors for speed and space; this sound, reaching its peak, is soon overtaken by a Chorus of Screaming Kids*)

KIDS VOICES   Yaayyyyyyy!

LEO'S VOICE   (*After a moment, deeply depressed*) George, is that a "yay"? What kinda "yay" is that? I ask for a "yay" you give me a death rattle. Come on—if you're gonna rehearse a "yay," rehearse a "yay".

KIDS VOICES   (*Screaming*) Yaayyyyyyyyy!!

LEO'S VOICE   (*Softly*) Death; we're dying; with that kind of a "yay" the show is dying, that's why the show is dying, the kids don't have a "yay" attitude; dead, dying, dead; death, doornail, dying, dead . . .

(During these last few lines, Lights have been gradually coming up on ARNOLD BURNS' *Office; part of a large theatrical agency of which* ARNOLD *is a rather successful member; modern, wood-paneling, non-objective paintings and framed photographs of his clients on the wall, spectacularly large window behind the desk with a twenty-second floor skyline view. A large bowl of fruit is on an end-table near the door. One of the two phones on* ARNOLD'S *desk is a special "speaker-phone," consisting of a small loudspeaker box on the desk which amplifies clearly the voice of whoever is calling. It can also be spoken into from almost any point in the room if one is facing it. As the following scene progresses the speaker-phone is treated by those present as if it were a person in the room, they gesture to it, smile at it, etc.* ARNOLD *is alone in his office, leaning against his desk, listening to the speaker-phone, from which we continue to hear the voice of* LEO HERMAN)

LEO'S VOICE *(Continued)* You hear that? You hear that, Arn? Nothin's workin' without the Big Murr' and the beautiful words. What am I without him?—a big mouth with nothin' in it: empty, zero, nothing, not. Mister Language, I need him; sweetie of a writer.

ARNOLD That was *last* year he won the Sweetie Award, Leo.

LEO'S VOICE *(Laughs good-naturedly)* Please excuse my little words. They slip out of my face once in a while. Arn, you got my voice comin' out of that speaker-phone in your office, huh? Comes out like the biggest phoney you ever met, right? That's how I sound, don't I? Big phoney.

ARNOLD No, Leo.

LEO'S VOICE I'm getting sick of myself. Hey Arn, you figure there's a good chance of Murray comin' back with me on the show?

ARNOLD Can't guarantee it, Leo; I've sent him to one other appointment today, fairly good offer—

LEO'S VOICE Well, I'm hopin' he comes back with *me*, Arn. Funny bit you being the agent for your own brother, what d'ya call that?

ARNOLD It's called incest. *(Intercom buzzes;* ARNOLD *picks it up)* O.K., send him in. *(Into speaker-phone)* Got a call, fellah; check back with you when Murray shows.

LEO'S VOICE Right, 'bye now.

*(*MURRAY *enters wearing new suit and carrying a pineapple)*

MURRAY Good afternoon, Mr. Burns.

ARNOLD *(Coming around the desk)* Good afternoon, Mr. Burns. Hey, you really did get a new suit, didn't you? How'd the appointment go with—?

MURRAY *(Putting pineapple on desk)* Arnold, every time I see you, the agency's put you on a higher floor. I swear, next time I come you'll be up in a balloon.

ARNOLD Murray, the appointment—

MURRAY I can't get over this office, Arnie *(sits on the window-sill)* Twenty-second floor. You can see everything. *(Shocked by something he sees out the window)* My God, I don't believe it—

ARNOLD *(Comes towards him)* What—?

MURRAY It's King Kong; he's sitting on top of the Time-Life Building. He . . . he seems to be crying. Poor gorilla bastard, somebody shoulda told him they don't make those buildings the way they used to . . .

ARNOLD *(Raising his hand in the air)* Hello, Murray. Welcome to Tuesday. Come *on*, how'd it go with Jimmy Sloan?

MURRAY He took me to lunch at Steffano's, East 53rd. Christ, it's been a coupla years since I hustled around Lunchland. There is this crazy hum that I haven't heard for so long, Arnie; eight square yards of idea men busily having ideas, eating away at their Chef's Salad like it's crackerjacks and there's a prize at the bottom.

ARNOLD And Sloan . . . ?

MURRAY *(Sitting on the sofa)* Sloan lunches beautifully, can out-lunch anybody. He used to be a Yes-man, but he got himself some guts and now he goes around bravely saying "maybe" to everybody. A killer, this one, Arnie, he's got notches on his attache-case. Wants me to be a permanent guest on his new Panel-Show. *(Doing Sloan)* "Every afternoon. Just talk. No sweat. Running bit for you. On the show. Honesty. Absolute honesty. Best trick of them all, babe; first thing outa your cockamamie head."

ARNOLD What'd you tell him about the offer?

MURRAY I told him good-bye. I don't think he noticed when I left; he focuses slightly to the right of you when he talks, just over your shoulder, so if you stay out of range he can't tell that you're gone. Probably thinks I'm still there.

ARNOLD Murray, you told me this morning to get any job I could; Sloan's offer wasn't so bad—

MURRAY Sloan is an idiot.

ARNOLD   *(Sitting next to him on sofa; angrily, firmly)* Listen, Cookie, I got *news* for you, right now you *need* idiots. You got a bad reputation for quitting jobs, I even had trouble grabbing Sloan for you. Why did you have to go and build your own personal blacklist; why couldn't you just be blacklisted as a Communist like everybody else?

MURRAY   Don't worry, Arnie; I figured I'd go back with Chuckles. He's ready to take me back, isn't he?

ARNOLD   Yeah, he's ready. I just spoke to him. *(Solemnly)* Hey, Murray, Leo says he came up to your place last January, a week after you quit him, to talk you into coming back with the show. And right in the middle you went into the kitchen and started singing "Yessir, That's My Baby." Just left him standing there. Your way of saying "good-bye."

MURRAY   Well, that was four months ago, Arnie—

ARNOLD   *(Attempts to conceal his amusement, then turns to* MURRAY, *smiling)* So, what'd you do with him, you just left him standing there? *(Starts laughing)* Like to have been there, seen that, must have been great—

MURRAY   *(Laughing with him)* Arnie, it was beautiful.

ARNOLD   *(His laughter building)* It's about time somebody left Leo Herman standing around talking to himself—I wish to God I didn't enjoy you so much. I don't do you any damn good at all— *(Abruptly solemn, pulling himself out of it)* O.K., O.K., Murray, no fun and games with Leo today, understand? He is absolutely *all* we got left before the hearing Thursday.

MURRAY   Yes, I understand.

ARNOLD   *(going briskly to pick up phone on desk)* I wish we coulda got something better for you, kid, but there just wasn't any time.

MURRAY   Well, Chuckles won't be so bad for a while—

ARNOLD   No, Murray. *(Puts phone down firmly)* Not just for a while. You'll really have to stick with Chuckles. I had our Agency lawyer check the facts for me. Most the Board'll give you is a probationary year with Nick; a trial period. The Board's investigators will be checking on you every week—

MURRAY   Every week . . .

ARNOLD   —checking to see if you've still got the job, checking with Leo on your stability, checking up on the change in your home environment.

MURRAY *(Softly)* Sounds like a parole board.

ARNOLD *(Into intercom)* Margo; get me Leo Herman on the speaker-phone here, the studio number. Thanks. *(To MURRAY)* He's waiting for our call. Look, Murray, maybe he's not the greatest guy in the world; but y'know, he really *likes* you, Murray, he—

MURRAY I have a way with animals.

ARNOLD *(Pointing at MURRAY)* That was your last joke for today. *(A click is heard from the speaker-phone; ARNOLD turns it on)* You there, Leo?

LEO'S VOICE Right, Arn. I'm down here in the basement, in my gymnasium; lot of echoing. Am I coming through, am I coming through O.K.?

ARNOLD Clearly, Leo. Murray's here.

LEO'S VOICE Murray! Murray the wonderful wild man; fellah, how-are-ya?

MURRAY *(takes his hat off, waving "hello" to speaker-phone)* O.K., Leo, how're *you* doing?

LEO'S VOICE Oh, you crazy bastard, it's damn good to hear that voice again. You're an old monkey, aren't ya?

MURRAY You sound about the same too, Leo.

LEO'S VOICE Not the same. I'm *more impossible* than I used to be. Can you imagine that?

MURRAY Not easily, Leo, no.

LEO'S VOICE Murray, I need you, fellah; I need you back with the show. Murr', we'll talk a while now, and then I'll come over to your place tonight, go over some ideas for next week's shows. It'll be great, sweetie—Oh, there's that word again: "Sweetie." I said that word again. Oh, am I getting *sick* of myself. Big phoney. The truth, fellah, I'm the biggest phoney you ever met, right?

MURRAY Probably, Leo.

LEO'S VOICE *(After a pause; coldly)* "Probably," he says. There he goes, there goes Murray the old joker, right? You're a jester, right? Some fooler. You can't fool with a scheduled show, Murray; a scheduled show with a tight budget. *(Softly, whispering)* Murray, come closer, tell you a secret . . . *(MURRAY comes closer to the box)* You're gonna hate me, Murray; I gotta tell you something and I know you're gonna hate me for it, but we can't have the same Murray we used to have on the show. Who appreciates a good joke more than anybody? *Me*. But who jokes too much? *(Suddenly louder) You!*

MURRAY   Leo, couldn't we talk about this tonight when we get together?

LEO'S VOICE   *(Softly again)* It hurt me, Murr', it hurt me what you used to do. When all those thousands of kids wrote in asking for the definition of a Chipmunk and you sent back that form letter sayin' a Chipmunk was a—was a what?

MURRAY   A cute rat.

LEO'S VOICE   *(Still soft)* A cute rat; yeah. I remember my skin broke out somethin' terrible. Some jester you are, foolin' around at the script conferences, foolin' around at the studio. Now, we're not gonna have any more of that, are we?

MURRAY   *(Subservient, apologetic)* No, we won't, I'm sorry, Leo.

LEO'S VOICE   Because we can't fool with the innocence of children, can we? My God, they believe in the little Chipmunk, don't ask me why; I'm nothing; God, I know that. I've been damned lucky. A person like me should get a grand and a half a week for doin' nothin'. I mean, I'm one of the big *no-talents* of all time, right?

MURRAY   Right—I mean, no, Leo, no.

LEO'S VOICE   Oh, I know it's the truth and I don't kid myself about it. But there'll be no more jokin'; right, Murr'? *(Suddenly loud)* Because I'll tell you the truth, I can't stand it.

MURRAY   Right, Leo.

LEO'S VOICE   *(Softly)* Good. Glad we cleared that up. Because my skin breaks out somethin' terrible. *(Brightly again)* You're the best, Murray, such talent, you know I love ya, don't ya? You old monkey.

MURRAY   *(To ARNOLD)* Please, tell him we'll talk further tonight, too much of him all at once—

ARNOLD   Say, Leo, suppose we—

LEO'S VOICE   Murray, I want you to put some fifteen-minute fairy tales into the show. You've got your Hans Christian Andersens there, your Grimm Brothers, your Goldilocks, your Sleepin' Beauties, your Gingerbread Men, your Foxy-Loxies, your legends, your folk tales—do I reach ya, Murr'?

MURRAY   *(Quietly)* Yeah, Leo—

LEO'S VOICE   Now, what I want in those scripts is this, Murray, I want you to give 'em five minutes o' action, five minutes o' poignancy, and then five minutes o' moral message: race-rela-tions-thing, world-peace-thing, understanding-brings-love-thing, love-brings-understanding, I don't know. Shake-em up a little. Controversy. Angry letters from parents. Kid's show with something to *say*, get some excitement in the industry, wild . . .

MURRAY   *(Leans over, very close to speaker-phone, whispers into it)* Hey, Leo, I might show up one day with eleven minutes a' poignancy, no action, and a twelve second moral message—

ARNOLD   Murray. Stop it—

MURRAY   *(Suddenly shouting into speaker-phone) And then where would we be?*

(There is a pause; no sound comes from the speaker-phone, then)

LEO'S VOICE   See how he mocks me? Well I guess there's plenty there to mock. Plenty mocking. Sometimes I try to take a cold look at what I am. *(Very soft)* Sweaty Leo jumping around in a funny cos-tume trying to make a buck out of being a Chipmunk. The Abominable Snowman in a cute suit. But I'll tell you something, Murray—sit down for a minute. (MURRAY *is standing;* LEO'S VOICE *is still fairly pleasant)* Are ya sitting down, Murray? (MURRAY *remains standing;* LEO'S VOICE *is suddenly loud, sharp, commanding)* Murray, sit down! (MURRAY *sits down)* Good. Now I'm gonna tell you a story—

MURRAY   *(Softly, painfully)* Arnold, he's gonna do it again—the story—

LEO'S VOICE   Murray—

MURRAY   *(Softly, miserably)* The story I got tattooed to my skull—

LEO'S VOICE   On June the third—

MURRAY   *(Hunching over in his chair, looking down at the floor)* Story number twelve—the "Laughter of Children" story—

LEO'S VOICE   I will be forty-two years old—

MURRAY   *(To ARNOLD, pleading)* Arnie—

LEO'S VOICE   And maybe it's the silliest, phoniest, cop-out thing—

LEO'S VOICE & MURRAY   *(In unison)* —you ever heard, but the Chipmunk, Chuckles, the little guy I pretend to be, is real to me—

LEO'S VOICE   —as real to me as—as this phone in my hand; those children, don't ask me why, God I don't know, but they believe in that little fellah— *(MURRAY looks up from the floor now and over at the speaker-phone which is on the other side of the room; his eyes are fixed on it)* Look, Murr', I do what I can for the cash-monies; but also, and I say it without embarrassment, I just love kids, the laughter of children, and we can't have you foolin' with that, Murr', can't have you jokin'— *(MURRAY stands up, still looking at the speaker-phone)* because it's this whole, bright, wild sorta child kinda thing— *(MURRAY is walking slowly toward the speaker-phone now. ARNOLD, watching MURRAY, starts to rise from his chair)* It's this very up feeling, it's all young, and you can't joke with it; the laughter of children; those warm waves, that fresh, open, spontaneous laughter, you can feel it on your face—

MURRAY *(Picking the speaker-phone up off the desk)* Like a sunburn—

LEO'S VOICE Like a sunburn—

ARNOLD *(Coming towards MURRAY as if to stop him)* Murray—wait—

LEO'S VOICE And it's a pride thing— *(MURRAY turns with the speaker-phone held in his hands and drops it into the waste-paper basket next to the desk. He does this calmly. ARNOLD, too late to stop him, stands watching dumbly paralyzed. LEO, unaware, goes right on talking, his voice somewhat garbled and echoing from the bottom of the wastepaper basket)* —so then how lovely, how enchanting it is, that I should be paid so well for something I love so much— *(Pause)* Say, there's this noise—there's this—I'm getting this crackling noise on my end here—what's happened to the phone?

ARNOLD *(Solemnly, looking down into the basket)* Leo, you're in a waste-paper basket.

LEO'S VOICE That you, Murray? —there's this crackling noise—I can't hear you—hello?—what's going on?—

ARNOLD *(Reaching down)* Leo, hold it just a minute, I'll get you.

LEO'S VOICE There's this funny noise—where'd everybody go? Where is everybody?—Hello, Murray—hello—come back— come back—

ARNOLD *(Fishing amongst papers in basket for speaker-phone)* I'll find you, Leo, I'll find you— *(Finally lifts speaker out of basket, holds it gently, tenderly in his hands like a child, speaks soothingly to it)* Look, Leo—Leo, we had a little—some trouble with the phone, we— *(Realizes that he is getting no reaction from the box)* Leo?—Leo? *(Shaking the box tenderly to revive it)* Leo . . . Leo, are you there? . . . Are you there? . . . It's dead. *(Turns to look at MURRAY, announcing the results of fatal surgery)* He's gone.

MURRAY   Well, don't look at me like that Arnie; I didn't *kill* him. He doesn't *live* in that box. Or maybe he does . . .

ARNOLD   A man has a job for you so you drop him in a basket.

MURRAY   Arnie, I quit that nonsense five months ago—

ARNOLD   Murray, you're a *nut*, a man has a job for you, there's a hearing on Thursday—

MURRAY   A fool in a box telling me what's funny, a Welfare Board checking my underwear every week because I don't look good in their files—and *I'm* the nut, right? *I'm* the crazy one—

ARNOLD   Murray, you float like a balloon and everybody's waitin' for ya with a pin. I'm trying to put you in *touch*, Murray—with *real things*; with—

MURRAY   *(Angrily, taking in the office with a sweep of his hand)* You mean like this office, *real* things, like this office? The world could come to an end and you'd find out about it on the phone. *(Pointing at two framed photographs on* ARNOLD'S *desk)* Pictures of your wife eight years ago when she was still a piece and your kids at their cutest four years ago when they looked best for the office . . . Oh, you're in *touch* all right, Arnie.

ARNOLD   *(Softly, soothing)* Murray, you're just a little excited, that's all, just relax, everything's gonna be fine . . .

MURRAY   *(Shouting)* Damn it—get angry; I just insulted you, personally, about your wife, your kids; I just said lousy things to you. Raise your voice, at least your eyebrows . . . *(Pleading)* Please, have an argument with me . . .

ARNOLD   *(Coaxing)* We'll call Leo back, we'll apologize to him— *(*MURRAY *goes to the end table, picks up an apple from the bowl of fruit)* Everything's gonna be just fine, Murray, you'll see—just fine—

MURRAY   Arnie?

ARNOLD   Huh?

MURRAY   Catch.

*(*MURRAY *tosses the apple underhand across the room.* ARNOLD *catches it.* MURRAY *exits)*

ARNOLD   Aw, Murray . . .

(He sits at his desk, alone now, defeated. Glances over at the framed pictures in front of him; a moment, then he places them face-down on his desk. He discovers the apple in his hand; bites into it.

We begin to hear NICK *humming "Yes Sir, That's My Baby" as the*

LIGHTS *fade quickly. This Music continuing in the darkness until the* LIGHTS *go up on* MURRAY'S *apartment;* NICK'S *humming and whistling fading back now so that it is coming from outside the window; the humming growing louder again after a second or two as we hear him descending the fire-escape ladder from Mrs. Meyers' apartment. It is early evening. No one Onstage. The apartment has been rather spectacularly rehabilitated by* SANDRA *since we saw it last. The great clutter of* MURRAY'S *nonsense collection, clocks, eagles, radios, knick-knacks, etc. has been cleared away, the books have been neatly arranged in the bookcases, a hat-rack has been placed above the bureau and* MURRAY'S *hats are placed neatly on it, there are bright new bedspreads on the two beds and brightly colored throw-pillows, one new curtain is already up at the windows and a piece of matching material is over the Morris chair. The beach-chair and swivel-chair are gone and the wicker-chair has been painted gold, the table has a bright new cloth over it. Pots of flowers are on the table, the bookshelves, the file-cabinets, head-board, desk, etc. and geraniums are in a holder hanging from the window-molding. The whole place has been dusted and polished and gives off a bright glow. After two lines or so of the song,* NICK *enters through the window from the fire-escape, carrying his pajamas and school books.* NICK *sees the curtain first, and then, from his position on the window-seat, sees the other changes in the apartment and smiles appreciatively.* SANDRA *enters from kitchen, carrying mixing-bowl and spoon; smiles, glad to see* NICK)

SANDRA Hello, Nick.

NICK Hello, lady. I came in from the fire-escape. Mrs. Myers lives right upstairs. I went there after school, I— *(Indicating her work on the apartment)* Did—did you do all this?

SANDRA Yes, Nick; do you like it?

NICK *(Goes to her, smiling)* I think it's superb. I mean, imagine my surprise when I saw it. *(Pause)* Where's Murray?

SANDRA *(Happily telling him the good news)* Nick—Murray went downtown to see your Uncle Arnold. He's going to get a job.

NICK Hey, no kidding?

SANDRA He'll be back at work in a couple of days.

NICK That's terrific. Hey, that's just terrific. (SANDRA *goes to the folded new curtains on the bed, sits down on the bed, unfolds one of the curtains, begins attaching curtain-hooks and rings to it;* NICK *sits next to her, helping her with the curtains as they talk together)* See, lady, he was developing into a bum. You don't want to see somebody you like developing into a bum, and doing nutty things, right? You know what he does? He hollers. Like we were on Park Avenue last Sunday, it's early in the morning and nobody is in the street, see, there's just all those big quiet apartment houses; and he hollers, "Rich people, I want to see you all out on the street for volleyball! Let's snap it up!" And sometimes, if we're in a crowded elevator someplace, he turns to me and yells, "Max, there'll be no *more* of this self-pity! You're forty, it's time you got *used* to being a midget!" And everybody stares. And he has a wonderful time. What do you do with somebody who hollers like that? Last week in Macy's he did that. *(Then, laughing)* If you want to know the truth, it was pretty funny. (SANDRA *smiles)* I think you're a very nice lady.

SANDRA   Thank you, Nick.

NICK   What do you think of me?

SANDRA   I think you're very nice also.

NICK   A very nice quality you have is that you are a good listener, which is important to me because of how much I talk. *(She laughs, enjoying him)* Hey, you're some laugher, aren't you, lady?

SANDRA   I guess so, Nick.

NICK   *(Trying to make her feel at home)* Would you like some fruit? We got lots of fruit.

SANDRA   No thank you, Nick.

NICK   If you want to call your mother or something, I mean, feel free to use the telephone—or my desk if you want to read a book or something—or *any* of the chairs.

SANDRA   I will, Nick, thank you.

NICK   O.K. *(Pause)* Are you going to be staying around here for a while?

SANDRA   I might, yes.

NICK   *(He rises, picks up the pajamas and books he brought in with him; indicates apartment)* Has . . . has Murray seen . . . all this?

SANDRA   No, not yet.

NICK   *(Nods)* Not yet. *(Goes to window, steps up on window-seat)* Well . . . Good luck, lady.

(He exits through the window, carrying his pajamas and school books, goes on up the fire-escape. SANDRA goes to the window-seat, straightens the curtain for a moment. MURRAY enters, unnoticed by her)

MURRAY   *(Standing still at the front door; to himself)* Oh God, I've been attacked by the *Ladies Home Journal.*

SANDRA   *(She hears him, goes to him happily)* Murray, what a nice suit you bought. How is everything, which job did—?

MURRAY   *(Looking around at her work on the apartment)* Hey, look at this . . .

SANDRA   Don't you like it?

MURRAY   *(Looking around, noticing his knickknacks are missing)* Sure. Sure. Lotta work. Place has an unusual quality now. Kind of Fun Gothic.

SANDRA   Well, of course I'm really not done yet, the curtains aren't all up, and this chair won't look so bad if we re-upholster—Come on, Murray, don't keep me in suspense, which one of the jobs did you—?

MURRAY   *(Takes her arm, smiles, seats her on the chair in front of him)* I shall now leave you breathless with the strange and wondrous tale of this sturdy lad's adventures today in downtown Oz. *(She is cheered by his manner and ready to listen)* Picture, if you will, me. I am walking on East Fifty-first Street an hour ago and I decided to construct and develop a really decorative, general-all-purpose apology. Not complicated, just the words "I am sorry" said with a little style.

SANDRA   Sorry for what?

MURRAY   Anything. For being late, early, stupid, asleep, silly, alive— *(He moves about now, acting out the scene on the street for her)* Well, y'know when you're walking down the street talking to yourself how sometimes you suddenly say a coupla words out loud? So I said "I'm sorry," and this fellah, complete stranger, he looks up a second and says "That's all right, Mac," and goes right on. *(MUR-RAY and SANDRA laugh)* He automatically forgave me. I communicated. Five o'clock rush hour in midtown you could say "Sir, I believe your hair is on fire," and they wouldn't hear you. So I decided to test the whole thing out scientifically. I stayed right there on the corner of Fifty-first and Lex for a while, just saying "I'm sorry" to everybody that went by. *(Abjectly)* "Oh I'm so
s   o   r   r   y   ,
sir . . . " *(Slowly, quaveringly)* "I'm terribly sorry, madam . . . " *(Warmly)* "Say there, Miss, I'm sorry." Of course, some people just gave me a funny look, but Sandy, I swear, seventy-five percent of them *forgave* me! *(Acting out the people for her)* "Forget it, buddy." . . . "That's O.K. really." Two ladies forgave me in uni-

son, one fellah forgave me from a passing car, and one guy forgave me for his dog. "Sophie forgives the nice man, don't you,
Sophie?" Oh Sandy, it was fabulous. I had tapped some vast reser-
voir. Something had happened to all of them for which they felt
*some*body should apologize. If you went up to people on the street
and offered them money, they'd refuse it. But everybody accepts
apology immediately. It is the most negotiable currency. I said to
them "I am sorry," and they were all so generous, so kind. You
could give 'em love and it wouldn't be accepted half as graciously, as unquestioningly.

SANDRA   *(Her amusement fading)*   That's certainly ... that's very
interesting, Murray.

MURRAY   Sandy, I could run up on the roof right now and holler "I
am sorry," and half a million people would holler right back
"That's O.K., just see that you don't do it again!"

SANDRA   *(After a moment)*   Murray, you didn't take any of the jobs.

MURRAY   *(Quietly)*   Sandy, I took whatever I am and put a suit on it
and gave it a haircut and brought it outside and that's what happened. I know what I said this morning, what I promised, and
Sandra, I'm sorry, I'm very sorry. *(She just sits there before him and
stares at him expressionlessly. He smiles warmly, takes her hand)*
Damn it, lady, that was a beautiful apology. You gotta love a guy
who can apologize so nice. I rehearsed for over an hour. *(She just
looks at him)*   That's the most you should expect from life, Sandy,
a really good apology for all the things you won't get.

SANDRA   Murray, I don't understand. What happens to Nick? What
about the Welfare Board—?

MURRAY   Sandra—

SANDRA   I mean, if you don't like the jobs your brother found for you,
then take *any* job—

MURRAY   *(Takes both of her hands, kneels down next to her chair)*   Oh,
Sandy . . . Nick, he's a wonderful kid, but he's brought the world
in on me. Don't you understand, Sandy, they'd be checking up on
me every week; being judged by people I don't know and who
didn't know me, a committee of ghosts; gimme a month of that
and I'll turn into an ash-tray, a bowl of corn-flakes, I wouldn't
know me on the street— *(Looks under chair)*   Have you seen
Murray? He was here just a minute ago— *(Looks at her, smiles)*
Hey, have *you* seen Murray? *(Pleading for her to understand)*   I
wouldn't be of any use to Nick or to you or anybody . . .

SANDRA *(She moves away from him, goes to window-seat, still holding the curtain she had been working on; she begins, absently, folding it neatly on her lap)* I've had no effect on you at all. I've made no difference . . .

MURRAY *(going to her at the window-seat; quietly, with love)* Oh, Sandy, you are a fine and jolly lady . . . please understand.

SANDRA When you left this morning, I was so sure . . .

MURRAY This morning— *(He sits next to her on the window-seat. His arm around her, his free hand gesturing expansively)* Oh, Sandy, I saw the most beautiful sailing this morning—the *Sklardahl*, Swedish liner, bound for Europe. It's a great thing to do when you're about to start something new; you see a boat off. It's always wonderful; there's a sailing practically every day this time of year. Sandy, you go down and stand at the dock with all the well-wishers and throw confetti and make a racket with them— *(Takes confetti from pocket, tosses it in the air)* Hey, Bon Voyage, Charley, have a wonderful time . . . It gives you a genuine feeling of the beginning of things . . . There's another one Friday, big French ship, two stacker . . .

SANDRA *(Quietly)* Murray, Nick will have to go away now, Murray. *(She looks away from him)* I bought new bedspreads at Altman's, I haven't spoken to my mother in two days, and you went to see a boat off— *(Smiles to herself for a moment)* My goodness; I'm a list-maker. *(She leaves him alone in the window-seat)* I have to have enough sense to leave you, Murray. I can see why Nick liked it here. I would like it here too if I was twelve years old. *(Puts folded curtain down on chair, picks up her jacket)*

MURRAY *(Coming down toward her)* Come on, stick with me, Dr. Markowitz, anything can happen above an abandoned Chinese restaurant . . .

SANDRA Maybe you're wonderfully independent, Murray, or maybe you're the most extraordinarily selfish person I've ever met.

(She picks up her handbag and starts toward the door)

MURRAY *(Tired of begging, angrily)* What're you gonna do now, go back and live in a closet? That's really gonna be quite thrilling— you and Albert, guarding the Lincoln Tunnel together.

SANDRA *(Turns at door, looks about the apartment for a moment; very quietly)* There are so many . . . so many really attractive things you can do with a one-room apartment if you're willing to use your imagination. Good-bye, Murray.

(She exits, closing the door behind herself)

MURRAY   *(He stands still for a moment; then rushes forward to the closed door, angrily. Shouting)* Hey, damn it, you forgot your files! *(Picks up her files from bureau, opens door; but she is gone)* The management is not responsible for personal property! *(Closes door, puts files back on bureau; stands at door, looking around at the apartment)* And what the hell did you do to my apartment? Where are my clocks? What'd you do with my stuff? *(Points to top of headboard)* Where's my eagle?! *(Comes Down Center, his back to us, shouting)* What've we got here; Goddamn Sunnybrook Farm?! What happened to my place? *(Suddenly realizes he's still wearing a new suit; he yanks off his jacket, rolls it up into a tight ball and throws it violently across the room. He stretches, inhaling a delicious freedom, then strides over to the window, leans out, shouting)* Everybody on stage for the Hawaiian Number, please! . . . Well, then if you're not ready, we'd better work on the Military March Number . . . *(Going briskly to his old phonograph, putting record on turn-table, continues shouting towards his neighbors in the alley)* Now the last time we ran this, let's admit it was pretty ragged. I mean, the whole Spirit Of Seventy-Six float was in disgraceful shape yesterday! *(An old and scratchy but spirited Marching Band rendition of "Stars And Stripes Forever" starts blasting from the phonograph,* MURRAY *prowling the room, yanking off the new bed-spreads, firing the fancy pillows into the closet, throwing plants in after them, shouting)* O.K. now, let's go, everybody ready, Grenadiers ready, Cossacks ready, Rough Riders ready, Minute Men ready . . . *(Shouting fiercely, stripping the new fabric off his chairs, the Music building louder with his voice, filling the room, a violent movement with each phrase)* Let's go, let's go, let's go, let's go . . . *(He continues as . . .)*

THE CURTAIN FALLS

Above, Robards,
Daniels, Harris

Right, Martin
Balsam and
Robards

ACT THREE

*In the darkness, before the curtain goes up, we hear the old recording
of the Marching Band playing "Stars and Stripes Forever."*

*The music diminishes somewhat as the curtain goes up and takes on
the tinny, crackling sound of* MURRAY'S *old phonograph on the wicker chair. It's about thirty minutes later and, though much of* SAN-
DRA'S *work on the apartment is still apparent, it is obvious that* MUR-
RAY *has been busy putting his place back into its old shape. The curtains and the tablecloths are gone and all the flower pots have been put
on top of the file-cabinets. The swivel-chair and the beach chair are
back in view and the spread-winged eagle is back on top of the headboard. Cluttered about the room again is much of* MURRAY'S *collection, clocks, radios, knick-knacks, stacks of magazines, etc., etc. As the
curtain goes up,* MURRAY *has just retrieved a stack of magazines, the
megaphone and the pirate pistol from the closet where* SANDRA *had
put them, and we see him now placing them back around the room
carefully as though they were part of some strict design.* ARNOLD
*enters, carrying his attaché-case; walks down to beach chair, sits, takes
his hat off. The two men do not look at each other. The music continues to play.*

ARNOLD   *(After a moment)* I didn't even bring a tangerine with me.
That's very courageous if you think about it for a minute. *(Looks
over at* MURRAY, *who is not facing him; points at record-player)* You
wanna turn that music off, please? *(No reply from* MURRAY)
Murray, the music; I'm trying to— *(No reply from* MURRAY, *so*
ARNOLD *puts attaché-case and hat on table, goes quickly to record-play-
er, turns music off;* MURRAY *turns to look at* ARNOLD) O.K., I'm a
little slow. It takes me an hour to get insulted. Now I'm insulted.
You walked out of my office. That wasn't a nice thing to do to me,
Murray. *(MURRAY does not reply)* You came into my office like
George God; everybody's supposed to come up and audition for
Human Being in front of you. *(Comes over closer to him, takes his
arm)* Aw, Murray, today, one day, leave the dragons alone, will
ya? And look at the dragons you pick on: Sloan, Leo, me; silly old
arthritic dragons, step on a toe and we'll start to cry. Murray, I
called Leo back, I apologized, told him my phone broke down; I
got him to come over here tonight. He's anxious to see you,
everything's O.K., we—

MURRAY   Hey, you just never give up, do you, Arnie?

ARNOLD   *(Tensely)* Murray, if you love Nick—or whoever it is he's
calling himself this week—you have got to take any kind of stu-

pid job to keep him. I even thought maybe Shirley and me could take him, but with our three she'd go crazy, I—

MURRAY   *(Realizing* ARNOLD'S *genuine concern)* Arnie, don't worry, I know how to handle it. I've got a coupla days to tell him. And don't underrate Nick, Arnie; he's gonna understand this a lot better than you think he is.

ARNOLD   Murray, I finally figured out your problem. There's only one thing that really bothers you— *(With a sweep of his hand)* Other people. *(Quietly, secretively)* If it wasn't for them other people, everything would be great, huh, Murray? I mean, you think everything's fine, and then you go out into the street—and there they all *are* again, right? The Other People; taking up space, bumping into you, asking for things, making lines to wait on, taking cabs away from ya . . . The Enemy. Well, *watch* out, Murray, they're *every*where . . .

MURRAY   Go ahead, Arnie, give me advice, at thirty thousand a year you can afford it.

ARNOLD   Oh, I get it, if I'm so smart why ain't I poor? You better get a damn good act of your own before you start giving *mine* the razzberry. What's this game you play gonna be like ten years from now, without youth? Murray, Murray, I can't *watch* this, you gotta *shape-up*—

MURRAY   Shape-*up*? *Shape-up*? Arnie, what the hell happened to you? You got so old. I don't know you any more. When you quit "Harry the Fur King" on 38th Street, remember?

ARNOLD   That's twenty years ago, Murray—

MURRAY   You told me you were going to be in twenty businesses in twenty years if you had to, till you found out what you wanted. Things were always going to change. Harry said you were not behaving maturely enough for a salesman; your clothes didn't match or something . . . *(Laughs in affectionate memory)* So the next day, you dressed perfectly, homburg, gray suit, cuff-links, carrying a brief-case and a rolled umbrella . . . and you came into Harry's office on roller skates. You weren't going to take crap from *any*body. So that's the business you finally picked—taking crap from *every*body.

ARNOLD   I don't do practical jokes any more, if that's what you mean.

MURRAY   *(Grabs both of* ARNOLD'S *arms, urgently)* Practical, that's right; a way to stay alive. If most things aren't funny, Arn, then they're only exactly what they are; then it's just one long dental appointment interrupted occasionally by something exciting, like waiting or falling asleep. What's the point if I leave everything exactly the way I find it? Then I'm just adding to the noise, then I'm just taking up some more room on the subway.

ARNOLD   Murray, the Welfare Board has these specifications; all you have to do is meet a couple of specifications—

MURRAY   *(Releases his grip on* ARNOLD'S *arms)* Oh, Arnie, you don't understand any more. You got that wide stare that people stick in their eyes so nobody'll know their head's asleep. You got to be a shuffler, a moaner. You want me to come sit and eat fruit with you and watch the clock run out. You start to drag and stumble with the rotten weight of all the people who should have been told off, all the things you should have said, all the specifications that aren't yours. The only thing you got left to reject is your food in a restaurant, if they do it wrong you can send it back and make a big fuss with the waiter. (MURRAY *turns away from* ARNOLD, *goes to window-seat, sits down)* Arnold, five months ago I was on the subway on my way to work; I was sitting in the express looking out the window same as every morning watching the local stops go by in the dark with an empty head and my arms folded, not feeling great and not feeling rotten, just not feeling, and for a minute I couldn't remember, I didn't know, unless I really concentrated, whether it was a Tuesday or a Thursday . . . or a . . . for a minute it could have been *any* day, Arnie . . . sitting in the train going through any day . . . in the dark through any year . . . Arnie, it scared the hell out of me. *(Stands up)* You got to know what day it is. You got to know what's the name of the game and what the rules are with nobody else telling you. You have to own your days and name them, each one of them, every one of them, or else the years go right by and none of them belong to you. *(Turns to look at* ARNOLD) And that ain't just for week ends, Kiddo. *(Looks at* ARNOLD *a moment longer, then pleasantly)* Here it is, the day after Irving R. Feldman's birthday, for God's sake— *(Takes hat, puts it on)* And I never even congratulated him. *(Starts to walk briskly towards the front door)*

ARNOLD   *(He shouts)* Murray!

(MURRAY stops, turns, startled to hear this loud a voice from ARNOLD. ARNOLD *looks fiercely at* MURRAY *for a moment, then* ARNOLD *too looks surprised, starts to laugh)*

MURRAY   What's so funny?

ARNOLD   Wow, I scared myself. *(After a moment, awkwardly)* I have long been aware, Murray . . . I have long been aware that you don't respect me much. I suppose there are a lot of brothers who don't get along, but in reference . . . to us, considering the factors . . . *(Smiles, embarrassed)* Sounds like a contract, doesn't it? *(Picks up his brief-case, comes over to* MURRAY*)* Unfortunately for you, Murray, you want to be a hero. Maybe if a fellah falls into a lake, you can jump in and save him; there's still that kind of stuff. But who gets opportunities like that in midtown Manhattan, with all that traffic. *(Puts on his hat)* I am willing to deal with the available world, I don't choose to shake it up but to live with it. There's the people who spill things, and the people who get spilled on; I do not choose to notice the stains, Murray. I have a wife and I have children and business, like they say, is business. I am not an exceptional man, so it is possible for me to stay with things the way they are. I'm lucky. I'm gifted. I have a talent for surrender. I'm at peace. But you are cursed; and I like you so it makes me sad, you don't have the gift; and I see the torture of it. All I can do is worry for you. But I will not worry for myself, you cannot convince me that I am one of the Bad Guys. I get up, I go, I lie a little, I peddle a little, I watch the rules, I talk the talk. We fellahs have those offices high up there so we can catch the wind and go with it, however it blows. But, and I will not apologize for it, I take pride; I am the best possible Arnold Burns. *(After a moment)* Well . . . give my regards to Irving R. Feldman, will ya? *(He starts to leave)*

MURRAY   *(Going towards him)* Arnold—

ARNOLD   Please, Murray— *(Puts his hand up)* Allow me once to leave a room before you do.

(ARNOLD *snaps on the phonograph as he walks past it to the front door, exits to the blaring music of "Stars and Stripes Forever."* MUR-RAY *goes toward the closed door; then turns and stands for a long moment looking at the phonograph as the music comes from it. After a moment or two,* NICK *enters through the window from the fire-escape, unnoticed by* MURRAY. NICK *looks about, sees that the apartment is not quite what it was an hour before)*

NICK   Hey, Murray . . .

MURRAY   *(Turns, sees* NICK*)* Nick . . . *(Turns Phonograph off)*

NICK   Hey, where's the lady?

MURRAY   Well, she's not here right now—

NICK   *(Stepping forward to make an announcement)* Murray, this afternoon at school I made a decision, right in the middle of Creative Geography class I decided that since *you* were getting a job today then I made up my mind it is time for *me* also to finish a certain matter which I have been putting off.

MURRAY Nick, listen, turned out the only job I could get in a hurry was with Chuckles—

NICK *(Nodding in approval)* Chuckles, huh? Well, fine. Just as long as I don't have to watch that terrible program every morning. *(Returning to his announcement)* For many months now I have been concerned with a decision, Murray—Murray, you're not listening.

MURRAY *(distracted)* Sure I'm listening, yeah . . .

NICK The past couple months I have been thinking about different names and considering different names because in four weeks I'm gonna be thirteen and I gotta pick my permanent name, like we said.

MURRAY Why don't you just go on calling yourself "Nick"? You've been using it the longest.

NICK Nick is a name for a short person. And since I am a short person I do not believe I should put a lot of attention on it.

MURRAY Whaddya mean, where'd you get the idea you were short?

NICK From people who are taller than I am.

MURRAY That's ridiculous.

NICK Sure, standing up there it's ridiculous, but from down here where I am, it's not so ridiculous. And half the girls in my class are taller than me. Especially Susan Bookwalter.

(NICK sits dejectedly in swivel-chair)

MURRAY *(Crouching over next to him)* Nick, you happen to be a nice medium height for your age.

NICK *(Pointing at MURRAY)* Yeah, so how is it everybody crouches over a little when I'm around?

MURRAY *(Straightens up)* Because you're a kid. *(Sits next to him)* Listen, you come from a fairly tall family. Next couple years, you're gonna grow like crazy. Really, Nick, every day you're getting bigger.

NICK So is Susan Bookwalter. *(Rises, continuing his announcement)* So for a couple of months I considered various tall names. Last month I considered for a while "Zachary," but I figured there was a chance Zachary could turn into a short, fat, bald name. Then I thought about just picking *any* name and putting "Captain" in front of it, to sorta jack it up a little. Then last week I finally, really, decided and I took out a new library card to see how it looks and today I figured I would make it definite and official.

(He takes a library card out of his pocket; hands it to MURRAY*)*

MURRAY   *(Looks at card in his hand, confused)* This is *my* library card.

NICK   No, that's the whole thing; it's mine.

MURRAY   But it says *"Murray* Burns" on it—

NICK   Right, that's the name I picked. So I took out a new card to see how it looks and make it official.

MURRAY   *(He looks at card, moved and upset by it, covering with cool dignity, he stands and speaks very formally)* Well, Nick, I'm flattered . . . I want you to know that I'm . . . very flattered by this. (NICK *goes to alcove to put schoolbooks and pajamas away)* Well, why the hell did you . . . I mean, damn it, Nick, that's too many Murrays, very confusing. (MURRAY *begins to shift the card from one hand to the other, anxiously)* Look, why don't you call yourself "George," huh? Very strong name there, "George" . . .

NICK   *(Shaking his head firmly)* No. We made a deal it was up to me to pick which name and that's the name I decided on: "Murray."

MURRAY   *(Urgently)* Well, what about "Jack"? What the hell's wrong with "Jack"? Jack Burns—sounds like a promising heavyweight—

NICK   I like the name I picked better.

MURRAY   Or Martin—or Robert—

NICK   Those names are all square.

LEO'S VOICE   *(From behind the door, shouting)* Is this it? Is this the Lion's Den, here? Hey, Murr'!

MURRAY   *(Softly)* Ah, I hear the voice of a Chipmunk.

NICK   *(Going into bathroom)* I better go put on a tie.

MURRAY   *(Goes to the door; looks over to the other side of the room at* NICK *who is Offstage in the bathroom; speaks half to himself, softly)* You coulda called yourself Charlie. Charlie is a very musical name. *(Then he opens the door.* LEO HERMAN *enters. He wears a camel's-hair coat and hat. The coat, like his suit, is a little too big for him. He is carrying a paper bag and a large "Chuckles" statue—a life-sized cardboard cut-out of himself in his character of Chuckles the Chipmunk; the statue wears a blindingly ingratiating smile)*

LEO   *(With great enthusiasm)* Murray, there he is! There's the old monkey! There's the old joker, right?

MURRAY *(Smiling politely)* Yeah, Leo, here he is. *(Shakes* LEO'S *hand)* It's . . . it's very nice to see you again, Leo, after all this time.

LEO *(Turning to see* NICK, *who has come out of the bathroom wearing his tie)* There he is! There's the little guy! *(Goes to* NICK *carrying the statue and the paper bag)* Looka here, little guy— *(Setting the statue up against the wall)* I gotta "Chuckles" statue for you.

NICK *(With his best company manners)* Thank you, Mr. Herman; imagine how pleased I am to receive it. It's a very artistic statue and very good cardboard too.

LEO *(Taking a "Chuckles" hat from the paper-bag; a replica of the furry, big-eared hat worn by the statue)* And I gotta "Chuckles" hat for you too, just like the old Chipmunk wears.

(He puts the hat on NICK'S *head)*

NICK Thank you.

LEO *(Crouching over to* NICK's *height)* Now that you've got the "Chuckles" hat, you've got to say the "Chuckles-hello."

NICK *(Confused, but anxious to please)* The what?

LEO "Chip-chip, Chippermunkie!" *(He salutes)*

NICK Oh, yeah—"Chip-chip, Chippermunkie!" *(He salutes too)*

LEO May I know your name?

NICK It's Nick, most of the time.

LEO Most of the time; great. *(Pulling two bags of potato chips from his overcoat pockets)* Say, look what I've got, two big bags of "Chuckle-Chip" potato chips! How'd ya like to put these crispy chips in some bowls or somethin' for us, huh? *(*NICK *takes the two bags, goes to kitchen)* And take your time, Nick, your uncle n'me have some grown-up talkin' to do. *(After Nick exits into kitchen)* The kid hates me. I can tell. Didn't go over very well with him, pushed a little too hard. He's a nice kid, Murray.

MURRAY How are *your* kids, Leo?

LEO Fine, fine. But, Murray, I swear, even *they* don't like my show since you stopped writing it. My youngest one—my six-year-old—uh— *(He can't quite remember)*

MURRAY Ralphie.

LEO Ralphie; he's been watching the "Funny Bunny Show" now every morning instead of me. *(Begins pacing up and down)* Oh *boy*, have I been bombing out on the show. Murray, do you know what it *feels* like to bomb out in front of children? You flop out in front of kids and, Murray, I swear to God, they're ready to *kill* you. *(Stops pacing)* Or else, they just stare at you, that's the worst, that hurt innocent stare like you just killed their pup or raped their turtle or something. *(Goes over to* MURRAY*)* Murray, to have you back with me on the show, to see you at the studio again tomorrow, it's gonna be *beautiful*. You're the *best*.

MURRAY   I appreciate your feeling that way, Leo.

LEO   This afternoon, Murray, on the phone, you hung up on me, didn't you?

MURRAY   I'm sorry, Leo, I was just kidding—I hope you—

LEO   Murray, why do you do that to me? Aw, don't tell me, I know, I make people nervous. Who can listen to me for ten minutes? *(Begins pacing up and down again, strokes his tie)* See *that?* See how I keep touching my suit and my tie? I keep touching myself to make sure I'm still there. Murray, I get this feeling, maybe I vanished when I wasn't looking.

MURRAY   Oh, I'm sure that you're here, Leo.

LEO   *(Pointing at* MURRAY*)* See how he talks to me? A little nasty. *(Suddenly smiles)* Well, I like it. It's straight and it's real and I like it. You know what I got around me on the show? Finks, dwarfs, phonies and frogs. No Murrays. The show: boring, boredom, bore . . . *(Cups hands around mouth, shouts)* boring, boring, sleepy, over, finished, gone, crashing . . .

(During these last few words, SANDRA *has entered through the partly open door.* MURRAY *turns, sees her)*

SANDRA   *(Staying up in the doorway area; reserved, official)* Murray, I believe that I left my files here; I came to get my files; may I have my files, please? I . . . *(She sees* LEO, *comes a few feet into the room)* Oh, excuse me . . .

MURRAY   *(Cordially, introducing them)* Chuckles the Chipmunk . . . this is Minnie Mouse.

LEO   *(Absently)* Hi, Minnie.

SANDRA   *(Looking from one to the other, taking in the situation)* You must be . . . you must be Mr. Herman.

LEO   *(Mumbling to himself)* Yeah, I must be, I must be him; I'd rather not be, but what the hell . . .

SANDRA   *(She turns right around and goes to the door)* Well, I'll be on my way.

(She exits. MURRAY *picks up her files from the bureau, goes to the door with them)*

LEO   *(Interrupting* MURRAY'S *move to door)*   Very attractive girl, that Minnie; what does she do?

MURRAY   She's my decorator.

LEO   *(Looking around the apartment)*   Well . . . she's done a *wonderful* job!   *(Indicating apartment with a sweep of his hand)*   This place is great. It's loose, it's open, it's free. Love it. Wonderful, crazy place. My God—you must make out like mad in this place, huh?   *(*MURRAY *closes door, puts files back on bureau;* LEO *is walking around the apartment)*   How come I never came here before?

MURRAY   You were here last January, Leo.

LEO   Funny thing, work with me for three years and I never saw your apartment.

MURRAY   You were here last January, Leo.

LEO   *(Stops pacing, turns to* MURRAY*)*   Wait a minute, wait a minute, wasn't I here recently, in the winter? Last January, I think . . . *(Goes over to* MURRAY*)*   Oh, I came here to get you back on the show and you wouldn't listen, you went into the kitchen, sang "Yes Sir, That's My Baby." I left feeling very foolish, like I had footprints on my face . . . You old monkey.   *(Smiles, musses up* MURRAY's *hair)*   You're an old monkey, aren't ya?   *(Starts pacing again)*   You know what I got from that experience? A rash. I broke out something terrible . . . Minnie Mouse?   *(Stops pacing)*   Minnie *Mouse!*   *(Laughs loudly, points at door)*   You told me her name was Minnie *Mouse!* I swear to God, Murray, I think my mission in life is to feed you straight lines . . . *(Taking in the apartment with a sweep of his hand)*   It's kind of a fallout shelter, that's what you got here, Murr', protection against the idiots in the atmosphere. Free, freer, freest—   *(Cups hands around mouth, shouts)*   Free, freedom, free, life, liberty, happiness—   *(Takes off his coat)*   Another year and I'm gonna cut loose from the Goddamn Chipmunk Show. Binds me up, hugs me. Finks, dwarfs, phonies and frogs. *(Following* MURRAY *to the window seat)*   Two of us should do something new, something wild; new kind of kids' show, for adults maybe.

MURRAY   You told me the same thing three years ago, Leo.

LEO   *(Sits next to* MURRAY*)*   Well, whaddya want from me? I'm a coward; everybody knows that.   *(Suddenly seeing the "Chuckles" statue against the wall next to him)*   Oh God! . . .   *(Points at the statue; in* *anguish)* Did you ever see anything so *immodest?* I bring a big statue of myself as a gift for a child! I mean, the *pure ego* of it. *(Covers his face with his hands)* I am ashamed. Murray, could you throw a sheet over it or something. *(Sees* NICK *who has just come out of the kitchen with two bowls of potato chips)* Mmmm, good! Here they are. *(Grabs one bowl from* NICK'S *hand, gives it to* MURRAY. *Then* LEO *turns to* NICK, *assumes the character and the voice of Chuckles the Chipmunk; a great mock-frown on his face, he goes into a routine for* NICK*)* Oh, goshes, kidderoonies, look at your poor Chippermunk friend; he got his mouff stuck. No matter how hard I try I can't get my mouth unstuck. But maybe—if you Chippermunks yell "Be happy, Chuckles," maybe then it'll get unstuck . . . *(*LEO *waits.* NICK *does not react.* LEO *whispers)* You're supposed to yell "Be happy, Chuckles."

NICK   Oh, yeah—sure— *(Glances quickly at* MURRAY; *a little embarrassed, he yells)* "Be happy, Chuckles!"

LEO   Oh *boy! (His frown changes to a giant smile)* You *fixed* me! Looka my mouff! *(He jumps up in the air)* Now I'm all fixed! *(Gets no reaction from* NICK. NICK *stands patiently in front of* LEO*)*

NICK   *(Offering the other bowl of potato chips to* LEO, *trying to be polite)* Mr. Herman, don't you want your—?

LEO   *(Not accepting the potato chips, stroking his tie)* That was a bit from tomorrow morning's show. You'll know it ahead of all the kids in the neighborhood.

NICK   Thank you.

LEO   That . . . that was one of the funny parts there, when I couldn't move my mouth.

NICK   Yeah?

LEO   Didn't you think it was funny?

NICK   Yeah, that was pretty funny.

LEO   Well, don't you laugh or something when you see something funny?

NICK   It just took me by surprise is all. So I didn't get a chance. *(Offering potato chips, politely)* Here's your—

LEO   Another funny part was when I jumped up with the smile there, at the end there. That was another one.

NICK   Uh-huh.

LEO   *(Pressing on, beginning to get tense)* And the finish on the bit, see, I've got the smile— *(*NICK *stands there politely as* LEO *switches back* *to his Chipmunk voice and puts a giant smile on his face)* Now I'm aaaall fixed, Chippermunks! *(Sudden mock-pathos in his eyes)* Ooooops! *Now* I got it stuck the *other* way! Oh, *oh*, now my face is stuck the *other* way! *(LEO throws up his arms, does a loose-legged slap-stick fall back onto the floor. Remains prone, waiting for NICK'S reaction. NICK stands there looking at LEO quite solemnly)*

NICK   *(Nods his head up and down approvingly)* That's terrific, Mr. Herman. *(With admiration)* That's all you have to do, you just get up and do that and they pay you and everything.

LEO   You didn't laugh.

NICK   I was waiting for the funny part.

LEO   *(Sitting up)* That was the funny part.

NICK   Oh, when you fell down on the—

LEO   When I fell down on the floor here.

NICK   See, the thing is, I was—

LEO   *(Gets up from the floor, paces tensely up and down)* I know, waiting for the funny part. Well, you missed another funny part.

NICK   Another one. Hey, I'm really sorry, Mr. Herman, I—

LEO   Forget it—I just happen to know that that bit is very *funny*. I can prove it to you. *(Takes small booklet from pocket, opens it, shows it to NICK)* Now, what does that say there, second line there?

NICK   *(Reading from booklet)* "Frown bit; eighty-five percent of audience; outright prolonged laughter on frown bit."

LEO   That's the analysis report the agency did for me on Monday's preview audience. The routine I just did for you got outright prolonged laughter; eighty-five percent.

MURRAY   You could try him on sad parts, Leo; he's very good on sad parts.

LEO   *(Goes to MURRAY at window-seat, shows him another page in booklet)* Matter fact, there's this poignant-type bit I did at the Preview Theatre: "Sixty percent of audience: noticeably moved."

MURRAY   They left the theatre?

LEO   *(Tensely, angrily)* There he is; there's the old joker; Murray the joker, right?

NICK   *I* do some routines. I can imitate the voice of Alexander Hamilton.

LEO   That's lovely, but I—

NICK   I do Alexander Hamilton and Murray does this terrific Thomas Jefferson; we got the voices just right.

(MURRAY *sits in Morris chair;* NICK *stands behind him*)

MURRAY   *(In dignified voice)* Hello there, Alex, how-are-you?

NICK   *(In dignified voice)* Hello there, Tom; say, you should have been in Congress this morning. My goodness, there was quite a discussion on—

LEO   Now that's *ridiculous*. You . . . you can't *do* an imitation of Alexander Hamilton; nobody knows what he *sounds* like—

NICK   *(Pointing triumphantly at* LEO*)* That's the *funny* part.

MURRAY   *(Shaking his head regretfully)* You missed the funny part, Leo.

LEO   *(Walking away from them)* I'm getting a terrible rash on my neck. *(Turns to them, growing louder and more tense with each word)* The routine I did for him was *funny*. I was workin' good in front of the kid, I know how to use my God-damn *warmth*, I don't go over with these odd kids; I mean, here I am right in *front* of him, in *person*, for God's sake, and he's *staring* at me. *(Moves towards them, on the attack)* It's oddness here, Murray, *odd*ness. Alexander *Ham*ilton imitations! Jaded jokes for old men. Murray, what you've done to this kid. It's a damn shame, a child can't enjoy little animals, a damn shame— *(Really on the attack now; waving at the apartment, shouting)* The way you brought this kid up, Murray, grotesque atmosphere, *unhealthy*, and you're not even guilty about it, women in and out, *decorators*; had he been brought up by a *normal* person and not in this *mad*-house—

NICK   *(Quietly, going towards* LEO*)* Hey, don't say that—

LEO   A certain kind of freakish way of growing up—

NICK   *(Quietly)* Hey, are you calling me a freak? You called me a freak. Take back what you said.

LEO   *(Walks away from them, mumbling to himself)* On June third I will be forty-two years old and I'm standing here arguing with a twelve-year-old kid. *(*LEO *quiets down, turns, comes toward* NICK, *sits on bed,* NICK *standing next to him; he speaks calmly to* NICK*)* See, Nicky, humor is a cloudy, wonderland thing, but simple and clear like the blue, blue sky. All I want is your simple, honest, child's opinion of my routine; for children are too honest to be wise.

NICK   *(Looking directly at* LEO; *calmly, quietly, slowly)* My simple, child's reaction to what you did is that you are not funny. Funnier than you is even Stuart Shlossman my friend who is eleven and puts walnuts in his mouth and makes noises. What is not funny is to call us names and what is mostly not funny is how sad you are that I would feel sorry for you if it wasn't for how dull you are and those are the worst tasting potato chips I ever tasted. And that is my opinion from the blue, blue sky.

(NICK *and* LEO *remain quite still, looking at each other. A moment; then* MURRAY *throws his head back and laughs uproariously.* LEO *stands; the bowl of potato chips tips over in his hand, the chips spilling in a stream onto the floor)*

LEO   *(Seeing* MURRAY'S *laughter, goes to him at Morris chair, angrily)* Murray, the joker, right? You didn't want to come back to work for me, you just got me up here to step on my face again! *(*NICK, *unnoticed by* LEO, *has gone quickly into his alcove and comes out now with his ukulele, playing and singing "Yes Sir, That's My Baby" with great spirit.* LEO, *hearing this, turns to look at* NICK*)* It's the *song.* It's the good-*bye song.* (LEO *grabs his hat and coat quickly as* NICK *goes on playing; starts for front door, shouting)* Getting *out, bunch of nuts* here, *crazy* people—

MURRAY   Leo, wait . . . *(Goes to door to stop* LEO*)* Leo, wait—I'm sorry—wait— *(*LEO *stops at the door;* MURRAY *goes down towards* NICK *who is near the alcove, still playing the song)* Nick, you better stop now—

NICK   Come on, Murray, get your uke, we'll sing to him and he'll go away—

MURRAY   *(Regretfully)* Nick, we can't— *(Gently taking uke from* NICK, *puts it on window-seat)* Just put this down, huh?

NICK   *(Confused by this; urgently)* Come on, Murray, let him go away, he called us names, we gotta get rid of him—

MURRAY   Quiet now, Nick—just be quiet for a minute. *(Starts to go back towards* LEO*)*

NICK   *(Shouting)* Murray, please let him go away! *(*NICK, *seeing the "Chuckles" statue next to him against the wall, grabs it angrily, throws it down on the floor)* It's a crummy statue—that crummy statue! *(Begins to kick the statue fiercely, jumping up and down on it, shouting)* It's a terrible statue, rotten cardboard—

(MURRAY *comes quickly back to* NICK, *holds both of his arms, trying to control him)*

MURRAY   Aw, Nick, please, no more now, stop it—

(There is a great struggle between them; NICK *is fighting wildly to free himself from* MURRAY'S *arms)*

NICK   *(Near tears, shouting)* We don't want jerks like that around here, Murray, let him go away, we gotta get rid of him, Murray, we gotta get rid of him—

MURRAY   *(Lifts the struggling* NICK *up into his arms, hugging him to stop him)* No, Nick—I'm sorry, Nick—we can't . . . *(*NICK *gives up, hangs limply in* MURRAY'S *arms.* MURRAY *speaks quietly)* I'm sorry . . . I'm sorry, kid . . . I'm sorry . . . *(Puts* NICK *down, still holding him)*

NICK   *(After a pause; quietly, in disbelief)* Murray . . .

MURRAY   You better go to your room.

NICK   This is a one-room apartment.

MURRAY   Oh. Then go to your alcove. *(*NICK *waits a moment, then turns, betrayed, walks over to his alcove, lies down on bed.* MURRAY *looks over at* LEO *who is standing dejectedly at the front door; he walks slowly over to* LEO, *looking down at the floor; humbly)* Leo . . . hope you didn't misunderstand . . . we were just kidding you . . . we . . .

LEO   *(Coming towards* MURRAY, *apologetically)* I, myself, I got carried away there myself.

MURRAY   We all got a little excited, I guess. *(Reaches out to shake* LEO'S *hand)* So, I'll see you at work in the morning, Leo.

LEO   *(Smiling, shaking* MURRAY'S *hand)* Great to have you back, fellah. You both hate me.

MURRAY   Nobody hates you, Leo.

LEO   I hollered at the kid. I'm sorry. I didn't mean to cause any upset. I don't get along too good with kids . . .

MURRAY   Don't worry about it.

LEO   Wanna come have a drink with me, Murray? We could—

MURRAY   No thanks; maybe another night, Leo.

LEO   Look, after I leave, you horse around a little with the kid, he'll feel better.

MURRAY   Right, Leo.

LEO   *(Pauses; then comes closer to* MURRAY*)* Murray . . . that bit I did was funny, wasn't it?

MURRAY   *(After a moment)* Yeah, Leo . . . I guess it was just a bad day for you.

LEO   Yeah, bad day for the old chipmunk. *(Pointing at the Chuckles statue on the floor; quietly, but giving a command)* You don't want to leave that statue lying around like that, huh, Murray?

MURRAY   No. No. *(Goes to statue obediently, lifts it up off the floor, leans it upright against the wall)* There.

LEO   Fine.

MURRAY   See you tomorrow.

LEO   *(Smiles, grabs MURRAY's shoulders)* O.K., see ya at the studio in the morning, you old monkey. *(Goes to door; stops; turns to MURRAY)* Hey, you're an old monkey, aren't you? *(LEO waits for an answer. MURRAY nods, accepting the definition. LEO exits briskly, leaving the door open. MURRAY stays near the door for a moment. NICK is still lying on his bed in the Alcove, his back to MURRAY)*

MURRAY   *(Walking over to NICK, trying to make peace with him)* Say, I could use a Pastrami sandwich right now, couldn't you, Nick? On rye, with cole slaw and Russian dressing.

(NICK does not reply. MURRAY sits down next to him on the bed. NICK refuses to look at MURRAY. They are both silent for a moment)

NICK   *(Softly, bitterly)* Guy calls us names. Guy talks to us like that. Shoulda got rid of that moron. Coulda fooled the Welfare people or something . . . *(SANDRA enters through the open door, unnoticed by them; she stays up in the doorway, watching them)* We coulda gone to Mexico or New Jersey or some place.

MURRAY   I hear the delicatessen in Mexico is terrible.

NICK   *(After a moment)* I'm gonna call myself *Theodore*.

MURRAY   As long as you don't call yourself Beatrice.

NICK   O.K., fool around. Wait'll you see a Theodore running around here. *(Silent for a moment, his back still to MURRAY; then, quietly)* Another coupla seconds he woulda been out the door . . . *(Turns to look at MURRAY)* Why'd you go chicken on me, Murray? What'd you stop me for?

MURRAY   Because your routines give me out-right prolonged laughter, Theodore.

SANDRA: *(After a pause)* Four-ninety-five for this table-cloth and you leave it around like this— *(Picks up discarded table-cloth from chair)* A perfectly new table-cloth and already there are stains on it. *(Sits on Morris chair, starts to dab at table-cloth with her handkerchief)* You know, it's very interesting that I left my files here. That I forgot them. I mean, psychologically, if you want to analyze that. Of course, last month I left my handbag in the Automat, and I have no idea what that means at all. *(MURRAY leaves alcove, starts toward her)* I think that the pattern of our relationship, if we examine it, is very intricate, the different areas of it, especially the whole "good-bye" area of it, and also the "hello" and "how-are-you" area . . . of it.

MURRAY *(Standing next to her chair now, smiles warmly)* Hello, Sandy, and how-are-you?

SANDRA *(Looks up at him, smiles politely)* Hello, Murray. *(Goes right back to her work, rubbing table-cloth with handkerchief)* You're standing in my light.

MURRAY Oh. *(Retreats a step)*

NICK *(Walking over to her)* Hello, lady.

SANDRA Hello, Nick.

NICK *(Indicating her work on the table-cloth)* Lady, can I help you with any of that?

SANDRA Matter of fact, Nick— *(She stands; her arm around NICK, she goes to Center with him)* Nick, I don't think the effect, I mean the overall design of this room is really helped by all these— *(Gesturing to MURRAY's stuff around the bed)* these knick-knacks.

NICK You mean the junk?

SANDRA Yes.

NICK Yeah, not too good for the over-all design.

SANDRA So if you'd just put them away in that carton there— *(Indicates carton near bed)*

NICK Sure, lady.

(NICK goes quickly to the carton, begins to put MURRAY'S junk into it, some radios, a megaphone, some clocks, an eagle. SANDRA starts putting table-cloth on table)

MURRAY *(Moves forward, trying to halt the proceedings)* Hey, Sandy, now wait a minute— *(She goes on with her work, putting a piece of material over the Morris chair. He turns at the sound of one of his radio-cabinets being dropped into the carton by NICK)* Listen, Nick, I didn't tell you to—*Nick*—

NICK *(Looking up from his work)* Wilbur— *(Drops a clock into the carton)* Wilbur Malcome Burns.

(SANDRA is putting the flowers back around the room, picking up magazines, etc.)

MURRAY   *(Protesting)* Hey, now, both of you, will ya wait a minute here, will ya just wait . . . ? Hey . . . *(They ignore him, going on with their work. He gets an idea, smiles, strides confidently over to the window. Meanwhile* SANDRA *and* NICK'S *work accelerates; the Prussian Helmet and the Pirate Pistol disappearing, throw-pillows and seat-covers re-appearing, etc.* MURRAY *leans out the window shouting with great gusto)* Campers . . . the Entertainment Committee was quite disappointed by the really poor turn-out at this morning's Community Sing. I mean, where's all that old Camp Chickawattamee spirit? Now I'm sure I speak for all of us here this evening when I say . . . *(He hesitates, about to come up with something.* NICK *and* SANDRA *join in throwing the giant, bright new bedspread over the bed, smoothing it out, removing the eagle from the headboard, etc.* MURRAY, *haltingly, tries again)* Yes, I'd like to say right now that I . . . that . . . that I . . . *(Silence for a moment; then he sits in the window-seat; his voice is soft, vague)* Campers . . . I can't think of anything to say . . .

(We begin to hear the sound of an oncoming Subway Train, his home continuing to disappear as SANDRA *and* NICK *go on happily with their work;* MURRAY *quite still, slumped, his arms folded, seated as he was when he described forgetting what day it was to* ARNOLD; *the Subway Sound builds to a clattering roar and then is quickly overtaken by the more powerful roar of Mid-Town Rush Hour Traffic; the wail of sirens, desperate honking, screeching trucks and groaning buses filling the stage as . . .)*

THE CURTAIN FALLS

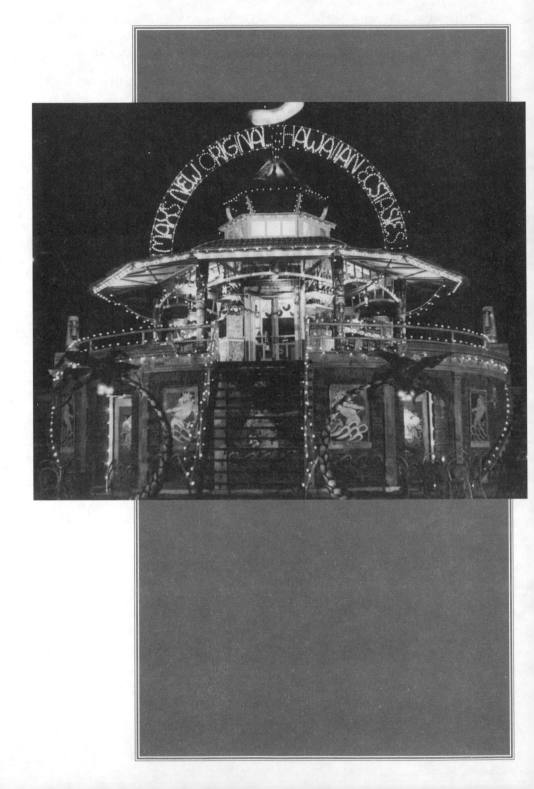

THE GOODBYE PEOPLE

THE GOODBYE PEOPLE

A long time ago, roughly twelve or thirteen years before the birth of Christ, I got my first copy of *The Goodbye People*. Herb Gardner wanted me to play the only woman in the play and I accepted — and then backed out because a movie I was to direct was green-lighted, or green"lit" as they said in those days. While I was in pre-production *The Goodbye People* opened on Broadway and closed.

I guess I shouldn't have been surprised. It was such an unconventional play. The first act was very long, the second act was very short. The late Bill Hickey described the central character Arthur as a man who goes crazy in order to pull himself together. The play, itself, celebrates impracticality, recklessness, irrational hope, stubbornness, and the refusal to listen to reason — with no warning to young people that these qualities might be injurious to their income. All the characters speak eloquently and at length, in the tradition of Shaw and Shakespeare. It wasn't really what they were looking for on Broadway that season.

And then, many years later, just after the defeat of the Spanish Armada, Herb Gardner sent me *The Goodbye People* again. He had reworked it, trimmed it, balanced out the first and second acts, and asked if I would direct it somewhere out of town to see how it played. And so, with a cast that included Gene Saks, Zohra Lampert and Gabriel Dell, we went to The Berkshire Theatre in Stockbridge, Massachusetts and opened this intensely Jewish play about New Yorkers in Coney Island.

The first preview audience consisted of the most sedate and well-mannered gentiles I have ever seen gathered in an East Coast theatre. Herb and I watched them in silence as they filed in. Not one woman over fifty had strawberry hair. Not one man was without a tan. Everyone was smiling. Nobody talked about how full they were. It looked like a catastrophe.

And then, somewhere near the end of the first act, this civilized, courteous audience began to behave as though they were at a revival meeting. They spoke aloud, they took sides in arguments, they applauded, they cried "no!" when bad things happened and "don't do it!" when there was danger. They came back again — just to see if the characters had taken their advice. They became — almost Italian.

Since then *The Goodbye People* has been done many times. It was revived in New York; it has played in Chicago, Los Angeles and throughout this country. It has had long runs in France, Germany and Czechoslovakia; and it has been made into a movie. And, through the centuries, I have watched the audience response. And then, finally, as I sat down to write this introduction, it dawned on me that *The Goodbye People* is not a special play about New York Jews. It is a quintessential play about America, about discounting the odds, about having hope without evidence, about the refusal to accept old age or anything else without an argument, about thumbing your nose at death with dignity and, in fact, thumbing your nose at dignity. It is about the tough, unregenerate, screw-you exhilaration of the old West, still alive and doing business in Coney Island.

— ELAINE MAY
New York City

Judd Hirsch with Herb Gardner on location for
the film of *The Goodbye People*.

The Goodbye People opened at the Ethel Barrymore Theatre, New York City, on December 3, 1968. It was produced by Feuer and Martin and directed by Herb Gardner, with sets and lighting by David Hays and costumes by Alvin Colt. The cast was as follows:

ARTHUR KORMAN	Bob Dishy
MAX SILVERMAN	Milton Berle
NANCY SCOTT	Brenda Vaccaro
EDDIE BERGSON	Jess Osuna
MICHAEL SILVERMAN	Tony Lo Bianco
MARCUS SOLOWAY	Sammy Smith

The Goodbye People was presented at the Solari Theatre in Los Angeles, opening January 2, 1979. It was directed by Jeff Bleckner. Sets were designed by James Freiburger, lighting by John Beilock. The cast was as follows:

ARTHUR KORMAN	Peter Bonerz
MAX SILVERMAN	Herschel Bernardi
NANCY SCOTT	Patty Duke Astin
EDDIE BERGSON	Bruce Weitz
MICHAEL SILVERMAN	Michael Tucker
MARCUS SOLOWAY	Sammy Smith

The Goodbye People, produced by Joseph Kipness and Maurice Rosenfield at the Belasco Theatre in New York City, opened May 1, 1979. It was directed by Jeff Bleckner, with sets, lighting and costumes by Santo Loquasto, Jennifer Tipton and Elizabeth Palmer. The cast was as follows:

ARTHUR KORMAN	Ron Rifkin
MAX SILVERMAN	Herschel Bernardi
NANCY SCOTT	Melanie Mayron
EDDIE BERGSON	Marvin Lichterman
MICHAEL SILVERMAN	Michael Tucker
MARCUS SOLOWAY	Sammy Smith

CHARACTERS

    ARTHUR KORMAN

    MAX SILVERMAN

    NANCY SCOTT

    EDDIE BERGSON

    MICHAEL SILVERMAN

    MARCUS SOLOWAY

SCENE: A part of the Boardwalk and Beach in Coney Island, February, 1968.

ACT I: Just before dawn.

ACT II:

    Scene 1: Early evening of the same day.

    Scene 2: Three days later, early evening.

    Scene 3: Dawn, the following day.

ACT ONE

Before the curtain goes up, we hear about twenty seconds of an old Al Jolson recording of "Toot, Toot, Tootsie, Goodbye".

The sound is loud and clear, but it is obviously a scratchy old record.

JOLSON'S VOICE

"Toot, Toot, Tootsie! Good-bye.
Toot, Toot, Tootsie, don't cry.
The choo-choo train that takes me
Away from you,
No words can tell how sad it makes me.
Kiss me, Tootsie, and then
Do it over again.
Watch for the mail,
I'll never fail,
If you don't get a letter
Then you'll know I'm in jail . . . "

The music is joined by the sound of rolling surf, gulls, a winter wind, a distant buoy bell, and then the curtain goes up . . .

Scene: The beach at Coney Island. It is late February, a few minutes before dawn. The boardwalk lamps are lit, the surf crashes, the winter wind whistles. The audience is where the ocean would be and the beach angles down toward us. Upstage is a section of boardwalk; a wide wooden stairway leads down from it to the beach at right, disappearing into drifts of sand. Far left are two battered phone booths, back to back under the boardwalk, with sand banked against them like gray snow. Above the boardwalk we can see the open sky, and below it the boardwalk planks drop striped shadows on the sand. Under the boardwalk, to the left of the stairs, is a boarded-up refreshment stand, obviously closed for the winter but old and faded enough to indicate that it has been closed for an even longer time. The front of the stand is about fifteen feet wide; it shows years of being battered by wind and water. Above the stand is an old, faded sign; originally silver letters against a blue background, it is now a mixture of the many colors of age, wear, rust, and strong sun. We can just about make out that the sign says "Max's Hawaiian Ecstasies." At center, a weather-beaten pier extends about four rows into the audience.

At rise: The Jolson song continues for a few moments . . .

JOLSON'S VOICE

"Toot, Toot, Tootsie, don't cry,

Toot, Toot, Tootsie, good-bye,
Good-bye, Tootsie, good-bye . . . "

The music fades into the sound of wind and ocean; the stage is empty for a few moments and then ARTHUR KORMAN *enters, running breathlessly along the boardwalk and down the steps.* ARTHUR *is about forty, wears a Mackinaw with the hood up and a pair of dark glasses, and is carrying a banjo case and a folded newspaper. He is in a great hurry as though late for an important appointment. He goes quickly into the shadows under the boardwalk, emerging in a moment with a folded beach chair, striped with the colors of summer. Moving quickly down center, he drops everything in the sand, unfolds the beach chair, and sits on the edge of it expectantly, looking anxiously out at the off-stage horizon where the audience is. A moment; then he checks his watch; then he looks at a page in the newspaper as though to verify something, nods to himself, and returns to his vigilant pose, leaning forward, his eyes squinting with concentration on the horizon. Another moment and then he jumps up, moves down to the edge of the pier for a closer look at the horizon. He is getting annoyed.*

ARTHUR   *(Quietly)* "Goddamn New York Times" . . . *(Going quickly to phone booths)* Who ya supposed to believe any more? Who ya supposed to trust? *(Deposits coin, dials angrily, glancing over his shoulder from time to time as though something might suddenly happen on the horizon. Speaks into phone)* Hello, *New York Times*? I think we got a problem. We got a definite problem here. Your Late City Edition says here, page 70, column 3: "February 22; sunrise: 6:41." O.K., well, it's six forty-*eight* right now, and I don't know what's happening in *your* neighborhood, lady, but down here we got darkness . . . Well, if you're just the operator, then who's responsible, who's on top of the sunrise situation over there? . . . City Desk? Fine. Lemme speak to them. . . Who's this? Mr. Mallory? Mr. Mallory, look out your window. What do ya see? That's called darkness, Mr. Mallory. That's nighttime you got goin' on out there. My name is Arthur Korman, a regular subscriber to your publication, come at great inconvenience to myself to witness the birth of a new day, come on the B.M.T. in quest of beauty and gettin' my ass froze off in total blackness down here! What the hell're you guys usin' for weather information up there? What're ya, a buncha *gypsies* up there!

(During these last few lines, MAX SILVERMAN *has entered from under the boardwalk. A short man, about seventy-five years old, he wears an overcoat, a fishing hat, and an unlit cigar that appears to be part of his face. He carries a shopping bag from which he takes a folding ruler and begins to measure the front of the old refreshment stand; nodding*

and murmuring in total agreement with everything ARTHUR *is say-ing.* MAX *speaks in a rich, full-bodied, tasty Russian-Jewish accent)*

MAX   Sure . . . sure . . .

ARTHUR   Great. Beautiful. You're sorry. Meanwhile I'm down here at Coney Island, alone in the dark, and you guys're up there in leather chairs, drinkin' hot coffee and makin' the news up outa your head!

MAX   Sure, that's the story . . .

ARTHUR   Of *course* you wanna hang up on me now. What difference do *I* make, right? You don't need *me* . . .

MAX   *(Measuring)* Sure . . . sure . . . they don't need you . . .

ARTHUR   I'm just a victim of your imaginary weather reports, the hell with *me*, right?

MAX   *(Nodding)* Sure, the hell with you . . . the hell with *all* of us . . .

ARTHUR   The sunrise, the sunset; that's a responsi*bility*, fella . . .

MAX   A big organization . . . who cares? . . .

ARTHUR   Hello? Hello? Hello, Mallory? . . . They hung up.

MAX   *(Folding his ruler)* Sure they hung up. A Mallory will hang up on you.

ARTHUR   *(Seeing this stranger for the first time, but continuing his anger)* Goddamn it, Goddamn gypsies . . .

MAX   You called them at the wrong time, buddy. *(Looks at pocket watch)* I'll tell you the right time to call them. Never.

ARTHUR   *(Shouting, pointing to horizon)* I mean, look at that, will ya!

MAX   *(Shouting)* Disgraceful!

ARTHUR   What the hell is *that?*

MAX   Blackness! Blackness and darkness!

ARTHUR   I mean, am I being un*reason*able?

MAX   You're being reasonable! Reasonable and cold and lied to!

ARTHUR   What about the front page here? What about "President Buoyed by Senate Support of Asia Policy"? I don't believe *that either* now!

MAX   He could be sitting around at this moment, not buoyed! What do *we* know? We know what they *tell* us!

ARTHUR   Far as I'm concerned they've thrown a doubt on their entire Late City Edition!

MAX   The *Daily News* too! You can forget *them* also!

ARTHUR   I mean, really, who ya supposed to *trust* any more?

MAX   This city, forget it! It's a miracle even that the telephone worked!

ARTHUR   The Goddamn B.M.T., we sat stalled thirty minutes in the tunnel this morning!

MAX   Garbage in the river, smoke in the lungs, and everywhere the Mallorys are hanging up!

ARTHUR   And who do ya *talk* to? What do ya—

MAX   They don't care, they cover up! It's a scientific *fact* that every minute the entire island is gradually sinking into the ocean! Do they *mention* it? Do they *do* anything? Next week we'll all be on Sixth Avenue breathing through *straws*; and nobody *mentions!*

ARTHUR   *(Quieting down; becoming more aware of the stranger he's been talking to)* Funny, I'm usually the only one around here at this hour; do you—

MAX   *(Still angry)* A big organization, they don't *care!* *(Close to* ARTHUR, *confidentially)* I'm last night at Katz's Delicatessen; forty-six tables, what they take in there, one night, unbelievable. It's 1 A.M., two frankfurters, I'm a happy man. Suddenly they're closing up, they say go finish your hot dogs outside; in a flash of an eye I'm on the street. A big store, who needs you? A little store, they let you finish. But do you know who owns a little store these days? I'll tell you who. Nobody. And that's the whole story today. How-do-you-do-sir, Max Silverman right here!

(Suddenly shoots out his hand)

ARTHUR   *(Shaking his hand)* Arthur Korman.

MAX   What're ya hangin' around here?

ARTHUR   Well, actually, I've come to see the sunrise . . .

MAX   Sure. Why not? A sunrise is nice. What line are you in? I'll bet you're in the art line. *(ARTHUR nods)* Sure, I figured the art line. Where are you located? *(ARTHUR hands him a card;* MAX *holds it up close to his eyes)* "The Jingle Bell Display Company. Bill Fairchild, President. Arthur Korman, Designer." I'll tell you right now, I like the sound of the whole organization. *(ARTHUR sits in beach chair, looks off at horizon)* Right, you better get ready. Because a sunrise out here'll run you, tops, ten, fifteen minutes. *(Sits next to him on chunk of driftwood)* A whole week now I see you here, who knew we could be such terrific pals? With your odd behavior; what is that to sleep here in February?

ARTHUR   I don't *sleep* here Mr. Silverman; sometimes while I'm waiting for the sunrise I—

MAX   A whole half hour I spoke to you yesterday. With them dopey glasses, who knew the eyes were closed? I'm having a gorgeous and terrific conversation, right in the middle you say, "Goodbye, Bill..."

ARTHUR   *(Rises, begins to fold beach chair as though to move on; politely)* Talked in my sleep, eh? Well, that's—

MAX   A fella comes in February to dream about Bill. Funny glasses. Goodbye, Bill. Jingle Bells. Arthur, you'll pardon me, but maybe you're a fairy?

ARTHUR   Mr. Silverman, Bill is my employer's name, I—

MAX   Arthur, you'll be what you want to be, I'm still your pal! *(Rises, a sympathetic hand on his arm)* Listen, you'll make a life for yourself. I'll tell you somebody who doesn't have problems. Nobody. *(His arm around* ARTHUR, *leading him up center;* ARTHUR *carrying the chair)* O.K., O.K., you're being straight with me, I'll be from the shoulder with you ... It's time I revealed to you my true identity ... *(Points to boarded-up stand)* You see that sign? That place? "Max's Hawaiian Ecstasies"? Well, that Max from there ... and this Max ... are one in the same Max. *(Turns to him, quietly)* *I* am that Max, of Max's Hawaiian Ecstasies ... Yessir.

(MAX *steps back, waiting for a big reaction to this revelation)*

ARTHUR   *(Politely)* Oh ...

MAX   Of course, we been closed now awhile for various alterations, remodeling, renovations, and modernization ...

ARTHUR   Uh-huh. How long?

MAX   Twenty-two years. A special place, you gotta wait for the right moment.

ARTHUR   *(Attempting, politely, to disengage himself)* Mr. Silverman, I think the sunrise is about to—

MAX   We had here a class operation ...

ARTHUR   I see a bit of light on the—

MAX   *Al Jolson.* Yessir, Jolson himself comes once for a frankfurter— *two* frankfurters and a large coconut drink; July 10, 1943, he's here on the boardwalk for a War Bond Rally. Gives you an idea the type clientele. *(He slaps the side of the stand; the small building shudders with age)* We had 'em all here; your various show business greats, your various underworld personalities, a couple artists, tenors from the opera, some of your top politicos, they come running from all walks of life. You're asking "Why?" and the question will be answered. Because we had here . . . ecstasy. Grass on the walls, lush; hanging from the ceiling, jungle novelties; tropical foliage; had a record playing with your various exotic-bird noises. A coconut drink costs a dollar. Can you imagine what that was in 1943, a dollar for a soda? Musta been some terrific soda, right? And frankfurters—ground special, my own meat—frankfurters that you could soar to the sky, one bite you need a pilot's license! Hamburgers I wouldn't even discuss, *tears* would come to your eyes . . . (ARTHUR *has put down his beach chair, listening)* And crowds, crowds all the way back to Tenth Street, on Saturday nights back to Neptune Avenue. They ate on the beach here, pineapple paradise under the moonlight, summer nights that last forever . . . and up above the store, with soft blue lights, put a shiver in your neck, my sign, my credo, with silver letters for Silverman, it said, "Without a Little Ecstasy, What's Life? Don't Worry about the Prices!"

ARTHUR   Well, that must've been—

MAX   Unfortunately, they started worrying about the prices . . . *(Goes to stairway, taking in the whole neighborhood with a sweep of his hand)* And the big places started to open on the boardwalk—aluminum nightmares! Fifteen cents for a frankfurter! Coney changes under my feet; comes in garbage, goes out style. Who needs ecstasy? My place becomes here a ghost and haunts itself. *(Moves up the stairs, points lovingly to an area of boardwalk above his store)* Was once, right there, Soloway's Bath, Beach, and Sports Club. Guided by the hand of Marcus Soloway, a gentleman and a genius; with columns, pillars, almost marble, rising up. On top, a roof built like a pagoda would make even a Chinaman happy . . . and, oh, oh, on this roof a sea lion, buddy, almost marble, with green eyes that looked out at the sea . . . *(A sweep of his hand; shouting)* And now gone! The only Roman Jewish Oriental bathhouse the world will ever know! *(He sits on the top step of the stairway, for the first time like an old man. ARTHUR is at bottom of steps, listening)* You want to know who ends up twenty-two years with a job manager of the Burger Circus, cheap food on Lexington Avenue? Me. Max. The same Max. And Marcus Soloway is today a salesman sports goods in Jersey. You want to know God's job? To give every great man a squash! *(He* *stands, angrily)* Yessir, I got *that* boy's number! He's a joker, a fool-er, a whimsical fella, and a rascal altogether! *(Moving down the steps to* ARTHUR*)* What kinda monkey business that without Max to give it a spin, the world turns anyway? How come the ocean is still there without Soloway's sea lion watching it? *(Poking* ARTHUR'S *chest)* I'll tell ya what, mister; the difference between me and God is that I know how to run a class operation.

ARTHUR   Mr. Silverman—

MAX   Would you let me talk, please? I have only recently recovered from a serious and delicate operation on my only heart— *(Gives* ARTHUR *a slight shove;* ARTHUR, *off-balance, sits back down on the beach chair)* I'm buddies with the angel of death, I'm operating on a very tight schedule, so close-'em-up-the-mouth—

ARTHUR   I'm sorry, I—

MAX   You came here to see the sunrise; but today, mister, Max Silverman *also* rises! *(Leans close to him)* I notice that don't take your breath away . . . but they almost took *mine* away altogether. Two months in Mount Sinai Hospital—all day my family sits around the bed watching me with funerals in their eyes. Every lively move I make is to them a miracle and a wonder. I lift a cup of tea, I get an ovation. Suddenly I'm a talented man and my talent is that I'm not dead. What I got to look forward is in ten years I'll be my brother Harry whose big accomplishment is that he's eighty years old and he gets outa bed every morning! Look at Harry, they say, will you look at him how he eats his *soup*, look how *cute*, look how he hears almost ten percent of what you say to him— *(Suddenly, rushing to* ARTHUR*)* And they almost had *me!* *(Grips* ARTHUR'S *arm urgently)* I'm lying in the bed there and I'm starting to think I'm terrific just because I'm *breath*ing! *(As though in the hospital room)* I look around at them . . . my wife, God bless her, a silly person . . . Joey the Bum and Michael the Bore . . . Rhoda and Barbara . . . or Barbara and Rhoda . . . married to Harold and Arnold . . . or Arnold and Harold . . . A *gross* of grandchildren: Sean, Adam, Kate, Mary-Jane, Mindy, Mandy, Molly; it's an Irish lullaby! "Dad," says Rhodabarbara, "not a *bunch* people—a bunch *of* people—you can hear that, can't you, Dad?" From the whole crowd *one* person who ain't ashamed—*likes* even how I sound, and that's Shirley, Crazy Shirley. I used to think the whole family isn't a total loss there's one Crazy Shirley in there— *(Shouting)* The hell with *her also!* A whole year I don't hear from her! She run away from her husband—O.K., her used husband with his used-car lot, *him* you run away from—but why from Max? Max who is adorable! *(Exhausted, leans back against the dune)* She wasn't there . . . and in the bed I look around at the rest of them, with their blank faces you could write a message on their foreheads like on a sheet of paper . . . and I'm thinkin', if I die, when I die, this here is all I leave, this is all the world will know of me, this bunch American beauties here . . . so *then*, right *there*— *(Shoves himself upright off the dune; shouting)* —buddy, I make-'em-up my mind—right there in Mount Sinai Hospital, Room 423, semiprivate—I decided *not* to die! Halt! Stop the horses! Rip it from the schedule! Max has got business to do! First I gotta leave something you should know I been around; somethin' says I was alive, somethin' terrific, somethin' classy . . . somethin' beautiful; can't just leave behind this crowd of Silvermans. *(The lights have gone out along the boardwalk; and now the sun begins to rise, throwing a pink glow on the sand and the edges of the boardwalk)* And what's it gonna be?! *Yessir*— *(He points to the boarded-up stand)* —rising up from the ashes—fresh, thanks God, like a daisy—awakened like a sleepin' princess—here ya go, whatta ya say—the grand and gala reopening of—the *Original Max's Hawaiian Ecstasies!* (ARTHUR *murmurs something)* I'll tell ya who's not gonna die! *Me*; the original Max! (ARTHUR *murmurs, shifts in his chair)* I'll tell ya—

ARTHUR   *(Murmuring)* Goodbye . . . goodbye, Bill . . .

MAX   *(Goes to chair, looks at* ARTHUR; *then lifts up* ARTHUR'S *sunglasses.* ARTHUR *is sound asleep)* Out like a light. You rotten kid. Well, it's your misfortune, buddy; you missed a lot of terrific conversation. *(*MAX *notices the sunrise, now a rich, red-orange glow filling the stage)* Stupid, you're missing the sunrise! A spectacle, what you came here to see! *(Shakes* ARTHUR, *shouting urgently)* Wake up! You're missing it! Beautiful view, beautiful words . . . you're missing it . . . *(Sadly; lets go of* ARTHUR'S *arm)* You people are always missing it. *(*MAX *is silent for a moment, quite still; then he shrugs)* What the hell; sleep. I can't bother you. I got business. *(Picks up the shopping bag, starts up the boardwalk steps)* Contacts to make. Money to raise. Business. *(A* GIRL *steps forward from the striped shadows under the boardwalk; she is wheeling a brightly painted bicycle, a foreign-made racer called a Peugeot. The* GIRL *is a thirty-three-year-old who dresses like sixteen: jeans, serape-sweater, beads, little white boots, everything out of place with her adulthood and the February weather.* MAX *reaches the top of the steps; looks down, sees her)* What is it, girlie? What can I do for you? *(She shakes her head)* You're lost? *(She hesitates; shakes her head again)* The bicycle path is over by Ocean Parkway. Now you'll excuse me, I got business . . . *(He hoists his shopping* *bag up under his arm, walks left down the boardwalk . . . stops, looks out at the horizon. The sunrise fills the stage with a red-golden glow. He looks up at the sky, angrily)* A joker, a fooler, a rascal. Also a show-off!

(MAX exits to the left of the boardwalk, singing as he disappears from sight)

"Toot, Toot, Tootsie, good-bye,
Toot, Toot, Tootsie, don't cry . . . "

GIRL *(Singing softly)*

"The choo-choo train that takes me
Away from you . . . "

ARTHUR *(In his sleep)*

"No words can say how sad it makes me . . . "

GIRL *(Smiles; wheels her bike toward ARTHUR)*

"Kiss me, Tootsie, and then . . . "

ARTHUR *(After a moment)*

"Do it over again . . . "

GIRL "Watch for the mail . . . I'll never fail . . . "

(Silence. She moves closer, testing the depth of his sleep)

"Watch for the mail . . . I'll never fail . . . "

(Silence. She rings her bicycle bell. Silence; he is deeply asleep. She feels the sunrise on her face; looks out at it; awed, whispering)

GIRL What'd he call ya—Arthur? Arthur, you're missing a beauty . . . *(Glancing up and down the deserted beach)* Oughtta be a bigger crowd for a show like this . . .

ARTHUR *(Singing)*

"If you don't get a letter
Then you'll know I'm in jail . . . "

(She laughs. He murmurs) Quitting, Bill . . . leaving organization . . . goodbye, Bill . . . *(He moves restlessly in his sleep)* Light, light . . . shade is up...

(She holds her hand in front of his eyes, shielding him from the sun. He relaxes peacefully)

GIRL *(She lays her bike down near him, sits next to him in the sand; leans against his chair, continuing to hold her hand in front of his eyes)* Tell ya what, Arthur . . . altogether, so far, it's the best relationship I've had with a man this year. *(He murmurs)* Nancy. Nancy Scott. *(He murmurs)* Yes, I'm married; but maybe we can work something out.

ARTHUR   Bill . . .

NANCY   Bill will just have to understand. That was never a very healthy relationship, anyway. *(Leans more comfortably against his chair)* Oh, beach buddy, we have got something very valuable here. Dr. Berman says I've got trouble relating to people. Well, he's wrong. I relate terrific. It's when they all start relating *back* at me, *that's* when the—

ARTHUR   Leaving organization, Bill . . .

NANCY   Nobody blames you.

ARTHUR   Quitting, Bill. *Had* it . . . Quitting . . .

NANCY   You took as much as you could.

ARTHUR   Up to here, Bill. Quitting now . . . no more, goodbye—

NANCY   *(Indicates banjo case)* I think it's time you concentrated on your music anyway— *(A phone rings. She glances about)* Phone. Where? *(The phone rings again)*

ARTHUR   *(Cordially, in his sleep)* Hello. How are ya?

(A third ring; she spots the two booths under the boardwalk, runs for them)

NANCY   Jesus, who calls up the beach? *(Opens the door to first booth; grabs phone)* Hello, Atlantic Ocean. *(Sits down in booth)* Huh? Well, who is *this?* . . . Sounds like rolling surf because it *is* rolling surf. Arthur Korman; yeah, just a second— *(Leans out of booth)* Arthur! For you on "one"! Arthur! Phone! Hey, Arthur! *(He remains motionless)* Sorry, he's asleep. That's right, on the beach. Who shall I say called? Oh . . . Bill. Look, Bill, hate to break it to ya like this, but he's quitting. Yeah, leaving the organization. Well, what can I tell ya, Bill, he seems very definite about it. Yeah, O.K., 'bye.

(She hangs up)

ARTHUR   Leaving, Bill . . . leaving . . .

NANCY   You left. *(She leaves the booth, unaware that* EDDIE BERGSON *has just entered at the top of the boardwalk steps. A tall man, about forty, he wears an overcoat and carries two containers of coffee.* NANCY *looks back at the phone booth, suddenly regretful about what she's done. She moves toward* ARTHUR*)* Mr. Korman . . . I think you better wake up now, I—

EDDIE   Shirl . . . ?   *(She freezes, her back to him)*   Shirley . . . ?   *(After a moment, she turns to him)*   Oh. Oh, excuse me, miss, I was . . . *(He is about to leave; he stops, looks at her for a long moment)*   Hey . . . *(He takes a step down the stairs)*   Hey, is that you, Shirl?

NANCY   Can you start with an easier question?

EDDIE   Jesus . . . the nose . . .

NANCY   Yeah; how about that?

EDDIE   And you musta lost . . .

NANCY   Twenty pounds. Five in the nose alone.

EDDIE   Your . . . your hair, it's . . .

NANCY   Mr. Gaston calls it "Dazzling Midnight."

EDDIE   Jesus . . .   *(Coming slowly down the steps)*   I mean, you warned me on the phone, but . . . I was still lookin' for, y'know, Shirley.

NANCY   That makes two of us.

EDDIE   *(At bottom of steps)*   Well, hello.

NANCY   Hello, Eddie.

ARTHUR   *(Cordially, in his sleep)*   Hello. How are ya?

NANCY   *(Shrugs)*   I think he's a friend of my father's.   *(Going to the dune, far from* ARTHUR*)*   Appreciate your coming down here, Eddie. I thought, y'know, a divorce isn't something we should talk about on the phone, right?   *(He nods, following her to the dune)*   I mean, we owe each other a better goodbye than that, don't we?

EDDIE   Yeah. Kinda cold here, though, isn't it?

NANCY   Come down to see Pop, he's been sick—

EDDIE   Yeah, I know—

NANCY   Finally got the nerve to call home and Ma told me; she's going crazy—he's out here every day, supposed to be home resting—

EDDIE   Well, you know Pop, he—

NANCY   She figures maybe he'll listen to me . . . Fact is, I've been comin' down here a lot myself this winter. I thought it would be a good place for us to talk.   *(Looks out at horizon)*   So lovely here, it's . . . it's like every morning you get your money back, Eddie.

EDDIE   Yeah. It's very nice. Very cold here, though. Maybe we could—

NANCY   That was Pop's store there. When I was a kid I used to come here at this hour to help cut the French Fries . . . *(With* MAX'S *accent)* "Crispy, curly edges, please!" *(Looking at store)* Funny, it gets smaller every time I—

EDDIE   Cold. You want my coat?

NANCY   No thanks. *(Sits)* Here, pull up a dune, Eddie.

EDDIE   *(He sits opposite her. They are silent for a moment)* Long time, Shirl. *(She nods)* Here. Coffee. I think it's still warm. *(She accepts one of the containers; nods thank-you)* Fact is, I got over here pretty fast. Took a '66 Chevy hard-top off my lot, come over on the Belt Parkway. You take your East Side Drive down to your Brooklyn-Battery Tunnel; then— zing— you shoot right out on the Belt till you hit the Coney Island exit. *(Silence; they sip their coffee)* So what ya been doin' with yourself, Shirl?

NANCY   Been working on television, Eddie. Acting.

EDDIE   No foolin'.

NANCY   Yeah. Me and my new nose. I do that commercial for Wonder Suds where they say, "Did you know washday could be paradise?" I play the girl who didn't know.

EDDIE   Hey, no foolin'.

NANCY   Here, I'll show ya— *(Flashes a blank, wide-eyed stare)* That was me, not knowing.

EDDIE   Great eyes.

NANCY   What?

EDDIE   You still got the same eyes. Great eyes. *(Silence; they sip their coffee)* Does it hurt a lot when they do it—fix up your nose? *(She shrugs)* Yeah, I figured it must hurt a lot. Look, how about you come back with me, stay married and everything—

NANCY   Eddie—

EDDIE   I got the car right out on Neptune, we could—

NANCY   No, Eddie— *(Then gently)* Eddie, we decided; we agreed—

EDDIE   Right.

NANCY   I'm sorry, I—

EDDIE   Right. Right. *(He sips his coffee)*

NANCY   Believe me, Eddie, I've thought about it a lot; even been to an analyst, I—

EDDIE   What does he say?

NANCY   I do most of the talking, he just listens—

EDDIE   Then come home, Shirl, I can do that for ya at home—

NANCY   Eddie—

EDDIE   Jesus, Dazzling Midnight, a new nose, what do ya—

NANCY   "What do ya need it for?" Your favorite question, Eddie; they're gonna put it on your tombstone: "Here Lies Eddie Bergson; What Did He Need It For?"

EDDIE   Fact is, I love you, Shirl. And I loved you just the way you were, too.

NANCY   Dear, sweet Eddie . . . you were in love with a midget. I'm what I'm asked to be, see, and you were asking for a little toy lady. Eddie, I had to get outa there before I got too short to reach the doorknob. *(Grips his hand urgently)* Oh, Eddie, there's so much maybe I can be, so much I want to— *(She looks at him for a moment)* Gettin' any of this, Eddie?

EDDIE   Gettin' the sound of it. Sounds like leaving.

NANCY   Oh, Eddie; dear, sweet—

EDDIE   *(He stands)* That's enough "dear, sweet Eddie" for today. I'm startin' to take offense at it. *(Crushes his coffee container, drops it in the sand)* Look, Shirl; it's what people do: being married. It's what there is. Not fantastic, but what there is. Six years we had no chairs in the dining room because you were waiting for fantastic ones. You're lookin' for fantastic, Shirl, and there isn't any. But there *is* the Bergsons, and that knocks me out. Just seein' it on your driver's license, "Shirley Bergson," just knocks me out. *(Walking to the stairs)* You still got the same eyes but they look frightened to me. Out in the cold with frightened eyes; you'll for-give the expression, kid—but what do ya need it for? *(Checks watch)* Gotta open the lot by eight . . . *(Going quickly up the stairs)* Probably make it in forty, forty-five minutes. No traffic comin' out, but goin' back you get your rush traffic building up on the parkway. Course, I could always just shoot straight out on the— *(Stops at top of stairs; turns, looks down at her)* This doctor you go to; he just listens, huh? *(She nods)* Uh-huh. *(He puts his coat collar up)* Well, I think you better go to one who talks to you; because, fact is, Shirley, it's really very cold out here. *(He shoves his hands deep into his coat pockets, turns left down the boardwalk, and exits quickly. Silence. There is the sound of a lone and distant buoy bell. A gust of wind; she hugs herself against the cold)*

NANCY   Well; looks like you and me, Art.

ARTHUR   Goodbye.

NANCY   *(Shrugs)* These seaside things never last . . . *(Going to her bike)* Listen, Arthur, we tried, we hoped . . . but let's be sensible; it's over. I think the best thing is a simple "goodbye" . . .

ARTHUR   Goodbye.

NANCY   Never really felt like a woman with you, anyway. I think it had a lot to do with your calling me Bill all the time . . . *(She suddenly lets go of her bike, buries her face in her hands, trembling. The bike falls over in the sand. After a moment she looks up, frightened, surprised by her own behavior)* Goddamn it . . . *(She marches angrily to the two phone booths, enters one of them, deposits coin, dialing fiercely. A gust of wind: she shivers; speaks into phone)* Hello, Dr. Berman? Nancy Scott. Look, I'm sorry to bother you at this hour, but I want my money back. It's not working out, Berman; I asked you for happy and fulfilled and you gave me lonely and frightened. *(Sits in booth, shivering)* Listen, I . . . I think Nancy Shirley Silverman Scott has gone and flunked the freedom test. The alone thing; I can't seem to handle the alone thing. It's not the dark I'm afraid of; it's the light, it's the mornings, it's the goddamn mornings. I wake up next to lovers with noses as strange to me as my own. I know they must be lovers because they never look like friends. Maybe I should go back to Eddie, huh? I mean, he's still got the same face . . . *(Quietly; hugging herself against the cold)* Listen, keep the money; just give me an estimate—I'm thirty-three, how many years are gonna be left by the time I figure out how to live them? Make me happy, Wizard; make me happy and we still got a deal . . . a happy above happy that guilty can't reach; a happy so high that the guilties'll die on their way up after me . . . Hello? Hello? . . . God damn you, *wake up!* Everybody up! *(She stands, shouting into the phone)* I don't care *how* early it is! Don't you know a crazy lady when you hear one? O.K., Berman, that's it. We've *had* it. We're finished! You *bet* I'm serious. Goodbye; I don't need you any more. I don't need you . . . So I'll see you at two o'clock, O.K.? Boy, are you lucky I can't make a decision. *(Hangs up sharply. Quietly, to* ARTHUR*)* Problem now is what to do till two o'clock. *(Going to her bike, which lies in the sand next to* ARTHUR'S *chair)* This is the difficult period, see: between doctor's appointments. *(Settles herself down in the sand between the chair and the bike)* Pop'll be back. I'll wait for Pop. *(Rests her head against the bike)* No sleep all night . . . *(Closes her eyes.* ARTHUR *suddenly moves in his sleep—she whispers urgently)* No, no, don't go— *(He relaxes again, murmuring peacefully)* Good. Tell ya the truth, I hate to sleep alone. *(Closes her eyes, drowsily)* Just don't wake up, see . . . As long as you don't wake up, m'friend, you are the best there is . . . *(Her voice trailing off)* Hey, don't feel the wind down here . . . no wind, the best . . . the best . . .

(She is asleep. Silence. ARTHUR *awakens; he stares out at the horizon for a few moments, trying to remember where he is. He looks down sleepily, sees the bicycle wheel; he studies it curiously for a few moments—suddenly startled to see a pair of feet next to the wheel and an entire girl connected to them)*

ARTHUR   Oh . . .

NANCY   *(Opens her eyes, also startled)* Oh . . .

ARTHUR   Hello. Hello there.

NANCY   Arthur, you're awake.

ARTHUR   Yes. Yes, I am. Yes.

NANCY   *(Rising)* Hello.

ARTHUR   Hello. How are ya? *(Rising)* Good morning. *(Stumbling over the bicycle)* Your bike?

NANCY   Yes.

ARTHUR   Nice bike.

NANCY   Ten-speed Peugeot with handle brakes.

ARTHUR   Hey, the old guy—the old guy, Silverman, where's— ?

NANCY   It's a curse. All night long I'm an old Jewish man and in the morning I turn into the beautiful girl you see before you.

ARTHUR   *(To horizon)* Oh, God. Oh, my God—

NANCY   What—

ARTHUR   The sun! Looka that! It's up! It's up already! Goddamn sunrise, they slipped another one right past me. *(Slumps defeated in beach chair)* Looka that. Six mornings in a row . . . *(Jumps out of his chair)* Excuse me. You wanna sit down? Forget it, stranger on the beach; who knows, right? I don't blame you. I'm Arthur Korman, I'm harmless, how-are-ya? *(Holds out his hand—withdraws it before she can respond)* Right. Watch out, I could be anybody. A nut. This city; I know how you feel. *(She sits down on the beach chair)* Beautiful. Look, you sat down. I'm Arthur Korman; I'm completely, completely harmless. *(Shakes her hand vigorously)* Don't worry about it. You're free to leave any time. You're a very pretty girl. Exceptional.

NANCY   Thank you, I—

ARTHUR   Don't worry about it. *(Sits opposite her, on sand dune)* I'm just going to sit here and you sit there and everything'll be beautiful. You want some coffee?

NANCY   Great; yes.

ARTHUR   Oh; I don't have any. How did you know my name? You must be freezing. Hey, I'll give you my coat.

NANCY   Truth is, I am cold, if it isn't—

ARTHUR   Beautiful. Beautiful. *(Taking off his coat)* Situation like this, believe me; you know how to handle yourself. May I ask your name?

NANCY   Nancy Scott.

ARTHUR   Beautiful. I like the way you handle yourself. *(He has forgotten to give her the coat)*

NANCY   Excuse me…

ARTHUR   Right, baby.

NANCY   Your coat, I—

ARTHUR   Oh, my God, of course—

(Rolls it up, tosses it to her like a basketball)

NANCY   Thank you.

ARTHUR   So what're ya doin' around here? I come to see the sunrise, but I fall asleep.

NANCY   Don't worry; great thing about the sun is that it comes back every morning.

ARTHUR   Even fell asleep on this crazy old guy today.

NANCY   He's my father.

ARTHUR   Weather like this, how come you don't wear a coat or something?

NANCY   That crazy old guy, he's my—

ARTHUR   I mean, it's February.

NANCY   Well, when I go to buy coats I think I'm very tall. I've got six tall coats and they all look terrible on me.

ARTHUR   Beautiful.

NANCY   So if I was tall I'd be warm. Meanwhile I'm short and cold.

ARTHUR   Beautiful. Beautiful. See what we're doing? We're talking.

Opening up. This is terrific. *(After a moment)* You got to let it happen. Letting it happen is what it's all about. *(Silence; he picks up his banjo case, opens it, takes out banjo)* This is called a Whyte Lady, this banjo. Great sound. Haven't made 'em for thirty, thirty-five years. *(Sits next to her on chunk of driftwood, holding the banjo with great affection)* See this here; carved bone pegs . . . pearl inlay on the frets . . .

NANCY   Would you play something for me?

(He holds the banjo in playing position; plucks one of he strings, listens to it critically, tightens it. Silence for a moment. He puts it back in the case)

ARTHUR   Tell ya what, it wouldn't be a good idea.

NANCY   Why not?

ARTHUR   Because I don't play the banjo.

NANCY   What are you doing with it?

ARTHUR   Carrying it. I carry it.

NANCY   Oh.

ARTHUR   I carry things. Idea is you carry something around long enough you become obligated to it, see; to learn what to do with it. Got the instruction book in there too. And my sculpture tools. Used to do sculpture and I'd like to get back to it, so I carry my tools in there and it reminds me. Of my obligation. *(He snaps the case shut. He looks off at the horizon for a few moments; sings softly to himself)*

"If you don't get a letter
Then you'll know I'm in jail . . . "

(Silence) Well; 'bye now. *(Rises; picks up banjo case)* Yessir, that ol' clock really ticks away, doesn't it? *(Shaking her hand vigorously)* This was great. Talking to you. Beautiful to meet you. Beautiful experience here. *(Walking briskly to the stairs)* Right; but now it's time to start the ol' day goin', huh?

NANCY   Your . . . your coat, I . . .

ARTHUR   *(Going up the stairs)* Keep the coat. It's your coat. I want you to have it; it's February.

NANCY   *(Unbuttoning the Mackinaw)* Take your coat. I don't want it—

ARTHUR   *(At the top of the stairs; he turns to her)* Please. Please keep it—

NANCY   *(Holding the coat out to him)* I really don't want it. Here—

ARTHUR *(A casual wave of his hand)* Hey, keep the coat—*(Suddenly, desperately, clutching the banjo case)* Please—Keep it—Keep the goddamn coat, will ya? Lady, I gotta leave now. The gaps. The gaps in the conversation. The gaps are coming! Get out while you can! Believe me, you're in for a losing experience. That's it, lady; that's all I do. You've just seen everything I do. That was it. I don't follow up with anything. I'd like to play you a song on my banjo or invite you for a swim but I don't play I just carry and it's too cold. Forgive me, I'm sorry; goodbye.

(He starts to exit left down the boardwalk)

NANCY *(Shouting)* This is a four-thousand-dollar nose! *(Throws his coat down on the sand)* You're walkin' out on a four-thousand-dollar nose here, dummy! *(He turns, startled by her outburst)* Don't stand there! Go away! Alla you! I don't need *any* of you! This is Dr. Graham's nose! A top nose! This is Mr. Gaston's hair! Mr. Gaston of Lexington Avenue! This is my agent's name and this is Dr. Berman's attitude and this voice I'm talking to you with is from Madame Grenier, the vocal coach! I'm not just a pretty girl, I'm a *crowd* of pretty girl! A convention . . . a parade . . . a . . . *(There are tears in her eyes. She turns away from him, sits down on the beach chair)* So who needs you; I got company . . . *(She hugs herself against the cold, trembling)* Go away, goodbye; we're goin' over great here . . . Graham, Gaston, Bennan, my agent, the madame and me.

(Silence. A gust of wind)

ARTHUR *(Gently)* Lady, I . . .

NANCY You still here?

(She remains seated with her back to him)

ARTHUR Listen, all those people . . . I want you to know something, they did a terrific job on ya. *(Silence)* You really look . . . fine. Just fine. *(Silence; he comes down the stairs, picks up his coat, stands behind her)* Here. You're shivering. Please take this . . . *(She does not respond; he drapes the coat very delicately over her shoulders)* When it gets windy you can put the hood up, O.K.? *(She reaches behind her head, letting her longish hair fall outside the coat. He assists her carefully with a strand or two)* Very real; the hair. *(She continues to look the other way. He touches her shoulder gently)* I'm sorry that I upset you. You mustn't take it personally. Believe me, you're a pretty girl. You must be a pretty girl because I can't talk to you. I can't talk to you people . . . There's a special code. Some guys know the code. I don't know the code. *(Silence)* Please, give me your number. I'll call you. I'm terrific on the telephone. *(No reply. He shrugs sadly, turns to leave)* I know I could have a great life if there was just some way to phone it all in.

(Starts to walk slowly away)

NANCY   *(Quietly)* The hair, y'know . . . the hair *is* real. *(He stops, delighted to hear her voice)*

ARTHUR   I thought so. It had to be.

NANCY   It's just the color that was changed, see.

ARTHUR   Well, it's very suitable.

NANCY   Thank you.

ARTHUR   I think it's *all* very suitable.

NANCY   Thank you. *(After a moment)* It's just the nose, actually, that's not mine.

ARTHUR   Really? It certainly *looks* like—

NANCY   I know it's not mine because yesterday at Bloomingdale's I saw another girl with it. Dr. Graham, he does a certain style of nose and it turns out there's a Goddamn *army* of us walking around New York with it. *(They both laugh at this for a moment.)* Yukon five, six, one, four, one.

ARTHUR   What?

NANCY   That's my number.

ARTHUR   Thank you.

NANCY   If you ever want to visit your coat.

ARTHUR   Coats. *(Looks up at the sky)* Tall coats, you've got six of them . . .

NANCY   Yes, I—

ARTHUR   The old guy . . . the old guy, you said he was your father . . .

NANCY   I thought you didn't hear that.

ARTHUR   I didn't. I just heard it now. It takes about twenty minutes for sound to reach me. *(She laughs, enjoying him)* See what you're doing? You're listening. How do ya do that? You even *look* like you're listening. That's the hard part. I gotta work so hard on that part I can't hear a thing—there's one now—

NANCY   What?

ARTHUR   A gap. And that's just the beginning, that was just a little one—

NANCY Hey, Arthur—

ARTHUR Wait'll the big ones come, they can kill ya—

NANCY Take it easy, we've got plenty to talk about—

ARTHUR Seems like we've covered everything—

NANCY About me being pretty, we could talk about that some more. That's always good for a coupla minutes. *(He smiles, relaxing a bit)* What's really fascinating, see, is that nobody seems to know me any more . . . *(He sits opposite her, nodding attentively)* My own father, for example. Truth is, I was afraid to introduce myself to him. Sees my new nose, hears my new name—I'll wake up at the bottom of the Atlantic with fifty pounds of frankfurter tied to my foot. *(He continues nodding)* You hear any of that, Art?

ARTHUR Parts. Parts of it.

(Silence. He glances about anxiously)

NANCY Chrissake, that was a *pause*. Pauses are O.K.— *(Another silence. They both glance about anxiously)* Uh—work—our work, let's about our—

ARTHUR O.K.—

ARTHUR and NANCY What kind of—

NANCY You're first, Arthur.

ARTHUR Well, I've got this sorta silly job . . . I'm with the Jingle Bell Display Company, see; I run this department there called Santa's Workshop—

NANCY *(Suddenly, remembering)* Jesus, your *job*—

ARTHUR I *told* you it was silly—

NANCY Arthur, do you . . . how do you like it there?

ARTHUR Eighteen years of Christmas? It's a nightmare. I'm slowly turning into an elf. *(Pacing in the sand)* Pixies, pixies, I'm a fella lives with pixies. You hang around with pixies too long, something happens to your head. Planning to quit any day now.

NANCY How about today?

ARTHUR Today?

NANCY *(A bit of strained laughter)* Arthur, this funny thing happened, *(After a moment)* A nutty, impulsive, funny sorta . . . *(Turning away)* Arthur, forgive me, I had no right, I . . .

ARTHUR *(Gently)* What is it? Tell me.

NANCY   See, this guy Bill called . . .

ARTHUR   Bill, right.

NANCY   And you seemed so definite there . . . in your sleep . . .

ARTHUR   Definite in my sleep, right.

NANCY   So I told him you were quitting.

ARTHUR   Quitting, right.

NANCY   Arthur, I'm sorry— I was in a crazy mood, I—

ARTHUR   Is *that* what's worrying you? Is *that* what you're worried about? Quitting my *job?* That dumb, silly *job?* I was going to quit *any*way! I was *going* to quit! Not right *now* maybe, not this very *minute;* but I was going to quit! *I was going to quit!* He thought you were kidding, he thought you were crazy, right? Some nut making a joke, right?

NANCY   He *must* have, Arthur, he—

ARTHUR   Eighteen years of my *life*, he couldn't've just—

NANCY   Arthur, he said he'd call *back*, he—

ARTHUR   *When? When?*

NANCY   In a little while, he—

(ARTHUR *collapses into his beach chair*)

ARTHUR   *(After a moment, quietly)*   Good. Good. That's nice. *(Recovering, with a grand sweep of his hand)* Style, see, it's just that I meant to leave with a little style. Eighteen years, you don't just walk out and slam the door, right?

NANCY   Of course not.

ARTHUR   *(Opens banjo case, takes out stack of letters)*   Wrote him twenty-six really fine letters of resignation this year; it's just a matter of selection. *(Looks fondly through letters)*   Been working on my style. Even got one here in sonnet form—listen; ends with— *(Reading, lyrically)*

> "The blossom is fruitless for he who seeks the lotus
> And I, Arthur Korman, give you two weeks' notice."

(Rises, points to horizon)   That's what I was gonna use it for, the sunrise, see; as a whattayacallit: inspiration. Said in the "Times", "Sunrise: 6:41," so I sent Bill a telegram with the number here to call me twenty minutes later. I figured all that beauty comin' up . . . and I would quit so great. The world being born again; the world and me . . . *(Smacks his fist into the side of the dune)*

Damn it, lady, you want a great life, you gotta have like that book, *Great Whattayacallits*, first!

NANCY *Expectations.*

ARTHUR Right! That's why I started coming here. I got up last Wednesday and I noticed I didn't have any. It was my birthday, forty-one years old and I wasn't even expecting *that*.

NANCY Come on, forty-one's not old—

ARTHUR I know; but it happened the day after I was twenty-three, so naturally I was a little shocked. Wednesday morning—zappo—forty-one. I felt like I'd left a wake-up call for thirty and I musta slept right through it. *(Turns to her, urgently)* Something terrific was supposed to happen by now, see—some terrific reason for shaving and buying shoes and keeping the clocks wound—something terrific, a dazzler, a show of lights, a— *(Grips her arm)* I had this whole other fella in mind once; you would been crazy about him. I was gonna be a sculptor, I had in my mind once . . .

(His voice trails off; he turns away)

NANCY What, Arthur? Tell me . . .

ARTHUR Monuments . . . I had in my mind once, monuments. How do ya like that?

NANCY Sounds wonderful.

ARTHUR *(His spirits soar)* I wanted to sculpt those heroes like you see in the park, guys on horses with swords, terrific guys outa bronze and metal and they stay there in the park forever . . . forever, lady . . . *(Running to the top of the dune)* They got bronze eyes looking outa their heads and bronze fingers pointing somewhere in particular, and if it's a good statue, a really great one, you can see five hundred people in the air behind the guy, looking where his eyes are looking and ready to go where his finger is pointing . . .

NANCY Wonderful . . .

ARTHUR So I went to this school to study sculpture. Trouble is, I was in that school for five years and by the time I came out they were all outa them.

NANCY All outa what?

ARTHUR Heroes and parks. They were all outa them. Seems like the world run outa heroes and the parks run outa space and I come outa school all at the same time. *(Slides to bottom of dune)* I mean, there just didn't seem to be any call for what I did. Truth is, there's not a helluva lot of action in the monument field. *(Picks up the letters of resignation)* So I took this job meanwhile ... eighteen years of meanwhile and every year they give you a birthday party. *(Going to end of pier, carrying the letters)* Except Wednesday it was special; besides the beer there was champagne in paper cups because I been there longer than anybody. Everybody singing "Happy Birthday"; Bill, the fellas, the secretaries, everybody around me in a circle singing, and all of a sudden I couldn't remember what I'd meant to do with it ... my, y'know, life. Stood there trying to remember and they went on singing like a machine I couldn't stop, "Happy birthday," they're singing, "happy birthday, dear Arthur," and I wanted to rip the building down, *hit* something, *crush* something, and then I thought I was crying but it turned out I'd squirted champagne in my face from squeezing the paper cup. *(Suddenly, violently, he crushes the letters in his hands. He whispers)* What am I waiting for? *(Turns to her, shouting)* Hey, lady, what am I waiting for? *(Points to phone booth)* Today ... today I get out! When he calls back, I get out! When he calls back, I *quit!* Not another day dying alive! Arthur says goodbye! *(He tosses the letters high up over his head)* Santa's little helper says goodbye! *(The letters spin in the air like confetti;* NANCY *bursts into applause)* A week late, but here's my birthday and you're at the party!

NANCY   Happy birthday!

ARTHUR   Thank you, thank you—

NANCY   And many happy returns—

ARTHUR   And how about *that*—?

NANCY   What— ?

ARTHUR   No gaps! *(He races across the beach to her, grips her hands in delight. She laughs, kisses him spontaneously on the cheek)* My God, things are going well here.

(The phone rings. A moment; then he lets go of her hands—starts across the beach to the phone booth. She picks up the banjo, roughly plucking the notes for "Happy Birthday" as he marches to the booth, opens the door ... He puts his hand on the phone, she smiles expectantly ... he does not pick up the phone; he stands in the booth with his hand on the phone while it continues to ring)

NANCY   *(Quietly, putting down the banjo)* Arthur ... *(The phone continues to ring; she shouts urgently)* Arthur! *Arthur!*

ARTHUR   *(He sits in the booth; very quietly)* Damn cold here, isn't it?

NANCY   *(Coming toward him)* Arthur—answer it—

ARTHUR   *(Turning away)* The sunrise—I missed the sunrise—

NANCY   I saw it, it was gorgeous, now answer the Goddamn *phone*— *(Shouting above the phone)* Arthur, you're using the sunrise as a *crutch*—

ARTHUR   *(Shouting)* I know, but I'm a cripple, so it's O.K.—

NANCY   Arthur, you said not another day— *(She grips his arm)* You said you were dying alive—

ARTHUR   *(Leaves booth, moving away from her)* That listening you do, it has some terrible disadvantages—

NANCY   O.K., go ahead, run away from the truth—

ARTHUR   The truth! The Goddamn *truth!* They keep tellin' ya how beautiful it is but they never tell ya what the hell to *do* with it— *(Shouts at the ringing phone)* Stop! Stop! My God, will ya please stop— *(He runs to the booth, slams the door, stands with his back against it; shouts to her above the muffled but insistent ringing)* Here's the truth, lady! Ain't it gorgeous? It's eight o'clock. At eight o'clock I go to work. At seven thirty I dream, and at eight o'clock I go to work. *(The ringing stops. His back against the booth, he slides down, sitting in the sand; bows his head)* You see the truth comin', take my advice—run home, lock your doors, paint your mirrors black. The son of a bitch'll kill ya.

NANCY   *(Moving toward him)* Oh, baby, you're a wailer—

ARTHUR   Right. Also a coward and a—

NANCY   *(She kneels next to him in the sand)* Arthur, people can change their whole lives; I believe that . . . their whole lives if they want to . . .

ARTHUR   Don't you get it, lady? I blew my time. I used up my turn. My cool talk and my kid's clothes, it doesn't work. Only young is young and they don't let you do it again . . .

NANCY   Arthur it's—

ARTHUR   *(Nodding sympathetically)* I see you got the same kinda problem . . .

NANCY   Huh?

ARTHUR   Excuse me, but I couldn't help noticing the funny clothes . . .

NANCY   What funny clothes?

ARTHUR   The funny clothes you got on . . . the kid's clothes . . .

NANCY   Wait a second, buster—

ARTHUR   I mean, you must be what now: thirty-one, thirty-two?

NANCY   Arthur, you're a charmer . . .

ARTHUR   Forgive me, Nancy; it's just I've been the route, I can save you some pain. *(Gently, touching her arm)* There's things we can't change. Believe me, they ain't lettin' either of us into the world at half-fare any more. Keep telling yourself you're a kid and— *(She rises; starts to take his coat off)* Hey, what're ya doin' ?

NANCY   Giving your coat back.

ARTHUR   Hey, what're ya doin'?

NANCY   It's called "leaving." You will recognize it by how I won't be here any more.

(She drops his coat in the sand)

ARTHUR   Hey, where ya goin'?

NANCY   *(Lifting up her bicycle)* I'm taking my funny clothes and getting the hell outa here.

ARTHUR   *(Scrambling to his feet)* Hey, I—I alienated you, right?

NANCY   Alienated? I came here a cute girl and I'm leaving a nervous old lady!

ARTHUR   See, it's just—I thought we had this problem in common, I—

NANCY   The only thing we got in common is sand in our shoes! *(Wheeling her bike to the left under the boardwalk)* I'm not climbing into any cookie jars with *you*, buster! Too late, years passing, that's all you talk about! It's like hangin' around with the Hunchback of Notre Dame—he doesn't have much to say, but you always know what time it is! *(Gets onto to her bike, turns to him)* Mister, I'm sorry, but I have looked inside your head this morning and it's fulla bluebirds. Unfortunately, not one of them is the bluebird of happiness. *(Starts to ride to the left under the boardwalk)* And for your information, I happen to be twenty-six . . .

MAX'S VOICE   *(Approaching, off left; singing)*

> "Is it true, what dey say about Dixie,
> Does de sun really shine all de time . . . ?"

(She immediately stops, gets off her bike, starts wheeling it in the opposite direction from MAX)

ARTHUR   Nancy, you've come back—

NANCY   I haven't come back, you idiot! My God, I'm surrounded by crazy old men!

(She starts to drag her bicycle up the boardwalk steps)

MAX'S VOICE   *(Coming closer, at left on boardwalk)*

"Do de sweet magnolias blossom
At ever'body's door . . . "

NANCY   Where the hell is he *coming* from—?

(Turns around, dragging her bike back down the steps, wheeling it to the right under the boardwalk, away from MAX'S voice)

MAX'S VOICE   *(Coming closer)*

"And do de folks keep eatin' possum,
Till dey cain't eat no mo' . . . ?
Is it true what dey say about Swanee
Is a dream, by dat stream, so sublime . . . ?"

(She stops; deciding to face him, wheels her bike back to the bottom of the stairs, stands there with it proudly as though with her gallant steed, awaiting MAX)

"Do day laugh, do dey love,
Like dey say in every song . . . ?"

(She abruptly lets go of the bike; grabs up ARTHUR'S coat from the sand, puts it on, zipping the hood up over her head so that only her eyes are exposed; returns to her proud position at the bottom of the stairs)

"Well, if dey do, then yessir,
Dat's where I belong . . . "

(MAX appears on the boardwalk, singing with great gusto. Caught up in the finish of the song, he proceeds down the steps like a vaudeville performer, one at a time; and once, for effect, moving back up a few steps before proceeding down for the finish of the song. This performance is not necessarily for anyone's benefit; it's something he would do even if the beach were empty)

MAX   *(Singing)*

"Do dey laugh, do dey love,
Like dey say in every song?
Well, if dey do, then yessir . . . "

(Going for a big finish)

"Dat's where I beloooooong . . . "

(He takes off his hat and bows to no one in particular)

ARTHUR   *(After a moment)* Uh . . . very nice.

MAX   Nice? Nice? What's wrong with wonderful? That's a song, sir. With a melody. Who since Jolson? Who? Nobody is who. Since Jolson, a wasteland of pipsqueaks. (MAX *breaks into a warm smile, comes down the step his arms outstretched.* NANCY *turns to him as he approaches, takes the hood off.* MAX *passes* NANCY *without any sign of recognition; goes to* ARTHUR, *grips his shoulders in greeting)* Arthur, my sleeper, my darling, you're awake; terrific! I see you and my heart, what's left of it, skips a beat. *(Indicating* NANCY*)* Good. Good. You got yourself a girl friend. *(Moving down to pier, his arm around* ARTHUR, *confidentially)* What happened, it's all finished with Bill? Good. (NANCY *sits on the bottom step of the stairway, zips up her hood)* You got yourself a shy one. Do me a favor, you got a match? *(Indicates his cigar;* ARTHUR *lights it)* Good. Now one more thing I need from you. Ten thousand dollars.

ARTHUR   Huh?

MAX   I'm lookin' for who's gonna get in on the ground floor, get a nice percentage of Max's Hawaiian Ecstasies. Who's gonna be the lucky fella? Two days now, I been on the telephone calling; turns out there's not a lot of lucky fellas around. Arthur, ten thousand dollars.

ARTHUR   I—

MAX   I'm on the telephone calling up some of my former business associates; any one of them would *jump* at the opportunity. Unfortunately, they're all dead. *(Outraged)* It's only twenty-two years; everybody died! *(Sits at edge of pier, takes list of names from shopping bag)* Al Glickman, my meat supplier, *gone*—I'm speakin' to Al Glickman *Junior.* Kramer's Kitchen Supplies, I'm speakin' to Kramer Junior. Cantor and Sons, the contractor, I'm on the phone with "and Sons." How long I been gone? All of a sudden I'm living in New York Junior! And these Juniors, these winners, senior voices on the phone with junior guts, wouldn't advance you credit for a Hershey bar. Gotta know first, for *sure, every-*thing— *(Imitating their voices)* "Max *who?*" they say, "Hawaiian what? We'll see first how you do—after you open—maybe then . . . " Cold voices, people born for telephones . . . (NANCY *approaches him at the pier, removing her hood. He looks at her, then at* ARTHUR, *suddenly laughing)* The joke is, what's payin' the phone bills for these darlings is a business they got from their fathers who wouldn't *trust* a voice on a telephone! Billy Gallino, Gallino Rolls and Buns—I'm talking yesterday to William . . . Gallino . . . Junior—a hundred receptionists answer the phone he shouldn't catch cancer from my voice—I ask him for credit, two months' goods, he gives me a cute maybe on the telephone. (NANCY, *assuming that* MAX *doesn't recognize her, moves closer to him, becoming involved in what he is saying*) His father, I'll tell you frankly, was a thief. Overcharged me, sometimes delivered me stale merchandise; I'm sure he's not resting easy right now because he didn't steal the ground he's buried in. But Monday I'm on the phone with Junior and I'm sorry Billy isn't still alive to sell me yesterday's bread . . . (*Suddenly standing, shouting; using the pier tie as support*) I'm sorry *none* of them are alive, those hondlers, those hustlers, those *faces!* Now I got the Maybe Babies! A dozen numbers I dialed and each place the *same fella* answered! You couldn't tell who, what, which one! Could be they all got together, hired a fella to make a record? O.K., their fathers had accents, but *they* got no sound at *all!* Billy Gallino, he read a bread order aloud, you could *tango* to it! We had a fight once on Canal Street. I hit him, he hit me— (*Points to a mark over his eye*) Here's a scar from Gallino. We did business! Junior with his micey voice, he nibbles, he nibbles, he noshes on my soul. Billy, I knew what he was— Junior, he could be anything, a sea captain, a potato chip, a corn muffin, what? (*A sudden burst of energy brings him to the end of the pier*) Ah-hah! But at the end of the conversation, these sweethearts'll do a "Goodbye" for you—oh *boy*, it's *beautiful!* "Hello," they don't do so good; and after "Hello," nervous and rotten . . . but "Goodbye," will *they* do a job for you on "Goodbye"! (*He blows a goodbye kiss into the air*) "Goodbye . . keep in touch . . . so long . . . " All of a sudden warm and personal and terrific . . . (*Waving goodbye*) "Goodbye to ya . . . alla best to ya . . . we'll have lunch . . . see ya around . . . " All of a sudden it's happiness, it's sweetness, it's their best number, it's the goodbye people and they're feelin' terrific; they got through a whole phone call without promising anything, without owing, they lived another day without getting into trouble. (*He takes off his hat and waves it toward the ocean*) "Goodbye . . . goodbye . . . we're rootin' for ya . . . goodbye . . . " (*He puts his hat back on; turns to them*) I'll tell ya the truth, buddy—the old days wasn't so terrific, but God help me from the new ones. (*He picks up his shopping bag as if to leave; suddenly turns to* ARTHUR) Arthur, ten thousand dollars, I could open the store in two weeks; whaddya say?

ARTHUR   Ten thousand dollars, Jesus, I—

MAX   Eight then; seven—

ARTHUR   So suddenly, I—

MAX   Five. O.K., *five*. A full partnership for five—

ARTHUR   You see, it's —

MAX   Three! My final offer is three!

ARTHUR   Mr. Silverman, I'm—

MAX   Forget it! You lost it! It's finished!

ARTHUR   A sum like that, you can't expect a perfect stranger—

MAX   How perfect should a stranger be? Please, Mr. Sunrise, forget
it. *(Squeezing* ARTHUR'S *face gently, as though he were an infant)*
Arthur, darling, relax . . . sleep, my child. *(Hoists the shopping bag
up under his arm, turns to leave)* You just missed an opportunity,
pure gold. *(Walking briskly to the stairs)* I just figured you were in
a generous mood. I mean, since you gave my daughter your coat,
I figured maybe you'd give *me* a little something too . . .

(He starts quickly up the steps)

NANCY   *(Startled, whispering)* Pop . . .

MAX   *(He continues up the steps, singing)*

> "Do de sweet magnollias blossom
> At ever'body's door?
> And do de folks keep eatin' possum,
> Till dey cain't eat no mo' . . . ?"

(He turns left on the boardwalk, about to exit, still singing . . .)

NANCY   *(Shouting up at him)* No guilt, Silverman! Forget it! I'm
booked ahead solid! I'm not free to feel guilty about you till the
first Saturday in August! So forget it!

*(He continues walking, ignoring her, about to leave. She turns angri-
ly, wheeling her bike under the boardwalk, about to leave)*

ARTHUR   Hey, wait . . . Nancy . . . Mr. Silverman . . .

MAX   Nancy? Nancy? *(He turns)* Who's Nancy? Where's Nancy?

NANCY   *(Stepping out from under the boardwalk)*. Me. I changed my
name to Nancy Scott.

MAX   Terrific.

NANCY   I kept the *S*.

MAX   Wonderful.

(He turns to leave)

NANCY   Pop, wait—hey, Silverman—

MAX   Silverman? Who's Silverman? There's no Silverman here— *(He turns to them)* Allow me to introduce myself. Ricky Rogers. How do you do?

NANCY   O.K., Pop—

MAX   I kept the *R*.

NANCY   O.K., Pop, get it all out; now tell me about my new nose. Go ahead—

MAX   What nose? I don't see a nose. Arthur, do you see a nose?

NANCY   It's not that small—

MAX   First try and hold up a pair of glasses with it, then we'll talk. Whatsa matter, they couldn't leave you with something? They took away a nose and left a message. Listen, Mary-Lou, I'll tell ya—

NANCY   It's *Nancy*—

MAX   Excuse me, it's hard to remember a name when you don't know the face.

NANCY   It happens to be a damn good job, Pop—

MAX   Sure it's a good job. For a pixie. For a person it's ridiculous.

ARTHUR   Actually, Mr. Silverman, a pixie's nose is quite—

MAX   Ah, the daredevil speaks! What's with you and Captain Courageous here; funny business on the beach?

NANCY   Pop, *Jesus*—

MAX   Right, that's the name; Jesus. Used to be Max, but I changed it to reach a bigger crowd. *(Standing firm at the top of the stairs, he stares off at the horizon now, refusing to look down at her)* Some people are in the hospital for three months. Some people don't come to visit them. That's some people.

NANCY   Pop, I didn't even *know*, I—

MAX   Some people didn't even know. So out of touch, certain parties are. That's certain parties.

NANCY   O.K., Pop, you got all the aces . . . *(Sits, defeated, on bottom step)* The hospital, I didn't know; I never think of you as being sick. Pop, I listen to you talking about the guys you spoke to on the phone . . . and I realize how much I need you to be alive. *(He remains looking the other way; makes an elaborate business of shifting his shopping bag from one hand to the other)* Silverman; you gonna keep standing up there like that?

MAX   You; you gonna keep sittin' down there like that?

NANCY   *(Taking a deep breath)* The air; you can taste it here . . . damp and salty and full of Silverman pride.

MAX   Silverman? I see only one Silverman! One Silverman and one runaway nose-fixer in a stranger's coat! The victim of a recent massive coronary stands here waiting for an explanation.

NANCY   *(She suddenly stands, shouting)* O.K., Silverman, I have seen your vengeful moods before! Your ears close, your accent gets thicker, and Zorro rides again! You don't *want* an explanation; you just want me to stand here and keep feeding you straight lines! Either you warm up a little and *talk* to me or I'm on my way.

MAX   Threats, ultimatums . . .

NANCY   Well, what's it gonna be, Silverman?

MAX   Deals, negotiations...

(He remains silently looking the other way, straightening his hat. ARTHUR *looks tensely from one to the other)*

NANCY   Well, I tried . . .

(She turns sharply, wheeling her bike quickly off left under the boardwalk)

MAX   Sally-Ann— *(She stops)* You see that stairway there? *(Still not looking her, he gestures toward the stairs)* It has got, by actual count, twenty-two steps. You show up on step number eleven, and maybe I'll meet you there shortly. *(She looks up at him)* I heard a weather report on the radio this morning. Says cold air masses are coming down from Canada. *(He turns, holds out his arms to her)* Quickly, quickly, before they get here . . . *(She laughs, drops her bike, and races up the steps into his arms)* Devochka, devochka . . . welcome to the top of the stairs.

NANCY   "Devochka," doesn't that mean—?

MAX   It means, "You fixed your nose but I love you anyway."

(They sit on the top step; she holds his hands in hers. ARTHUR, *unnoticed by them, has been moved almost to tears by their reconciliation; sits on dune, watching with pleasure and fascination)*

NANCY   O.K. now, Pop, admit it; I don't look so bad.

MAX   Certainly you are a pretty person. But once you were a novelty item; now regular merchandise.

NANCY   Pop, I just wanted things to be new—

MAX   Must be a good attitude because I got the exact same attitude; that's why I'm opening the store again.

NANCY   Pop, the store—

MAX   I'll tell you what chance you got to talk me out of it. No chance.

NANCY   But you're not well—

MAX   Not well is twenty-two years workin' for somebody else, that's a disease you can die from.

NANCY   How ya gonna do it alone?

MAX   What's alone? Comes back with me, once a partner, still a gentleman and a genius, Marcus Soloway!

NANCY   You spoke to him . . .?

MAX   Well, not for a couple years—but I'll fix the store like it was, he'll see it, he'll join right up! I know what's in that classy Soloway head! He owns still fifty percent of the property, it's valuable, it's beach-front. Like me, a hundred times Marcus coulda sold his share. But he keeps it twenty-two years. Why? Because, like me, he's got the same idea! Because, like me, he waits for our turn to come again. *(He stands)* You're thinking I'm crazy, why open? Who'll come in the winter? People come; for the best, people come, for ecstasy they show up.

NANCY   But, to fix up the store, where will you get the money from?

MAX   Where will I get the money from? I'll . . . I'll *tell* you where I'll get the money from!

ARTHUR   From me . . .

MAX   From him! I'll get the money from *him!* *(Turns, looks down at* ARTHUR*)* From *him?*

*(*NANCY*, also surprised, looks down at* ARTHUR. ARTHUR *stands on top of the dune, a little surprised himself)*

ARTHUR   *(Quietly)* I've been thinking about it . . . and I've decided to invest in this . . . *(Gestures to store)* this project here, yes. *(Slides to bottom of dune)* Property, yes . . . property at the beach . . .

(He touches the store; the little building shudders with age)

MAX   *(Coming quickly down the stairs to him)* Congratulations, Mr. Sunrise, you just made a first-class investment.

NANCY   Arthur, why the hell're you—

MAX   Close-'em-up-the-mouth, Mary Jane.

ARTHUR   Actually, I *would* like to tell you why. You see, Mr. Silverman, I've—

MAX   For ten thousand dollars you can call me Max.

ARTHUR   O.K., Max, I—

MAX   I said for ten thousand dollars. Until I get the check keep calling me Mr. Silverman.

NANCY   Let him finish what he's *saying*, I wanna know why the hell he's—

MAX   *(Sharply, aside)* No-sir, this kinda fella you let him open his mouth he'll talk himself right out of it.

ARTHUR   *(A slight tremor in his voice)* You see, a time comes when one must—

NANCY   *(Coming urgently down the steps)* Arthur, it's *February*, he's not *well*; what do ya think you're *doing?* Being *nice?* Doing us a *favor?*

MAX   *(Offended; gesturing grandly)* What nice? What favor? He's waltzing into a gold mine!

ARTHUR   *(With genuine admiration)* Jesus, Mr. Silverman, how do ya do it? You just *believe* that everything's gonna work out for ya, you just—

MAX   *Crap!* I don't believe in *noth*ing or *no*body! Including *you* till I get my check. *(As he busily takes shopping bag from stairs, begins removing items from it: blueprints, deeds, sandwiches, pens, contracts, a thermos bottle, zoning maps, etc)* I believe in *me*, Max; and why's that? Because I'm terrific? No-sir. Because I'm what's left. Hello and goodbye; I look around, what's left is me. I believe in Max Silverman, and when the weather is nice I believe in God; a couple days in the spring and that's *that*. *(Takes two new pamphlets from bag)* Meanwhile, darling; if God don't work out . . . there's contracts. Sign this and a check and then we'll *all* believe. *(Smooths out a plateau of sand on the side of the dune, lays out the contracts on it, hands ARTHUR a pen)* The signed contracts you'll take to Michael David Silverman, a lawyer and a son.

NANCY   *(Approaching them)* Pop, wait—

MAX   His address is on the top there.

NANCY   Both of you, please—look; the Alamo with pineapples, *look*—

MAX   *(Ignores her, reading contract softly to Arthur)* "Joint Venture Agreement . . ." Beautiful, all poetry; "The party of the second part, hereinafter referred to as Joint Venturer . . . " That's you, darling; yesterday a sleeper, today a party and a venturer! Says here also, "Right of Survivorship"; means one of us dies, the other one gets the entire kaboodle. Arthur, if you don't drop dead, you got a terrific deal here.

NANCY   Snow, it's gonna snow next week . . .

MAX   Now the best part . . . paragraph Seven: *(Softly: a hymn)* "The party of the first part does hereby grant joint ownership of the property to the party of the second part . . . and to all his heirs and successors forever." Ah, such words; a contract like this you don't need a lawyer, you get a mixed chorus to sing it to you. (ARTHUR'S *pen is poised over the contract)*   Your name is Arthur Korman . . .

(ARTHUR suddenly signs. MAX snaps it away and flashes a second copy under ARTHUR'S *pen.* ARTHUR *signs the second one)*

NANCY   *(Sits helplessly on the stairs)*   Oh, God . . .

ARTHUR   *(Quietly)*   A short name . . . what a short name I've got.

MAX   *(Softly)* Arthur, you know what this means . . . ? *(They have been seated at the dune;* MAX *rises now and extends his hand to* ARTHUR*)* It means shake the hand . . . (ARTHUR *rises unsteadily, takes* MAX'S *hand)*   Shake the hand and you own a piece of the world forever. . . .

(There is a gust of whistling wind; it rattles the papers on the beach. The men stand with their hands joined, the lights dim; NANCY *shivers, looking up at the winter sky as . . .)*

THE CURTAIN FALLS

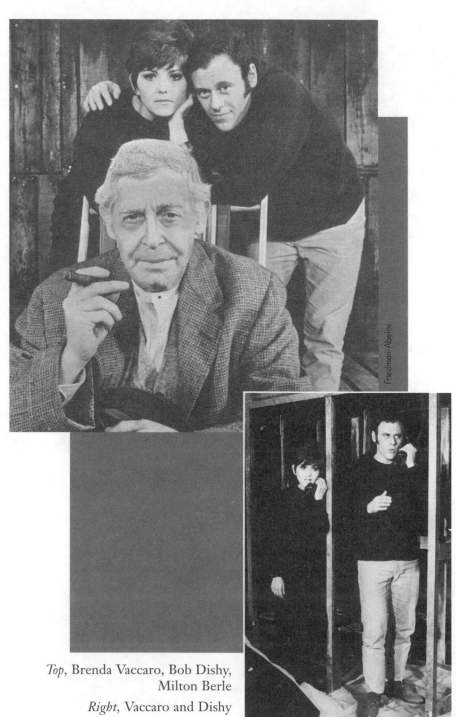

Top, Brenda Vaccaro, Bob Dishy,
Milton Berle

Right, Vaccaro and Dishy

Friedman-Abeles

Friedman-Abeles

Top, Pam Reed and Judd Hirsch
Above, The Dixieland Devils

ACT TWO

Before the curtain goes up we hear a scratchy old record of Al Jolson singing a Hawaiian love song . . .

JOLSON'S VOICE

"Down Hawaii way
Where I chanced to stray
On an evenin' I heard a
Hula maiden say . . . "

(ARTHUR'S *voice joins in softly*)

ARTHUR and **JOLSON'S VOICE**

"Yaaka hula hickey dula
Yaaka hula hickey du . . . "

(As the curtain rises)

"Down Hawaii way
By the moonlit bay
Where I lingered awhile, she
Stole m'heart away . . . "

(It is early evening; the boardwalk lamps are lit, there is moonlight and a gentle glow on the sand. Everything else is as it was, with one extraordinary exception—to the left of the store is a rather well sculpted seven-foot palm tree; it is arched gracefully over the store and over ARTHUR, *who sits beneath it holding his banjo and singing quietly in the moonlight. To his right, tacked onto one of the boardwalk pillars, is his designer's "rendering" of the projected Hawaiian Ecstasies, in which the store is seen in all its imagined glory—many palm trees, tables and chairs spread along the beach; the store itself is pictured as a multicolored grass hut, the roof features a glowing Hawaiian volcano, and towering above that is a neon frankfurter. The actual steps toward realizing the rendering are small at this point, but promising; there is the tree that* ARTHUR *is building, and just downstage of it a wicker table and two small wicker chairs; an open carton marked "Colby's Outdoor Products—Everything under the Sun" stands nearby. Several of the boards have been removed from the front of the store, partially revealing the old counter; an ancient portable Victrola rests on the counter, from which the music continues . . .)*

"Yaaka hula hickey dula
Yaaka hula hickey du . . . "

(He hits two chords on his banjo; chuckles with satisfaction, goes on with the song)

Oh, I don't care if you've loved the ladies
Far and near . . . "

(Rises, continues work on the tree, molding swirls of bark around the trunk)

"You'll forget about 'em all if
You could hear
Yaaka hula hickey dula
Yaaka hula hickey du . . . "

(There is a gust of wind; the tree begins to sway. He hugs the tree to steady it. The phone rings. He continues to hold on to the tree, singing softly)

"Yaaka hula hickey dula
Yaaka hickey du . . . "

(The phone continues to ring, piercing the gentle moonlit setting and the soft music. ARTHUR *finally lets go of the tree, turns the music off, walks decisively to the phone booth, humming a bit more of the song . . . shifting unconsciously to "Jingle Bells" as he reaches the booth. Grabs phone; speaks briskly)*

ARTHUR   Arthur Korman here! Right, *Bill;* how the hell are ya, fella? Well now, where were we? We haven't talked so we couldn't be anywhere, right? O.K., here's the situation, Bill; here's how it shapes up . . . That's because it *is* rolling surf, Bill . . . Right, but this is a very nice time of year also: Picturesque . . . Glad that amuses you, Bill; but the fact is . . . *(Looks at horizon for inspiration. There is only the moon)* The fact is I'm involved in a very interesting project here at the beach, Bill . . . a design project of my own, and I might well continue to . . . A restaurant, I guess you might call it a sort of an outdoor restaurant, a sort of an out-door-restaurant-beach-design project is what I'm involved in here, Bill . . . I wish you wouldn't do that . . . Bill, I'd really rather you didn't laugh at this . . . *(Sits in booth; quietly)* Don't laugh, please . . . *(*NANCY *enters on boardwalk, at right, wearing his Mackinaw and carrying a portable electric heater. She stands at the top of the stairs, unnoticed by him, listening)* Quitting? Quitting? Who said that? Oh; well, she's an associate of mine here at the project, poor kid's been under a lot of pressure; fact is, we're all under a lot of pressure here at the project right now, so I'd appreciate your calling me back in ten minutes because there's something important I have to discuss with you, Bill, a whole area of discussion. Beautiful; finish your dinner and call me back. That'll be beautiful. I really appreciate your cooperation on this, Bill. Later, man. Beautiful. 'Bye. *(Hangs up quickly; slumps in booth, exhausted.*

Sees NANCY *at the top of the stairs)* Oh . . . *(Leaves booth)* Good evening. I'm glad to see you. *(She remains at the top of the stairs, looking the other way)* I was just discussing the quitting area with Bill. *(Silence. He gestures about)* Well, Max and I—we've begun. How do you like the tree? The tree here . . . *(Silence. No reply)* It's just Celanese strips over aluminum armature, but I think you still get this graceful-tree feeling. *(Touching the tree)* Used all of my old tools . . . *(He bounds over to the wicker table)* Hey, first table sample in from Colby's— *(Takes umbrella from under table; fits it into center of table, opens it. It is in the shape of a small palm tree)* Sort of a follow-through here on the graceful-tree feeling see, it's—

NANCY   *(Quietly, calmly)* You've gone mad.

ARTHUR   I'm sorry you feel that way.

NANCY   You have set sail on the banana boat.

ARTHUR   I really wish you'd consider the—

NANCY   *(Shouting)* Crazy! The word is "crazy"! A man who can't play the banjo and an old man who can't lift one are gonna sell frankfurters on the beach in the dead of winter!

ARTHUR   Well, it's a unique enterprise, that's true, but—

NANCY   Graceful-tree feeling! Oh, my God—

ARTHUR   And you're wrong; I can play the banjo— *(Picks it up, strums two chords)*

NANCY   Oh, Jesus—

ARTHUR   Well, I'm still learning—

NANCY   Dead of winter! Dead as in dying! As in dying old man! I saw you with my own eyes, I saw you give him a check for ten thousand dollars! That's not a *business* investment, that's *funeral* expenses, that's—

ARTHUR   How much did *you* give him?

NANCY   Two thousand. *(Sits on top step; quietly)* How could I do that? I don't understand; I went with him to deposit your check, to talk him out of it, and the next thing I knew . . . How could I do that? I asked Dr. Berman about it this afternoon.

ARTHUR   What did he say?

NANCY   He said the best he could do was three hundred.

MAX'S VOICE   *(Approaching, at left, singing)*

"Moonlight becomes you,

It goes with your face,
You certainly know how
To fix yourself up terrific . . . "

NANCY   I'm trapped, mister. I can't stop him, and I can't leave him either, I . . .

MAX   *(Enters on boardwalk, carrying two large toolboxes; singing)*

"Moonlight becomes you,
I'll tell you right now . . . "

(Sees ARTHUR'S *tree; stops, deeply impressed. He takes a step down the stairs, looks at the tree in the moonlight; whispering)*

Oh . . . oh, boy . . .

NANCY   Pop, you shouldn't be carrying all those—

MAX   *(Quietly, to* ARTHUR*)*   What can be said? O.K., a partner—a friend even, I figured. But an artist, a great artist, I was not prepared. *(Coming quickly down the stairs)* The Last Supper? Forget it! A comic strip! The *Mona Lisa* is a bimbo! Move over, God, we got another fella here makes trees! *(Squeezes* ARTHUR'S *face)* Your check goes today into Irving Trust, smooth . . . smooth like an egg into a cake, and all day my ear is filled with "yes" . . . "yes" from Auerbach Refrigeration, "yes" from Holiday Juice Machine, "yes" from—

NANCY   *(Trying to take one of the toolboxes)* Here, let me—

MAX   Same nose from this morning? Good. I'm getting used to it. *(Goes to counter with toolboxes, sets them down)* Partner, up the street by Shatzkin's Famous Knishes, is James Carlos Velásquez— a Spanish gentleman, a cab-driver, and a visionary. A small percentage, deferred, he does our deliveries here— *(Points to street)* Go; look for a young fella, sixty-eight, with a Dodge, Sixty-Four—inside is a new sign for the store, unpainted. Bring it and paint it!

ARTHUR   *(Indicates rendering)* Max, I'd like to discuss—

MAX   At my earliest possible convenience— *(Points, under boardwalk)* Shirley, two blocks down Stillwell, a Pittsburgh Paint Outlet. They're open ten more minutes; establish credit and bring me a rainbow. *(He looks at them both)* What I got here? Sand castles? *(Claps his hands)* Move—Move—Time. Time. A couple weeks we open here! *(*NANCY *exits reluctantly under the boardwalk.* ARTHUR *hesitates on the stairs)* O.K., I'll look at the picture . . . *(Goes to rendering; studies it for several moments. Turns solemnly to* ARTHUR*)* I'll tell ya what you're talkin' here, mister . . . you're talkin' ecstasy.

ARTHUR   I think we need some really big palm trees, Max—

MAX   No others would be acceptable!

ARTHUR   The volcano on the roof, I—

MAX   Guaranteed, a volcano!

ARTHUR   *(Going quickly up the stairs)*   Grass huts!

MAX   I love it!

ARTHUR   *(Exits to right, on boardwalk)*   Tribal masks!

MAX   A must! Whatever they are! *(Alone now; looks at rendering)* A little dull; but he'll learn.

(Takes crowbar from toolbox, begins prying loose the first of the boards covering the front of the store; singing)

> "Moonlight becomes you,
> I'm not kidding around . . . "

(The phone rings. He grabs it, instinctively distrusting the instrument)

What is it, who is it? I'm busy here! . . . The beach project? Correct, yessir, this is the beach project. I'm the chairman. State your business . . .   He's not here. Later, call later. Sunrise is a good time . . .

(During these last few moments, a MAN *has entered on the boardwalk at left. He stands in the spill of light from one of the boardwalk lamps, a silhouette carrying a briefcase, looking down at the proceedings. During the next few lines he comes down the stairs, looking solemnly about at the palm tree, the wicker table, the rendering. A rather neatly dressed man in his late thirties, his air of efficiency and organization is immediately at odds with the beach and the open sky. His attitude and his clothes belong to closed rooms. He will be constantly brushing sand off his shoes and his well-pressed overcoat. He very carefully places his briefcase out of sight under the wicker table, then watches* MAX *finish his conversation)*

Who may I say rang? Who? Bill? Bill, from "Goodbye, Bill"? Listen, he's got a girl friend now, leave him alone. Palm trees, girls, a healthy life by the sea; it's not too late for *you*, either. *(Sits in booth)*   Tell me something, what line are you in? . . . Jingle Bells? Sounds risky. Seasonal and risky. Listen to me, you want to get involved with something sturdy, with a foundation? Do yourself a favor, Billy; come down, give a glance here; Tenth Street and the boardwalk. Look for the volcano! *(Hangs up)*

MAN   My God . . . what's this?

MAX *(Turns to him)* What's this? What does it look like? It's paradise. Who are you? *(Leaves booth, studying the* MAN'S *face)* Wait, I know you from someplace . . .

MAN *(sits on wicker chair)* Take a second, Max. It'll come back to you.

MAX Atlantic City, nineteen fifty-eight . . .

MAN No.

MAX Sure; business. I know you from business . . .

MAN No.

MAX Wait, wait, a *relative* . . .

MAN Right.

MAX A cousin, a nephew, a . . .

MAN A son. I'm your son.

MAX Which one?

MAN Michael.

MAX *(Snaps his fingers)* Of course, my son Michael. Must be him. Looks just like him. *(Shakes his hand, cordially)* How-do-you-do-sir.

MICHAEL Max, there are some urgent legal matters—

MAX Sure, now I remember. My lawyer, the son. See, at first I couldn't recognize; because a son, you make a simple cash request— *(Points to store)* —an investment in paradise, he doesn't tell you to go to hell—

MICHAEL Max, I refuse to finance your suicide—

MAX Even a lawyer, what's the good? I give you something to handle, a simple divorce—

MICHAEL A simple divorce? My mother and father; a simple divorce? Max, I told you, this insane divorce, you have no right to ask me. You'll have to get a stranger—

MAX With a son like you, who needs a stranger?

MICHAEL Max, get another lawyer—

MAX What do I pay you?

MICHAEL Nothing.

MAX Then I'll wait till I get a better buy.

MICHAEL Max, there is another, quite imperative matter which I have attempted, unsuccessfully, to bring to your attention—

MAX   Who stops you?

MICHAEL   Max, I came to the house last week and you threw me out. I came in, you hollered, "Yich! Briefcase-carrier!" And shoved me out the door.

MAX   You shouldn't bring a briefcase to dinner. It's not nice.

MICHAEL   And now the matter has increased in urgency. *(Taking* ARTHUR'S *contract from his overcoat pocket)* Max, some fellow named Korman left this on my secretary's desk this morning—

MAX   *(Glancing about)* Hey, where you got it?

MICHAEL   What?

MAX   The briefcase, where you got it?

MICHAEL   Out of sight, don't be concerned.

MAX   *(Pleasantly)* Where you got it? Let me see . . .

MICHAEL   *(Lifts it out from under table)* Here, I've—

MAX   *(Shouting)* Yich! Briefcase-carrier! Old man! Go away!

MICHAEL   *(Quickly putting case back under table)* It's gone, Max, it's gone—

MAX   In a briefcase comes always bad news. Now you got worse anyway; that suit. A suit for old people. A suit to be buried in. Or to bury somebody. *(Sits opposite him; quietly)* Tell me . . . you came here to bury somebody?

MICHAEL   Max, if we're finished with my briefcase and my suit, there is an urgent legal matter—

MAX   The tone, the voice, I don't like it—

MICHAEL   What *do* you like about me?

MAX   Since eighteen: nothing. You went into the boredom business, became a pioneer in the field— *(Bangs on the table)* The *looks* of you. Old. Old. Go eat a hamburger, get a *stain* on yourself, wear the wrong *tie, something.* What happened to sloppy kids?

MICHAEL   I'm not a kid, Max—

MAX   Sure, a kid—

MICHAEL   Max, I have a profession, a wife, two sons—

MAX   Two? How nice for you; I don't have *any. (Rising)* Now you'll excuse me, I open here soon, there are touches to finish—

MICHAEL   Max, wait, we've got to talk. *(Quietly)* Max, have you spoken to Soloway?

MAX   What's to speak? When I finish the store, I'll call him, he join right up.

MICHAEL   Max, to begin with . . . believe me, I never expected you to be able to get *anybody* to invest in—

MAX   What's to tell me?

MICHAEL   It seemed reasonable to assume—

MAX   *(Coming toward the table)* What's to tell me, Michael?

MICHAEL   Please remember, you were in the hospital, you were not expected to survive—

MAX   What, the cemetery is suing me for breach of promise?

MICHAEL   The store had just been sitting here for years—of no use to anybody—there was Mother to consider, an income to consider—

MAX   What, what—?

MICHAEL   Max—

MAX   What, what, what—?

MICHAEL   Max, the property was sold. A month ago, when you were in the hospital . . . *(MAX is quite calm; he sits opposite MICHAEL at the table)* Max, please understand, it's just this week you've talked about reopening . . . after all these years . . .

MAX   *(Quietly, calmly)* Sold. To who, sold?

MICHAEL   The Mister Hot Dog stores, it's a chain of—

MAX   I have seen them.

MICHAEL   They're always interested in beach-front locations, they—

MAX   You have received a check? You have cash in the hand?

MICHAEL   Not yet.

MAX   And Marcus. He agreed? He is selling his share?

MICHAEL   Yes.

MAX   *(Lights his cigar; leans back calmly in his chair)* Uh-huh.

MICHAEL   Max, I hope you understand; I acted in what appeared to be the best interests of . . .

MAX   Certainly.

MICHAEL   You see, we all thought . . .

MAX   Certainly; you all thought I was passing away . . . *(Without rising, MAX suddenly grabs the lapels of MICHAEL'S overcoat and pulls him across the table)* Well, I passed back *in* again, Sonny Boy! *(Pulling him closer)* Tell Mister Hot Dog the deal is off! Tell him Max had a change of heart—it's still beating!

MICHAEL   Max, listen to me—

MAX   There's no conversation. *(Lets go of him)* Refuse the money.

MICHAEL   Max, you don't have to *take* the money, they're quite willing to offer you a percentage of the profits instead. They'll put one of their stores here this summer, you'll share in all the—

MAX   Here? In paradise? *(Rises from table)* They'll put up a Mister Hot Dog in paradise?

MICHAEL   Please, Max—don't you see, you won't have to knock yourself out. And you'll still be in *business*, you'll be a *partner*, you'll drop around from time to time—like your brother Harry and the hardware store.

MAX   I don't want to do business like my brother Harry, and don't wanna shimmy like my sister Kate neither! Partners with *them?* Garbage merchants! The answer is out of the question.

(Goes to front of store, continues prying board loose with crowbar)

MICHAEL   *(Follows* MAX *to store)* Max, I *told* you, they're getting Soloway's share, they'll *be* your partners whether you sell or not. They're going to want one of their chain stores here by June 15, for the summer season—

MAX   *(Turns to him with crowbar)* My regrets to Mister Hot Dog, also *Mrs.* Hot Dog.

MICHAEL   Max, unless you can prove you're running a profitable business here by June, they've got the legal right to put up one of their own—

MAX   Profits; there'll *be* profits!

MICHAEL   How, Max? From what?

MAX   From business! From customers! It's almost springtime!

MICHAEL   Max, they'll take you to *court*, it's—

MAX   Gorgeous! Court is gorgeous! *(Delighted, he grips* MICHAEL'S *arm)* Everybody sues everybody! Meanwhile the store is open, meanwhile profits! They'll take you to court, you'll *keep* them there. Delays and stalling, legal monkey business. You'll do it, Michael; you and the magic briefcase. Get me time, get me the summer, and I'll show you profits!

MICHAEL   Max, there won't *be* any profits . . . not here . . . there never were.

MAX   Take a sniff that breeze, there's gold in the air . . .

MICHAEL   Max, no . . . we can't . . .

MAX   Why *no?* Why *can't?* (*Holding* MICHAEL'S *arm, shaking him*) Do it, Michael! Do this thing! Do a silly thing! Get a wrinkle in your suit! Give me a sign I'll know you're alive!

MICHAEL   (*Quietly*) Max, please . . . this place won't last a month. And if *it* does, *you* won't. It's foolish, it's impossible . . . it'll kill you, Max.

MAX   (*Lets go of his arm*) When you were a baby, you were smart. At three months you knew to wave bye-bye . . . (*Walks away from him to counter*) It's still the thing you do best.

MICHAEL   Max, I'm trying to—

MAX   Soloway, he made a contract?

MICHAEL   Not yet, they're negotiating; but by the end of the week they—

MAX   (*Delighted*) He's negotiating. Perfect. (*Returns to work, prying board with crowbar*) Now you may leave the premises.

MICHAEL   Max, I'm—

MAX   (*Shouts*) Kindly leave the premises!

MICHAEL   It never varies, Max. Whenever I see you, you say the same three things to me: "Hello," "Who are you?" and "Leave the premises." (*Going to table*) Actually, Max, since eighteen I haven't been too crazy about *you* either. (*Picks up briefcase*) You keep telling me I'm ashamed of your accent. I never was. Only mystified. I just can't figure out why it's thicker now than it was twenty years ago. (*Turns to him*) The anger too. Thicker and thicker. Today I'm trying to talk you into staying alive, and you're angry. You were angry last year, and year before that, and three years ago you came to my house for dinner—and asked me to leave the premises. My own home, Max; y'know, the one with the two sons? (MAX *ignores him, busily prying board with crowbar.* ARTHUR *enters at right on boardwalk carrying large wooden sign. Stops, listens, unnoticed by them*) Tell me, Max; what is it? Solve the mystery. What makes you perpetually angry with me? (MAX *continues his work.* MICHAEL *raises his voice, almost shouting*) Come on, Max! I'm *asking you*—my client, the father! *What the hell is*— (*Checks himself; regains control; speaks quietly again*) Well, it's certainly not going to accomplish anything for *both* of us to get angry. *(Picks up his briefcase, about to exit)* No point in—

MAX   *(Quietly)* Wait a minute . . . *(Points with crowbar)* What you were just doing here—*that* was angry? What kinda angry is that, I don't know till you tell me? Here, I'll show you angry . . . *(MAX suddenly smashes one of the boards with his crowbar, shouting)* This is angry! *(Then quietly, smiling)* You see that? There's no mix-up. *(Coming toward MICHAEL)* *There's* the mystery, *that's* why I'm angry—because I never know when *you* are. I look in your face: what's up? If that's angry, it's not enough. I look in your face, I don't see anybody. I look for Max, I don't see him either... that's why I got a store. The accent? Was a time, there were neighbor-hoods in this city I could cash checks with it. Whatta *you* got tells you you're not somebody else? An American Express card? The store is foolish, the store is silly, but the store is mine. Whatta you got belongs to *you*? A briefcase fulla bad news and an old man's suit. Go away from me, you're breaking my eyes. Wave bye-bye, sonny, I'll see you in a million years . . .

(MAX takes ledger pad from overcoat pocket, sits at table with his back to MICHAEL, checking figures with a pencil stub. MICHAEL turns to leave, stops)

MICHAEL   Max, you're going to open the store . . .

MAX   Of course.

MICHAEL   Then I'm quite certain I won't see you alive again.

MAX   Get a Polaroid. Take a picture.

MICHAEL   I don't understand . . . *(Shouts)* God damn you, Max . . . why do you want to die here with a bunch of palm trees! *(Covers his eyes with his hand)* Damn you, damn you, old man; I'm cry-ing . . .

MAX   You feel so bad, help me to open the store.

MICHAEL   I can't help you to kill yourself, Max.

MAX   *(Turns to him)* Yessir, you're crying . . . but not enough! *(Turns abruptly back to the ledger, immediately absorbed)* "Six counter grills, double weight, two hundred eighty, installed . . . " *(Michael steps forward violently, about to smash his fist into the table—checks himself, composes himself; turns to leave)* "Malt mixers, eight-speed, gallon size, with filter . . . " *(Michael remembers that he has left his brief-case, picks it up, exits quickly under the boardwalk at right, brushing the sand off the briefcase)* Quart-size, twenty-two eighty, repairs up to one year . . . "

NANCY'S VOICE　Pop . . .

(She steps solemnly out of the shadows under the boardwalk, at left, carrying a carton of paints. She has apparently been standing there for some time)

NANCY　Pop, I was . . .

MAX　*(Rises, goes toward her)*　Ah, the colors.

NANCY　Pop, I heard . . .

MAX　All?

NANCY　Enough.

MAX　Good. Then you know there's nothing to worry. *(Smiling, takes carton of paints from her)*

NANCY　*(To* ARTHUR, *who is carrying the sign down the stairs)*　Arthur, Soloway's selling his share to the Mister Hot Dog chain—

ARTHUR　Oh, God—

MAX　I don't need "Oh, God" from you, I can get "Oh, God" from her. *(Happily opening the carton of paints)*　Nothing to worry, plenty time. He's not *selling*, he's *negotiating*. Like people *breathe*, Soloway negotiates. In a subway he negotiates the carfare—

ARTHUR　Max, if he sells—

MAX　Darling, darling, if he knew we were opening he wouldn't enter*tain* such an offer, wouldn't even give it a cookie. Be advised, sir; we are talking here of Marcus Soloway . . . a man built temples in the sand, sea lions, pillars toward the sky. *(His arm around* ARTHUR*)*　Arthur, wait'll he sees your volcano, your trees . . . *(Points to rendering)*　How much can we do in three days?

ARTHUR　Well . . . some, I—

MAX　"Some" is exactly enough! *(Shakes* ARTHUR'S *hand)*　It's settled; we open in three days!

NANCY　Oh, God . . .

MAX　See how good she does it? *(His hand on* ARTHUR'S *shoulder)*　Arthur, all we gotta do is show Marcus we're in business, show him we're alive—I promise you, he'll join right up. *(Quietly)*　Partner... do you trust me on this?

ARTHUR　Well, yes, I—

MAX　Then what're ya hangin' around for! *(Points to sign)*　The letters are there, fill me in the colors! Sunrise, Arthur, colors like the sunrise! *(Hands crowbar to* NANCY*)*　Quickly, the boards come off the store; tomorrow equipment arrives! Installations! *(Walking briskly to stairs)* Some words in English are beautiful. "Installations" is beautiful. "Deliveries" is beautiful. *(Going up the stairs)* "Goods," "equipment," "counter," "register" . . .

NANCY   Where are you going?

MAX   The première has been advanced, I must go now to Margolis on the corner—formerly tailor of Florenz Ziegfeld, "Flo" to him—makes me an outfit for the opening, stripes; stripes to dazzle the eye.

NANCY   Pop, wait —

MAX   "Wait" is not a beautiful word— *(As he exits)* "Wholesale" is a beautiful word. "Contract" is another beauty . . . *(Disappearing to the left down the boardwalk)* "Percentage," "price," "bargain," "customer," "sale" . . .

NANCY   *(Quietly)* I can't do it. *(To* ARTHUR*)* Nope. Sorry. Can't. *(Shakes her head.)* Uh-uh. *(He approaches her)* I can't. I can't watch this. I thought I could; but I can't . . . *(She hands him the crowbar)* I have to leave now. *(Points to heater she brought earlier)* That's portable; make sure he uses it to keep warm . . . *(Going left, under boardwalk)* Promise me . . .

ARTHUR   Nancy, I think we should try to—

NANCY   Arthur, you're a nice man, a gentle man; but you're quite crazy. You're both crazy and I have to leave now.

ARTHUR   *(Gestures to store)* The three of us together, maybe we could—

NANCY   It's a wonderful group. I don't know who I am, he's dying, and you can't quit your job.

(She starts to exit left under the boardwalk. ARTHUR *suddenly hauls back and smashes the crowbar against the stairway railing; the sound rings in the air—she turns, startled)*

ARTHUR   All right, goddamn it, that's it! *(He flings open the phone booth door)* Gotta be done, the time has come! *(Deposits coin, dialing fiercely)* No more foolin' around here, damn it!

(The phone in the second booth starts to ring)

NANCY   Arthur, he's calling you back! Arthur, the other phone! *(He ignores her, bent on his mission)* Arthur! *(She races to the second booth, grabs the phone)* Bill, listen; Arthur's calling you on the other—

ARTHUR   Hello.

NANCY   Hello. Listen, he's—

ARTHUR   Hello, Nancy?

NANCY   Who is this?

ARTHUR   It's me, Arthur.

NANCY   Arthur . . .

ARTHUR   Look, I tell ya why I called . . .

NANCY   Arthur, I'm hanging up now . . . *(Leans around corner of booth; speaking directly to his back)* Arthur, I'm hanging up now, O.K.?

ARTHUR   Nancy, don't go— *(He grips the phone tensely)* Nancy, I'm twenty minutes late for *everything*; conversations, trains, sunrises, people . . . Being alive; I'm twenty *years* late on that one. So don't go, Nancy, not now . . . not now, I just got here. *(Touched by what he has said, she delicately, soundlessly hangs up her phone, leaves her booth, stands behind him. Unaware, he continues on the phone)* Hello? Hello, Nancy . . . ?

NANCY   *(Quietly)* Hello. *(He turns to her)* I came as soon as I got your call. *(Sadly)* Arthur, forgive me, I can't do it. You and me, the store; it's too late. It got too late . . .

ARTHUR   People can change their whole lives if they want to—

NANCY   You just heard that—

ARTHUR   I've been hearing it all day—

NANCY   Arthur, I'm married—

ARTHUR   Oh.

NANCY   I was getting a divorce, that's why I came to the beach today—

ARTHUR   Wherever you get it, I'm delighted—

NANCY   Arthur, I want to go back . . . *(Crossing to dune)* My old buddy, Shirley, I want her back. She didn't expect a helluva lot, but she didn't shake like this either . . . My husband's got a used-car lot on Fourteenth Street; nothing'll ever be new there, but I know I'll never be scared . . . I . . .

ARTHUR   No.

NANCY   Huh?

ARTHUR   *(Quietly, shaking his head)* No. You can't go back. *(Comes toward her, at dune)* We've gone too far. I built a tree, you built a nose, and we can't go back now. *(He takes her hand)* I built that tree today, and while I was doing it I heard this fella laughing . . .

laughing with joy . . . and I looked around and it was me. I love you, Nancy. Nancy, Shirley, alla you, I love you and I love my Goddamn tree. Please, if your hand trembles, take mine. If you want love, take mine. If you want to love somebody, love me. *(After a moment)* Believe me, none of that was easy without a telephone. *(He touches her cheek)* You're beautiful. Forget pretty. Beautiful . . .

NANCY   *(Softly)* Arthur, it's all new, it's—

ARTHUR   No, looks to me like you been beautiful a long, long time.

NANCY   Arthur, at night my old nose comes back to haunt the bedroom . . . *(He carefully pulls the hood of the Mackinaw back off her face)* It snifles and moans all night . . . *(He holds her face in his hands)* It's terrible, you'll hate it . . . *(He kisses her tenderly. They lean back against the slope of the dune, their arms around each other, the palm tree arched gracefully over them in the moonlight. She talks softly into his shoulder)* Arthur... Arthur, you figure we got a chance?

ARTHUR   Lady, I learned five chords on the banjo today—*any*thing is possible.

(She laughs, she kisses him; holding on to him tightly. They are silent for a moment, lying against the dune, their arms around each other)

NANCY   Arthur, God help us, we love each other.

ARTHUR   Right.

NANCY   We love each *other*, of all people. *(Silence. They hold each other. Only the sound of the surf for a few moments)* Arthur, if you're asleep, I'll kill ya.

ARTHUR   Awake, I'm awake— *(He suddenly lifts her up in his arms, celebrating)* Awake!

NANCY   Hey, what're ya doin'?

ARTHUR   Carrying you. I told you, I'm very big on carrying things—

MAX'S VOICE   Put that daughter down! One partner with a coronary is enough!

(ARTHUR puts her down, but they continue to hold hands. MAX enters on boardwalk, at left, wearing a red-and-white-striped blazer and a straw skimmer, his overcoat over his arm. He makes a small spin, fashion-show style, at the top of the stairs)

MAX   And *this*—this is why they call it a blazer! *(Starts jauntily down the stairs, continuing the fashion parade)* Yessir, and here's Max again—this time in smart and tasty opening-night apparel, he—

NANCY   Max, put your goddamn *coat* on, it's—

MAX   Well . . . *(Takes note of them holding hands)* Looks to me like goodbye Eddie, huh?

NANCY   Pop, I—

MAX   Listen, you want turtle soup, you gotta hurt a couple turtles, right? *(Coming down the stairs)* Because while we're on the subject of people breaking up . . . there's certain other news . . .

NANCY   My God, not Mike and Sandra . .

MAX   No; not Mike and Sandra . . . *(Picks up crowbar, returning to work, removing boards at front of store)* Max and Rosie.

NANCY   Who?

MAX   Me and your mother, Max and Rosie; in three and a half weeks we're getting a divorce. *(Shouting to* ARTHUR*)* What's with my sign? The organization is getting loose here! *(Hands the stunned* NANCY *a crowbar)* Come, the boards. Three days! We gotta move here!

NANCY   Max, you—

MAX   *(As* ARTHUR *takes paint cans from carton)* Get ready with the reds, get ready with the yellows; and I'll give you a tip, gold! *(Begins prying loose one of the boards covering the front of the store)* Nancy, the boards—

NANCY   Pop, I don't believe it—

MAX   Believe it, and then help me with the boards.

NANCY   *(Holding his arm)* Pop, you've been married now for—what is it?—Forty-three *years*—

MAX   What can I do, the marriage isn't working out.

NANCY   Pop, forty-three *years, five* children—

MAX   Well, you can't say we didn't try, right? *(Shouting to* ARTHUR *who works on the sign downstage, near the pier)* Silver! Use also silver! For Silverman!

NANCY   *(Draping the overcoat on his shoulders)* Max, *why* . . . after all these years, why *now?*

MAX   Because the woman looks funny at me . . . *(Turns to her)* Shirley, the woman looks funny at me. Since I come from the hospital, she looks at me like she misses me . . . and I *didn't leave* yet! *(Whacks the first board; it falls to the sand. Begins prying second board)* These ladies, one little heart attack, they start right away learning to live without you. Trouble is, they learn a little too good and a little too early and all of a sudden you wake up one morning in the same bed with your own widow! *(Shouting to* ARTHUR, *who has turned from his work to listen to* MAX*)* The sign! What's with the sign? You wanna be known only for your trees?

NANCY   *(Gently)* Pop . . . Pop, maybe if you talk to her . . .

MAX   *Talk* to her? Shirley, every morning I come in for breakfast, the woman is reading the obituaries. I say, "Good morning, Rosie!" She says, "Guess who died." I say, "Who died?" She says, "Bing-bing. One minute he was here and then, bing-bing, he was gone." I say, "*Who*, Rosie, *who?* Who is Mr. Bing-bing today?" And then she tells me . . . And, Shirley, I swear to God, *I never heard of him!* *(Another whack, the second board falls to the sand)* For Rosie, anybody who died is automatically a buddy! *(Puts crowbar down, grips* NANCY'S *arm tensely)* Shirley, Shirley . . . in my neighborhood they're gonna put up soon a lotta new apartment buildings; they paint these big X's on the windows of the old houses they're gonna rip down . . . *(He is frightened)* Last week we're watching the TV; I'm sittin' there in front of the set like a fish they took all the bones outa, fillet of person . . . and I catch Rosie lookin' at me . . . Shirley, she's lookin' at me like she sees X's on my eyes; like she sees 'em painted right on there, like she hears the wrecking crew coming from blocks away. *(Shouting to them both)* Maybe I'm gonna die, but I guarantee you it's not gonna be in the middle of the Late Show! Maybe it's the truth what she sees—but if that's the truth, I don't wanna hang around with it! *(Turns sharply to* ARTHUR*)* Gimme that sign! *(Goes quickly down to* ARTHUR, *throwing his overcoat off on the way)* The coat! The coat covers my outfit!

(He grabs the sign from ARTHUR, *lifts it easily onto his shoulder, starts up the boardwalk steps with it. The sign is about five feet by four and does not face the audience at this point)*

ARTHUR   Max, let me help you with—

NANCY   Pop, damn it, you shouldn't be—

*(*MAX, *ignoring them both, moves briskly to the top of the stairway and then a few steps along the boardwalk until he is directly over the store; he lifts the new sign up over the railing, intending to hook it in place over the old one—he suddenly stops, staggers. He turns away from them and us, grips the railing for support.* NANCY *and* ARTHUR *stand paralyzed for a moment, terrified.)*

NANCY   *(Whispering)* Oh, my God—

ARTHUR   Max—

*(They both rush forward to the stairs—*MAX *suddenly turns to them, quite calmly, smiling)*

MAX   Don't make funeral arrangements. I just stopped to take a breath. *(He looks at them both; then looks at* NANCY *for a long moment. Her back is to us; he sees something in her face that we cannot see. He shakes his head)* Shirley . . . son-of-a-gun . . . you're lookin' funny at me. *(Quietly, to them both)* Oh, my sweet children; won't you be shocked . . . my darling children with your frightened eyes, won't you be surprised when I live forever. *(He turns the new sign around, hooks it onto the railing over the old one. The gold and silver letters against a deep-red background are not completely painted in, but still clearly announce: "Max's New Original Hawaiian Ecstasies."* MAX *moves to the side, takes a few steps down the stairs to view the bright new sign above the old store)* Twenty-two years, every day, somebody asks me, "What's new?" I say, "Nothing's new." Next week they'll ask; I'll say . . . "Me." *(Shouting)* The sign is up, the sign is up and then the business starts again; look, look my darling babies . . . soon it begins again.

(His arms raised, shouting, as . . .

There is a BLACKOUT.

Immediately in the darkness, we hear the Dixieland Devils, an eight-piece Dixieland marching band—trumpet, trombone, clarinet, tuba, snare, cymbals, field drum, and marching drum—they go into a strong and strutting introduction to "Over the Waves."

To the beat of this music, light bulbs start to pop on, one at a time, along the perimeter of the pier. In the light of these first few bulbs we begin to see more clearly that it is MAX *who is putting these bulbs in, taking red, yellow, and orange bulbs from his shopping bag and placing them along the pier; they light up in time with the music.*

Toward the end of the intro, there are three downbeats to the march itself; on the first downbeat, colored footlights go on across the stage. On the second, the pier lights pulse on brighter; and on the third MAX *marches from the pier to the beach as . . .*

A sunrise begins in the blackout; a four- or five-minute blossoming of light; from gray to pink, from pink to vivid red, and from red finally to a golden orange . . . In this gradual revelation of light we will see the old stand being transformed into the new one, all of it done by MAX, NANCY, *and* ARTHUR *working in unison. All of their work should be completed when the sunrise reaches its peak and then—the sky goes night-black, the entire stage brightly illuminated, amid the dark, deserted beach around it.*

It is three days later, early evening; all three people are just complet-ing the last of the tasks we have watched them perform through the changes of light and time; and there, beautiful and ugly and glorious, is the New Original Max's Hawaiian Ecstasies. The motif is, of course, Hawaiian; the stand appears brightly repainted and it is hung with grass matting, native-hut style; long blades of plastic grass engulf the store, they glisten and rustle in the February wind. The store is framed on either side by two palm trees now, the trunks running up the sides of the building and bursting with enormous palm fronds that dovetail across the roof of the stand; two smaller trees frame the sign above. The counter, hung with fronds and grass, polished and shining, has been outfitted with two new grills, a bubbling tank of coconut drink, and other bright new counter fixtures. The interior of the stand has been decorated with imitation jungle birds, tropical vines, and Tahitian tribal masks. On the sand in front of the store are two round, wicker beach tables surrounded by wicker chairs; umbrellas rise up from the tables, the poles painted like palm bark and the umbrella tops covered with plastic palm fronds. There are colored lights everywhere, the most outstanding light display being a neon frankfurter that forms an archway between the two lampposts on either side of the top of the stairway; each time the frankfurter blinks on and off, it grows small-er, as though bites are being taken out of it—three huge bites; on the fourth bite the frankfurter is gone, and then it reappears whole again. The Dixieland music is coming from a record player on the counter, the record spinning, the music continuing through part of this next scene.

As the lights shift from sunrise to the early evening of this scene, each one of the three people is completing a final task, the music building to a peak . . .

ARTHUR *turns on a glowing red light at the center of a small plaster volcano that he has just placed on the roof of the store.*

NANCY *staples a final large palm frond on the second palm tree.* MAX *takes a furled banner from inside the store and, half marching, half strutting, carries it to the end of the pier, hooking it onto the tallest of the pier ties, then lets it unroll facing the ocean and the audience; it has silver letters against a blue background and a silver arrow at the bottom; it says: "TO ALL BOATS: STOP HERE FOR MAX'S." At the same moment that the banner unfurls,* ARTHUR *turns on his vol-cano light and* NANCY *staples the palm frond, their three tasks com-pleted simultaneously.*

MAX *turns from his banner now as the Dixieland music builds to a finish; he looks at the store, at* ARTHUR *and* NANCY. *He takes his hat off to it, to them, and to himself. Then, as if by mutual signal, all three leave their separate positions and rush forward to the center of the beach, where they join in a huge three-person hug)*

MAX   *(Kissing them both; then squeezing one face with each hand)* I love everything here, each item, everything and everyone here . . . until further notice. *(Crossing to coconut drink on counter)* Now the toasts . . . *(Pours out three drinks in coconut-shell goblets)* I understand '68 is a very good year for coconut drink.

NANCY   Silverman, I'd appreciate it if you'd put on your coat, it's—

MAX   *(Raising his goblet)* To what we did here . . . *(They all raise their goblets, gathering around one of the wicker tables)* To three days that have changed the face of the North Atlantic coastline . . . to Shirley's palm leaves, each a beauty . . . to Arthur's volcano, which I am considering at this moment for a loan-out to the Metropolitan . . . also to Arthur's frankfurter sign, which if I wasn't talking right now would leave me speechless . . . and to Benny Kalsheim . . .

ARTHUR   Benny Kalsheim?

MAX   He come over with me on the boat from Russia, I include him in all toasts. *(Raising his goblet higher)* And to Mr. Marcus Soloway, who comes tonight . . .

ARTHUR   You spoke to him— ?

MAX   Spoke? Sang! We *sang* to each other! A duet! Twin Cantors on the telephone!

NANCY   Did he say he'd—?

MAX   Soloway don't do business on the phone. He is a person, in person, with a face and no lawyers. He comes to argue, to holler, to hustle; business! I wouldn't miss a minute!

ARTHUR   Yes, but did he say he'd—

MAX   *(Gesturing about with goblet)* The truth, partner: do you see a "no" here anywhere? Even a "maybe"? *(Raising his goblet)* To all those present, relatives and associates, lovers and partners . . . and to all Hawaiians everywhere! *(They clunk glasses and drink. Sips thoughtfully)* Another dash rum, some more shreds coconut, we got here easy a dollar-fifty item.

ARTHUR   I have a toast . . . *(They raise their goblets again)* To the

Silvermans, both of them; and to the sun rising tomorrow on our land . . . the land of Silverman, Soloway, and Korman . . . the blessings of a new day . . . to Coney, island of dreams, island of—

MAX   Wrap it up; we got work here. *(They clunk goblets and drink)* Now you, Shirley, a toast.

NANCY   *(She turns to them, raises her goblet)* To the store, to the Ecstasies . . . and to the men I love most.

MAX   The best one. She did the best one. *(They clunk goblets and drink)* O.K., party's over! *(Crossing to phone booth)* Tomorrow we open, Soloway comes soon.

ARTHUR   O.K. *(Clapping his hands)* Nancy, Lafayette Electric closes at eight. I've arranged for ten heaters at eighteen-fifty a unit; tell them we'll take a dozen if they come down a dollar each—

NANCY   *(Stacking goblets on counter)* A dozen if they come down a dollar, right—

ARTHUR   Velásquez is parked on Stillwell, he'll help you carry them. *(To* MAX, *who is in booth, dialing)* Max, when Soloway comes, seat him at Table 2, it's the best view of the area.

MAX   Yessir.

ARTHUR   *(Gathering stack of posters and tape)* O.K., thirty left, that makes about four hundred posters spread around the—

MAX   Velásquez, he put 'em in the high schools? *(ARTHUR nods)* Good. For the young people, out here will be the *in* place. Moonlight and coconuts— *(Into phone)* Hello, Abrams? Then get me Abrams. *(To* ARTHUR*)* The posters, Arthur—Stillwell, Tenth, and don't forget the boardwalk. Soloway should see them whichever way he comes.

ARTHUR   Max, we'll surround him.

*(*ARTHUR *starts upstairs with posters,* NANCY *heads under boardwalk to street)*

MAX   *(Shaking the phone)* What's with Abrams? I gotta tell him where the parade starts . . .

NANCY   *(About to exit)* Parade . . . ?

MAX   Yessir; comes down the avenue at dawn, a fine organization, the Dixieland Devils, to advertise the opening. Rampart Street on Coney Island Avenue! From the land of Dixie, led by Irwin Abrams, what a sound, clean and perfect, everybody struttin' along . . . What, you don't recall those devils? That's them on the record, Shirley; same group when I opened thirty years ago, you marched with me in the parade, you and Michael.

NANCY   *(Remembers, smiling)* Jesus; they must be very—

MAX   O.K., a tuba died since; also a clarinet; but tomorrow Irwin himself leads, still spunky, a trumpet takes your heart away. *(Gestures with receiver)* Takes a little while to get to the phone, otherwise perfect. *(*NANCY *and* ARTHUR *enjoying the romance of it as* MAX *rhapsodizes)* The selection, naturally, is "Over the Waves"; what could be better? Tomorrow at dawn, windows go up, doors open, everybody looks: "What's that?" A band, eight pieces, a float with a sign "Come to the Ecstasies! On the Beach at Tenth Street!" *(*NANCY *blows a kiss to* ARTHUR *and they exit to their separate tasks.* MAX *speaks into the phone)* Hello, Abrams? Silverman! I said *Silverman* . . . That's right, I'm still alive. Yeah, still since yesterday . . . *Yesterday,* Abrams, I spoke to you *yester*day! *(Shouting into phone)* Batteries, Abrams; get new *batteries* for your machine! *Spend* a dollar . . . Good, it's coming back to you; good, Silverman's parade; you remember. Between the memory and the ears, you're charging too much; how about you come down fifty dollars? . . . Oh, *that* you heard, you heard that one! Abrams, I love you! *(There is the burst of a match flame on the boardwalk, at left. The flame lingers on the face of* MARCUS SOLOWAY; *lighting his cigar, slowly, elaborately. He is an old man wearing a very new fur-collared ski coat. He blows out the match, steps forward into the light of* ARTHUR'S *frankfurter sign at the top of the stairs. He looks up at it, thoughtfully. All this as* MAX *continues on the phone)* Abrams, you and the boys, you'll rendezvous with the float at Surf and Stillwell. Then you'll start down the avenue; you got that? Good, good. And, Abrams, *loud;* you'll play loud! *Loud,* goodbye! *(Hangs up; shakes his head)* Old people...

MARCUS   *(Shouting)* Silverman! Soloway is here!

MAX   Soloway! *(Leaves booth)* Soloway! *(Steps forward to bottom of stairs)* Soloway, look at you!

MARCUS   Silverman, look at you! Oh boy, *old!*

MAX   Look at *you! Older!*

MARCUS   *(Coming down steps)* I heard you was sick.

MAX   They put me in a new ventricle.

MARCUS   Oh boy.

MAX   Dacron.

MARCUS   Oh boy.

MAX   Plastic. Can you believe it?

MARCUS   I believe it. They put me in a pacemaker.

MAX   Oh boy.

MARCUS   Makes me a pace.

MAX   The coat. I like the coat. Sporty.

MARCUS   Thank you. Your coat I don't like. Coats, you never knew. *(Sits at a table, looking around at store, nodding)* Coconuts, you know. But not coats. *(Pointing at boardwalk)* I seen a poster on the boardwalk.

MAX   Good.

MARCUS   A fella is standing next to it; pointing and smiling.

MAX   My partner.

MARCUS   A partner. A pointer and a smiler.

MAX   *(After a moment, indicating the store)* Well . . . ?

MARCUS   *(Nods)* Nice. *(Looks about at the lights, the tables; nods)* Nice.

MAX   *(Pouring him goblet of coconut drink)* Here. Taste.

MARCUS   *(He sips the drink. Reflects on it a moment; then nods)* Nice.

MAX   Well . . . ?

MARCUS   Close it up. Max, take the money and close it up.

MAX   You! From the devil! You're taking money from the devil!

MARCUS   Why not? I never heard from him before. Twelve thousand dollars; when it comes, I'll take it. At my age, that's a good salary; could be a thousand dollars an hour. You gather me, Max? You gather my meaning? *(Leans forward at table)* I come to tell you personally: take the money and close it up.

MAX   Marcus, you won't take the money, you'll join me here . . . I got an instinct and a feeling, it's our turn again . . .

MARCUS   Max, when it was our *turn* even, it wasn't our turn. *(Rising from table)* Twenty years ago we was flops in July; how come we'll be such winners in February? Take the instinct, take the feeling, take the money, and close it up. *(Crossing to water's edge)* You know what you got here? *Wintertime.* Coldness, Max. And I'm not talkin' in the soul; I'm talkin' in the toes, the nose, and the elbows. Who'll come to shiver with a frankfurter? *(Turns to him)* Even alone, Max; what's the hurry? You can't wait for sunshine?

MAX   A Dacron ventricle don't wait for sunshine.

MARCUS   *(Nods)* This is a point.

MAX   *(Comes toward him)* You'll come back. *(Shouting)* What's wrong with you? The season is by the doorstep! Every day it gets warmer!

MARCUS   Listen to you! Max, I don't see you now a long time because you make me nervous! Always excited and you holler too much! Three years ago, the hurricane; I come around here the next day, I'm hoping this place would blow away. The sea should come and get it, it wouldn't aggravate me any more. You gather me? But it didn't blow away and neither do you! You're still around hollering and you make me nervous, Silverman. *(Crosses to MAX)* Take my advice, I come to tell you personally: be an old man, you'll live longer. *(Takes his arm)* Max, listen to me . . . this year I started doing old-man things. I tell stories for a second time, just like an old man. Sometimes for a third time. It's coming out of my mouth about how I got a good buy on my new car, the third time I'm telling it to my daughter and her husband. I *know* it's the third time, but I go right on, it don't bother me; just like an old man. I fall asleep in front of people like it's my right and my privilege, just like an old man. I can remember what I did, what clothes I wore, names of people from when I was eighteen, and if you told me I was in Hong Kong yesterday, I would believe you, because I don't remember; just like an old man. So, I finally figured it out. The reason I'm behaving like an old man . . . is because I'm an *old man.* A *revelation* to me, Silverman; and for the first time in *years* I'm not annoyed with myself. Silverman, I was not a top businessman. I was good, but not first-class. I was an O.K. husband; and as a father, not a knockout. But, Max . . . I'm a *great old man.* I do that the best. I was born for it. I'm seventy-four, Max, and it fits me like a glove. You, you're a crazy. I wish you well with the business; but I can't join you . . . *(He smiles)* I'm too old for it. *(He crosses under the boardwalk at right to leave; turns, points to one of the tables)* The tables. How much you paid?

MAX   Thirty-eight fifty; Colby's on Fourth Street.

MARCUS   Dumb! Coulda got from Harold's for twenty-five, on Canal Street. You coulda made— *(He stops himself, turns)* Now I'm leaving. Best good wishes to you and yours . . . *(Walking into the shadows under the boardwalk at right)* Notice how I don't take the stairs. Regard me, how I take the easy way under the boardwalk. I'm seventy-four, Max, and I got one interest in life: seventy-five. You gather me, Silverman? *(He exits. MAX looks around at the store for a moment, then shouts in the direction of MARCUS'S exit)*

MAX   The hell with you! A gold mine like this; who needs you anyway? The coat; I lied to you about the coat. I didn't like it! *(He
nods to himself, satisfied with his outburst. He looks up at the boardwalk, sees an unlit bulb on the string along the railing)* A red bulb is
out. Leaves a dark spot. *(Rummaging among bulbs in box on the
table)* Must be no dark spots. *(Finds a red bulb, starts up the stairs
with it. He stops about halfway up)* How come yesterday twenty-
two steps . . . today a thousand?

(He sits on the top step)

ARTHUR'S VOICE   Beautiful . . .

*(He walks into the light of his frankfurter sign at the top of the stairs,
carrying the roll of tape, the posters apparently distributed)*

ARTHUR   Max, you can see this whole place glowin' half a mile away.

MAX   That was the intention.

ARTHUR   *(Coming down the steps)* Everything dark, the whole beach,
and just this place glowin' like a jewel, Max.

MAX   Like a jewel was the intention.

ARTHUR   Neighborhood's covered with those posters, nobody'll be
able to walk down a street without—

MAX   Arthur, listen; Soloway was here . . .

ARTHUR   Well . . . ?

MAX   Good news, Arthur. He's selling his share.

ARTHUR   *(Sitting next to him on steps)* Doesn't sound like good news,
Max.

MAX   You gotta have an ear for it. *(Turns to ARTHUR, smiling)* Arthur,
we're rid of him! The man was unfortunately an invalid. A liabil-
ity to the organization. *(Taps his chest)* A pacemaker in waltz time.
(Snaps his fingers) Suddenly old.

ARTHUR   Max, that means Mister Hot Dog is our partner . . .

MAX   Why not? We open *our* store, we give *them* a percentage, and
we don't have an old man hanging around. All we gotta do is show
profits by June. *(Holds ARTHUR's arm, happily)* The good news,
partner . . . the good news is honor. Honorable battle with Mister
Hot Dog. Arthur, if we do good here by June, if we stop them,
that is a number one victory! A world covered with plastic and we
make a dent! It's a public service! *(He stands)* A whistle is blown
in the face of the junk parade! Everywhere Mister Hot Dog, but
not *here*, Arthur, never *here*.

ARTHUR *(rises, goes a few steps down the stairs, looking about at his work)* It's really . . . it's so beautiful . . . we've got three months, we've got a chance.

MAX When I pick a partner, I pick a partner! *(Sits back down on the steps)* Poor old Marcus, he lost the eye for paradise.

ARTHUR *(Touching the palm next to the stairs)* Gotta say so myself, I did a terrific job on these trees. It's the angle of them that does it, I think.

MAX *(Handing him the red bulb)* Here, there's a light out on the railing— *(ARTHUR takes bulb, going quickly up steps to boardwalk railing)* Look for the dark spot.

ARTHUR *(As he puts the bulb in)* Listen, did anybody happen to . . . has anybody said anything to you about my trees?

MAX References were made.

ARTHUR Yeah, it's mostly the angle of them that does it. The shape and the angle; I mean, you *know* it's a palm tree.

MAX Velásquez brings the tables yesterday, I give you verbatim, he says, "Look what you got here—*palm* trees."

ARTHUR Tell ya what we need, Max. *(Crossing left, on boardwalk)* One more tree, right here . . . right up here . . . something you can see from the street. Whaddya think? *(No reply)* Thing is, I'm gonna have to work out some kinda weatherproof glaze for the plaster; it's—

MAX Now I can't talk. I'm busy.

ARTHUR O.K., later; but it's—

MAX Not later either. I'm busy having a heart attack.

ARTHUR What?

MAX A regular heart attack.

ARTHUR Max—

(He races across the boardwalk to the steps)

MAX I'll tell you what I'm doing. I'm dying.

ARTHUR *(Running down the steps, about to go past MAX to the phone)* I'll call your doctor—an ambulance—

MAX *(Grabbing ARTHUR'S hand)* No-sir. No time. No-sir.

ARTHUR Max, the phone, I'll be a second—

MAX No-sir—

ARTHUR   (*Kneels next to him on step*)   Max, what should I do, I—

MAX   I don't know. I never died before.

ARTHUR   (*His arm around* MAX)   Oh, my God . . .

MAX   Look at you. If I don't hurry, you'll beat me to it.

ARTHUR   Max, can I . . . can I . . . how do you feel?

MAX   Not in the pink. (*He stands*)   Too busy! Who needs this? It's stupid! So stupid! (*Staggers down the few steps to the sand*)   I got business. There's business . . . (ARTHUR *moves down in front of him, trying to hold him*)   I got business. I got business . . . (*He is spent; he falls into* ARTHUR'S *arms.* ARTHUR *holds him, kneels with him on the sand. There are a few short bursts from a car horn offstage*)   Arthur . . .

ARTHUR   Yes, Max . . .

MAX   Tell Rosie, say to her . . . (*He suddenly laughs; a whispered, desperate, delighted laugh*)   Say to Rosie . . . guess who died. (*His head falls against* ARTHUR'S *chest. He is dead.* ARTHUR *holds him. There is a gust of wind;* ARTHUR *automatically puts* MAX'S *coat collar up to protect him.* NANCY *enters at the top of the steps*)

NANCY   The heaters are in the car; you'll have to help . . . (*She sees immediately what has happened. She stands quite still.* ARTHUR *looks up at her. She begins to nod; slowly, quietly*)   Sure . . . sure . . . (*She comes down the steps, stands near* ARTHUR *and* MAX; *she continues to nod, almost hypnotically, whispering*)   Sure . . . sure . . .

(*The carnival lights go out; leaving only dim moonlight for a moment, and then there is a . . .*

BLACKOUT

Immediately in the darkness we hear NANCY'S *voice*)

NANCY'S VOICE   To all boats. Stop here for Max's . . .

(*During this next speech we will see a gradual change of light lasting the several minutes of her dialogue, the darkened beach turning slowly to bright dawn.*

In the first beginnings of light we discover NANCY *sitting at the edge of the pier next to the silver and blue banner on the pier tie that reads "TO ALL BOATS . . . "* MAX *is gone, but* ARTHUR *remains seated at the bottom of the steps where we last saw him. The effect is such that* NANCY *has been seated at the edge of the pier all night, speaking through the night till dawn. There are no tears left*)

NANCY   (*As the dawn lights begin to dim up; she touches the banner*)   Sure.

The *Queen Mary* was gonna stop here, right? Frankfurters at the captain's table. You wanna know who was gonna show up here? *(Imitating* MAX'S *accent)* I'll tell you who. Nobody. (ARTHUR *comes to the end of the pier, stands behind her. She continues, angrily)* How dare you, Silverman. How dare you go and die. I paint forty-eight palm leaves and then you . . . Sneaky, sneaky, crazy old man, how dare you die. You hustled me, Silverman; you said you were gonna live forever, and you didn't. So all bets are off, Max. No more crying. I did that last night. That's all you get . . . Am I talking to myself, Max; or am I talking to you? Well, I couldn't tell the difference when you were alive, either. (ARTHUR *sits next to her; the sunrise grows brighter)* This crazy place. He conned us, Arthur. Alive and hollering he made it look possible: palm trees in February, lovers on sand dunes. But now you are dead, and where are the customers, Max? *(She close her eyes, whispering)* Listen to the ocean, Arthur; the noise it makes; it roars. If it had an accent I'd think it was him . . . What do I do now? I don't how . . . *(A blank, wide-eyed stare)* Here's me, not knowing. It's my best number . . .

(The phone rings)

ARTHUR   *(Rises, going to phone)* That'll be Gallino's; I better cancel the bread order. And Glickman's Meats, gotta call them also. *(Picks up phone)* Hello . . . *(Quietly; awkwardly)* Bill; how are ya? . . . Jesus, has it been three days? Sorry about that, I . . . The beach project? Well, it didn't work out very well, no . . . Bill, it's not really funny. Not funny at all . . . *(There is the sudden sound of an eight-piece Dixieland Marching Band hitting a loud downbeat, off-stage.)* Jesus . . . *(The band hits a second downbeat; he turns to* NANCY*)* Jesus, the Dixieland Devils; I forgot to cancel the parade . . . *(Into phone)* Hang on a second, Bill; be right back. *(He races up the stairway; as he reaches the top of the stairs the band hits a third downbeat and swings into a strutting, blasting arrangement of "Over the Waves." The offstage music grows gradually louder as the band marches up the unseen avenue parallel to the boardwalk.* ARTHUR, *at the top of the stairs, cups his hands around his mouth and shouts in the direction of the music)* Mr. Abrams! Mr. Abrams! Stop! Hey! Mr. Abrams *(ARTHUR'S hands drop to his sides; he begins to smile)* Jesus Christ, that's the oldest bunch of musicians I ever saw. *(The music grows louder;* NANCY *crosses anxiously to the foot of the stairs)*

NANCY   Arthur, you better go down there and tell them.

ARTHUR   Jesus, look at 'em go.

NANCY   Arthur . . .

ARTHUR   They've got this sign; it says "Come to the Ecstasies" . . . all that noise . . . people'll see the sign . . . maybe they'll . . .

NANCY   Arthur, listen to me . . .

ARTHUR   And there's posters everywhere . . .

NANCY   Arthur, Arthur . . . nobody's gonna come . . .

ARTHUR   Every day it's getting warmer . . .

NANCY   *(Shouting above the music)* Arthur . . . you're not gonna open the store, it's crazy . . .

ARTHUR   *(Shouting down to the open phone)* Hey, Bill! Ya hear that, Bill? That's a parade! Hey, Bill; got a great idea for our Easter display! How about a bunny nailed to a cross? By the ears! Ya like that one, Bill? Are ya laughing, Bill? Just keep laughing, Bill! Goodbye, Bill! Goodbye! Merry Christmas to all, and to all a good night! *(Shouting to* NANCY*)* Hang up the phone!

NANCY   Arthur—

ARTHUR   Hang up the phone, Shirley! *(She hangs up the phone; he turns to look at the parade again, bouncing with the rhythm)* Boy oh boy, what a class operation . . . Come look, come on . . .

NANCY   *(Shouting)* Arthur! Listen to me! This place, it's hopeless! It's a monument to hopelessness!

(The music reaches a strutting, blasting, swinging peak)

ARTHUR   *(Turning to her, smiling)* I told you, lady . . . I'm crazy about monuments. *(Shouting above the music)* Come on . . . just come and look . . . come see the parade . . . come on . . . come on . . .

(Holding his hand down to her, shouting, as . . .)

THE CURTAIN FALLS

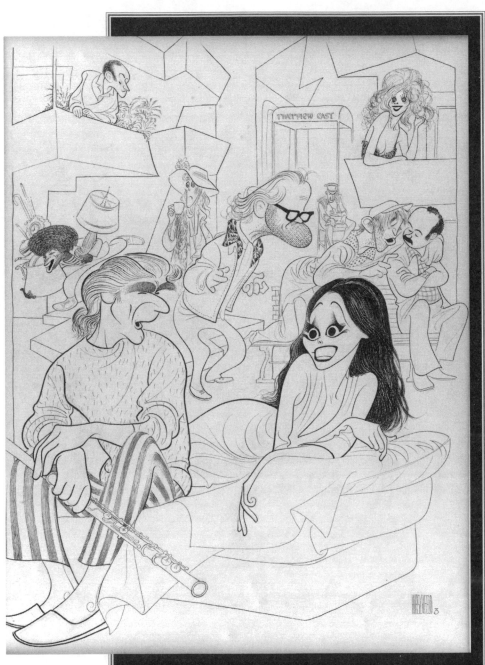

THIEVES

THIEVES

It was the winter of 1974. I got a phone call from my friend, Marlo Thomas, who told me that our mutual friend Herb Gardner's play, *Thieves*, was in trouble out of town. The star had gone, and the understudy was playing out the run; the director, Michael Bennett (who a year later would direct *A Chorus Line*) had gone, saying he had done everything he could; and the producers had one foot out the door. Herb had asked Marlo if she would consider taking over the starring role to try to help turn the situation around. Marlo said she would do it if I would come in as the director. We both knew Herb had worked on the play for a long time, and I'd read it and was surprised to hear of its reception. I agreed to fly to Boston to give my opinion.

I did not like the way the play was being presented. For reasons I'm still not sure of, it was fairly dark on-stage (the play took place at night, but still ...), and most of the cast was too far away from the audience, to whom they were directly shouting (another idea I had trouble with). Somewhere in all this darkness and distance was the extraordinarily gifted Herb Gardner's play. After the performance, I told Herb and Marlo and the producers that I didn't know how good I could help make it, but I knew how to make it better than it was. Herb seemed heartened, Marlo, who has an indomitable spirit, was ready to go in, and the producers headed out the door.

I now became the director and the producer, along with my old friend Dick Scanga, who flew up to Boston to help. I began to split my time between working with Herb on the script and directing Marlo into the part. Also, I had the lights turned up, moved the cast closer to the audience, and asked everyone to talk to each other and not to us out front.

I sat in the back of the theater with Herb every night watching the play, with the understudy playing the role Marlo would eventually play. One evening, when the performance was over, two ladies came up the aisle, the last to leave. They spotted Herb and me sitting in the back of the theater with our yellow pads and assumed we were involved with the production. They started to laugh, and in a ridiculing whisper exclaimed: "They're trying to fix it!"

About a week later, with Herb's script changes and Marlo in the

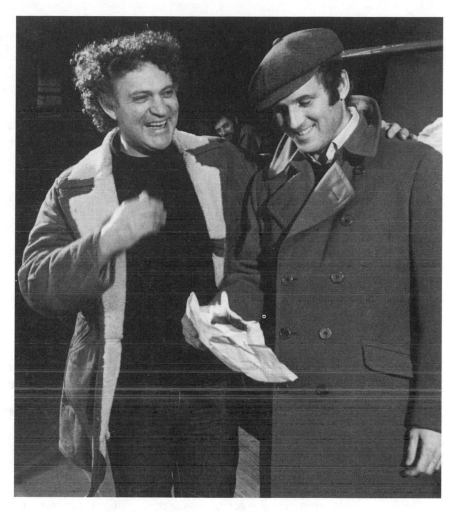

role, the response of the audience changed dramatically. We invited the critics to review it again. They did, and this time they liked it. People began to line up for tickets! Herb and I would sit in a restaurant across the street from the theater and stare at each other in astonishment as the lines grew larger. A legal closing notice had been placed on the backstage bulletin board of the Shubert Theatre by the departing producers. That Saturday night, in a happy on-stage ceremony, Herb and I burned it.

The show opened to mixed reviews in New York, but we decided to stay, hoping the audience would like the show enough that maybe we'd catch on. And we did. With the enormous skill of our general manager, Jim (Keep On Truckin') Walsh pulling one rabbit after another out of the hat,

Thieves continued to run.

One Saturday morning shortly after the show opened, Herb called to tell me that William Hickey, who was playing the part of the old alcoholic bum in the play, had badly hurt his ankle and couldn't go on for the Saturday matinee. I asked Herb who the understudy was, and he replied that there was none. In all the confusion of getting the show in shape and on to New York, the subject had never come up. I had just assumed that all that had been done before I arrived on the scene since the play had already played in two cities. It hadn't.

Herb said, "One of us will have to go on."

I said, "What do you mean, 'one of us'? You're not even in the union." I couldn't say he wasn't an actor, because even though Herb's a Tony Award-winning playwright (*I'm Not Rappaport*), he's also a wonderful actor. But there was no question, union regulations being what they were, that when the curtain went up and the old bum came out that Saturday afternoon, it was going to be me.

The part wasn't very big. I quickly went into my closet and found the oldest, most beat-up-looking clothes I had. Since I rarely got rid of old clothes at that time, I had a selection. I put them on and jumped into a cab.

Herb was standing in front of the theater when I arrived. He looked at me semi-approvingly and began to pick up I-don't-know-what from the gutters of 45th Street and put it all over my clothes and face. A few minutes later, as the curtain went up, there I was lying in the gutter. After twenty years in the theatre, thanks to my friend Herb, I had become a bum on Broadway.

The weeks went by. The audiences continued to enjoy the play, to laugh and be moved by it; they kept on coming.

They identified with Sally's free spirit, or they identified with Martin's fear of the implicit danger of that spirit. They were intrigued by the characters that only Herb Gardner could create. People emerged from the theater quoting their favorite lines, "Men like young girls because their stories are shorter," "Get out of the traffic and you're dead, Charlie." Eventually *Thieves* became the longest running play on Broadway that season and was bought for the movies. Being involved with it all remains the most gratifying experience I've had in the theater.

— CHARLES GRODIN
Westport, Connecticut

Thieves was first presented by Richard Scanga and Charles Grodin at the Broadhurst Theatre, New York City, April 7, 1974. It was directed by Charles Grodin, with sets by Peter Larkin, costumes by Joseph G. Aulisi, lighting by Jules Fisher, and sound by Sandy Hacker. The cast was as follows:

STREET MAN	William Hickey
CARLTON DANFIELD II	Haywood Nelson
MAN ABOVE	Dick Van Patten
HARRY	Pierre Epstein
FLO	Alice Drummond
MARTIN CRAMER	Richard Mulligan
SALLY CRAMER	Marlo Thomas
NANCY	Ann Wedgeworth
STANLEY	George Loros
JOE KAMINSKY	Irwin Corey
GORDON	David Spielberg
STREET LADY	Susie Bond
PEREZ	Pierre Epstein
POLICEMAN	George Loros
DEVLIN	Sammy Smith

The play takes place between one A.M. and seven A.M. on a warm June night in the upper East Side of Manhattan.

ACT ONE

Distantly, gracefully, someone is playing "The Streets of Laredo" on a flute. The melody drifts gently for a few moments, followed by the sound of city traffic, and then the curtain rises.

One A.M., mid-June, we see pieces of a piece of the city, the upper east side of Manhattan asleep in the heat. At Center is the entrance and the seventeenth and eighteenth-floor terraces of a modern luxury apartment building. A sign over the entrance says that this is "Riverview East," but the only view is of other terraces and the only sign of a river is in the name of the building. At Right and Far Left, we see the jutting terraces of two similar, Off Stage buildings. The columns of terraces face each other like the unmeshed teeth of opposing gears. GORDON'S terrace at Far Left, MARTIN'S terrace at Center in Riverview East, and NANCY'S terrace at Right all have the same skeletal railings, plastic deck-chairs and redwood picnic-tables. Down Stage, the street level spills cut onto the apron and down towards the audience. A ramp runs across, forward of the apron, from Center to Right, disappearing down into the pit, supposedly to the river level. At Right, under NANCY'S terrace, is a park-bench, an open phone-booth and the ornate railing of a balcony over the unseen river. Up Left, between GORDON'S terrace and Riverview East, is the indication of a dim alley or side-street.

At rise: MARTIN CRAMER stands alone on his terrace at Center, playing his flute. He is about forty, wearing pajama-bottoms and an old, red N.Y.U. sweatshirt. He plays gently, with his eyes closed. Below him, on the side-street at Left is the indication of an old DeSoto Sky-View Cab. The DRIVER is asleep on the front seat, cap pulled down, only the white stubble on his chin visible. At Center a very old Irish DOORMAN sleeps on a chair in the doorway of Riverview East, his ancient face in contrast to his shining new uniform. An old BUM sleeps on the bench at Right. A battered fishing-hat over his face to protect him from a recent rain. He wears an oversized double breasted jacket and stolen shoes.

After a moment there is the soft, cackling laughter of someone below the apron, and the crazy old STREET LADY enters, coming up the ramp from below. She wears a ragged, floor-length velvet dress, a sailor's windbreaker, sneakers, a large straw sunhat, and carries two huge shopping-bags, her face like a rouged antique. She stops at the top of the ramp, delicately picks up a discarded box of wooden matches, delighted by her treasure. She continues to rummage about the street for further prizes, her selections are thoughtful, her actions precise, items to be placed in her shopping-bags are chosen with a con-

noisseur's taste. She will laugh periodically at particular, secret jokes. CARLTON DANFIELD, *a twelve year-old black kid, enters Up Left from the shadows of the sidestreet. He wears freshly laundered jeans and jean-jacket, a white polo shirt, lensless glasses, and carries two large children's books to complete his impersonation of an innocent schoolboy. He stops at the cab, his eyes flick professionally from the* DRIVER'S *sleeping face to the coin-changer on the seat next to him and then back again. He checks the street, then reaches into his jean-jacket and takes out a wire coathanger which has been fashiond into a long-handled hook, his eyes never leaving the* DRIVER'S *face. At Right, the* STREET LADY *has moved up to the* BUM *on the bench, studying his hat. She wants it. The* DRIVER *stirs slightly;* CARLTON *steps back, calmly adopting his schoolboy pose again. The* STREET LADY *removes the fishing-hat from the sleeping* BUM'S *face, puts it in her shopping bag, chuckling softly.* MARTIN *turns Up Stage with his flute, swaying slightly with the music. A Man enters on the terrace above* MARTIN *carrying a small T.V. set and a bowl of soup, puts his things down on his picnic table and reaches out over the edge of his terrace to feel for rain. Their terraces are constructed in such a way that* MARTIN *and the* MAN FROM ABOVE *can never see each other.* CARLTON *reaches into the cab with the wire hook, removes the glistening coin-changer. The* STREET LADY *moves from the* BUM *to the sleeping* DOORMAN *at Center, contemplates the umbrella under the* DOORMAN'S *chair.* CARLTON *opens one of his books, "The Wizard of Oz"; we see that it has been hollowed out, leaving only an outside frame of pages. He places the coin-changer quickly in the hollow space, puts the book under his arm and, adjusting his fake glasses, walks casually down towards the ramp. The* BUM *awakens, glances about for his hat, spots* CARLTON, *watches him with great fascination as the kid sits at the edge of the stage, takes the coin-changer out of the book, begins to "click" out the coins, counting the loot. The* STREET LADY *deftly removes the umbrella from under the* DOORMAN'S *chair. The* BUM *leaves his bench, approaching the ramp as* CARLTON *counts his coins. The* STREET LADY *moves to the bench with her umbrella, opens it, laughing victoriously.*

BUM   *(Shuffling over to* CARLTON*)* Lotta quarters, lotta quarters . . . *(Sits next to him)* Some lotta quarters there, boy. (CARLTON *calmly puts his hand into his jacket-pocket*) I'm a commercial fisherman, see. Gotta get to Sheepshead Bay by four o'clock. Also, my eyeballs need fixin'. White Stallion is a very fine sauterne which is also a good eye-ball fixer. For one dollar and twenty-five I can get to the Bay and get my eye-balls fixed too. *(Silence)* Total on that is one dollar and twenty-five. *(The old* BUM *and the twelve-year-old* *boy look into each others eyes for several moments, judging)* Quarters alone, you got nine, ten dollars in there, boy . . . *(Suddenly reaching for the book)* Kid like you don't need all that—

CARLTON   *(Quickly, quietly, taking knife from his pocket)* You lookin' to get cut, juice-head?

BUM   *(Studying the knife)* No, sir. *(Shakes his head mournfully)* Sweet Jesus, this has been a bad night. *(Rises, withdrawing into the shadows of the building)* Never shoulda come uptown. Trouble with me, I never worked out no specialty for myself. You want to make it in this town, boy, you got to have a specialty . . .

MAN FROM ABOVE   *(Looks down in* MARTIN'S *direction)* My terrace is flooded from the rain. They forgot to put drains in these terraces. *(Silence. No reply)* They build these buildings too quickly and they forget things. I was wondering if you had a similar problem down there. *(No reply. He goes to the plant box at edge of terrace)* Don't try to grow any vegetables out here. Especially tomatoes. What you get are these tough little New York tomatoes. Gotta chop half-way into the damn things before you get to a tomato. You feed them, you nurture them, you care for them, and you end up with a box full of little red handballs. *(Sits at picnic-table, turns on T.V. set)* Forget tomatoes.

*(*NANCY GRESHAM, *attractive, skimpy nightgown, comes out on terrace opposite* MARTIN'S *in the building at Right. She smiles at the flute music and the gentle night, holds her hand out delicately to feel for rain.* CARLTON *continues to count his coins below)*

STANLEY'S VOICE   *(From inside* NANCY'S *terrace-doorway)* Hon'? You up, hon'?

NANCY   *(Graceful Southern accent)* Uh-huh. The rain woke me. The rain and the air-conditioners. Sounded like applause. I swear, love, like a standin' ovation. *(The* STREET LADY *chuckles softly)*

MAN FROM ABOVE   *(Eating his soup)* Vichyssoise. Good. Cold soup on a hot night. Perfect.

*(*GORDON, *moustached, early forties, bathrobe, appears in the light of a Japanese lantern on the highest terrace in the Far Left building. He is looking out at us through binoculars)*

GORDON   *(Quietly)* God bless shortie nighties.

MAN FROM ABOVE   Another thing you can forget about in this building is good television reception. Every night it snows on Randolph Scott. *(Switches dial)* Look, it's snowing on the Morning Prayer. It's snowing on the Rabbi.

HARRY'S VOICE *(Approaching)* Can you believe that, Flo? *(HARRY and* FLO, *a middle-aged couple in formal party clothes, enter at Right, going towards the entrance.* HARRY *is pointing at the sleeping* DOORMAN*)* Look at that. Will you look at that, Flo?

FLO *(Entering building)* Come on, Harry.

BUM *(approaching them)* Sir, pardon me, but could you spare thirty thousand dollars?

HARRY What?

BUM O.K., I'll settle for fifty cents.

HARRY Go away, go away.

BUM *(Drifting back into shadows of building)* Gotta get myself a specialty.

HARRY *(Leans close to sleeping* DOORMAN*)* Devlin . . . Devlin, I want you to know how reassuring it is to see you asleep in front of this open doorway while approximately fifty thousand thieves, junkies, rapists, madmen and students are roaming the city. *(Leans closer)* I want you to know that. *(Follows* FLO *into building)* I told him, Flo, I told him . . .

FLO Sure you told him. Because he's asleep. *(As they exit)* Asleep or deaf or dead; that's when you tell them, Harry . . .

*(*CARLTON *crosses quickly to the sleeping* DOORMAN, *feels carefully along the pockets of the* DOORMAN'S *jacket. The* STREET LADY *on the bench and the* BUM *in the shadows observe with interest.* CARLTON *slips his hand smoothly into one of* DEVLIN'S *pockets, removes a large set of tinkling keys. The* STREET LADY *chuckles approvingly.* CARLTON *opens the entrance door with one of the keys, slips quietly into the building)*

BUM *(Softly)* Kid's gonna make it in this town; he's got himself a speciality.

MAN FROM ABOVE Look. My Vichyssoise has turned black. Five minutes out here and it turned black. *(No reply)* Please stop with the trumpet. Every night with the trumpet. You're making me crazy with that trumpet.

MARTIN *(Stops playing)* This is not a trumpet, sir.

MAN FROM ABOVE Sure, talk tough. You're safe in your apartment. I know you people. I remember the voices . . . *(As* MARTIN *exits into his darkened apartment)* I remember all the voices . . .

(The MAN FROM ABOVE *is lost in shadow as lights come up on* MARTIN'S *apartment. The large bedroom is completely empty except for a*

stepladder with a geranium plant on it, a huge cardboard carton, a box-spring, a mattress and somebody asleep under the blanket, MAR-TIN *gets into the bed, drifting towards sleep.* SALLY *sits up, looks at his sleeping form for a moment, turns on the lamp which is set on a suitcase next to the bed. She is in her mid-thirties and has the kind of face that doesn't know how pretty it is. His eyes are closed. She studies his face for a moment)*

SALLY   Can I ask you a question?

MARTIN   Yes.

SALLY   Who are you?

MARTIN   Martin.

SALLY   *(Thoughtfully)*   Martin, Martin . . .

MARTIN   Martin Cramer.

SALLY   Martin Cramer. Right.   *(After a moment)*   And where do I know you from?

MARTIN   I'm your husband. You know me from marriage.

SALLY   *(Nodding)*   Right, right . . .

MARTIN   *(Opens his eyes)*   Sally, the forgetting game. I hate it. You have no idea how much I hate it.

SALLY   O.K., O.K., I—

MARTIN   *(Sitting up at edge of bed)*   Sally, at least once a week now you wake me up in the middle of the night and ask me who I am. I hate it.

SALLY   You used to think it was charming.

MARTIN   I thought a lot of things were charming.

SALLY   *(Nodding thoughtfully)*   Dr. Matthew Spengler talks about this in his book, in "Marriage and Modern Society," he calls it "the inevitable decline from charm to nightmare . . . "

MARTIN   Sally, there is no such book and there is no Dr. Spengler.

SALLY   I know.

MARTIN   Sally, why do you keep—

SALLY   I do the best I can to class up the conversation.

MARTIN   But you don't just do it with me, you do it with everybody. Last month with my mother you made up a whole country. A whole country that doesn't exist.

SALLY   I thought she'd be happy there.

MARTIN   But there *is* none. There is no Hungarian West Indies.

SALLY   My countries, my books; you used to think they were funny . . .

MARTIN   I thought a lot of things were funny.

SALLY   What happened? We—

MARTIN   O.K., Sally. *(He rises decisively, goes to Center of room)* I was going to wait till morning, but why wait . . .

SALLY   Let's wait.

MARTIN   First, Sally . . . First, I want you to know how much I appreciate the wonderful work you've done on our apartment here. How you've managed to capture, in only five short weeks, the subtle, elusive, yet classic mood previously found only in the Port Authority Bus Terminal. *(Pacing about the room)* In addition, Sally, you have, somewhat mystically, lost or forgotten the name of the moving and storage company with whom you placed nearly fifty-five thousand dollars worth of our furniture.

SALLY   It's an Italian name, I know that.

MARTIN   This, coupled with the fact that you disappeared eight days ago on what was ostensibly a trip to Gristede Brothers to buy some strawberry yogurt, and did not return until this evening, has led to a certain amount of confusion for me . . .

SALLY   I went to Gloria's place to think things out, to—

MARTIN   *(Opens crumpled letter)* All confusion, of course, vanished with the arrival last week of this simple, touching, yet concise note from the Misters Morris, Klien, Fishback and Fishback . . . *(Reading calmly, evenly, only the slightest tremor in his voice)* "We have been retained by your wife, Sally Jane Cramer, hereinafter referred to as "Wife," to represent her in the matter of your divorce. Said wife having requested that her whereabouts remain unknown to you at present, we therefore . . ." *(Carefully folding letter into paper airplane)* After eight days of staring into the air-conditioner, wondering which Santini Brother had my furniture, which Gristede Brother had my wife, and which Fishback owned my soul, a light began to dawn . . . or maybe one went out . . . and I realized that nobody was hiding you from me, that your whereabouts, said wife, have been unknown to me for years . . . that you make a fine letter-writer, a great decorator, and a perfect stranger. *(Going to terrace-doorway)* You said you came back tonight to talk about the divorce. You didn't mention it. Neither did I. And the habit, the habit of being together, began again. *(Turns to her)* But

I couldn't sleep. I couldn't sleep and I thought about it and tonight, Sally, I have decided to retire from the games. The Olympics are over, lady, the torch is out . . . and you are free. *(He tosses the paper airplane through the terrace-doorway, it sails into the street)* Said husband, hereinafter referred to as "gone," has had it. *(*MARTIN *goes out onto the terrace. Below, the* STREET LADY *scurries out of the shadows to pick up the paper airplane, disappears again)*

SALLY   *(After a moment, quietly)* Marty, I came back tonight because I'm pregnant and I'm terrified.

MARTIN   Can't hear you from out here.

SALLY   I know. *(Rises from bed, wearing robe, going to terrace doorway)* Marty, I came back tonight . . . Did I buy you that sweatshirt? *(No reply)* It's a size too big. If we're getting a divorce why did we make love tonight?

MARTIN   Goddamn wine . . . why'd you bring a Goddamn bottle of wine to discuss a divorce?

SALLY   Why'd you light a candle?

MARTIN   It goes with the wine.

SALLY   *(She smiles. Remains in doorway, quietly)* Marty, it was lovely tonight. Like a surprise party. Like a lovely party with two hosts . . . If you've got any material of your own on this I'd be glad to hear it.

MARTIN   Look, it goes without saying—

SALLY   No, *don't* let it go, *not* without saying— *(Grabs his arm)* Come on, keep me company, show an emotion! Emotions, Marty, *you* remember. Come on, scream at me for walking out! Holler, or cry, or—Christ, how many years since I've seen a tear outa ya!? *(Shaking him)* Come on, Marty-baby, you can do it; break something, throw a plate at me—

MARTIN   I *can't* . . . They're all packed. *(He goes sadly back into the room)* This beautiful place, you never moved in . . .

SALLY   *(Following him)* You keep *moving* us, another room, a higher floor—

MARTIN   This beautiful place . . .

SALLY   Poor shmuck, we'd just be back up to our ass in French Provincial—

MARTIN   Do you have to talk like that, are you *compelled*—

SALLY   That's how I *always*—

MARTIN   When we're out with people, I cringe, I literally—

SALLY   I've seen ya, you go off in a corner and pretend you're an onion-dip—

MARTIN   All these years, that loud, embarrasing—

SALLY   That's how I talk to everybody—

MARTIN   What about at school, what about those little—

SALLY   P.S. Twenty-*Nine*, Marty. Canal Street, have you forgotten what those kids *sound* like down there? *(He walks away)* Dummy, you bought yourself a new mouth and kept the same old wife. *(She follows him)* It's *me*, Sally Jane Kaminsky, I know ya from before, fellah. I know ya from coppin' goodies off of every open counter in the neighborhood, I know ya from knockin' over DeSapio's Grocery with the Golden Avengers, I—

MARTIN   Sally, I was sixteen years old—

SALLY   *(Laughing)* I remember your jacket. the red one with the big pockets sewn inside. You'd come dragging out of Woolworth's, the only Jewish pelican in New York . . . *(Silence for a moment. He turns to her)*

MARTIN   I didn't think you even noticed me in those days.

SALLY   Sure I noticed you.

MARTIN   I mean, I thought it was years later that—

SALLY   I was crazy about you.

MARTIN   I always thought it was at Marilyn Krasney's party that you first— *(She shakes her head)* All this time, how come you never talked about—

SALLY   Who talks? We don't talk, we move. We're movers. I also saw you following me home all the time.

MARTIN   I didn't.

SALLY   I saw ya.

MARTIN   You couldn't have. I cut in and out of doorways, Peter Lorre taught me how.

SALLY   Woulda stopped and talked to you except I was scared of all you guys from the Golden Avengers. I mean, you weren't as tough as Whitey Arkish, but still I was scared. *(She puts her arms around him)* Could've had me at fifteen. How about that? We could've been divorced by now.

MARTIN   *(His arms around her)* Whitey Arkish wasn't so tough . . .

SALLY   *(Tenderly)* First real date we had was four years later . . . we broke into Loew's Delancy with a crow-bar . . .

MARTIN   Take Whitey's knife away he fell apart . . .

SALLY   We pried open the fire-door at three in the morning, you put me in the middle of the eighth row . . . and then you got up on the stage and played your flute for me, "Blue-Tail Fly" and "The Streets of Laredo," fantastic repertoire . . . and over your head on the curtain, it said . . .

MARTIN   *(Softly)* "Loew's Delancy, Home Of The Stars . . ."

SALLY   And then the cops came— *(Holds him tightly, inspired)* Jesus, sirens . . . sirens and everything . . . runnin' through alleys, all those alleys, half-way across town, outa breath, gettin' away with it, gettin' away clean . . . *(Tenderly)* Oh, Marty, how'd you do it?

MARTIN   What?

SALLY   Get to be so boring. *(He walks away, she pursues him)* You had a knife and a flute and you wanted to be a teacher, you were a Goddamn interesting person—

MARTIN   What the hell is going *on* here, where's all this *coming* from!?

SALLY   We were gonna *stay* down there, we promised, we were gonna teach in the neighborhood—

MARTIN   Sally, that was *years* ago—

SALLY   *(Racing out onto terrace)* And here he is, ladies and gentlemen— *(Announcing to the neighborhood)* For the first time on any terrace—the principal of the Little Bluebell School—see him pick up his check— *(He races after her)* watch him do the totally unnecessary for the completely unneeding—

MARTIN   *(Pulling her back into room)* Sally—

SALLY   You blew it, you lost your privates to a private School—

MARTIN   Damn it, the Little Bluebell School happens to be a first rate—

SALLY   My God, Marty, the Devil maybe I could understand—but you sold your soul to Bugs Bunny.

MARTIN   *(Finally raising his voice)* You're a bigot, Sally! You hate rich kids! Maybe that's why we don't have any. All we've got is Crazy Carmen and Danfield the Dealer—

SALLY   You only let Carlton stay a week, he really liked you—

MARTIN   I know he liked me. But he loved my typewriter; that's why he took it—

SALLY   He's intelligent, confused—

MARTIN   So was Willie Sutton—

SALLY   We're not alone here, Mister. You used to believe in something, you used to care. Just a few years ago, Civil Rights Day, you marched down Fifth Avenue with me—

MARTIN   Not a *few* years ago! Fifteen. That was fifteen *years* ago. I cared. Sure I cared. A long time ago. Another time. Marches that never got past the Six O'Clock News, carrying placards that nobody remembers. You gotta be young, you gotta be in the world just long enough to think it's still worth saving. *(Pacing, loudly) Canal* Street, you're not teaching down there, you're a *cop.* You're a Goddamn policeman. I wait in terror every night for you to come home dead. Don't you know there's a Puerto Rican down there with your number on it? The neighborhood, the precious neighborhood, all I ever got from the neighborhood was four knife scars, two broken noses and a fruitcake wife! And they all hurt when it rains. *(Rushes to her, urgently)* I got *out*, Sally, don't ya see? I got outa there alive and I won't go back. I'm too old to be a Golden Avenger, I'm too young to be Albert Schweitzer. I don't get hit anymore and I don't hit back, I don't change the world and it doesn't change me . . . *(Grips her arm, quietly)* Don't you get it, Sally? Don't you know what's going on out there? This rotten little island is slowly sinking into the sea. Nobody listens, nobody cares, none of it's the same. It all got . . . older. The survivors are up here, lady, way up here. Please, Sally, the only kids I want to save are us. What's my crime, what's wrong with wanting something better for us? A new life, a view of the river—

SALLY   What river? *(Stalks out onto terrace)* Show me the Goddamn river!

MARTIN   *(Shouting)* O.K., forget it! Go back! Go back to our first place, Seventy-Eight Orchard Street, the one room roach festival!

SALLY   Glad you remember the address, Marty . . . because that's where I sent the furniture. *(Silence for a moment. She remains on terrace with her back to him)*

MARTIN   *(Quietly)* In other words, Sally, what you have done . . . what you have done is sent five rooms of antique furniture to a one room, cold water flat that we have not lived in for ten years. *(She nods)* Unusual.

SALLY   Apartment Four B.

MARTIN   I think you're crazy.

SALLY   So did the old guy in Apartment Four B.

MARTIN   All . . . all of our furniture . . .

SALLY   Don't worry, I gave the old guy a coupla bucks to keep his eye on it. I mean, he can hardly *not* keep his eye on it, right?

MARTIN   *(Nodding)* Right, fine, fine . . .

SALLY   *(Goes quickly to him)* Four B, Marty— *(Holds his arm)* We made terrific promises and gorgeous love there. And we had nice, loud fights and threw inexpensive things at each other and hugged a lot and . . . *(Sees his blank face, shrugs)* Well you had to be there. *(Moving about the large, bare room)* I woke in the middle of the night last week. This empty room woke me like an alarm bell and for a minute I didn't know who we were. Without our coffee-table, I didn't know. Without our couch . . . And then I remembered. We're the Cramers. We're this couple. And we're staying together because we're expected to dinner next Friday by some other couples; and the next Friday we're expecting them. We're the Cramers. We don't love each other so we love other couples, and they love us. Held together by other couples, married to other marriages, travelling in fours, sixes, eights, shoulder to shoulder at each other's tables, boy, girl, boy, girl, boy, girl, close, close, so nobody slips away. We're this couple; I remembered and I fell asleep . . . The next morning I heard somebody scream in the subway. Rush hour, the train stopped dead between Union Square and Canal and somebody blew; if the train stops for more than a minute somebody always blows. It was this high, nutsy scream, like somebody certain they're gonna die right there under the city. It scared the hell outa me and I put my hand to my throat and I felt it throbbing and I saw everybody looking and I knew it was me. It was me screaming, and I couldn't stop. And that night I went to Gristede Brothers and kept on walking. *(Silence for a moment)* If you want to visit your furniture, the keys to the apartment are in the bookcase. *(Goes to pick up shoulder-bag on terrace picnic-table, as though to leave)*

HARRY'S VOICE   *(From above)* Finished. Finished. Finished. *(She looks up)* Over. Over. Ended. Finished.

SALLY   Did you hire a narrator?

MARTIN   *(In terrace-doorway; gently)* Sally, why did you come back tonight?

SALLY   *(Turns to him)* Okay, Marty, I got some news for ya . . .

MAN FROM ABOVE   Hello? Hello? Hello there . . . ?

SALLY   Chrissake . . .

MAN FROM ABOVE   What do you people look like? Have I seen you in the lobby?

MARTIN   Sir, we would appreciate—

MAN FROM ABOVE   Are you the short people? Are you the midgets?

MARTIN   Look, Mister, we—

MAN FROM ABOVE   You're the midgets, aren't you? You sound like the midgets.

MARTIN   Please, sir—

MAN FROM ABOVE   One of you plays the trumpet and one of you giggles in the elevator. Why do you do that? Why is everybody so crazy? It wasn't always like this—

MARTIN   *(Shouting up)* Damn it, will ya please—

MAN FROM ABOVE   You're angry. You're angry because you're short.

(SALLY *laughs.* MARTIN *chuckles in spite of himself, they suddenly hug each other, holding on silently)*

NANCY   *(On her terrace)* Hey, huggers . . .

STANLEY'S VOICE   What, hon'?

NANCY   Huggers, love. We got some huggers over there.

STANLEY'S VOICE   Huh?

NANCY   People huggin'.

STANLEY'S VOICE   Oh.

MARTIN   What did you want to tell me?

MAN FROM ABOVE   Well, I drink a little . . .

SALLY   There's something we oughta talk about . . .

MAN FROM ABOVE   Who am I kidding? I drink a lot. I sit out here with my Vodka and I try to understand what's going on. I'm sorry to intrude, but do you know what's going on? Do you know why everyone has gone mad? Would you like some Vodka?

MARTIN   Sally, what is it . . . ?

MAN FROM ABOVE   *(Whispering)* I'm sorry, I'll go inside now . . . good night . . .

MARTIN   Have you been unfaithful to me? Is that it?

SALLY   Unfaithful sounds awesome. Ask if I've been foolin' around.

MARTIN   Have you?

SALLY   No. What about you?

MARTIN   I haven't been fooling around, either.

SALLY   How about unfaithful? *(Phone rings on picnic-table. She picks it up, whispers into it)* No, Jim, no . . . I told you, not here, never here . . . *(Smiles, turns to him)* I'm kidding, it's Gloria . . . *(Into phone)* Sorry, Glo, I shouldn't've disappeared without telling you . . .

MARTIN   Tell her she'll get used to it . . .

SALLY   Good, let me speak to him . . . Barry! That's right, Barry, it's me. How ya doin', kid? Miss me? Sure, I miss you. Uh-huh . . . uh-huh . . . that sounds great. So what did . . . uh-huh. Yeah, just a sec' . . . *(To* MARTIN*)* Barry wants to speak to you . . .

MARTIN   I don't want to speak to Barry.

SALLY   Why not? He—

MARTIN   Sally, I would like to remind you that Barry is a German Shepherd. He does not speak, he barks. He barks because he is a dog. A very large—

SALLY   You wouldn't let him live in the new apartment with us, the least you could do is—

MARTIN   Hang up, it's a dog.

SALLY   *(Into phone)* Just another sec', Barry . . . *(Covering phone)* What should I tell him?

MARTIN   Don't tell him *anything*! He's a *dog!* And he is a *great* dog, but he makes a *terrible person!*

MAN FROM ABOVE   My God, speak to the poor animal!

MARTIN   *(Shouting up)* I thought you went inside!

MAN FROM ABOVE   I went inside. There's nobody there.

SALLY   He's heard your voice already, I can't just—

MARTIN   *(Shouting)* Sally, stop it! For Chrissakes, we've got more important . . . *(She holds the phone out to him)* Sally, we're right in the middle of a *very* important . . . *(Grabs phone)* Okay, Okay, if you'll stop . . . *(Into phone, quickly)* Hello, Barry, how are you? . . . Good . . . I'm fine. Okay, Barry, gotta go now; 'bye. *(Hangs up)* I can't tell you how much that depresses me.

SALLY You shouldn't just hang up on him like that.

MARTIN I know I shouldn't. I'm not capable of a complete relationship.

SALLY I don't think he's really happy with Gloria . . .

MARTIN You and that dog, it's so damn sad.

SALLY What's wrong? I love him. He loves me. He trusts me, he never asks—

MARTIN *(Gently)* Sally . . . you treat him like he's your child . . . you always have.

SALLY Maybe we should do that.

MARTIN What?

SALLY Have some children. We'll start with one. *(Quietly; sitting at picnic-table)* See, I've been thinking . . . I thought maybe, y'know, something new between us, a way to begin again . . .

MARTIN All these years, you never—

SALLY I wasn't sure.

MARTIN And now that we're separating, now you're sure?

SALLY *(After a moment)* Sounds crazy, doesn't it?

MARTIN I'm afraid so. *(Gently)* Sally, look at us . . . we've been leaving each other for years . . . piece by piece. The way things are between us, a child would end up being a kind of souvenir.

SALLY You're right, of course. *(They stand silently on the terrace for a few moments)* Well, that doesn't leave us much more to talk about, does it?

MARTIN I guess not.

SALLY I better get dressed and go now. *(She goes through terrace doorway, exits through doorway at Left of main room, where she has left her clothes. MARTIN, alone now, paces about awkwardly, shifting his flute from one hand to the other. Then he stands quite still, turns to doorway)*

MARTIN Are you pregnant, Sally? *(No reply. She enters the main room, dressed to leave)*

SALLY No.

MARTIN Then why did you come back tonight?

SALLY I guess it was a social call. *(She goes to front door; picks up suitcase. MARTIN remains in the terrace doorway, the large, empty room between them)* Well, now we're at the goodbye part. How do we do this?

MARTIN   I'm not sure.

SALLY   I guess we'll keep in touch.

MARTIN   Of course we will. You'll be staying at Gloria's, I imagine.

SALLY   For a while. And I guess you'll be staying here.

MARTIN   Yeah *(After a moment)* Sally . . . after Gloria's, where will you go?

SALLY   I don't know. I'm not sure. *(Silence)* You were crazy. You were the craziest kid in the neighborhood. *(She exits)*

(MARTIN sits at picnic-table; only the sound of distant, late-night traffic for a few moments)

MAN FROM ABOVE   *(Softly)* Martin, I think that you should both seriously consider the—

MARTIN   *(Rising violently, flute held over his head like a weapon, screaming)* Shut up, will ya!!

(Sudden silence again. Lights up on NANCY'S terrace as she moves to the edge, watching him, still wearing skimpy night-gown, a man's shirt over her arm. MARTIN sits down again at picnic-table, pours glass of wine)

NANCY   They stopped huggin'.

STANLEY'S VOICE   *(From inside NANCY'S terrace-doorway)* Huh?

NANCY   The people who were huggin'. They ain't huggin' no more.

(Lights up on GORDON'S terrace, focusing binoculars on NANCY)

STANLEY'S VOICE   Hon', I'll have to go home and get my pills. I've got this thing with my back, see.

NANCY   She went away and he did his hollerin'. Sometimes when he's alone he does this hollerin' . . .

GORDON   *(Whispering)* Now just lean over a little, darlin' . . .

NANCY   They've got the same picnic-table I've got. Redwood. *(Leans forward at railing)*

GORDON   Forget the others, there is only you . . .

NANCY   Way they were huggin', Lord, I thought they were gonna do it right there on the picnic-table. *(She starts to put the shirt on)*

GORDON   No, no, my love . . . I ask for so little really . . .

STANLEY'S VOICE   Thing is, hon', by the time I get down there it'll be two o'clock and I've got to be up by seven.

NANCY   Y'know sometimes I come out here in the middle of the night and I just stand here and think about all these buildin's and all the people who must be doin' it at that exact moment . . .

(GORDON *exits.* MARTIN *finishes his glass of wine, pours another. Although his actions remain muted his presence will be felt through this scene)*

STANLEY'S VOICE   So I think the sane thing'd be for me to stay down there, hon'.

NANCY   You see, in Daytona Beach, I thought I was the only one who did it. My momma gave me that impression. I mean, the only one who *wanted* to do it; I didn't *do* it in Daytona Beach, I only wanted to do it in Daytona Beach, I didn't start doin' it till I got to New York . . . Minute I got off that bus, I knew that everybody was doin' it in New York. It's a feeling you got. First job I had I knew that everybody in that office was doin' it. I mean, I wasn't really sure till I did it with some of them, but I had the feeling. I was in Daytona Beach for Thanksgiving and, I swear, they still don't do it there. It's very reassuring in New York. It's a comfort to know you're not alone.

STANLEY'S VOICE   Did you hear what I said, hon'?

NANCY   About what, love?

STANLEY'S VOICE   Well, I have to go home and get my pills, and the sensible thing'd be, since it's so late, that I stay there. Hey, I'll give you a wake-up call, a warm good morning. Would you like that?

NANCY   A warm good morning would be very nice.

STANLEY'S VOICE   Jesus, where's my shirt?

NANCY   *(She smiles, holds the collar of the shirt closer around her neck)* What color are my eyes?

STANLEY'S VOICE   Your eyes? Your eyes, hon'? Blue. *(After a moment)* Jesus, they're brown. I had it mixed up with your hair.

NANCY   *(Pleasantly)* You thought I had blue hair? *(Quietly)* Anyway, they're green; so now you lose your shirt.

STANLEY'S VOICE   Can't hear you, hon' . . .

NANCY   I said, we spilled some liquor on your shirt while we were doin' it so I threw it in the incinerator.

STANLEY'S VOICE   You threw it away? You threw my *shirt* away?

NANCY 'Fraid that's what I did. (MARTIN *pours another glass of wine*)

STANLEY'S VOICE (*After a moment*) Well, I think that was a very hostile thing to do, love.

NANCY No, I know when I'm being hostile. My doctor tells me I'm just havin' fun. Us blue haired ladies have all the fun.

STANLEY'S VOICE Jesus, where . . . where the hell is my jacket? (*No reply*) It's a checked sports jacket . . .

NANCY What's my name, love?

STANLEY'S VOICE Chrissake, *Nancy*.

NANCY Nancy what?

STANLEY'S VOICE Graham.

NANCY Gresham. You lose.

STANLEY'S VOICE (*After a moment; quietly*) You're not gonna tell me you threw my jacket away too? You're not gonna tell me *that*, are ya . . . ? (*No reply*) Oh, terrific. Getting a cab is gonna be just terrific . . . Running around half-naked on First Avenue . . . (*Closer; urgently*) Listen to me, I've got . . . I've got to go home, see . . .

NANCY I was smack in the middle of tellin' you about my life . . .

STANLEY'S VOICE Nancy, the jacket . . .

NANAY Okay, here's my story . . . (*She is silent for a moment*) Oh, I guess I told you my story. I guess that's all there was. Your jacket is in the closet next to the kitchen.

STANLEY'S VOICE Thank you.

NANCY Goodness, finished my story and I didn't even know it.

(MARTIN *moves off into his now darkened apartment, softly playing his flute*)

STANLEY'S VOICE Christ!

NANCY What is it, love?

STANLEY'S VOICE Christ, this *closet* . . . all these *shirts* . . .

NANCY (*Smiling at flute music*) He's playing his piccolo again . . .

STANLEY'S VOICE Shirts, shirts, shirts . . .

NANCY He plays so sweet . . .

STANLEY'S VOICE Jesus Christ . . . it's like a Goddamn de*part*ment store in here . . .

NANCY He plays so sweet, but so sad . . . maybe its the . . .

STANLEY'S VOICE   *(Coming closer)* Nancy, that's a creepy closet . . .

NANCY   Think of it this way, love, if you saved earrings, how many would you have?

STANLEY'S VOICE   Nancy, that closet is a pathological closet. I personally think you're in a lot of trouble.

NANCY   Come on, you figured me for a wacko up front; that's why you hit on me at the office this afternoon.

STANLEY'S VOICE   You're just being hostile because I can't remember the color of your Goddamn eyes.

NANCY   Okay now, Stan, you just go on home to your pills or whatever it is you're callin' your wife this year. Go home and wash me off and tell Mary-Lou how you lost your shirt gamblin'. Dawn's a long time comin' after you boys leave and I like thinkin' about that till I fall asleep. *(Goes to terrace-railing)* So God damn my eyes and forget my name but never, never take me for a dumbo. I got smarts I ain't used yet, I am the Wonder Book of Knowledge, don't give me no wake-up calls, baby, I been up for hours . . . Looky here, come see the view; everybody's out there cheatin' t' beat hell. Everybody's out there cheatin' and I know it. Old city lookin' to get young, straights lookin' for crazy, low lookin' to get high, everybody lookin' to get out and I got the keys to the city. Ain't a marriage I can't get into, ain't a Mary-Lou I can't bust . . . Wowie, it's two A.M. in Manhattan, honey-babe, and everybody's lookin' for some nice, new, good old days. *(She is silent for a few moments. No sound from the doorway)* I shall assume by your silence, sir, that you have decided to break off our engagement. *(No reply)* Hey there, ol' Stan . . . Hey Stan? . . . *(No reply. She starts to unbutton the shirt)* Listen, you can have your shirt back, I was only funnin' . . . *(No reply. She sees something far below in the street. She leans forward, squinting)* Lord . . . *(Leans over the edge, shouts down)* Hey! . . . Hey, you! . . . Hey, you without a shirt! *(Louder)* Hey, you forgot to kiss me goodnight! You forgot! *(MARTIN stops playing his flute. NANCY takes the shirt off, rolls it angrily into a ball, and tosses it sharply down towards the street. She looks silently down into the street for several moments. Whispering)* God damn . . . you didn't even kiss me goodnight.

(The STREET LADY *scurries out from the shadows below, snaps up* STANLEY'S *shirt, darts over to bench at Far Right, chuckling over her new treasure, sits on bench, putting shirt on over her coat.* MARTIN *moves out onto his terrace, playing his flute again.* NANCY *becomes aware of him, smiling at the gentle music, watching him, zeroing in. Lights up on* GORDON *watching them with binoculars)*

GORDON   *(Quietly)* Losing her . . . losing Shortie-Nightie . . .

CAMILLE'S VOICE   *(From inside* GORDON'S *terrace-doorway)* Gordon, let me give you a perfect example of how well I understand this relationship . . .

GORDON   What is this guy . . . some kinda Goddamn Pied Piper?

CAMILLE'S VOICE   Monday night when I woke up and said these things were stabbing me and you said they were paperclips and I saw they were hairpins, I did not pursue the issue . . .

BUM'S VOICE   Hey, what's goin' on here, what time is it . . . ? *(Lights up on* BUM *sprawled in shadows Down Left)*

GORDON   I could play my guitar, but I'm too far away . . .

(Lights up on SALLY *at open street-phone near* STREET LADY'S *bench at Far Right, her suitcase next to her,* STREET LADY *listening with great interest.* MARTIN *moving to terrace-railing as he continues playing flute,* NANCY *watching him)*

BUM   *(Quietly, to no one in particular)* I'm a commercial fisherman, gotta get to Sheepshead Bay . . .

CAMILLE'S VOICE   I did not pursue the idiotic idea that you sleep in a bed full of paper-clips . . .

SALLY   *(Into phone, reading from notebook)*

"If you're a bird, be an early bird,
And be sure to fill your breakfast plate.
If you're a bird, be an early, early bird,
But if you're a worm, sleep late."

(She laughs, the STREET LADY *laughs with her. The Flute music, and lights on* MARTIN, NANCY *and* GORDON *gradually fading during* SALLY'S *call)* Nice, huh? Gloria, you have just been privileged to hear number One Hundred and Eighty-One in my ever-popular and yet to be published collection of children's poetry. I'm reading them to you because they protect me from muggers out here. It's like Wolfbane . . .

BUM   *(Takes tattered wristwatch from pocket)* What time is it? I'm late, I'm late . . .

SALLY   Yeah, we had a nice talk and I think he'll make a great first husband. *(After a moment)* O.K., I guess it's on for tomorrow morning. Eight o'clock. Listen, you don't have to stay for the whole thing, just come at the end and take me back to your place. Dr. Gerstad says I'll be rocky for a coupla days . . .

BUM   Ain't no hands on this watch . . . What time is it? Anybody got the time here . . . ?

SALLY   I don't know. Nervous. And I've got this terrible, creepy sense of freedom.

BUM   It's like May or June or something, right?

SALLY   Look, the . . . tomorrow, the procedure, how long does it take? . . . Gloria, "zappo" is, not my favorite surgical image . . . I *know* it's nothin' and I know it's legal, but it still ain't throwin' away a stale corn-muffin, right?

BUM   Anybody got the time here? . . .

SALLY   Listen, I'll see ya in a coupla hours, O.K.? Just leave the couch, Glo, I'll open it myself. Thought I'd sorta walk around for a coupla hours. Don't worry, I'll be fine— *(Indicates* STREET LADY*)* my mother is here. *(She laughs,* STREET LADY *laughs with her)* I'm fine. Really. I'm O.K. . . . *(Suddenly shaky)* No, I don't want to speak to Barry . . . Because he's a *dog,* because he's a Goddamn dog! *(She hangs up sharply)*

NANCY'S VOICE   *(A loud whisper)* Watch it, Mister! *(Lights up on* MAR-TIN *playing his flute, his eyes closed, at edge of terrace.* NANCY *moving quickly into her terrace light as* SALLY *exits with her suitcase at Right,* STREET LADY *following her.* MARTIN *opens his eyes, stops playing flute)* You keep your eyes closed you'll go right over.

MARTIN   Oh, yes . . . *(Turns to her)* Thank you very much, Miss . . . appreciate that. *(He sits at his picnic-table. She starts to go inside . . . A loud whisper)* Excuse me . . . Miss?

NANCY   *(Turns to him)* Yes?

MARTIN   Hello.

NANCY   Hello.

MARTIN   How ya doin'?

NANCY   Fine. How *you* doin'?

MARTIN   Fine. I'm Martin Cramer.

NANCY   Nancy Gresham.

MARTIN   Hello, Nancy. *(Indicates the wide space between them)* I'd shake your hand but I'd kill myself.

NANCY   Yes, you would. And I surely would miss your piccolo music.

MARTIN   Thank you. It's a flute, actually. *(They are silent for a moment.*

She becomes aware of her fading make-up; touches her cheek. He begins polishing his flute with the sleeve of his sweat shirt)

NANCY   You really must forgive me for appearin' before you in this fashion.

MARTIN   You look fine. Really.

NANCY   I was just about to do my arts and crafts . . . *(Points to huge make-up kit on her picnic table)*   Make-up. That tool chest there; that's my make-up kit.

MARTIN   All that? Hardly seems necessary.

NANCY   Kills the time . . . *(Smiles, touches her cheek)*   on my face. *(After a moment)*   Sure some hullabaloo last week.

MARTIN   Beg your pardon?

NANCY   Lord, you come runnin' out on that terrace, hollerin'. Thought you was hollerin' *at* somebody, but you were all alone, wavin' this piece of paper and hollerin' 'bout some Fishback fellah—

MARTIN   Pardon me—

NANCY   Then you was hollerin' 'bout Gristede Brothers—

MARTIN   No, Miss, that wasn't here—

NANCY   Then later, there was this cryin' sound—

MARTIN   No, not possibly; you see I was alone here at that time and—

NANCY   That's why most people cry.

MARTIN   *(Raising his voice)*   It must have been another apartment, or perhaps a television set. *(They are silent for a moment)*

NANCY   Yeah; musta been the TV. . . . Sorry for making a personal remark.

MARTIN   That's quite all right, really. *(Silence. MARTIN searches his mind for the proper words and the courage to say them. He finds neither. Sound of distant siren, rising, then fading away)*

NANCY   Well, g'night now.

MARTIN   Yes, goodnight.

NANCY   You keep your eyes open, hear? I surely would miss that piccolo music.

MARTIN   Thank you. *(She goes to the other end of her terrace, sits at pic-*

nic-table, her back to MARTIN. *He sits at his picnic-table; quietly, to himself)* It's a flute, actually.

(CARLTON *suddenly appears at the edge of the terrace just above* MAR-TIN'S, *holding the* DOORMAN'S *pass-keys in his hand. He glances about quickly, grabs an ice bucket and a portable radio from the terrace and disappears quickly back into the shadows,* NANCY'S *lights dim, we can still see her as she studies her reflection in the mirror on the lid of her make-up kit and begins a very precise make-up ritual which she will continue throughout this next scene. There is a sudden creaking noise from inside* MARTIN'S *darkened apartment. A small, forbidding silhouette appears in the light of the open front-doorway.* MARTIN *remains quite still at first, his fingers, tense on his flute. Then* MARTIN *enters quietly through the terrace door, stands still in the darkened room, his hand gripping his flute like a weapon at the ready.* THE SILHOUETTE *holds quite still in the rectangle of light)*

THE SILHOUETTE *(Gravel voiced, tough)* Come closer. (MARTIN *does not move)* Identify yourself.

MARTIN Who are you?

THE SILHOUETTE Identify yourself, Goddamnit.

MARTIN Who the hell—

THE SILHOUETTE Are you Martin Cramer?

MARTIN Why do you want to know?

THE SILHOUETTE Because if you're Martin Cramer, then I'm your father-in-law, and if you're not, you're a junky or a darky or a spic with a club and I'm in a lot of trouble.

MARTIN *(Turning the main light on)* Joe . . . (JOE KAMINSKY *steps into the room. He is a small, tough, fast-moving old man between seventy and eighty with a true New York street voice. He wears an Air Force leather jacket, sun glasses, an old cap, and a white silk scarf worn in World War One Air-Ace style)*

JOE *(clapping his hands)* Okay, Stiffo, what's up?

MARTIN Joe, it's three o'clock in the—

JOE I drive a cab all night. For me it's lunch time. *(Gesturing at the room)* What happened. Did I miss the auction? *(Goes into bedroom)* Where's my daughter? Where's the furniture? Where's Barry? Not even the dog is here . . .

MARTIN *(Following him)* Joe, what're you—

JOE Two months, Charlie. Nobody calls. New place, no invite. Something's wrong. *(Going out onto terrace)* I'm driving, I see lights, I come up. Whatta they get for a place like this, five hundred, six? *(Sits at picnic-table)*

MARTIN *(Sits opposite him; quietly)* Joe, what's happened is rather simple, really. Your daughter and I—

JOE *(Jumps up from table)* Wait a minute, I'm getting depressed here! *(Claps his hands, pacing)* Whatta they get here, six hundred, seven? I love the protection. Downstairs they got a leprechaun sleepin' in a general's uniform. Upstairs the door is open—

MARTIN I must've forgotten to—

JOE Maybe that's how your wife got away. This here porch, ya got no view here.

MARTIN You can see the river—

JOE I got news for ya. That's a building with bricks. A river you get water with boats.

MARTIN No, no, see— *(Leans over railing)* Right down there, see, and around there—

JOE You been gypped, fellah . . .

MARTIN Look, it's—

JOE Gypo, Charlie, gyperoonie . . .

MARTIN Joe, it's right *there* . . .

JOE Hey, wait a minute . . . you really believe you *can* see the river, don't ya? *(Touches his face, affectionately)* Shmuck, you been robbed. Goddamn porches . . .

MARTIN Actually, its a terrace—

JOE Charlie, for seven hundred bucks you can call it a Lazy Susan. Who's the tootsie? *(Indicating NANCY. She remains on her terrace with her back to them, doing her makeup)* I seen ya lookin' at the tootsie.

MARTIN That's a neighbor, we—

JOE I love how dumb you think I am.

MARTIN I think you've misunderstood the—

JOE Wait a minute . . . *(Sits next to him; quietly)* You think I'm knockin' the tootsie? The tootsies, the bimbos, they are the blood of life; they are hopefulness itself, without which I suggest you go sit in the closet and talk to your suits. *(Bangs on the table)* I am now seventy, seventy-five, maybe eighty; a tootsie gets in the cab, no brassiere, the bouncing alone keeps me alive another month.

They wink at me and a young fellah winks back at them from a million years ago; Kaminsky lives! *(Pounding on the table)* A nice tush moves tomorrow on the avenue, I'll be there to see it! There's a lotta guys dead because they got nothin' better to do, dying is their *hobby*. *(Stands, takes his cap off)* I am a God damn dirty old man; but a dirty old man beats a dead old man every time out. *(Sits; pats* MARTIN'S *hand)* How's the marriage going?

MARTIN   Well, Joe, not splendidly. I'd like to talk to you about—

JOE   Sure, right . . .

MARTIN   See, I guess people change, and—

JOE.   *(Jumps up)* I'm getting depressed again! *(Pacing)* I'm seventy-five, maybe eighty, and I don't want no more bad news!

MARTIN   I was hoping you could give me some insight into Sally's behavior—

JOE   *(Shoves* MARTIN *back in his chair)* My daughter is crazy, always was. So is her mother, and the other two girls is total ding-dongs. There's nobody to talk to, that's why I come here. *(Sits next to him)* Let's establish a little Goddamn *contact* here, Charlie . . . *(Quietly, confidentially)* I will tell you at this time about a tootsie . . . from the old days, when there was *tootsies*. I had this act in vaudeville, perhaps I mentioned it to you . . .

MARTIN   Yes, you have, Joe, I—

JOE   You lookin' bored at me?

MARTIN   No, I'm just trying to talk to you about me and—

JOE   You was lookin' bored at me— *(fiercely; grabs* MARTIN'S *arms, shaking him)* You look bored at me one *second* I'll crack open your head! One shot and you got a porch fulla brains! Don't you *dare*—

MARTIN   *(Prying* JOE'S *hands off)* Stop shakin' me, will ya? Christ, what *is* that, a family tradition?

JOE   *(Shouting)* We gotta *discuss!* *(Shoves him back down on bench)* Let's have a Goddamn relationship here! *(Quietly, smiling, sitting next to him)* We had this act, see. Dancing and jokes; me and Florabelle Newsome . . . Florabelle Newsome, to this day the name alone gives me a chill. Adorable Florabelle Newsome. Ginger hair and a face fulla secrets; terrific secrets, also the best tush in all of Newark, New Jersey . . . *(Suddenly depressed)* Trouble is . . . Florabelle, on May fourth, nineteen twenty-one . . . I did this terrible thing to her . . . *(*JOE *lapses into silence, looking away.* MARTIN *leans close to him)*

MARTIN   Joe . . . what did you do?

JOE.   I married her . . . *(Banging on the table)*   I *married* her, Goddamnit! I loved her and I married her! *There*, I *told* you! I had to tell somebody.

MARTIN   Joe, I had no idea that you had a wife before Helen.

JOE   Dummy, *that's Helen!* *(Bangs his fist on the table)* Florabelle Newsome, formerly the top tush in all of Newark! Helen Kaminsky! Can you believe it!? That crazy old lady who drives me up the Goddamn wall! That, *that* is adorable Florabelle Newsome. I mean, for Chrissakes, she must be *what* now, seventy, seventy-five . . . ? *(Whispers)* My God, will ya look at that tootsie over there? She puts on her makeup and hope springs eternal . . . *(Stands, shouting)* Hey, tootsie! Hey, tootsie on the porch! *(No reply. He speaks quietly, romantically)* Don't she know she's a tootsie? Don't she know, right now, this minute, I would get in my cab and take her to the moon? *(Shouting, anguished)* Love! Marriage! Children! I left show business! *(Outraged)* Safe! Safe! Howd'ya-do, three daughters and a hundred miles of linoleum! I wake up every morning shocked! *(Pounding on the table)* Love, Charlie, Goddamn love! Half the murders in New York, they say it's for love! *(Grips MARTIN's arm urgently)* That's why I wanted to talk to ya tonight. What should I do, Marty?

MARTIN   About what exactly, Joe?

JOE   My marriage. I gotta get *outa* there; that crazy old dame. Been sleepin' in the hack five days runnin'. This is it, Charlie; over and out—

MARTIN   *(His hand on JOE's shoulder)*   Joe, Helen loves you, she—

JOE   *(Going to edge of terrace)* Hey, tootsie! Hey, you . . . *(No. reply; he shrugs)* Maybe it's a fella. *(Goes to MARTIN, urgently)* I want your frank opinion; how about a trial separation? Little place uptown, my own place, a little freedom; Goddamnit, a little time to think things out. Hey— *(Grabs MARTIN's arm, inspired)* If you're gonna be alone, what about here! Perfect! You and me, Marty, terrific! Who knows, in a little while I'll see the river too! *(JOE is suddenly silent, exhausted, he leans against the terrace railing. He sits at the picnic-table, his energy gone; very quietly)* Charlie, what the hell am I talkin' about? I ain't goin' *no*where. Fact of the matter is, I'm a crazy old man and I ain't goin' nowhere. *(Looks up at MARTIN)* Christ, what *am* I, seventy, seventy-five . . . ?

MARTIN   You're seventy-eight, Joe.

JOE *(After a moment, quietly)* Already? *(Rising)* Jesus, I better get outa here. *(Going into room)* Ya leave a cab alone five minutes it turns into a taco stand. *(Stops, turns)* How the hell do ya know Helen loves me? How do ya know that?

MARTIN Because she—

JOE I'll give the broad a call; *one* call. Been sleepin' in the Goddamn *cab* for five days; got robbed tonight. One quick nap and somebody clips my coin-changer! Reminds me— *(Goes to* MARTIN*)* got ya a little somethin' for the new place, a household item— *(Takes a .38 caliber revolver from his pocket, hands it to* MARTIN*)*

MARTIN Joe, I can't—

JOE Don't worry, I got six more— *(Pointing to street)* There's a war down there, Charlie. Darkies, Puertos, junkies; war. *(Shaking* MARTIN'S *hand)* Marty, a pleasure; good night and God bless ya. *(To* NANCY*)* Good night, tootsic ... *(No reply; he shouts)* Hey, tootsie with the towel! *(She turns to him; he whispers to* MARTIN*)* See, she knows . . . the tootsies know. *(Goes to edge of terrace; grandly, removing his hat with a flourish)* Dear girlie . . . tootsie of the night . . . I pause here to say good-bye. For future reference I can be reached by the Supreme Radio Cab Company, Taxi Number Forty-One, Kaminsky. Wherever you want to go, love and Kaminsky will find a way . . . *(She smiles warmly. He whispers tenderly)* Looka that . . . Oh sweet tootsie, you *are* good news . . . *(As he exits through terrace-doorway)* Enough good news and a man could live forever. *(*MARTIN *goes quickly to doorway to give the gun back.)*

MARTIN Joe . . . Joe . . . *(But* JOE *is gone. He hesitates; then goes out on terrace, looks up at* NANCY. NANCY *snaps shut the lid of the make-up kit; she has done well with her work, the edges are softened; she touches her hair delicately.* CARLTON *appears in a slice of light on the floor above* MARTIN; *he is pulling a small dolly-platform, the caster wheels rolling audibly behind him; the dolly-platform carries the ice bucket and the portable radio, a lamp, a seventeen inch television set and two hi-fi speakers. He disappears into the shadows above, followed by his loot.* NANCY *and* MARTIN'S *terrace lights are the only remaining illumination on stage now, other than the bit of night sky between them. The lights in the terraces and windows of the other apartments have long since gone out)* Nancy, you look . . . fine.

NANCY Thank you.

MARTIN Your face; there was hardly any time for you to kill at all . . . A matter of minutes, I would say.

NANCY   Thank you,

MARTIN   Nancy, I would like to suggest . . .

NANCY   I'd feel a hell of a lot better if you put that gun down.

MARTIN   Oh, yes; of course. *(Puts gun down on picnic-table. Then, quietly)* Nancy, I would like to suggest . . .

NANCY   *(Quietly)* I live in apartment Seventeen N.

MARTIN   *(Leaning forward)* I . . . I can't hear you . . .

MAN FROM ABOVE'S VOICE   She lives in apartment Seventeen N.

MARTIN   Just mind your own damn—

MAN FROM ABOVE   *(Stepping into his terrace-light)* I live in apartment Eighteen B . . . does anybody care?

MARTIN   Chrissake, will ya—

MAN FROM ABOVE   I've been listening to your voice, Martin, and I know now that you're *not* one of the short people.

MARTIN   Fine, fine; well—

MAN FROM ABOVE   No, you're the one who took a cab away from me last Monday.

MARTIN   I wasn't even—

MAN FROM ABOVE   I remember the voice; say "taxi".

MARTIN   Now, look, mister—

MAN FROM ABOVE   Jumped in. Slammed the door in my face. "Taxi! Taxi!" and slam in the face. It was raining. Bet ya thought you'd never run into *me* again, Marty-baby.

NANCY   Mister, it wasn't him . . .

MAN FROM ABOVE   You, *you're* the one with the loud records. Why should I listen to *you?* Dancing, dancing, dancing—

NANCY   Look, mister, I—

MAN FROM ABOVE   *(Shouting)* Be quiet, dancer! This is between me and the door slammer!

MARTIN   *(Leaning over the edge)* Hey, fellah, I don't appreciate at all the way you're talking to the young lady!

MAN FROM ABOVE   How about you come up *here* and not appreciate it! Eighteen *B;* as in *bone* crusher!

NANCY   *(Shouting)* Go ahead, *holler*—and tomorrow night just try and find the *sunset!* *(Silence for a moment)*

MAN FROM ABOVE   *(Quietly)* What have you done with the sunset?

NANCY   We're *watchin'* it, baby; from where you can't see it! You're on the wrong side of the buildin'! *(MAN FROM ABOVE is silent. She smiles triumphantly)*

MAN FROM ABOVE   *(Shattering the silence)* Great! *Keep* the sunset! You want the Goddamn sunset; its *yours!* I don't expect any better! I know this city! The door-slammers get the cabs and the dancers get the sunset!

NANCY   *(Quietly, to* MARTIN*)* I live in apartment Seventeen N.

MARTIN   Seventeen N.

NANCY   As in neighborly.

MARTIN   I'll be by.

(NANCY exits through terrace doorway to await him within. Lights dim on MARTIN as he sits at picnic-table contemplating his departure to join NANCY. The MAN FROM ABOVE continues, unaware that no one is listening)

MAN FROM ABOVE   *(Still shouting)* I've got a rotten view of the rotten *parking* lot, but I'm a human *being* and my conscience is clear! *You*, you could have the Goddamn Grand *Canyon* out there and you'd still be miserable! I know alla you twitchy, screwed-up New York guys! You and your faggotty sunset! It's *yours!* *(After a moment)* Think about that. *(Another moment)* Nothing to say, Martin? . . . No smart talk, Seventeen N? *(Silence. Then, quietly)* Actually, I want you to feel free to discuss this with me. I'm willing to listen to your point of view . . . *(After a moment)* Because, you see, there's a lot of this that I don't . . . understand.

(A phone rings. Lights up on GORDON alone on his terrace, scanning the city with his binoculars. Phone on his picnic-table rings again. He will continue to look through binoculars during this scene)

CAMILLE'S VOICE   Aren't you going to answer that?

GORDON   Two in the morning. Must be a nut. *(Phone stops in middle of third ring)*

CAMILLE'S VOICE   Maybe it's the same nut who uses paper-clips in her hair. *(Silence)* Anyway, I'm going home now. Because what I have asked for is a definition of this relationship. This relationship here, and if we're not going to have that discussion then I'm going home now. *(Sound of retreating foot steps, a door opening)* Gordon, I'm going home now and don't expect to hear from me. Goodbye. *(Silence)* If you should want to discuss this with me I will be at the office number during the day and from five to about seven-thirty I will be at the Russian Tea Room, they can page me. If there's any of this you want to discuss. Goodnight, Gordon.

GORDON *(Turning from binoculars)* Goodnight. *(Sound of door closing; the phone rings, he picks it up immediately)* Hello. *(Silence)* Hello . . . Hello . . . ?

(Lights up on SALLY *at Far Right street-phone;* STREET LADY *on bench near her, listening intently to* SALLY'S *call)*

SALLY *(After a moment, tensely)* Hello.

GORDON Who is this? Who's calling?

SALLY Hello, Gordon . . . ?

GORDON Yes.

SALLY Gordon, it's Sally, of all people.

GORDON Sally?

SALLY Did I wake you?

GORDON No.

SALLY You said to call anytime. And here it is, anytime.

GORDON Right.

SALLY Sally Cramer, from the park. I mean, the bench. You read some of my poems last week . . . said you published children's books, we—

GORDON Sally Cramer, with the lovely poems. The lovely lady with the lovely poems.

SALLY That's the one. The lovely one.

GORDON I was hoping you'd call.

SALLY I was hoping I wouldn't.

GORDON Sally, where are you now? *(No reply)* Sally, where are you?

SALLY At the bench, I—

GORDON Would you like me to come down there, Sally?

SALLY No.

GORDON Would you like to come up here?

SALLY No.

GORDON What would you like?

SALLY I would like you to fall madly in love with me and think I'm wonderful and throw yourself at my feet; and I would like you to do it on the phone.

GORDON   *(Laughing)*   Sally, I'll be right over.

SALLY   No, I don't think—

GORDON   I'll be right over.

SALLY   Hold on now, let's— *(He hangs up. Lights out on* GORDON'S *terrace as he exits.* SALLY *stands still for a moment with the phone in her hand, realizing what she has just done. She hangs up, turns to* STREET LADY*)* Wait'll ya meet him, Ma; you're gonna love him. *(Lights dim on* SALLY. *The three people are illuminated in their isolated positions on the stage—the* MAN FROM ABOVE *on his terrace;* MARTIN *at Center seated at his picnic-table, lighting a cigarette, about to leave for* NANCY; SALLY *below at phone, waiting for* GORDON; *quite still. The* STREET LADY *goes to the phone-booth, delighted to find a few loose coins which have been left there; exits into the shadows at Right, chuckling over her treasure)*

MAN FROM ABOVE   *(Quietly)*   I had this habachi stove out here; steaks, chops, frankfurters, you name it. I loved that habachi stove. Then, last month, I went to Camp Young-Fun for the weekend. I saw the ad, what the hell, I went. I drove sixty eight miles upstate and when I got there everybody was old and there was no fun. And when I got back my habachi stove was gone. *(Glancing about)*   Who is taking all the things away? Martin, do you know? . . . Seventeen N? Any of you? . . . Feel free to answer please . . . *(Quietly)*   Miss Gerber, the receptionist with daisies on her blouse and sad, sad eyes; gone one day without a word and now there's a strange old woman answering the phone with a baby's voice. Who is taking all the things away? . . . Who are they? . . . Who are they? . . . *(Shouting)*   Who are they? *(The three people remain quite still, a siren wails distantly, the sound growing louder as . . .)*

THE CURTAIN FALLS

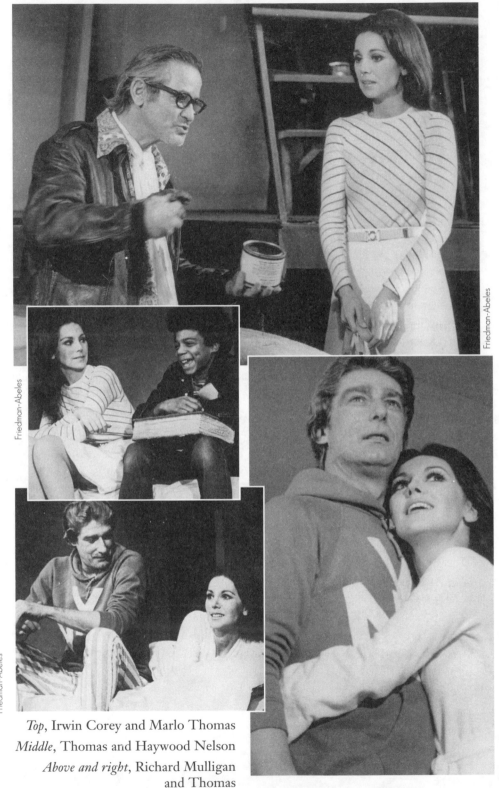

Top, Irwin Corey and Marlo Thomas
Middle, Thomas and Haywood Nelson
Above and right, Richard Mulligan
and Thomas

ACT TWO

Before the curtain rises there is the sound of flute music and gentle, late night traffic.

At rise: It's about an hour later on this quiet summer night. GORDON *lights a cigarette at Center, waiting. He wears carefully faded jeans and a sweater. The flute music fades as he moves into the light of the bench on the small balcony over the river at Right. He sits on the bench. Sound of a distant ferry-whistle from the invisible river below him. The* BUM *enters from the shadows at Far Left, wearing a base-ball-cap; he shuffles towards* GORDON. GORDON *turns to him.*

BUM   *(Cordially, tipping his cap)* 'Evenin'. *(Sits next to* GORDON *on bench, crosses his legs, leans back comfortably, looks out at the river. He smiles sociably at* GORDON. GORDON *tries to ignore him. He looks at* GORDON *for a long moment)* I'm in the goin' away business. You give me a dollar and I go away. *(*GORDON *sighs; give him a dollar.* BUM *remains seated, looking at him)* I'm also in the stayin' away business. For another dollar, I never come back. *(*GORDON *gives him another dollar. The* BUM *is very pleased; tips his cap, rises)* It's a pleasure doin' business with you. *(*SALLY *enters near phone, carrying a bag of Chinese take-out food and her suitcase; unnoticed by them, watching. The* BUM *is triumphant, inspired as he exits off into the shadows at Far Left)* I found it . . . I found one . . . A specialty! I got me a specialty! *(*GORDON *watches him leave; turns, sees* SALLY *standing near phone)*

SALLY   Hello.

GORDON   *(He rises)* Hello, Sally.

SALLY   That's not really a river, y'know.

GORDON   It isn't?

SALLY   No, it's an isthmus. It has no source, see. Just connects the Atlantic back up with the Atlantic. That makes it an isthmus.

GORDON   I see.

SALLY   That's what I came to tell you. *(He laughs warmly. She remains near phone, he remains several feet away at bench)* Well, everybody showed up.

GORDON   Yes.

SALLY   Kind of a tension in the air, ya notice that? *(He smiles)* Certainly is different from meeting here during the day.

GORDON   It's more exciting.

SALLY   Yes. It is.

GORDON   More possibilities.

SALLY   You bet.

GORDON   Also it's the beginning for us. That's the best part; hope, anticipation, the beginning.

SALLY   I figure you fool around a lot, right?

GORDON   I just try to arrange for as many beginnings as possible.

SALLY   "Fool around"; are they still saying that? I don't know what they're saying anymore. I've been away a long time. Fact is, there's a good chance I was never even there. *(He laughs)* Hey, I'm really goin' over pretty good here. *(She moves to the bench; sits, busily opening cartons and distributing food. He sits opposite her)* I hope you like Chinese food. I always like Chinese food. It makes me feel optimistic somehow. There's this place on First that's open till three A.M. and I wanted to bring something besides myself. The spareribs are great. They put honey on them. God, there's nothing in my fortune cookie. Do you suppose that means anything? *(Follows his gaze to the suitcase)* Oh, I'm crazy about big handbags. Actually, I just left my husband. I was gonna go to my girlfriend's place but she talks about abortions all night. Nothing's more boring than other people's abortions, right? I'm getting one tomorrow. At Bloomingdale's. There's a sale. You haven't touched your egg-roll. Did you really like my children's poetry? Do you remember the first line of "The Flying Festoon?" I mean, did you really like my poems or were you just trying to make out? I bet they're not saying *that* anymore either . . . *(Softly, looking away)* Well what the hell *are* they saying . . . ? *(Puts down spare-rib, near tears)* Damn it, what do people do? I don't know how to do this . . . *(She rises, picks up suitcase)* I hate not knowing, I've always been the smartest one in my class. Especially now, they're all twelve. *(Starts to walk away)*

GORDON   Sally, please stay—

SALLY   Look, I'm feeling crazy.

GORDON   That's O.K.—

SALLY   And I can't shut up—

GORDON   That's O.K.—

SALLY   And I'm not even going to sleep with you—

GORDON   Stay anyway—

SALLY   Christ, don't you have *any* standards? *(She walks briskly away, to Right)*

GORDON *(Softly)* "Oh, I'm going to fly with the Flying Festoon, I'll jump on his back and I'll whistle a tune . . . " *(She stops, smiles)* "Oh, I'm taking an apple, a ball and a prune, And we're leaving this evening, precisely at noon, 'Cause I'm going to fly with the Flying Festoon . . . Just as soon as he learns how to fly."

SALLY Okay, let's go to bed. *(He laughs. She returns to the bench)* Hey, I'm really very flattered . . .

GORDON *(Sits on bench)* Memorized it on my way over here. *(Takes pages from pocket)* The stuff you gave me; you said it was your favorite so I figured I could score a coupla points with it.

SALLY *(Sits opposite him)* Oh.

GORDON I also don't publish children's books. When I met you here you were writing children's poems, so that's what I was. If you'd been flying a kite I'd be an astronaut.

SALLY Aren't you giving away a lot of trade secrets here?

GORDON Part of my routine; when all else fails, I try honesty.

SALLY You're amazing.

GORDON Just dedicated.

SALLY Tell me, do you . . . do you get alot of drop-in business like this?

GORDON Some.

SALLY What about somebody to care about, somebody *there* . . .

GORDON You mean like marriage? Something always stops me.

SALLY What?

GORDON My wife. She's very much against it. And then there's the children. *(Rises, pacing in front of bench)* You look surprised. Well, imagine how I feel; I thought I was twenty-six. Sitting here waiting for you, I thought I was twenty-six. Me and the kids, we have dinner together every other Sunday; they sit there, growing, calling me Daddy and other vicious names.

SALLY Your wife won't give you a divorce?

GORDON Not even for Christmas. *(He stops pacing)* Truth is, Sally, I've stopped asking. Most of the ladies I see prefer it this way. It's like the fire law; all the exits are clearly marked. *(Gestures in the* BUM'S *direction)* I'm in the goin' away business. Give me a future, and I go away. *(He is silent for a moment. He turns to her, gently)* Sally, you don't belong here.

SALLY I've got a feeling this isn't part of your routine.

GORDON It isn't. Sally, I like you.

SALLY I sorta like you too. *(They are silent for a moment)* Well, that's it. That's the smallest small talk I've got. At least ya gotta give me credit for not telling you my life story . . . I think men like young girls because their stories are shorter. *(After a moment)* Look, am I too old for this?

GORDON For what?

SALLY *(Looking away)* I mean, I figure you generally get a much younger crowd here.

GORDON Sally, you're lovely . . . *(Moving to the bench)* Funny and warm and straight and lovely . . . *(He leans forward, kisses her; perfunctorily at first, and then it becomes more tender, more involved. He holds her face in his hands; he is upset, speaks quietly)* Sally, listen, I . . . see, I like you . . . I really like you.

SALLY I know, that's why I didn't run away.

GORDON *(Sits next to her)* Sally, you don't belong here. Run, do not walk; this is for terminal cases.

SALLY I know that too. Mister, I've got a rotten marriage on Eighty-First Street and a German shepherd on Seventieth . . . you look like my best bet tonight. *(Quietly, tensely)* Be glad, will ya? I'm askin' ya to be glad to see me. *(He touches her hand gently. Silence for a moment. He rises, picks up her suitcase, turns in the direction of his building. She rises. They stand quite still for a moment)* Look, I'm nervous.

GORDON I'm nervous too.

SALLY I can't help you.

GORDON My hand is shaking . . . can you imagine that? *(Comes towards her)* What happened is . . . I think what happened is, we talked . . . we became friends . . .

SALLY And you never screw your friends, right? *(He laughs, hugs her warmly)* Just keep laughing, Gordon, and we'll be O.K. *(He starts walking towards his building, carrying her suitcase. He stops, turns, holds out his hand to her. She hesitates a moment, then joins him. As they exit, hand in hand, into the shadows at Left)* Jesus, it's hard to make this look like an accident.

(The STREET LADY scurries out from the shadows at Right, grabbing up the remains of the Chinese food and carrying her prize to the curb at Center where she sits portioning out the food into two paper-plates

from her shopping-bag; carefully giving equal amounts to her Imaginary Guest. During the STREET LADY'S *picnic the lights cross-fade gradually to the colors of pre-dawn, indicating the passage of several hours in about fifteen seconds, flute music rising and then fading into the dawn light.* NANCY *comes out on her terrace wearing* MARTIN'S *red, N.Y.U. sweatshirt. She sips at a glass of red wine, smiles at the gentle pre-dawn colors. Although the light onstage has been altered enough to indicate the passage of time, there is still enough pre-morning darkness to isolate the individual terrace areas with light, and to fade in and out of these areas during the next few scenes)*

NANCY   *(Quietly, looking at the* MAN FROM ABOVE'S *darkened terrace)* Poor ol' Eighteen B . . . Can't see the sunrise neither. *(Silence for a moment)*

MARTIN'S VOICE   *(Sleepily, from inside* NANCY'S *terrace doorway)* Nancy . . . ?

NANCY   Yes, neighbor?

MARTIN'S VOICE   Did you . . . did you happen to see where I put my shoes?

NANCY   *(Takes a sip of wine)* What color are my eyes, neighbor?

MARTIN'S VOICE   *(After a moment)* Green. With flecks of gray.

NANCY   Son-of-a-gun . . . ain't had a winner in a long time.

MARTIN   What?

NANCY   I said your stuff's out here. Your shirt too.

MARTIN'S VOICE   Oh. *(Comes to doorway wearing his jacket; remains standing awkwardly in doorway, raises his hand)* Hi.

NANCY   Kinda partial to your sweatshirt; d'ya think I could—

MARTIN   Please, keep it. Glad for you to have it.

NANCY   Lord, we *slept* together . . . for hours. Regular ol' beddy-bye sleepin'. We made it till dawn . . . and that makes you the winner . . . *(Handing him his shoes as though presenting an award)* the all-time, champeen, winner.

MARTIN   *(Accepting the shoes)* Uh . . . perhaps some other time we could—

NANCY   *(Kindly, but not believing a word of it)* Sure. *(Handing him a bottle of wine)* We finished your red, here's some of my white.

MARTIN   Thank you. Unfortunately, I have to leave now. You see, I have some very valuable furniture downtown, that I have to check on, it's—

NANCY   *(Gently)* Sure, honey.

MARTIN   No, really, it's a rather valuable collection of antiques; it's relatively unguarded at the moment and I was planning to—

NANCY   *(Smiling)* Good night, honey.

MARTIN   Good night . . . *(His hands filled with the shoes and the wine, gesturing to flute on her picnic table)* Uh . . . my . . . piccolo.

NANCY   *(She hands it to him; smiling)* It's a flute, actually.

(MARTIN exits; light remains on NANCY, alone again on her terrace. She sips her wine. Lights up on STREET LADY below on the curb continuing her picnic, deeply engaged in a very animated though mute conversation with her imaginary guest)

MAN FROM ABOVE'S VOICE   *(Quietly)* Hello? . . . Hello . . . ? *(Lights up on his terrace, he is talking into the phone. Lights gradually fading on NANCY and STREET LADY while he continues)* Good morning, Speedy's All Night Pizza? Good. I tell ya, I'm the kinda guy I feel like a pizza at five-thirty in the morning, I order a pizza; because that's the kinda guy I am. I go with the moment . . . Oh, I'm sorry; of course, what kind of pizza. I mustn't keep you . . . uh . . . I imagine you're handling the phones and the pizza all by yourself at this hour . . . Of course, forgive me, I'll be brief. May I ask who I'm speaking to . . . ? *(Smiling broadly)* Speedy? Speedy himself? My goodness. Well, Speedy, let me tell you, your ad in the Yellow Pages is really quite an eye-catcher. Wonderful design; A smiling pizza with wings! Y'know, I really . . . Hello? . . . Hello, Speedy? . . . Speedy? . . . *(Lights up on GORDON'S terrace; SALLY alone at railing, wearing GORDON'S bathrobe, looking out at us and the city through his binoculars. Her hands begin to tremble, she puts the binoculars down; she is crying)* Hello? . . . Hello, Speedy? . . . Hello? . . . Hello . . . ? *(Lights fade on MAN FROM ABOVE. SALLY grips the terrace-railing tensely, still crying softly. A piece of the railing comes off in her hand; she grips the small piece of railing in anguish and surprise, drops it on the terrace-floor, covers her eyes with her hand)*

BUM'S VOICE   My own specialty! . . . *(Lights up on BUM entering at Left and STREET LADY on curb at Center eating spare-rib, as lights fade on SALLY. BUM approaches STREET LADY)* See, lady, I used to work Third and Fourteenth . . . hustlin' cars at the light; wipe the windshield, get a quarter, somethin' . . . *(Sits next to her on curb, takes a spare-rib)* Down there, see, they *expect* to see ya there; that's Bum-turf, that's Wino-land for sure . . . but up here, uptown, they want you out and gone; up here they will shell out to see me go . . . a dollar, maybe two, *disappearin'* money! They don't want to see them bad faces, lady, no sir; gets 'em thinkin' on hard times, gets 'em thinkin' on time comin' and time gone . . . gets 'em to lay out that beautiful go-away money. Sweet Jesus, I got me a specialty! *(Looks at her a moment)* Give ya a tip . . . *(Leans towards her confidentially)* Ladies up here, face like yours, I bet you could get five dollars to go away, easy.

(SALLY enters at Left with suitcase, crossing to entrance of Riverview East. The STREET LADY watches as SALLY places her suitcase inside the entrance doorway and comes back out to the still sleeping DOOR-MAN)

SALLY   Devlin, I'm leaving my suitcase in the lobby for a coupla minutes. I'll be right back, keep an eye on it for me, will ya . . . ? Devlin . . . ? *(Leans closer to him)* Devlin . . . ? *(Shrugs)* Sleep tight, Devlin, darling. *(SALLY exits into the building. The STREET LADY rises from the curb carrying her shopping bags, carefully passing behind DEVLIN and going into the building. She has left behind the umbrella she stole earlier; it rests on the curb next to the BUM. The BUM grabs up the umbrella and scurries off into the shadows, Far Left. The STREET LADY comes out of the building carrying SALLY'S suitcase, walking slowly at first and then racing off into the shadows at Right.)*

MAN FROM ABOVE   My TV is gone . . . *(As lights come up on his terrace)* I was right, it *is* the midgets! Stood here and watched one of them. A small, dark midget with a little truck . . . came right into the living room and took the Late Show away.

SALLY   Marty . . . *(Light fades on MAN FROM ABOVE, as SALLY appears in the doorway of the darkened Cramer apartment; a silhouette in the rectangle of light. The shape of the blankets on the bed give her the impression that MARTIN is lying there. She remains in the doorway)* Marty, it's me . . . Sally Jane Cramer; moving and storage . . . Well, how's the separation going so far? *(No reply)* Look, there's something I didn't think we should talk about on the phone. There's something I'm gonna do tomorrow and all of a sudden it seemed sorta unconstitutional that you never got to vote on it or anything—

CARLTON   *(From the darkness)* Mrs. Cramer . . .

SALLY   *(Startled, whispering)* Who's that . . . ?

CARLTON   Man, you been cleaned out. Somebody clean you out good here.

SALLY   *(Going toward light-switch)* Carlton—

CARLTON   *(Rushing to her)* Hold it—don't turn on the light yet—

SALLY   What the hell're you—

CARLTON   Been comin' around here a week now. Where you been?

SALLY   Where have *I* been? You haven't been in *school* for two months, I haven't been able to find you *any*where.

CARLTON   Got a deal for ya—

SALLY   No more deals, Carlton. Look, I've got a lot on my mind tonight; my own troubles— *(Going through the darkened room to the lighted terrace, reaches for phone on picnic-table)* I'll call your father, he'll take you home—

CARLTON   Wait a minute— *(Coming quickly toward her)* Here's the deal. I been in grade six three years now. Long time in grade six. Now all you gotta do is move me smooth into grade seven *(Goes back into room)* And this here's yours . . . *(CARLTON turns on the light. Placed about the room are three T.V. sets, two hi-fi speakers, several lamps, an ice-bucket, some portable radios, an electric broiler, a gold-leaf mirror, an oriental vase, a set of bongo-drums, the rest of* CARLTON'S *loot and the dolly-platform he brought them on.* CARLTON *gestures grandly)* Well, how do ya like the deal?

SALLY   I don't.

CARLTON   What's wrong?

SALLY   Everything. *(Her hand on his arm)* Carlton, all this stuff, we gotta—

CARLTON   *(Ducking away from her hand)* Why you always *do* that?

SALLY   What?

CARLTON   That *touchin'*.

SALLY   O.K., Carlton, get this straight. I am your teacher, I am not your fence. On my birthday the other kids bring an apple, you bring a color television set. *(Urgently, close to him, needing him to understand)* Oh, Carlton; this is not the way outa grade six. I put a lot of time in on you, three hours a week trying to teach you to read, trying to—

CARLTON   *(Picks up one of his books)* How'm I gonna read this here? "The Wizard of Oz." Three years now I been with that stoned chick, dumbass dog, an' all them freaks.

SALLY   Carlton, I just can't deal with this tonight. *(Goes to phone)* I'll call your father, he'll come and—

CARLTON   He dead. Somebody blow him away.

SALLY Oh, God . . . Carlton, I'm sorry, I . . .

CARLTON Seven years ago.

SALLY Seven *years* ago—who've I been speaking to on the—

CARLTON Friend James. Old wino cat. Live in the basement there.

SALLY But how do ya live? Where do ya—

CARLTON My daddy's on the Welfare. Wasn't doin' me no good dead, so I put him on the Welfare. Daddy's been on the Welfare 'bout two years now. James pick up the check, me an' him split it.

SALLY *(Sits, exhausted, at picnic-table)* Carlton, what am I gonna do with you?

CARLTON You re gonna move me into grade seven— *(Gesturing about the room)* And I'm gonna get you a couch, coupla chairs, coffee-table—

SALLY Carlton, I'm not in shape for this tonight, I'm—

CARLTON Four years in grade six; that's pushin' it. They gon' start checkin' up on ol' Carlton here, gon' find out 'bout my Welfare scam, gon' re'bilitate my ass. Livin' loose now, lady, livin' good; city livin' is the best—

SALLY *(A sudden burst of anger, gripping his arm)* Carlton, stop it! You can't *live* like this, ya—

CARLTON No touchin'!

SALLY Okay! *(Continues forcefully)* Carlton, here's the score. You can't just come waltzing back into school after two months; they're looking for you, they're gonna slam you right into one of those correctional schools. . .

CARLTON *(Taken aback, frightened)* Now that's bad . . . that's the lock-up . . . *(Sits on bed; silent, upset)*

SALLY Okay, okay . . . *(Sits next to him; comfortingly)* What I could do, see, is get them to place you in my custody. They'd give you a year's probation; means I'd be responsible for you. But if you're gonna hang around with me there's gotta be some rules, see; like about stealing—

CARLTON *(Indignantly)* There ya go with that *stealin'* talk. This custody scam, maybe I try it a while, but you got to get things straight. Lady, maybe *you* the one can't read. Check out the "Daily News", look what it say there—*every*body takin'. Cops takin', Welfare takin', school takin'; whole city takin'. All kinda scam goin', but Carlton the best . . . because he is scammin' the *scammers. (Leans back on bed)* No sir, ain't gon' end up no ol' guy bummin' dimes on the street, no James in the basement . . . *(*NANCY *comes out on her terrace, sipping wine, still wearing* MARTIN'S *sweatshirt.* SALLY *sees* NANCY *and the sweat shirt, rises from bed, moves toward terrace;* NANCY *sees* SALLY, *retreats quickly into her apartment.* SALLY *remains frozen at terrace-railing, more sad than shocked.* CARLTON *closes his eyes, his voice drifting into sleep)* Sign say "Irving Trust; Save For A Rainy Day" . . . Yeah, ain't no rainy day gon' blow *me* away . . . no storm neither, no cyclone gon' blow me to Oz . . .

(There is a blackout and then the sound of someone playing "Streets Of Laredo" on a flute from the back of the theatre we're in as a huge, tattered old motion picture screen drops down in "one" covering the entire set; a glaring work-light goes on at the downstage edge of the apron, above the screen a faded banner reads "Loew's Delancy—Home Of The Stars." MARTIN *comes down the aisle from the back of the theatre, playing his flute, moves up On Stage and then to Center, stops playing, bows gracefully.* MARTIN *puts flute in one pocket of jacket, takes wine-bottle out of the other. Drunk, unshaven, punchy, he looks about at the orchestra, the balcony, the ceiling with fondness, even love. His face reflects that beneath the peeling paint, the torn plush seats, the ghostly angels on the ceiling, he still sees the glories of this once grand movie palace. He raises his wine bottle, a celebration and a salute)*

MARTIN   Here's to ya . . . here's to ya, Loew's Delancy; better known as Low-wees Dee-lancy . . . Home of the stars, home of the galaxies, home of the moon, home of the good guys and the bad guys, a hundred years of Saturday, home sweet home . . . *(Sips the wine; turns, touches the old screen tenderly)* Hey, baby . . . hey, Dodge City . . . Iwo Jima . . . Casablanca, Shangri-La, Transylvania . . . hey . . . *(Sees his enormous shadow thrown on the screen by the work-light)* Hey, big guy, how's the big guy? *(Watching his shadow, Frankenstein's walk, Karloff's voice)* "I don't remember . . . only the flames . . . the flames . . . " *(His jacket a cape, Lugosi's voice)* "Good evening . . . I don't drink . . . wine, my dear . . . "

MAN'S VOICE   *(Puerto Rican accent; from pit below)* Hey, what you do here, mister? Hey . . .

MARTIN   *(Looks down in direction of voice; cordially)* Any requests . . . ?

MAN   *(His head and shoulders appearing from pit)* Hey, you break in here, I call the cop, they come soon; I'm tellin' you mister.

MARTIN   *(Takes flute from pocket)* Could I interest you in the theme from "Spellbound"?

MAN   I'm tellin' you, the cop come soon; I call them, mister.

MARTIN   May I ask your name, sir?

MAN   My name Perez, I call the cop, you better go now.

MARTIN   And in what way are you employed here, Mr. Perez?

PEREZ   I'm the Ni' watchman here, I think you better go now. I see you break in here.

MARTIN   You bet your ass I broke in here—zap, up the fire ladder—wam, through the fire door-zing, down my aisle—

PEREZ   The cop come, I tell the true, mister.

MARTIN   Mr. Perez . . . *(Peering out over the glaring light to the back rows of the theatre; gently)* Please go up to the second balcony and tell Ruthie Kaplan . . . Ruthie, I appreciate all favors done me at a time of desperate need . . . she will be wearing this powder blue, sorta fuzzy sweater—

PEREZ   Mister—

MARTIN   *(Gently)* And while you're up there, tell Brucie Cohen . . . Brucie— *(Shouting)* you don't lay off I beat the shit outa you!

PEREZ   Is a sin; you talk like that in a house of God, a sin.

MARTIN   Huh?

PEREZ   This here Reverend Elija Lincoln's Universal Church Of The Lord. You talk bad on holy ground here.

MARTIN   Jesus . . .

PEREZ   That's *right*, Mister. This a blessed place.

MARTIN   What happened to Loew's Delancy?

PEREZ   Gone. Long time now. This here Eglesa now. Religion place. You go now; okay, mister?

MARTIN   It was always a religious place. *(Holds bottle down towards Perez)* Come have some wine with me, Perez, let's talk a little . . . *(Perez exits, frightened, into the darkness below)* Come on, join me . . . wait . . . a little wine. . . *(MARTIN stands silently for a moment, looking out at the old theatre, alone, confused, homeless; he speaks quietly)* It's gone, Sally; don't ya see? Long, long gone . . . Loew's Delancy is closed, Bogart is dead, and Robinson is dead, and Bendix and Lou Costello, and Gail Russell and Betty Grable . . . Peter Lorre is gone, and Harpo and Sidney Greenstreet, and Whitey Arkish became an accountant and lives in Forest Hills. We don't belong here. Everybody went away and it's too late . . .

COP'S VOICE   (*Calmly, from back of theatre*) Good morning. (MARTIN *looks out in the direction of the voice*) Good morning, I'm Officer Colletti and this is Officer Simmons, and what we'd like very much is for you to put down your club and—

MARTIN   This is a flute . . .

COP'S VOICE   Good. We got flutes, too. Officer Simmons and me, we've *both* got flutes.

MARTIN   Jesus, this is silly. (*Laughing shakily*) See, I came for a little visit here, I—

COP'S VOICE   That's called breaking and entering, fellah. Now, if you'll just—

MARTIN   (*Laughing, suddenly aware of his rumpled pants, his jacket over his bare skin*) Look, I know what this looks like . . . whole thing's really misleading . . . you see, I'm the Principal of the Little Bluebell School . . .

COP'S VOICE   That's good. I'm Robin Hood and this is one of my Merry Men. (*Coming closer*) And since you won't come down here, we're gonna have to—

MARTIN   I used to live in the neighborhood, see, and I was—

COP'S VOICE   Good. Give us all the details when we book ya.

MARTIN   Oh, no—no that would be very unfortunate—at this time— (*Takes* JOE'S *gun out of his pocket*) I'm terribly sorry about this . . . but you really must not come down here . . . (*Points gun*) I would rather you didn't move at all. (*Looks at his enormous shadow on the screen, twirls the gun with his trigger-finger; smiles at his shadow's; whispers*) Jesus, Colletti, you got no idea how many times I saw myself on this screen holding a gun . . . no idea . . .

COP'S VOICE   (*Quietly*) Don't fool with this one, Ralph . . . wait him out . . . (*Louder, carefully, as to a madman*) See, what you don't know is that all the little bluebells miss you—they're havin' this party, they want to see ya and—

MARTIN   (*Trying to be pleasant, dignified*) I can see that there's no point in attempting to explain these circumstances to you . . . at this time . . . (*Moving towards wings at Right, carefully; holding the gun on them*) I'm sorry, there would be an incalculable amount of awkwardness involved in my coming with you . . . Forgive me, I have to go now, goodbye . . . goodbye, I don't live here any-more . . .

(*Sudden sound of a wailing siren . . .* MARTIN *exits, racing into wings, his shadow following, as the siren grows louder and the screen goes up . . . revealing the set at the beginning of dawn. The* BUM *is asleep on the bench, Far Right, his baseball cap pulled low over his eyes. The DeSoto is parked at left on the street.* JOE *is busily involved in a chrome-polishing ritual, an open can of Noxon metal polish rests on the hood; the grill and hubcaps have already been buffed to a glistening shine.* SALLY *follows* JOE *about the DeSoto as he fondly, delicately buffs the bumpers and doors.* CARLTON *is asleep on the back seat, we see him through the open back seat door as* JOE *polishes the handle. The sound of the pursuing siren from the preceding scene fades down as the dialogue from this scene begins)*

JOE   *(As lights come up, pointing to* BUM*)* Now *that's* an old man. You want to talk about *old; that's* old.

SALLY   Pop, do you have to polish the cab at this very moment?

JOE   *(Continues polishing)* This is Wednesday. Wednesday is cab polishing, Tuesday is washing. You know how many DeSoto Skyview Cabs they got left in the world? It's like eagles. You gotta save 'em from extinction. What's the emergency? Where'd you want me to take you?

SALLY   Look, I really appreciate this—

JOE   Used to talk to me, you don't talk to me no more.

SALLY   Tell ya the truth, Pop, last coupla years I get the feeling you don't really hear most of what I—

JOE   *(Turns to her)* What's up? Cash? You need cash?

SALLY   Just company, really. Got an hour before I have to be there.

JOE   Why ya goin' to the doctor?

SALLY   Guess you'd call it female trouble . . .

JOE   My female trouble, I got no doctor for.

SALLY   *(Smiling)* Everything's about the same at home then.

JOE   Except I'm gonna be a great grandfather.

SALLY   Hey, terrific. Who?

JOE   The one who hums to herself; y'know, what's her name; with the sweater says "Peace" on it.

SALLY   Beth? Jesus, is she married?

JOE   Nobody knows. You ask her and she just hums to herself. Frankly, I don't worry about dying, I only worry that the world will come to an end before I do. *(Comes over to her, points back to cab)* What're ya doin' with the jungle darky?

SALLY   Damn it, Pop, you're—

JOE   Don't worry, he's asleep. Asleep and dreaming about moving into my neighborhood. You and your Goddamn strays, even when you was a kid; dogs, cats, Italians—

SALLY   Fact is, Pop, I'm thinking about adopting him.

JOE   Adorable. That's adorable. What's Marty say?

SALLY   That's another piece of news. Looks like we're . . . y'know, splitting up.

JOE   Oh, adorable. This is an adorable morning.

SALLY   See, me and Marty—

JOE   Shoulda had children. How come no children?

SALLY   Children?

JOE   Yeah, you see them in the park a lot; they're the small ones in the carriages.

SALLY   Way things worked out, it's damn lucky I—

JOE   Lucky, lucky; it's a winning streak. *(Turns away from her, goes back to his cab)*

SALLY   *(Comes over to him)* Pop, I called you this morning . . . I called you because I'm going to get an abortion and I don't want to be alone.

JOE   Uh-huh. *(Continues polishing the front fender)* What else is new?

SALLY   See, Pop, we—

JOE   You're getting a divorce, a darky, and an abortion. That's some full morning we got here.

SALLY   And I thought afterwards you could take me and Carlton over to my friend's place.

JOE   Sure; what father would want to miss such an experience? *(Picks up rag and polish can)* This one! *(Sits in front seat of cab)* This one's gonna miss out on all the fun.

SALLY   Pop, *listen* to me—

JOE   *(Slams the cab door)* Get the darky out. You and the darky, *out!*

SALLY   Even if you're against the—

JOE   I'm not for, I'm not against, I just don't want the fare, lady! *(Takes car keys from pocket, puts them in ignition)*

SALLY Pop, *listen—*

JOE *(Shouting)* Since you been a minute old ya could hustle me into *any*thing! Not this, I'm not partners with this venture, I'm—

SALLY *(Hits a short burst on the horn)* Hold it, will ya?! *(Shouting)* I need your help! How about a little father action here!?

JOE That's how ya talk to an old man?

SALLY Christ, you're not gonna pull *that* one on me, are ya?

JOE Okay, forget that one. *(Shouting)* But I remain firm on all other points covered! Understood? *(Folds his arms, sits back)* All right. Proceed. I'm listening. *(She is silent. There are tears in her eyes. He gets out of the cab; quietly)* Look. It's okay, say anything you want.

SALLY Well, about the abortion . . .

JOE Except that!

SALLY I'm not sure I'm right, but I—

JOE I'll save you a lot of trouble. You're wrong.

SALLY Pop, ya know who I've been thinking about all night? . . . Uncle Abe. Uncle Abe, with the stomach trouble. There was that year he slept in the same room with me, I musta been about five at the time; he'd wake up in the middle of the night and he'd sit at the edge of his bed and he'd holler— *(With a Russian accent)* "Sally, Sally, what's it all *for?*" Just like that, Pop, "Sally, Sally, what's it all *for?*" *(Shrugs)* What the hell did I know, I was five at the time, I thought maybe it was all for Saturday afternoons; chocolate chip cookies was another strong possibility. Pop, it's thirty years later, and he's been askin' me all night . . . "What's it all *for?*" *(Turns to him)* Look, don't be offended, but I'm sure you haven't heard much of what I said.

JOE. I'm not offended. I'm deaf.

SALLY What?

JOE Four years ago the left ear went, one year ago the right. I receive only the picture portion of the program. *(Goes back to cab)* Looks to me like I'm not missing a thing.

SALLY Pop, you never told anybody.

JOE, Deaf means old; people stay away from what's old.

SALLY But how do ya—?

JOE Lips. I read the lips and the faces. Nobody knows. *(Points to huge, rear view mirror)* Triple-size, with a magnifier, I see what they say to me. *(Picks up tiny transistor earphone attached to radio-intercom)* This goes in the ear; sounds like a mouse being raped, but I don't miss any calls. The Company catches on, I'm out on my ass. With your mother it's easy, all I gotta do is nod a lot and say "they don't appreciate you" every ten minutes. *(Opens door, steps out)*

SALLY Pop, I'm really sorry.

JOE *(Crossing towards bench, at Right)* Dummy, I'm into my sixth life and you're still sitting in a pickle barrel! Listening was always in my way anyway. *(Goes to balcony over the river)* What's anybody got to tell me I ain't heard already? *(He leans on the balcony railing. The dawn light is gentle, the street is quiet and empty; they are alone except for the BUM asleep on the bench)* The quiet is good. Sometimes even beautiful. At night, all night it's like driving through new snow. *(Closes his eyes)* Listen. Listen to the quiet . . . quiet on quiet . . . in an hour the rush hour starts. *(Opens his eyes; smiling)* Beautiful, Sally, I love it. The traffic starts, the rush hour starts and I love it. Turning, hollering, moving, tells you you're around. Alive ain't enough, you gotta have ways to know it. Traffic, some kinda traffic— *(The BUM rises from bench—JOE shouts)* Un paso mas, estas muertos, Carlos! *(The BUM lies down again)* Good.

SALLY What did you say to him?

JOE I said, "One more step and you're dead, Charlie!" I know just enough Spanish to get me around the city.

SALLY Pop, he was just—

JOE I don't gamble! Only the horses. Got a thirty-eight under the dashboard and a billy-club on the seat— *(Turns to her, shouting)* What keeps *you* alive? I got a great grandchild comin'; don't know where it's comin' *from*, but it's comin'! Whatta *you* got to remember yourself by? How do ya know you're not an ashtray? What's it all *for?* It's for staying alive! Ya heard it here first, girlie! That's the trick, that's the ball game. Get outta the traffic and you're dead, Charlie! *(Grabs her arm; shaking her)* Am I talkin' loud enough? Estas muertos, Carlos? *(Quietly)* I see your face . . .

SALLY Pop . . .

JOE You're still goin' to the doctor, right?

SALLY Pop, you don't understand, it's—

JOE Okay, that's it! You're . . . you're *fired!* *(He walks briskly away towards the cab)*

SALLY   *(Following)* You can't fire a daughter.

JOE   I got *plenty* o'daughters! *All* kinds! *(The* BUM *starts toward them from the bench;* JOE *shouts at him)* No money! I got no money! No tango dinero! *(The* BUM *is frightened away, exits to the Right.* JOE *opens door, gets into cab)* Hey, he's gone. Your darky skipped! He's gone, and so's my new coin-changer! Adopt him? *Adopt him? Arrest* him! *(*SALLY *goes quickly to the cab, looks in at the empty back seat, upset)*

SALLY   Jesus . . . *(Shouting to the empty street)* Hey, Carlton . . . ! Carlton . . . ? *(But he is gone. She opens the cab door sadly, about to get in next to* JOE*)*

JOE.   Where the hell ya think *you're* goin'? Out, out!

SALLY   All I'm askin' ya to do is—

JOE   Ain't no door to door abortion service; Out.

SALLY   *(Points to lobby)* Wait a second, I'll just get my suitcase, and we'll—

JOE   You'll *walk.* You'll *think!* *(Puts key in ignition)* Only booked fifteen on the clock all night. I'm in the transportation field here. *(She doesn't move, still holding door open. He shouts)* I'm seventy-eight! My time is limited! Out!

SALLY   Damn you. *(She slams the door) Damn* you. *(She walks sharply away down the street to the Right)*

JOE   *(Shouting after her)* Years from now, Sally, believe me—you're gonna thank me for this!

SALLY   *(Stops, turns sharply)* The hell I will— *(Fiercely, bitterly)* I won't be thanking you for this. Not now, and not later. You missed a big chance here, Kaminsky. You had a Chance to hug me, to understand me, to know me a little, but you were off duty and you missed it . . . *(He turns away)* Don't you *dare* turn away from me! Watch the lips, Joe! You were deaf to me twenty years before your ears went. Daughters who love you, Joe; do you know how many there are left in the world? They're like eagles; you gotta save them from extinction. Keep your billy club and keep your thirty-eight, but you still won't be safe. Turn your clock on, Pop, feel it tick; *that's* the thief. That's the biggest thief in town. *(She turns and walks away, about to exit at Left)*

JOE   *(Shouting)* Hold it! *(She stops)* You want help, I got something for ya— *(Gets out of cab)* How old are you?

SALLY   You know damn well how—

JOE How old?

SALLY Thirty-three.

JOE Wrong. When you was four, the house was crowded; Abe, Benny, the cousins, all the girls to look after. Helen says to me we gotta get you into school a year early. Okay, Benny gets a blank certificate from his friend works for the city. We make you a year older. You're a kid, we're afraid you'll spill the beans at school, we don't tell you the truth. Coupla years go by, keep meanin' to tell ya but I start to notice I'm not rich—and I think, what would I ever give you? Money; forget it. Property; unlikely. I figure I'll give you time, when you need it. You got married, I figured it for a dowry; but you were happy and you didn't need it yet . . . Finally, I put it in my will; three grand for each girl and a year for Sally. But today I figure you need it. So there it is; you're thirty-two. *(Going back to cab)* You got a year. Don't blow it.

SALLY *(Smiling, gently)* Thanks, Pop . . . Thanks for the extra year.

JOE *(Shouting)* Dummy, don't ya know?—they're *all* extra years. *(Turns on ignition; puts his foot on the gas)* Listen to that, quietest damn motor in town. *(Lights out on DeSoto Far Left, as* JOE *backs the cab Up Stage and into the shadows)*

HARRY'S VOICE Taxi! Taxi! Goddamnit! . . . Taxi! *(Lights up on entrance to Riverview East as Harry steps out onto the street, waving wildly in the direction of* JOE'S *departed cab)* Goddamnit, *wait!* Don't you *see* me! What *am* I, the Goddamn Invisible Man?! *(Goes back to lobby to sleeping* DOORMAN*)* Goddamn you, Devlin . . . wake up and blow your Goddamn *whistle,* for Chrissakes! . . . *(*SALLY *comes towards entrance)* What the hell am I *paying* for? *(He shakes* DEVLIN'S *shoulder)* Missed four *cabs;* four, Devlin . . . I've got to get to *work.*

SALLY Leave him alone, mister, he's just sleeping, he—

HARRY Oh, he's *sleeping,* is he? Well, thank you very much for the information— *(She has gone into the lobby for her suitcase; finds that it is gone)*

SALLY Hey . . . Devlin, my suitcase. *(She shakes his shoulder gently)* I'm late for a very important appointment—where'd you put my— *(Slowly, quietly,* DEVLIN'S *very old and very dead body falls off the chair and onto the street, the braided cap rolling.* SALLY *kneels next to him, touching his ice cold hand. Harry begins to back away involuntarily towards the door, his briefcase held close like a teddy bear)*

HARRY Oh, my God . . . oh, my God . . .

SALLY   *(Quietly)* Poor dear man . . .

HARRY   Oh, my God.

SALLY   *(Kneeling close to him, touching his hand gently)* So cold . . . All this time, all night he's been : . .

HARRY   *(Still backing away)* Oh, God, he's . . . he's . . .

(GILBEY, *another harried businessman with a briefcase, comes briskly out of the building and onto the street, glancing briefly at the group behind him, then scanning the street for a cab)*

GILBEY   *(Shaking his head)* Devlin loves his bourbon. *(Shouting up the street)* Taxi! Hey, taxi! *(Shakes his head at the loss of his cab; turns to* DEVLIN'S *chair, takes whistle tied to thin strap around the chair, wipes off the mouthpiece, blows the whistle at an Off Stage cab . . . turns back to the group,* SALLY *kneeling next to* DEVLIN, *Harry frozen several feet away)* Hey, what's wrong with him? *(No reply)* He . . . he looks . . . uh . . .

SALLY   *(Not looking up)* Dead, I think the word we're all looking for is "dead." *(Silence for a few moments; nobody moves. She looks up at them)* Well, what've ya got in mind, fellahs?

HARRY   *(Whispering)* I'll . . . I'll get the superintendent . . .

SALLY   This isn't maintenance. *(She rises, commanding)* Pick him up, both of you; gently. Put down your briefcases and pick him up, put him on the couch in the lobby . . . gently . . . and give back his whistle . . . give him his whistle back! *(Backing away slowly toward the street-phone, at Right)* I'll call the police, stay with him till they come . . . *(The two men approach the body awkwardly; they avoid looking at each other.* GILBEY *reaches forward, holding* DEVLIN'S *shoulders. Harry reaches for* DEVLIN'S *feet.* GILBEY *nods and they lift the body up slowly, carefully.* SALLY *reaches phone, deposits coin, dialing as Harry and* GILBEY *exit into the building carrying the body)*

GILBEY   *(Politely)* My name's Gilbey, I'm in Fourteen C.

HARRY   Harry Soames, Seventeen J.

SALLY   *(Into phone)* Look, somebody died. His name is Devlin. He's in the lobby of Two-Sixteen East End Avenue. My name is Sally Cramer, same address. Okay. *(Hangs up, deposits another coin, dialing; speaks into phone as the* STREET LADY *appears on the street Up Right, approaches* DEVLIN'S *body, studying* DEVLIN'S *cap)* Hello, would you page Doctor Gerstad, please? Thank you. *(She waits; the* STREET LADY *leans over, picks up* DEVLIN'S *cap, looking it over.* SALLY *shouts)* Drop the hat, creep! *(The* STREET LADY *drops the cap, startled, very hurt)* I'm sorry, lady . . . I . . . (SALLY *points to the briefcases left by* HARRY *and* GILBEY*)* Take one of those. Take them both. They're yours. A present. *(The* STREET LADY *looks over at the two suitcases, studying them with interest.* SALLY *speaks into the phone)* Hello, Doctor Gerstad? Sally Cramer. Little transportation problem; but I'm calling a cab, I'll be there in ten minutes, okay? Did you get a good night's sleep? . . . No, I'm fine, really. Lenox Hill, Fourth Floor Admissions, okay. Wash up. 'Bye. *(She hangs up, deposits another coin, dialing. The* STREET LADY *puts down her two shopping bags, picks up the two briefcases, holds one in each hand like the shopping bags, and scurries off at Right.* MARTIN *appears on the street, Up Left. He is a wreck; unshaven, exhausted, hung over, his jacket open against bare smudged skin, black smudges everywhere from climbing, sweat stains from hard running, his sleeve ripped, his pants leg torn up to the knee, the material flapping as he stumbles along, glancing back furtively as though still pursued. Sally continues on phone)* Hello, Supreme Radio Cabs? Send a cab to Two-Sixteen East End Avenue; anybody but Kaminsky. No, he didn't say anything obscene to me. Two-Sixteen East End and hurry, I'll be waiting in front of the building. *(She hangs up.* MARTIN *stands at Far Left on street, unnoticed by her.* SALLY *walks sleepily to the curb in front of the building, picks up* DEVLIN'S *cap, sits on curb, hunched up, her arms around her knees like a tired street-kid. It is still very early, very quiet, no sound of traffic; the sun is not bright yet but it is there, warming and soft.* SALLY *closes her eyes, feels the sun on her face.* MARTIN, *still unnoticed by her, is trying to figure out what attitude to take. He decides on controlled dignity, buttons his torn jacket, sits at the edge of the curb some distance from her, puts his flute down, crosses his legs casually, holding his torn pantsleg together with one hand. Sound of a single, distant car driving by. Silence again)*

MARTIN   *(Calmly, looking away from her at the river)* Forget something?

SALLY   *(Not looking at him)* I've got a cab coming in five minutes.

MARTIN   Right.

SALLY   I came back for something. I thought I'd left something. But there was nothing here. *(After a moment)* Congratulations, Cramer. We did it. We joined the losers.

MARTIN   Sally, I . . .

SALLY   *(Turns to him)* Dead is dead, Mister. *(Suddenly aware of his appearance)* What the hell happened to *you?*

MARTIN   *(Calmly)* Interesting. You can still get from Loew's Delancy to the subway without being caught by the cops. Eight alleys, six basements. It still works.

SALLY   What were you doing on Delancy Street?

MARTIN   *(He shrugs)* Lookin' around

SALLY   For what?

MARTIN   Us, I guess; or me, or . . . anyway we weren't there. Neither was our furniture. That nice old guy you had watching the stuff . . .

SALLY   Yes?

MARTIN   He sold it *(She smiles)* He gave me the money, though.

SALLY   Well at least he gave you the—

MARTIN   Forty dollars. *(She laughs)* He said he was lucky to get that much for old junk *(She continues laughing)* I didn't find it very amusing.

SALLY   No, you wouldn't . . . *(She suddenly cracks, burying her face in her hands, shaking with sobs, the emotions of the night flooding in.)*

MARTIN   *(Rising)* Sally . . .

SALLY   *(Rising, moving away from him)* This isn't crying . . . this isn't really crying here. This is just crankiness; a cranky kid who's been up too late, or at the Zoo too long. *(Starting towards the bench, Far Right)* I'll wait for my cab across the street. You go up to the apartment and look for your river.

MARTIN   Sally, wait—

SALLY   *(Sharply, with finality)* Marty, the odds are against the House.

MARTIN   *(Calmly, controlled, his hand in his pocket)* Sally, I think we should take this opportunity to examine several of the issues . . . to discuss and examine several of the options available to us . . .

SALLY   *(Shouting, bitterly)* Christ, *listen* to you! Save it for the blue-bells, Marty! *(She walks briskly away toward the bench. The MAN FROM ABOVE comes out of the building carrying a briefcase, wearing a snappy business-suit and ready for the new day. MARTIN takes the gun quietly from his pocket, points it at the sky. A deafening shot shatters the still morning air. The MAN FROM ABOVE freezes, his eyes wide. SALLY turns sharply. MARTIN stands quite still, the thirty-eight pointed at the sky)*

SALLY   *(After a moment, to the MAN FROM ABOVE)* We're trying to get a cab . . .

MAN FROM ABOVE *(Turning sharply, walking back into the building; quietly, nodding)* Never . . . I'm never going out there again.

MARTIN *(Trying to remain under control)* As . . . as I began to say . . . We can't break up till we know whose fault it was. We have to decide who was wrong . . . *(Pointing)* You! You're wrong. I'm the right one, you're the wrong one. Let's remember that . . . Look, look at me, look what you did to me! . . . I went back to the past and it beat the crap outa me! Oh, God, I'm outa breath and I can't wear sneakers anymore . . . Look, look what you did . . . guns, *cops*, cops chasin' me . . . I broke my watch . . . I went up to a guy on First Avenue to ask him for the time. He gave me a quarter . . . I *kept* it! . . . Total for the night: forty dollars and twenty-five cents! . . . *(Suddenly, moving towards her)* Don't go, don't leave . . . God help me, I'm married to you . . . I'm married to sleeping next to you, I'm married to your Goddamn dumb jokes . . . I ran, I ran . . . *(Holding her, crying softly)* Running home, running to you, running, shouting, find her, find her . . . find her . . .

FLO'S VOICE *(Shouting, from above)* What's happening down there? I heard a gun! . . . Who is that? What's he *doing?* What's *wrong* with him?!

SALLY *(Holding MARTIN close, with love, delight, relief; looks up in the direction of FLO'S voice)* He's crazy . . . my husband is crazy . . . Crazy Marty . . . *(They kiss each other tenderly. Silence for a few moments as they embrace . . . a police siren wails distantly, Off Right, coming closer . . . SALLY turns towards the sound)* Marty, I think we better start walking now . . . that guy called the police. *(MARTIN starts towards the entrance, but SALLY leads him away Down Center)* Better not go in there, that guy'll identify us . . . and we've got an apartment fulla hot furniture. *(The siren grows louder, at Right . . . MARTIN gets rid of the gun on the curb at Center, picks up his flute; she grabs his hand, they start up the street to the Left)*

SALLY Better start walking quickly . . .

MARTIN Actually, running . . . running would be wise . . . *(Hand in hand they run to the Left up the street . . . Another siren starts to wail, Off Left, coming closer . . . they run to the Right, but that siren is wailing even closer now . . . they run back to the Center, not knowing how to escape. They finally race towards the ramp at Left, running down the ramp into the Pit.)*

SALLY *(Pausing on the ramp, delighted)* Marty, sirens . . . sirens and everything . . .

(As they disappear down the ramp and exit, the sirens grow louder and the gradually building sounds of Morning Traffic blend together with the following overlapped dialogue and movement; no distinct lines, the words are just more traffic noise, perhaps a phrase or two surfacing amidst the din, all action simultaneous as—the STREET LADY *scurries down Center to pick up the gun,* GILBEY *exits from the building to get a cab, the* BUM *approaches* GILBEY *for a handout, New Young* DOORMAN *comes out of building blowing a whistle,* JOE'S *Taxi-Light brightens as he turns on the ignition, Harry and* FLO *come to the edge of their terrace,* NANCY *and* GORDON *come out on their terraces with phones, the* MAN FROM ABOVE *comes out on his terrace in a bathrobe)*

GORDON I thought perhaps a little breakfast at my place—

HARRY Shoulda seen how I handled it; the guy keels over, everybody panics—

NANCY A *party?* At Eight O' Clock in the *mornin'?* I'll have to think on that—

FLO You're all heart, Harry—

BUM I'm in the goin' away business—

GILBEY Great, I'm *late*, Mac—

DOORMAN Taxi ! Taxi! Taxi—

GILBEY Driver, I'm going to Brooklyn—

JOE That's the difference between us—

BUM You give me a dollar and I—

JOE —*you're* goin' to Brooklyn and *I'm* not—

MAN FROM ABOVE *(Shouting above the others)* They've got guns now . . . of course . . . they've got guns . . . I'm having all my food sent *up* . . .

(These Voices lost now in the growing roar of heavy Morning Traffic as the City comes alive again and . . .)

THE CURTAIN FALLS

Liann Pattison, Harold Gould and Cleavon Little; set, Tony Walton

I'M NOT RAPPAPORT

I'M NOT RAPPAPORT

I was sent a script in 1986, of a play by Herb Gardner called *I'm Not Rappaport*; I had met him when in New York, and seen his play, *A Thousand Clowns*, which I liked tremendously. For me this was something worth seriously thinking about even before I'd read it. I plunged in. Two old men, one of whom was being offered to me to play. An eighty-year-old New York Jew of Eastern European origins. Was I good casting? Could I speak it correctly — this kaleidoscope of accents? Getting my tongue around and into a pot-pourri of cultures and cadences that were, except from my extensive view-ing of Hollywood movies in my early years, entirely unfa-miliar to me? But then there was the old man himself — gallant and perverse and touching, and, above all, funny. An inborn gaiety and youngness, and the courage to reject the world's percep-

Paul Scofield and Howard Rollins

tion of the "old folk" stereotype. A dancing mind, a sharp and sometimes wounding tongue, an unstoppable loquaciousness; his verbal ammunition let loose on a charming, friendly black counterpart, both sitting forever on benches in Central Park. Both enduring the importunate and sometimes menacing attentions of its regular wandering misfits; both unfazed and eternally optimistic. A story of superhuman courage and a certain mordant lightness of heart. So I did it; and at our first reading met Howard Rollins, my park bench companion. He was a young, handsome and vibrant American actor. Surprise — was *he* the actor for an eighty-year-old? Well yes, he was. Rehearsal began, our dualogues flowed, his sympathy and his perfect timing were moving and immaculate, and with make-up he was old and completely believable. It was a rare partnership, relaxed and flexible and trusting. The play was dense with talk, shared between Howard and Susan Fleetwood and myself. Other characters emerged and made important contributions, but we three did most of the talking, especially me; and we found we needed to extend rehearsal in order to be in shape for our first performances. Susan, who played my daughter, and who we have since, immeasurably sadly, lost, played the ambivalent relationship with her father, with a baffled tact and an infinite grace and honesty. Howard too has gone, and we have lost two luminous and beautiful actors.

We opened in London to amusement and delight, the audiences, though perhaps not all of the critics, understood the tragic and hilarious predicament of the story. We played I think for roughly one year — a year of unadulterated and exhausting pleasure. Thank you Herb, thank you Howard and Susan, and thank you Dan Sullivan.

— PAUL SCOFIELD
West Sussex, England

If you know Herb Gardner's plays then you won't be surprised to learn that all of his male lead characters are somewhat related, or perhaps I should say united: they all believe they are being pursued by time and silly people — a fact not surprisingly brought home to me after having played four of them. What may be surprising to learn, however, is that this playwright with his inescapable genius for finding humor in any human condition is utterly serious about these characters. He's lived their histories; he's met their families; cruised their neighborhoods; sampled their diets; and sung, played or hummed their songs; and, most notably, he's listened carefully to their memories of better times.

He does his character homework, or, more precisely his dogged research into their bloodlines, into the very bark of their family trees; in fact, he'll interview your mother if you're not careful — he interviewed mine! He was looking for some real-life background for a situation in his play, *Conversations With My Father*. But what he got was a shocking confession from my mother that she somehow killed my father's mistress (whom she called "the bum") with a frying pan! A revelation fascinating to Herb and particularly fascinating to me because she'd never mentioned it before.

But this dogged research, this unyielding involvement in the absolute wishes and dreams of these characters of his makes Herb Gardner all the more tenacious about protecting their rights and the ultimate frailty of their existence as real people — a concept I was to meet head-on in the summer of 1985 during rehearsal of *I'm Not Rappaport* at the American Place Theater in New York. I made the suggestion that Herb change the name of a character referred to by Nat, the 81 year old Jewish Don Quixote I was playing. Nat had already, and quite convincingly, described the character earlier as Hannah Perlman, a girl he'd only seen from a distance and whom he'd never had the courage to talk to, a fact he lamented the rest of his days since she eventually died, in loneliness and despair, by "taking the gas". But later in the play, in order to dissuade his daughter from declaring him incompetent, he uses the same Hannah Perlman in a preposterous and cunningly crafted lie — or "alteration" as Nat preferred to call it.

So, I suggested the name-change and even a change in circumstance so that the audience wouldn't catch on to the obviousness of the lie and start to react too soon, which I thought would spoil the emotional ingenuousness

Martha Swope

Judd Hirsch with Cleavon Little

of the moment. No matter how hard I argued for the change, Herb remained incredulous and adamant in his refusal to accede to what was now moving into the realm of an exhaustive plea-bargaining session.

"How else can I say it," I begged, "the audience will laugh with that all-knowing recognition that a ruse is in the making — the cover's been blown, the cat's out of the bag — and I, as the actor, will be fighting an uphill battle to remain serious enough to convince my daughter that every-thing is true. In other words, how the hell can I do that?!"

Herb's answer: "But Nat truly loved this woman — nothing could change that."

My reply: "But this is a play, we have choices — we can change any-thing."

His response (and here the playwright is succinct): "Nat wouldn't do that — he loved this hopeless girl — his memory of her is inviolable!"

Stalemate.

My heart sinks.

His is resolute.

He makes a request: "Couldn't you just keep them from reacting too soon?"

"How?"

"By making them believe that *this* story is the true one."

"Believe? For how long?"

"For as long as you can. Nat was as good an actor as you are, but his performance was his life; life presented as he wanted it to be, a past presented as he hoped it would have been. Like you have moments on stage — the best moments — when you believe you really are Nat, Nat also believes in the love that should have been with Hannah. Nat, like you at your acting best, never lies; he believes what he's saying, he *needs* to — and so will they."

An author makes his heartfelt plea, and it becomes my job — an actor's job — to accept the challenge.

Each night the audience held off longer and longer in their response. Each night, because of this playwright's faith in the old man's existence, I was able to make them think that *this* story about Hannah Perlman was the real one and not the one they had been convinced of previously. And then I started to believe it too; and continued to believe it for the next two and a half years.

I love this play. I think it's his best. I told him so.

His response ... well, I'll save that for the next collection.

— JUDD HIRSCH
San Francisco

I'm Not Rappaport was originally presented by the Seattle Repertory Theatre in December, 1984.

The play was subsequently presented by James Walsh, Lewis Allen, and Martin Heinfling at the American Place Theater in New York City on June 6, 1985. The cast was as follows:

NAT	Judd Hirsch
MIDGE	Cleavon Little
DANFORTH	Michael Tucker
LAURIE	Liann Pattison
GILLEY	Jace Alexander
CLARA	Cheryl Giannini
THE COWBOY	Ray Baker

Directed by Daniel Sullivan. Setting by Tony Walton. Costumes by Robert Morgan. Lighting by Pat Collins.

This production was transferred to the Booth Theatre in New York City on November 19, 1985 with the following cast:

NAT	Judd Hirsch
MIDGE	Cleavon Little
DANFORTH	Gregg Almquist
LAURIE	Liannn Pattison
GILLEY	Jace Alexander
CLARA	Mercedes Ruehl
THE COWBOY	Steve Ryan

CHARACTERS
NAT
MIDGE
DANFORTH
LAURIE
THE COWBOY
GILLEY
CLARA

Early October, 1982. A bench near a path at the edge of the lake in Central Park; New York City.

ACT I: Three in the afternoon.

ACT II: Scene 1: Three in the afternoon, the next day.

Scene 2: Six in the evening, the next day.

Scene 3: Twelve days later, eleven in the morning.

NOTE: All stage directions and set descriptions are given from the audience's left and right.

ACT ONE

SCENE: A battered bench on an isolated path at the edge of Central Park Lake, early October, 1982, about three in the afternoon. To the left of this center bench is a smaller even more battered one with several of its slats missing. Behind these benches is the Gothic arch of an old stone tunnel, framed above by an ornate Romanesque bridge which spans the width of the stage.

Before the curtain rises we hear the sound of a Carousel Band-Organ playing "The Queen City March."

AT RISE: Two men, MIDGE *and* NAT, *both about eighty years old, are seated at either end of the center bench; they sit several feet apart, an old briefcase between them.* MIDGE *is black and* NAT *is white.* MIDGE *wears very thick bifocals and an old soft hat; he is reading "*The Sporting News*".* NAT *wears a beret and has a finely trimmed beard, a cane with an elegant ivory handle rests next to him against the bench. The two men do not look at each other. A* JOGGER *runs by on the bridge above, exits at right. An autumn leaf or two drifts down through the late afternoon light. Silence for a few moments; only the now distant sound of the Carousel Music.*

NAT   O.K., where was I? *(No response. He smacks himself on the forehead)* Where the hell was I? What were we talking about? I was just about to make a very important point here. *(To* MIDGE*)* What were we talking about?

MIDGE   *(No response. He continues to read his newspaper for a moment)* We wasn't talking. *You* was talking. *(Turns page)* I wasn't talking.

NAT   O.K., so what was I saying?

MIDGE   I wasn't listening either. You was doing the whole thing by yourself.

NAT   Why weren't you listening?

MIDGE   Because you're a goddamn liar. I'm not listening to you anymore. Two days now I ain't been listening.

NAT   Stop pretending to read. You can't see anything.

MIDGE   Hey, how 'bout you go sit with them old dudes in fronta the Welfare Hotel, them old butter brains— *(pointing about the lake)* the babies at the Carousel, them kids in the boat—or some o' them junkie-folk yonder, whyn't you go mess with them? 'Cause

I'm not talking to you anymore, Mister. Puttin' you on notice of that. You may's well be talking to that tree over there.

NAT   It's a lamppost.

MIDGE   Sittin' here a week now, ain't heard a worda truth outa you. Shuckin' me every which way till the sun go down.

NAT   *(slapping the bench)* I demand an explanation of that statement!

MIDGE   O.K., wise-ass; for example, are you or are you not an escaped Cuban terrorist?

NAT   *(slapping the bench)* I am not!

MIDGE   O.K., and your name ain't Hernando—

NAT   Absolutely not!

MIDGE   So it's a lie—

NAT   It's a cover-story! *(Pause)* My line of work, they give you a cover-story.

MIDGE   Are you sayin'—?

NAT   All I'm saying, and that's *all* I'm saying, is that in my particular field you gotta have a cover-story. More than that I can't divulge at the present time.

MIDGE   Honey bun, you sayin' you're a spy?

NAT   I'm saying my name is Hernando and I'm an escaped Cuban terrorist.

MIDGE   But what kinda weirdo, bullshit cover-story is—?

NAT   You don't think I *said* that to them? That's what *I* said to them. I said to them, an eighty-one-year-old Lithuanian is a Cuban Hernando? That's right, they said, tough luck, sweetheart; yours is not to reason why. That's how they talk. Of *course* you don't believe it! You think *I* believe it? Such dopes. But it's a living. I beg you not to inquire further.

MIDGE   But why'd they pick an old—

NAT   Do *I* know? You tell *me*. A year ago I'm standing in line at the Medicaid, a fellah comes up to me—boom, I'm an undercover.

MIDGE   *(impressed)* Lord . . .

NAT   Who knows, maybe they got something. They figure an old man, nobody'll pay attention. Could wander through the world like a ghost, pick up some tidbits.

MIDGE   *(nodding thoughtfully)* Yeah . . .

NAT   So maybe they got something, even though, I grant you, they screwed up on the cover-story. All I know is every month a thousand bingos is added to my Social Security check.

MIDGE   Bingos?

NAT   Bingos. Dollars. Cash. It's a word we use in the business. Please don't inquire further. *(Silence)* Please, I'm not at liberty. *(Longer silence)* O. K.; they also gave me a code name, "Harry."

MIDGE   "Harry"?

NAT   Harry Schwartzman.

MIDGE   What's your real name?

NAT   Sam Schwartzman. *(Outraged)* Can you believe it? Can you *believe* it? That's some imaginative *group* they got up there, right? That's some bunch of geniuses! *(Then, shrugging)* What the hell, a thousand bananas on your Social Security every month you don't ask fancy questions.

MIDGE   Best not, best not. *(Leaning closer)* So, do ya . . . do ya ever pick up any information for them?

NAT   Are you kidding? Sitting on a bench all day with a man who can't tell a tree from a lamppost? Not a shred   *(Glances about, leans closer)* Fact is, I think they got me in what they call "deep cover." See, they keep you in this "deep cover" for years; like five, maybe ten years they keep you there, till you're just like this regular person in the neighborhood . . . and then, boom, they pick you out for the big one. Considering my age and general health, they're not too bright. *(Reaches into briefcase)* O.K., snack time.

MIDGE   *(nodding)* Yeah. Deep cover. I hearda that . . .

NAT   *(taking foil-wrapped sandwich from briefcase)* Here. Tuna salad with lettuce and tomato on whole wheat toast. Take half.

MIDGE   *(accepting sandwich)* Thank ya, Sam; thank ya.

NAT   Yeah, comes three o'clock, there's nothing like a nice, fresh tuna salad sandwich.

MIDGE   *(chewing)* Uh-huh.

NAT   *(chewing)* Crisp.

(Silence for several moments as their old jaws work on the sandwiches)

MIDGE   *(suddenly)* Bullshit! *(Sits upright)* Bullshit! Lord, you done it to me *again!* You done it! *(Throws the sandwich fiercely to the ground)* Promised myself I wouldn't let ya, and ya done it again! Deep cover! Harry Schwartzman! Bingos! You done it again!

NAT   *(smiling to himself as he continues eating)* That was nice . . . a nice long story, lasted a long time . . .

MIDGE   *(shouting, poking* NAT *sharply)* That's *it!* That's it, no more conversin'! Conversin' is *over* now, Mister! No more, ain't riffin' *me* no more!

NAT   Please control yourself—

MIDGE   *Move* it, boy; *away* with ya! This here's *my* spot!

NAT   Sir, I was—

MIDGE   This is *my* spot. I come here first!

NAT   I was merely—

MIDGE   Get offa my spot 'fore I lay you out!

NAT   *Your* spot? Who made it *your* spot? Show me the plaque. Where does it say that?

MIDGE   Says right here . . . *(Remains seated, slowly circling his fists in the air like a boxer)* You read them hands? Study them hands, boy. Them hands wore Golden Gloves, summer of Nineteen and Twenty-Four. This here's *my* spot, *been* my spot six months now, my good and peaceful till you show up a week ago start playin' Three Card Monte with my head. Want you *gone*, Sonny! *(Continues circling his fists)* Givin' ya three t'make dust; comin' out on the count o'three. *One*—

(MIDGE *rises, moving to his corner of the "ring")*

NAT   Wait, a brief discussion—

MIDGE   Sound of the bell, I'm comin; out. *You* won't hear it but *I will*. *Two*—

NAT   How you gonna hit me if you can't *see* me?

MIDGE   Dropped Billy D'Amato in the sixth round with both eyes swole shut. I just keep punchin' till I hear crunchin'. *Three!*

NAT   *(rising with dignity)* Please, sir—this is an embarrassing demonstration—

MIDGE   *(moving in* NAT'S *general direction, a bit of remembered footwork, jabbing)* O.K., comin' out, comin' out; comin' at ya, boy, comin' at ya—

NAT   *(moving behind bench for protection)* Sir, you . . . you have a depressing personality and a terrible attitude!

MIDGE   *Prepare* yourself, Mister, prepare yourself, get your—

(MIDGE *suddenly lunges, bumping against the bench, stumbling—he struggles to keep his balance, grabbing desperately at the air—then falls flat on his back in the path. He lies there silently for several moments)*

MIDGE   *(quietly, frightened)* Oh, shit . . .

NAT   *(aware that* MIDGE *is in danger, whispering)* Mister . . . ? *(No response. He leans forward urgently)* Mister, Mister . . . ? *(Silence. He moves towards* MIDGE *as quickly as possible)* Don't move, don't move . . .

MIDGE   *(trembling)* I know . . .

NAT   Could be you broke something . . .

MIDGE   *(softly)* I know. Oh, shit. Never fall down, *never* fall down . . .

NAT   *(kneeling next to him, trying to calm him)* It's nothing; I fall down every morning. I get up, I have a cup of coffee, I fall down. That's the system; two years old you stand up and then, boom, seventy years later you fall down again. *(Gently, firmly)* O.K., first thing; can you lift your head? *(MIDGE hesitates, frightened, then raises his head a bit)* Good sign. Put your head back. *(As* MIDGE *carefully rests his head back)* Good, good, good . . . *(Carefully, knowledgeably, touching* MIDGE, *checking for damage)* O.K., feeling for breaks, checking the pelvic area . . . feeling the hip now . . . If you like this we're engaged. *(MIDGE moans softly, frightened)* Don't worry; breaks is also nothing. Everybody breaks. Me, I got a hip like a teacup. Twice last year; I just got rid of my walker. *(Continues checking* MIDGE'S *left leg;* MIDGE *winces)* I was also dead once for a while. Six minutes. Also nothing; don't worry. They're doing a By-Pass, everything stops; they had to jump-start me like a Chevrolet. *(Starts checking* MIDGE'S *right leg;* MIDGE *apprehensive)* Six minutes dead, the doctor said. You know what it's like? Boring. First thing you float up and stick to the ceiling like a kid's balloon, you look around. Down below on the bed there's a body you wouldn't give a nickel for. It's you. Meanwhile you're up on the ceiling; nobody sees you. Not bad for a while, nice; you meet some other dead guys, everybody smiles, you hear a little music;

but mostly boring. *(He has finished checking* MIDGE'S *legs)* O.K.; can you move your arms? *(*MIDGE *demonstrates a few, short boxing jabs)* Excellent. O.K., good news: each item functional. Now, from experience, lie there and relax five minutes before you get up. *(*MIDGE *murmurs obediently)* O.K., best thing for relaxing is jokes— *(Rising to center bench near him)* Willy Howard, you hearda him? The best. O.K., years ago he had this great routine, see—

MIDGE   That was another lie, wasn't it?

NAT   What?

MIDGE   'Bout you bein' dead.

NAT   A *fact*, that was an absolute—

MIDGE   Man, you ain't even *friendly* with the truth! *Lies.* Goddamn *lies!* *(Slaps the ground)* It's your goddamn lies put me on the canvas here! Got me fightin', fallin' down—

NAT   *Not* lies— *(Sits upright on bench)* Alterations! I make certain alterations. Sometimes the truth don't fit; I take in here, I let out there, till it fits. The *truth?* What's true is a triple bypass last year at Lenox Hill, what's true is Grade Z cuts of meat from the A and P, a Social Security check that wouldn't pay the rent for a chipmunk; what's true is going to the back door of the Plaza Hotel every morning for yesterday's club-rolls. I tell them it's for the pigeons. I'm the pigeon. Six minutes dead is *true*— *(takes bunch of pages from briefcase)* here, Dr. Reissman's bills; here's the phone number, call him. A fact. And that was my last fact. Since then, alterations. Since I died, a new policy! This morning I tell the counterman at the Farm Fresh Deli I'm an American Indian. An Iroquois. He listens; next thing I know I'm remembering the old days on the plains, the broken treaties, my Grandpa fighting the cavalry. Not important *he's* convinced; *I* am, and I love it. I was one person for eighty-one years, why not a hundred for the next five?!

MIDGE   *(after a moment, resting on his elbows, thoughtfully)* Them club-rolls; how early you figure a fellah oughta show up down there to—

NAT   *Rolls, rolls*; you missed the whole *point*—

MIDGE   *(rising carefully to small bench)* The *point?* I *got* the point; the point is you're crazy, the point is you ain't never seein' your marbles again!

NAT   Ah, how fortunate, an expert on mental health. My daughter

Clara, she's another expert— *(holds up one of the pages)* here, wants to put me in a home for the ridiculous. "No sense of reality," she writes; "in need of supervision," she writes. This she writes to my therapist, Dr. Engels. Trouble is I don't have a therapist and I'm Dr. Engels. I give her the address of the Young Socialists' Club on Eighty-Sixth; I'm listed there as Doctor Friedrich Engels. *(Leans closer to him)* Crazy, you say? Listen to me, listen to Dr. Engels. You're a wreck. Look at you; is this who you want to be? Is this what you had in mind for old, this guy here? A man who obviously passed away some time ago? Whatta you got left, five minutes, five months? Is this how you want to spend it? Sitting and staring, once in a while for a thrill falling down? *(Urgently)* No, *wrong*; you gotta shake things *up*, fellah; you gotta make things *happen*—

MIDGE   *(truly outraged)* Hold it now! Hold that mouth right there! You tellin' *me* how to live? *You* tellin' *me*? You talkin' to an employed person here, Mister! *(Retrieving his newspaper from* NAT'S *bench, returning with great dignity to his own)* Midge Carter; you talkin' to Midge Carter here, boy—Super-in-tendent in charge of Three Twenty-One Central Park West; *run* the place, *been* runnin' it forty-two years, July. They got a furnace been there long as *I* have—an ol' Eric City Special, fourteen *tonner*, known to *kill* a man don't show he's boss. Buildin' don't move without that bull and that bull don't move without *me*. Don't have to make up nobody to be when I *am* somebody! *(Settling himself proudly on small bench)* Shake things up, huh? Don't shake *nothin'* up. How you figure I keep my job? Near fifteen years past retirement, how you figure I'm still super there? I ain't mentioned a raise in fifteen years, and they ain't neither. Moved to the night-shift three years ago, outa the public eye. Daytime a buncha A-rab Supers has come and gone, not Midge. Dozen Spic Doormen dressed up like five-star generals, come and gone, not Midge. Mister, you lookin' at the wise old invisible man.

NAT   No, I'm looking at a dead man! *(Points cane at him)* Fifteen years, no raise; it's a dead person, a ghost! You let them rob you!

MIDGE   They don't rob me; *nobody* robs me, got a system. You see that boy come every day, five o'clock? That's Gilley; give him three bucks, nobody robs me. Ten blocks from here to my place, walks me there, protects me.

NAT   From who?

MIDGE   Him, for one. Fifteen a week, he don't rob me—but nobody *else* neither, see; now *that's* Social Security—

NAT   *(laughing)* Oh, God—

MIDGE   Keep chucklin', sugar; ain't nobody dyin' of old age in *this* neighborhood.

NAT   Job! I see what your *job* is. Groveling! You're a licensed groveler!

MIDGE   *(rises from bench, shouting)* Super at Three Twenty-one, still got a *callin'*—only thing people got to call *you* is, "hey, old man!"

NAT   What do *you* know? What does a *ghost* know? *(Rising proudly)* People *see* me; they *see* me! I *make* them see me! *(His cane in the air)* The night they rushed me to Lenox Hill for the By-Pass, as they carried me out on the *stretcher*, six tenants called the Landlord to see if my apartment was available. Now, every *day*, every day at dawn I ring their bells, all six of them—the door opens, I holler "Good morning, Vulture; Four B is still unavailable!" I hum the first two bars of "The Internationale" and walk away.

MIDGE   *(moving towards him)* Old *fool*, crazy old fool; they can't see *you*. They can hear ya, but they sure can't *see* ya. Don't want to *look* at your old face; mine neither—I just help 'em out. Don't you get it, baby?—*both* of us ghosts only *you* ain't noticed. We old and not rich and done the sin of leavin' slow. No use to fight it, you go with it or you break, boy; 'specially bones like *we* got.

NAT   *(shouting)* Traitor! Traitor in the ranks! It's people like you give old a bad name—

DANFORTH'S VOICE   *(shouting)* Carter—

NAT   It's *your* type that—

DANFORTH'S VOICE   Carter— *(Peter Danforth enters on the bridge, Up Left, jogging; he is the same man who ran by earlier. Danforth is in his early forties and wears a newly purchased jogging outfit)* Carter . . . ah, good, *there* you are, Carter . . .

MIDGE   *(glancing about, not sure who it is or where the voice is coming from)* Midge Carter, here I am.

DANFORTH   *(slowing his pace)* Here, up here . . . on the bridge . . . *(jogging in place, cordially)* Danforth . . . Peter Danforth, Twelve H . . .

MIDGE   *(squinting up)* Danforth, right . . .

DANFORTH   *(breathlessly)* Been looking for you—several days now—they told me you might be in this area—our meeting, remember?

MIDGE   Our meetin', yeah . . .

DANFORTH   How about right here, soon as I finish my run?

MIDGE   Right here, you got it.

DANFORTH   Be right with you . . . *(Quickening his pace again)* Three more miles, be right with you, Carter; looking forward to it . . .

MIDGE   *(shouting up, as Danforth exits right)* Lookin' forward to the meetin', yessir; been on my schedule . . . *(Suddenly whispering, terrified)* Oh shit, the Man, the Man, he found me—

NAT   What man?

MIDGE   *The* Man, *the* Man, been duckin' him, he *found* me.

NAT   *What* man? What is it, Carter?

MIDGE   *(sits on center bench, trembling, brushing off clothes, adjusting hat, trying to pull himself together)* Mr. Danforth, Twelve H, Head o' the Tenants' Committee. Place is goin' Co-op, he says they got some reorganizin' to do, says he wants to see me private . . .

NAT   *(softly, nodding)* Ah, yes . . .

MIDGE   Last fellah wanted to see me private was when they found my wife Daisy under the Seventy-Ninth Street Crosstown. *(Buttoning sweater, trying for a bit of dignity)* See, problem is, it's been gettin' around the buildin' that I'm kinda nearsighted—

NAT   *(sitting next to him)* Nearsighted? Helen *Keller* was *near*sighted.

MIDGE   Got the place memorized, see. But last week I'm in the basement, lady from Two A sees me walk right smack into the elevator door. Mrs. Carsten, Two A, she's standin' in the laundry room watchin' me. Figured I'd fake her out, so I do it *again*, like I was *meanin'* to do it, like it's this *plan* I got to walk into the elevator door—dumb, dumb, *knowed* it was a dumb move while I was *doin'* it. Just kept slammin' into that elevator door till she went away. I'm shoutin', "gonna have this thing fixed in a jiffy, Mrs. Carsten!" Next thing I know Danforth wants to see me private. *(Hits himself on the head)* Panicked on the *ropes* is what I did; that's what blew it for me in the ring too . . .

(Silence for a moment)

NAT   *(quietly)* Are the cataracts in both eyes?

MIDGE   *(after a moment; quietly)* Yeah.

NAT   How many times removed?

MIDGE   Left twice, the right once. But they come back.

NAT   That's what they do. They're dependable. And how bad is the glaucoma?

MIDGE   Drops an' pills keep it down. 'Cept night-times. Night-times—

NAT   Night-times it's like you're trying to close your lid over a basketball.

MIDGE   No lie. No *lie*. When'd it start with you? Start with me four, five years back; nothin' on the sides. No p'ripheral vision, doc says. Five years back— *(he waves)* so long, p'ripheral vision. Then one mornin' there's this spot in the middle . . .

NAT   Ah, the spot, the spot . . .

MIDGE   Like the moon, this dead pearly spot . . .

NAT   The moon exactly . . .

MIDGE   And it gets to growin' . . .

NAT   Oh, yes . . .

MIDGE   Then, thank the Lord, it stops. Then what you got is the pearly moon spot, no p'ripherals, and this ring between 'em where folks come in and out.

NAT   Exactly; like birds. *(Leans close to him)* You get color or black and white?

MIDGE   Mostly blue. Blue shadows like. Weird thing is, all my dreams is still in full color, see everything real sharp and clear like when I was young—then I wake up and it's real life looks like a dream.

NAT   Exactly! Same with me *exactly!* I hadn't thought about it till this minute! *(His arm around* MIDGE*)* Carter, we're connected. Why? Because we both got vision. Who needs sight when we got vision! Connected! Yes, even with your cowardly personality and your chicken-shit attitude. Yes, I'm sure now. Our meeting with Danforth will go well, I'm convinced.

MIDGE   *Our* meetin'? What—

NAT   Yes, I have decided to handle this Danforth matter for you.

Don't worry, the Exploiters, the Land Owners, the Capitalist Fat Cats, I eat them for lunch.

MIDGE   *(alarmed)* Hold on now, boy, I never asked—

NAT   Don't thank *me*. I ask for nothing in return, only to see justice. Don't thank me; thank Karl Marx, thank Lenin, thank Gorky, thank Olgin—

MIDGE   Hey, don't need *none* o' you guys—

NAT   But mostly thank Ben Gold; in Nineteen-Nineteen I join the Communist Party and the human race and meet Ben Gold. He's the one, *that* was vision— *(as* MIDGE *starts to edge away from him on the bench)* Ben Gold, who organized the Fur Workers and gave them a heart and a center and a voice! What a voice, you thought it was yours. I'm matching skins at Supreme Furs, he makes me Assistant Shop Chairman; I'm at his side when we win. A ten percent wage increase and the first forty-hour week in the city! We win! *(Bangs his cane on the ground)* Where is he? Where is Danforth? Bring him to me. Bring me the Fascist four-flusher!

MIDGE   *(softly, covering his face)* Oh my God . . .

NAT   *(turns to answer* MIDGE*)* O.K., O.K., the Soviet Union, throw it up to me; everybody does. They screwed up, I'm the first one to admit it. I promise you, Carter, they lost me, *finished.* I gave up on them . . . but I never gave up on the ideas. The triumph of the proletariat, a workers' democracy, the ideas are still fine and beautiful, the ideas go on, they are better than the people who had them. Ben Gold, they hit him with the Taft-Hartley and the fire goes out, but the voice goes on; the conflict goes on like the turning of the stars and we will crush Danforth before suppertime.

*(*NAT *taps his cane with finality; sits back, crosses his legs, waiting for his adversary.* MIDGE *is silent for a moment. Then he turns to* NAT, *quietly, calmly)*

MIDGE   You done now? You finished talkin'? *(*NAT *nods, not looking at him)* O.K., listen to me; Danforth comes, don't want you speakin'. Not a word. Not one word. Don't even want you here. Got it? You open your face once I'm gonna give Gilley ten bucks to nail you permanent. Got that? Am I comin' through clear?

NAT   *(turns to* MIDGE, *smiling graciously)* Too late. I have no choice. I'm obligated. The conflict between me and Danforth is inevitable. I am obligated to get you off your knees and into the sunlight.

MIDGE   No you ain't. Lettin' you outa that obligation right now. *(Leans towards* NAT, *urgently)* *Please*, it's O.K., I got it all worked out what to say to him. Just gotta hang in till I get my Christmas tips, see—they only got to keep me three more months till Christmas and I'll be—

NAT   Christmas! Compromises! How do you think we lost Poland? Danforth has no right! The man has no right to dismiss you before your time—

MIDGE   Man, I'm eighty-*one*—

NAT   And when we finish with *him*, at five o'clock we'll take care of the hoodlum, Gilley. Together we'll teach *that* punk a lesson!

MIDGE   *(looks up at the sky, desperately)* Why, Lord? Why are you doing this to me? Lord, I asked you for help and you sent me a weird Commie blind man . . .

NAT   What Lord? Who is this Lord you're talking to? Oh *boy*, I can see I've got a lot of work to do here . . .

MIDGE   *(turning sharply up right)* Shit, here he comes, the Man comin' now . . .

NAT   *(turning up right)* Ah, good, I'm ready . . .

MIDGE   *(grips* NAT'S *arm)* Please, baby; I'm askin' ya, please be quiet—

NAT   Calm down, Carter—

MIDGE   Never done you no harm—

NAT   It's not him anyway. *(Leans to right, peering up at bridge)* No, definitely not him. It's a pretty girl.

MIDGE   How do you know?

NAT   Because of the glow. When I could see, all pretty girls had a glow. Now what's left is the glow. That's how you can tell.

(LAURIE enters Up Right on the bridge, and she is a pretty girl—soft, delicate, innocent, about twenty-five, wearing a dress to match the gentle October day. Carrying a large sketchpad and a box of charcoals, she crosses to an old stone ledge beneath a lamppost at the far left side of the bridge, unaware of MIDGE and NAT, who are some distance below her. Once at the ledge she closes her eyes and breathes deeply, inhaling the view of the lake; then she settles herself on the ledge and

proceeds briskly, studiously, to sketch the view—all this as MIDGE *and* NAT *continue their dialogue)*

NAT   Yes, definitely; a pretty girl . . .

MIDGE   *(rising urgently from bench)* Maybe so, but the Man comin' soon— *(pulling* NAT *to his feet)* time for the *Man*, time for you to go—

NAT   Calm down, Carter, you're hysterical—

MIDGE   *(moving* NAT *away from bench)* Ain't you got an appointment someplace? Whyn't you go tell somebody you're an Apache—

NAT   *(with genuine concern)* All right, all right, *you* will handle Danforth; I will permit it.

MIDGE   *(warily)* You mean that?

NAT   Of course, but first you must calm yourself—

MIDGE   I'll calm myself—

NAT   This is essential. In your present state the Land Baron will walk all over you; I cannot allow that. Here, this will do the trick— *(Reaches quickly into his jacket pocket, withdrawing small brown business envelope)* Here, some Government Grass to relax you. Official, legal; dope from Uncle Sam. The doctor prescribes, the government pays; two ounces a month for the glaucoma. Dilates the capillaries, relieves the pressure; everywhere. *(Takes a joint from the envelope)* Here. All rolled. Be my guest. Medicaid is paying.

MIDGE   *(peering anxiously off right)* Better not; makes me foolish sometimes. Ain't no time to get foolish—

NAT   Not foolish. Happy. I promise, you'll laugh at the Six O'Clock News. Even your children become amusing. *(Lights joint, inhales, hands it out to* MIDGE*)* Please, calm yourself. Here, take a hit, Danforth will be a piece of cake; one puff, the man is a Danish.

MIDGE   *(still very much on guard)* You swear you'll keep your mouth shut when the Man comes, shut *tight*—I'll take a puff.

NAT   Here, direct from the White House. *(MIDGE hesitates a moment; then takes a deep drag)* Good; now hold it in as long as you—

MIDGE   I know, I know; I was smokin' dope while you was eatin' Matzoh-balls, baby. *(Another deep drag, hands it back to* NAT*)* Fair stuff. Just fair.

(The distant sound of the Carousel Band-Organ begins off left as

though carried on the autumn breeze. LAURIE *looks up from her sketching for a moment, smiles, hearing the gently drifting melody of "That Old Gang of Mine."* MIDGE *and* NAT *will pass the joint back and forth between them as their dialogue continues, the grass gradually starting to reach them)*

MIDGE   *(glancing anxiously up right)* Man say three miles, he sure takin' it slow.

NAT   Maybe he dropped dead. *(On the inhale, handing joint to* MIDGE*)* A lot of these running people; boom.

MIDGE   *(on the inhale)* Young fellah like him?

NAT   They're the first ones; the young ones. Boom. They're running, they're smiling; boom. You should be here in the evening, they drop like flies . . . *(Chuckling, taking joint from* MIDGE*)* Boom, boom, boom . . . *(*MIDGE *chuckles along with him,* NAT *studies the joint fondly for a moment)* All my life I fought for Socialized Medicine . . .

MIDGE   Stopped smoking dope when I turned seventy . . .

NAT   *(peering up at* LAURIE*)* That girl just went from very pretty to beautiful . . .

MIDGE   Scared of goin' foolish. My Daddy went foolish five years before he died, didn't know his own name. Sad to see. Hope I ain't the only one hearin' that music.

NAT   *(moving towards bench, squinting up at* LAURIE*)* Now she's Hannah Pearlman . . .

MIDGE   Who?

NAT   *(sits on bench; softly)* Hannah Pearlman. She worked as a Finisher, stitched linings for yachting caps, Shiffman's Chapeaux on West Broadway. Nineteen Twenty-One.

MIDGE   *(joins* NAT *at bench; squints up at* LAURIE *for a moment)* No, ain't her. Tell you who you got there; that's Ella Mae Tilden . . .

(Both looking up at LAURIE *as they talk, getting more and more stoned; the gentle Carousel Music continuing, bringing the past with it on the breeze. Now, in this delicate, dappled, late-afternoon light,* LAURIE *truly seems to have the glow that* NAT *described)*

NAT   Very shy, shyer even than me. She would sit on her stoop in the early evening, a fine, fine face like an artist would paint . . .

MIDGE   Ella Mae; best wife I had, number three. Five all told. It's Ella

Mae give me John, it's John give me Billy, and it's Billy give me these teeth . . .

NAT   I passed that stoop a million times; I couldn't say hello. Funny-looking fingers from the stitching, she sat on the stoop with her hands hidden, like so . . .

MIDGE   Eight grandchildren professionals and Billy's the dentist. Billy give me this smile. *(He demonstrates)*   Put the teeth in, smiled, and left Ella Mae. Smile needed a new hat, and the hat made me walk a new way, which was out . . .

NAT   Also she was married. Yeah, went to work so her greenhorn husband could go to law school, become an American Somebody. Comes June, Arnold Pearlman graduates, suddenly finds out he's an attorney with a Yiddish-speaking wife who finishes yachting caps. Boom; he leaves her for a smooth-fingered Yankee Doodle he met at school. Four months later Hannah took the gas; a popular expression at that time for putting your head in an oven . . .

MIDGE   Poor Ella Mae cryin', me hearin' my new mouth say goodbye. She was near seventy then, but when my mind moves to her she is fresh peach prime . . .

NAT   September, a month before she took the gas, I see her in the Grand Street Library, second floor reading-room. A special place, quiet, not even a clock; I'm at the main table with *Macbeth*. I look up, there's Hannah Pearlman. She doesn't see me; her head is buried in a grammar book for a ten-year-old. She looks up, she knows me, she smiles. My heart goes directly into my ears, bang, bang, bang, I'm deaf. I don't speak. I can't speak. I'm there in the house of words, I can't speak. She puts her hands under the table, goes back to her book. After a while she leaves. I didn't *speak* . . .

MIDGE   *(bangs his fist on the bench)*   Goddamn smile got me two more wives and nothin' but trouble! Damn these teeth and damn my wanderin' ways . . . *(Takes out huge handkerchief, the Carousel Music fades)*

NAT   I didn't *speak*, I didn't *speak* . . .

MIDGE   *(blowing his nose)*   There's dope makes you laugh and dope makes you cry. I think this here's cryin' dope.

NAT   *(bangs his cane on the ground)*   Stop, stop! Nostalgia, I hate it! The dread disease of old people! Kills more of us than heart failure!

MIDGE   *(drying his eyes)* When's the last time you made love to a woman?

NAT   Listen to him, more nostalgia! My poor shmeckle, talk about nostalgia! It comes up once a year, like Ground Hog Day. The last time I made love was July Tenth, Nineteen Seventy-One.

MIDGE   Was your wife still alive?

NAT   I certainly hope so.

MIDGE   No, I meant—

NAT   I know what you meant. With Ethel it wasn't always easy to tell. *(Smacks his forehead) Shame* on me! A good woman, a fine woman, was it *her* fault I would always be in love with Hannah Pearlman?

MIDGE   See, last time for me I was bein' unfaithful. Damn my fickle soul, I cheated on them all. Daisy, I was seventy-six, still had somethin' on the side; somethin' new.

NAT   Carter, this is the most courageous thing I ever heard about you.

MIDGE   No courage to it, it's a curse. "Don't do it, Midge; don't *do* it," I kept sayin' while I did it. *Damn* my cheatin' soul.

NAT   No, no, you were *right!* You dared and did, I yearned and regretted. I *envy* you. You were always what I have only recently become.

MIDGE   A dirty old man.

NAT   A *romanticist!* A man of hope! Listen to me, I was dead once so I know things—it's not the sex, it's the romance. It's all in the head. Now, finally, I know this. The shmeckle is out of business, but still the romance remains, the adventure. That's all there *ever* was. The body came along for the ride. Do you understand me, Carter?

MIDGE   I'm thinkin' about it . . .

NAT   Because, frankly, right now I'm in love with this girl here.

MIDGE   *(after a moment)* Well, fact is, so am I. I got to admit. *(Peers up at* LAURIE *for a few seconds)* Son of a gun . . . First time I ever fell in love with a white woman.

NAT   The first? Why the first?

MIDGE   Worked out that way.

NAT   All the others were black? Only black women?

MIDGE   Listen, you ran with a wild, Commie crowd; where *I* come from you stuck with your own. Bein' a black man, I—

NAT   A what?

MIDGE   A black man. Y'see, in *my* day—

NAT   Wait. Stop. Excuse me . . . *(A beat; then* NAT *takes his bifocals out of his jacket pocket, puts them on, leans very close to* MIDGE. *He studies him for a few moments; then, quietly)* My God, you're right. You *are* a black man.

(Silence for a moment. Then NAT *bursts into laughter, pointing at* MIDGE*)*

MIDGE   *(after a moment, catching on to the joke, a burst of laughter)* Sly devil, you sly ol' *devil* . . .

NAT   *(laughing happily, pointing at* MIDGE*)* Hey, had ya goin', had ya *goin'* there for a minute, didn't I . . . ?

MIDGE   *(claps his hands, delighted laughter building)* Had me goin', had me *goin'*, yeah . . . Lord, Lord . . .

NAT   *(hitting his knees, roaring)* I love it, I love it, I love it—

(Fresh gales of stoned laughter; they rock on the bench)

MIDGE   Stop, stop, I'm gonna die . . .

NAT   I'm gonna drop dead right here . . . *(Suddenly stops laughing)* Wait a minute, Carter; is it *this* funny?

MIDGE   *(Stops laughing. Considers it. Bursts into laughter again)* Yes, it is. It is, definitely . . .

(They point at each other, laughing at each other's laughter, laughing now at the fact that they are *laughing; they fall on each other, shaking with mirth, threatening to roll off the bench.* MIDGE *suddenly leans back on the bench and abruptly falls asleep, snoring loudly)*

NAT   Carter, what are you doing? We're right in the middle . . . *(*MIDGE *keeps snoring)* How do you like that? One joint, look at this.

*(*MIDGE *suddenly wakes up and, as if by request, bursts into song)*

MIDGE   *(singing)*

> "I'm Alabamy bound,
>   there'll be no heebie-jeebies hangin' 'round . . .

(Rises to his feet, singing, strutting, gradually working in a small soft-shoe)

Just gave the meanest ticket-man on earth
all I'm worth
to put my tootsies in an upper berth.
Just hear that choo-choo sound,
I know that soon we're gonna cover ground . . . "

(NAT *rises to his feet, inspired, joining in the soft-shoe, finishing the song with him*)

MIDGE and NAT   (*harmonizing*)

"And then I'll holler so the world will know,
here I go,
I'm Alabamy booooouuuund!"

(LAURIE, *who has been listening to* MIDGE *and* NAT *sing their song from her ledge on the bridge, far above them, smiles at them now, nods her approval, holds her hands up in a brief moment of applause, then returns to her sketching*)

MIDGE   I think the woman's crazy about us.

NAT   Please, I knew it when she first showed up.

MIDGE   You got any more of that dope?

NAT   Now we're gonna do a Willy Howard routine. You think you were laughing *before*, wait'll you hear—

MIDGE   How about I do a Joe Turner song first, and *then* we do Willy Howard?

NAT   You just sang.

MIDGE   (*sitting* NAT *on bench*)   That was half an hour ago.

NAT   Really?

MIDGE   (*looking up, announcing this for* LAURIE)   "So Long, Goodbye Blues," by Big Joe Turner, Boss of the Blues—

(*Singing soulfully; a slow steady rhythm, snapping his fingers, performing for* LAURIE)

"Well now, so long, goodbye, baby
Yeah, well, soon now I'm gonna be gone
And that's why I'm sayin', baby—"

NAT   (*a burst of applause, rising*)   That was exquisite. Now here's Willy Howard— (*Glancing up at* LAURIE, *performing this for her*) O.K., Carter, I'm Willy Howard, you're the Straight Man. Whatever I say to you, you say to me, "I'm not Rappaport." You got that?

MIDGE   Yeah.

NAT   O.K., picture we just met.

MIDGE   O.K.

NAT   Hello, Rappaport!

MIDGE   I'm not Rappaport.

NAT   Hey, Rappaport, what happened to you? You used to be a tall, fat guy; now you're a short, skinny guy.

MIDGE   I'm not Rappaport.

NAT   You used to be a young fellah with a beard; now you're an old guy without a beard! What happened to you?

MIDGE   I'm not Rappaport.

NAT   What happened, Rappaport? You used to dress up nice; now you got old dirty clothes!

MIDGE   I'm not Rappaport.

NAT   And you changed your *name* too!

(A beat—then NAT *bursts into laughter; even if he wasn't stoned, this routine would leave him helpless.* MIDGE *regards him solemnly, thinking it over—then suddenly gets it, joining* NAT'S *laughter, pounding* NAT'S *shoulder)*

MIDGE   *(through his laughter)* "And you changed your *name too . . .* " Lord, Lord . . . *(Shouting up at* LAURIE *to make sure she got the punch-line)* "And you changed your *name too!*"

DANFORTH'S VOICE   *(shouting)* Right with you, Carter . . .

*(*DANFORTH *enters on bridge, at left, jogging)*

MIDGE   *(still laughing)* Oh, shit; he's here . . .

DANFORTH   Right with you . . .

NAT   *(laughing)* He's here! Good!

MIDGE   *(trying to control his laughter)* He's here, gotta shape up, boy . . . *(Scurries to bench to get* NAT'S *briefcase)*

NAT   *(delighted)* Don't worry, we'll take care of him—

MIDGE   No, no, there's no *"we"*; there's no "we" here— *(Grips* NAT'S *arm urgently, tries to stop himself from laughing)* You don't say *nothin'*, Mister, you don't open your *mouth . . . (A fresh burst of laughter)* You'll ruin me, boy; I'll be out on the street *tomorrow . . .*

(Danforth stops on bridge, winding down from his run, jogging in place, controlling his breaths, stretching himself against the bridge lamppost at right)

NAT   A piece of cake. The little I can see, the man is a wreck.

MIDGE   *(still chuckling softly)*   Please, *please*, baby . . . are you my friend?

NAT   Of course.

MIDGE   Then go over there, friend. *(Points to stone ledge, far left, at edge of lake)*   Sit over there and don't open your mouth. Not a word.

NAT   *(after a moment)*   You'll call me when you need me?

MIDGE   *(hands* NAT *his briefcase)*   Soon's I need you. Please, move it.

NAT   *(he has stopped chuckling)*   O.K., O.K. . . . *(Reluctantly, he starts down left)*   Remember, I'm ready.

MIDGE   I know that.

(DANFORTH, *having completed his winding-down ritual on the bridge, starts down towards* MIDGE *at the bench, entering through the Tunnel Archway, mopping himself with a towel.* NAT *settles himself with some dignity on the far left ledge, some distance from them, crossing his legs, his briefcase and his cane at his side.* LAURIE *has stretched out on the bridge ledge above, her eyes closed, a Walkman plugged into her ears, her shoulder-bag under her head)*

DANFORTH   Carter, hi.

MIDGE   Hi.

DANFORTH   Don't think we've ever really been formally introduced. I'm Pete Danforth.

(They shake hands)

MIDGE   Hi, Pete. They call me "Midge."

DANFORTH   Hi, Midge. Glad we decided to meet here. Chance to stay outside, y'know, after my run. Truth is, I hate running. Being immortal takes too much time. *(He chuckles)*

MIDGE   *(sitting on bench)*   "Midge" for Midget. My third wife give me the name; near two and three-quarter inches taller'n me, so she called me "Midge." Name stuck with me fifty years.

DANFORTH   Tell ya one thing, it's good to be reminded of what a great park this is. Goddamn oasis in the middle of the jungle.

MIDGE   Next two wives was normal-sized women, so it didn't make much sense. Name stuck with me anyway.

DANFORTH   Luckily my teaching schedule gives me two free afternoons this semester. Chance to really use this park. It's been years. I teach Communication Arts over at the Manhattan Institute on Sixtieth. No air in the place. Dreary. Been thinking about holding one of my classes out here in the—

MIDGE   What kinda arts?

DANFORTH   Communication. Communications of all kinds. Personal, interpersonal, and public; pretty much the whole range of—

MIDGE   You teach talkin'.

DANFORTH   *(smiles)* More or less; yes.

MIDGE   So you must know we 'bout at the end of the chit-chat section now; right?

DANFORTH   Right, right . . . *(Sits next to* MIDGE *on bench, carefully folding his towel)* Funny thing, by the way, I really didn't know—that is, I wasn't aware until just a few days ago—that you actually worked in the building; that you were employed there.

MIDGE   Keep to myself. Do my job.

DANFORTH   Of course. I just wanted you to know that the problem we've got here had not come to my attention sooner simply because you, personally, had not come to my attention. Frankly, I've been living there three years and I've never run into you.

MIDGE   I'm mostly down in the boiler room; don't get a lot of drop-ins.

DANFORTH   Of course.

(Silence for a moment)

MIDGE   Keep movin', boy, you on a roll now.

DANFORTH   Yes, well, as you know, Three Twenty-One will be going Co-op in November. We'll be closing on that in November. We've got Brachman and Rader as our Managing Agent; I think they're doing an excellent job. As President of the Tenants' Committee I'm pretty much dependent, the whole Committee is really, on their advice; we've basically got to place our faith in the recommendations of our Managing Agency.

MIDGE   And they're recommendin' you dump me.

DANFORTH   Midge, we've got some real problems about your remaining with the building staff.

MIDGE   Ain't that the same as dumpin' me?

DANFORTH   *(after a moment)* Midge, it's not for four weeks, it's not till November, but, yes, we will have to let you go. There are various benefits, Union Pension Plan, six weeks Severance pay; that's a check for six weeks salary the day you leave, that's . . . Midge, I'm sorry . . . *(sadly; shaking his head)* God, I hate this; I really hate this, Midge . . .

MIDGE   How 'bout *I* hate it first, then you get your turn.

DANFORTH   *(quietly)* Midge, think about it, isn't this the best thing for *every*body? The pressure on you, tenants' complaints, trying to keep up. *(His hand on* MIDGE'S *arm)* Time, Midge—we're not dealing with an evil Tenants' Committee or a heartless Managing Agent—the only villain here is time. We're *all* fighting it. Jesus, man, have you seen me *run?* It's a joke. I can't do what *I* did a few years ago either.

MIDGE   Hey, don't sweat it, son. See, Brachman and Rader, all due respect, is full of shit. Fact is, you need me. *(Leans back calmly)* Got an ol' Erie City boiler down there; heart of the buildin'. Things about that weird machine no livin' man knows, 'cept Midge Carter. Christmas. Take me till Christmas to train a new man how to handle that devil. *(Pats* DANFORTH'S *knee)* You got it, have the new man set up for ya by Christmas.

DANFORTH   Midge, we're replacing the Erie City. We're installing a fully automatic Rockmill Five Hundred; it requires no maintenance. *(Silence for a moment;* MIDGE *does not respond)* You see, the Rockmill's just one of many steps in an extensive modernization plan; new electrical system, plumbing arteries, lobby renovation—

MIDGE   Well, *now* you're *really* gonna need me. Pipes, wires, you got forty years of temporary stuff in there, no blueprints gonna tell you where. Got it all in my head; know what's behind every wall, every stretch of tar. *(Clamps his hand on* DANFORTH'S *shoulder)* O.K., here's the deal. My place in the basement, *I* stay on there free like I been, *you* get all my consultin' free. No *salary*, beauty deal for ya—

DANFORTH   Midge, to begin with, your unit in the basement is being placed on the co-op market as a garden apartment—

MIDGE   Don't you get it, baby? Blueprints, blueprints, I'm a walkin' treasure-map—

DANFORTH   Please understand, we've had a highly qualified team of building engineers doing a survey for months now—

MIDGE   *(suddenly)* Hey, forget it.

DANFORTH   You see, they—

MIDGE   I said forget it. Ain't interested in the job no more. Don't *want* the job. Withdrawin' my offer. *(Turns away; opens his newspaper)*

DANFORTH   *(moving closer)* Midge, listen to me . . .

MIDGE   Shit, all these years I been livin' in a garden apartment. Wished I knew sooner, woulda had a lot more parties.

DANFORTH   I have some news that I think will please you . . . *(His hand. on* MIDGE'S *arm)* Two of the older tenants on the Committee, Mrs. Carpenter, Mr. Lehman, have solved your relocation problem. Midge, there's an apartment for you at the Amsterdam. No waiting list for *you*, Mr. Lehman seems to know the right people. Caters especially to low-income senior adults and it's right here in the neighborhood you've grown used to—

MIDGE   Amsterdam's ninety percent foolish people. Ever been in the lobby there? Ever seen them sittin' there? Only way you can tell the live ones from the dead ones is how old their newspapers are.

DANFORTH   As I understand it from Mr. Lehman—

MIDGE   Amsterdam's the end of the *line*, boy.

DANFORTH   I'm sorry, I thought—

MIDGE   You ask Mr. Lehman *he* wants to go sit in that lobby; you ask Mrs. Carpenter *she* ready to leave the world. You tell 'em both "no thanks" from Midge, he's lookin' for a garden apartment.

DANFORTH   See, the problem is—

MIDGE   Problem is you givin' me bad guy news, tryin' to look like a good guy doin' it.

DANFORTH   *(after a moment)* You're right, Midge. You're right. You're dead right. *(Bows his head, genuinely upset)* I've handled this whole thing badly, stupidly, *stupidly*. I'm sorry, this whole thing . . . this is terrible . . .

MIDGE   *(patting* DANFORTH'S *hand)* Don't worry, Pete, you're gonna get through it.

DANFORTH   *(rises, pacing in front of bench)* Damn it, I tell you what I *can* do—what I *will* do—I'm getting you *ten* weeks Severance, Midge. *Forget* six, a check for ten weeks salary the day you go, I'm gonna hand it to you *personally*. And if the Committee doesn't agree, the hell with them; I'll shove it through, that's all. Least I can do. Ten weeks Severance—how does that sound to ya?

MIDGE   Well, better than six, I guess . . . *(Nods thoughtfully)* Sounds better, but I—

DANFORTH   *(shaking* MIDGE'S *hand with both of his)* That's a promise, Midge. Shove it down their throats if I have to. *(Moving briskly towards the stone steps at right to exit)* I'm sure we'll have no problem with—

NAT   Unacceptable. *(Calmly, rising from ledge at far left)* We find that unacceptable. *(*DANFORTH *stops,* NAT *moves slowly towards him)* Mr. Danforth . . . Mr. Danforth, I'll speak frankly, you're in a lot of trouble. *(Brisk handshake)* Ben Reissman; Reissman, Rothman, Rifkin and Grady. Forgive me for not announcing myself sooner, but I couldn't resist listening to you bury yourself. Our firm represents Mr. Carter, but, more to the point, we act as legal advisors to the HURTSFOE unit of Mr. Carter's union. HURTSFOE; I refer to the Human Rights Strike Force, a newly formed automatic-action unit who, I'm sorry to say, you're going to be hearing a lot from in the next few weeks. *(Sits next to* MIDGE *on bench,* DANFORTH *standing before them)* Personally, I find their methods too extreme; but I report and advise, that's all I can do. The ball is rolling here, Mr. Danforth.

MIDGE   Go away.

NAT   Mr. Carter keeps saying to us "go away"; we were arguing this very point as you ran by earlier. But, of course, as he knows, we are an automatic function of his union for the protection of all members. I have no choice.

MIDGE   *(grips* NAT'S *arm)* Man wants to give me ten weeks Severance—

NAT   A joke. The fellow is obviously a jokester.

DANFORTH   Mr. Reissman—

NAT   Speak to me.

DANFORTH   I'm not sure that I understand the—

NAT   Of course not. How could you? *(Crosses his legs, continuing calmly)* I will educate you. The situation is simple, I will make it simpler. We don't accept ten weeks Severance, we don't accept twenty. What we accept is that Mr. Carter be retained in the capacity of advisor during your reconstruction period, which I assume will take a year, maybe two. At this point, we'll talk further.

MIDGE   *(to* DANFORTH*)* I don't know him; I don't *know* this man.

NAT   Quite so; Mr. Carter is more familiar with Rifkin and Grady, the gentler gentlemen in our firm. It was thought best to send "The Cobra" in on this one. An affectionate term for me at the office.

DANFORTH   *(sharply)* Look, Reissman—

NAT   Speak to me.

DANFORTH   *(steps towards him, firmly)* I don't know what your game is, fellah, and I don't know your organization; but I *do* know Local Thirty-Two of the Service Employees Union—

NAT   And do *they* know you're planning to fire Mr. Carter?

DANFORTH   Not yet, but we—

NAT   And do *you* know that there's no mandatory retirement age in Mr. Carter's union? And do *you* know, further, that this means Carter has the right to call an arbitration hearing where he can defend his competence? And that you will have to get a minimum of four tenants to *testify* against him? Oh, that will be interesting. *Find* them. I want to *see* this, Danforth. Four tenants who want to be responsible—*publicly* responsible—for putting this old man out of his home and profession of forty-two years. *(His hand on* MIDGE'S *shoulder)* A man who was named "Super of the Year" by the New York Post in Nineteen Sixty-Eight: a man who fought in World War Two, a man who served with the now legendary Black Battalion of Bastogne at the Battle of the Bulge. The clippings will be xeroxed and circulated, the worms you find to testify will be informed. *(Rises from bench, pointing cane at* DANFORTH*)* And— and are you aware that for as long as you insist on pursuing this matter, for as long as this hearing lasts—and I promise you we will make it a *long* one—you can *make* no contract with Local Thirty-Two? That without a union contract you can *have* no co-op sale, no building corporation? Time, my friend, time will be *your* villain now. My firm will go *beyond* this hearing if justice fails us there. I'm talking *months*, cookie; I'm talking litigation, appeals, the full weight and guile of Rothman, Rifkin, Grady, and The Cobra. *(He lowers his cane to his side, moves slowly towards* DAN-FORTH; *quietly:)* Sir, I urge you to consider, win or lose, the massive and draining legal fees you will incur in pursuing this matter. I urge you to compare this time, cost, and embarrassment to the tiny sum it will take to keep Mr. Carter on salary. I urge you for *all* our sakes.

*(*DANFORTH *stands there in silence for a few moments, clearly confused.* MIDGE *has remained on the bench, listening with fascination)*

DANFORTH   Reissman . . .

NAT   Speak to me.

DANFORTH   I'm, frankly, a little thrown by this. I . . . I mean, you're asking me to just accept—

NAT   Accept or don't accept; I'm obligated to report this to HURTS-FOE immediately.

DANFORTH   I knew about the right to arbitration—Midge, I just didn't think you'd really want—

NAT   He wants. Meanwhile HURTSFOE goes after you tomorrow anyway. They'll make an example of you, you're perfect for them—

DANFORTH   But what have I—?

NAT   Idiot, you've hit every Human Rights nerve there is. I'm talking old, I'm talking black, I'm talking racial imbalance—

DANFORTH   Racial *imbalance?* The man was walking into *walls.* For God's sake, the man's an easy *eighty.*

NAT   There's nothing, I promise you, easy about eighty. Damn it, why am I even bothering to *warn* you? *(Picks up his briefcase)* Tomorrow you'll see it all. Time to let HURTSFOE out of its cage— *(Turns sharply, starts walking towards stone steps at right, to exit)*

DANFORTH   *(moves towards him, angrily)* Now look, Reissman, I find it hard to believe that I would be held personally responsible for—

NAT   *(starting briskly up steps)* You'll believe it tomorrow when they picket in front of your school. What was the name of that place, the Manhattan Institute? They'll believe it too. And then the demonstrations in front of your apartment building— *(Stops halfway up steps, pointing cane down at* DANFORTH*)* The name Danforth will start to *mean* something—you'll become an *adjective*, my friend, a symbol, a new word for the persecution of the old and disabled, the black and the blind!

DANFORTH Wait a minute—

NAT *Do* it, Danforth, *fire* him, it's your one shot at immortality! *Do* it . . . (MIDGE *holds his hand up in alarm)* Yes, Carter, forgive me, I *want* it to happen . . . I want to see HURTSFOE in action again . . . *(Tenderly, looking away)* Those crazy wildcats, it's hard not to love them. Those mad, inspired men. I want to hear the old words, alive again and pure . . . "Strike for a humane existence" . . . "Strike for universal justice"— *(His cane in the air, shouting)* Strike, strike—

DANFORTH *(shouting)* Hold it! Wait a minute! This . . . this whole goddamn mess has gotten out of *hand* . . . *(Continuing firmly)* Reissman, believe me, this was never my own, personal thing; I represent a *Committee*, the joint wishes of a—

NAT I'm sorry, the spotlight falls on you because it must. Because you are so extraordinarily ordinary, because there are so many of you now. *(Starts down steps towards him)* You collect old furniture, old cars, old pictures, everything old but old people. Bad souvenirs, they talk too much. Even quiet, they tell you too much; they look like the future and you don't want to know. Who *are* these people, these oldies, this strange race? They're not my type, put them with their own *kind*, a building, a town, *put* them someplace. *(Leans towards him)* You idiots, don't you know? One day you *too* will join this weird tribe. Yes, Mr. Chairman, you *will* get old; I hate to break the news. And if you're frightened now, you'll be terrified then. The problem's *not* that life is short but that it's very long; so you better have a policy. Here we are. Look at us. We're the coming attractions. And as long as you're afraid of *it*, you'll be afraid of *us*, you will want to hide us or make us hide from you. You're dangerous. *(Grips his arm urgently)* You foolish bastards, don't you under*stand*? The old people, they're the *survivors*, they *know* something, they haven't just stayed late to ruin your party. The very old, they are miracles like the just-born; close to the end is precious like close to the beginning. What you'd like is for Carter to be nice and cute and quiet and go away. But he won't. I won't let him. Tell him he's slow or stupid— O. K.—but you tell him that he is unnecessary, and that is a sin, that is a sin against life, that is abortion at the other end. *(Silence;* NAT *studies him for a moment)* HURTSFOE waits. The arena is booked, the lions are hungry . . .

DANFORTH　　*(quietly, earnestly)*　Ben, I'm glad you shared these thoughts with me. I'd never really—

NAT　　I'm through communicating with you, I'm communicating with Carter now. *(Sits next to* MIDGE *on bench)*　Carter, what shall we do with him? I leave it to you.

MIDGE　　I think . . . I think we should give him a break.

DANFORTH　　Ben, I'm sure that I can persuade the members of the Committee to reevaluate Midge's—

NAT　　Carter, what are you *saying?* What happens to the Cause? Are you saying you just want to keep your job and forget about the Cause?

MIDGE　　Frankly, yes; that's what I'm sayin'. Forget the Cause, keep the job.

DANFORTH　　*(perches opposite them on small bench)*　I think it's essential that we avoid any extreme—

NAT　　Carter, are you asking The Cobra *not* to strike?

MIDGE　　Don't want that Cobra to strike, no.

DANFORTH　　Next Committee meeting's in two weeks. I'll explain the—

NAT　　Mr. Danforth, my client has instructed me to save your ass. Quickly, the bomb is ticking . . . *(*DANFORTH *leans towards him intently)*　Two weeks is too late. Tonight. Jog home to your phone, call the members of your committee. Don't persuade, don't explain; announce. Tell them there's a job for Carter. Guide. Counselor. How about Superintendent Emeritus? Has a nice sound to it. Meanwhile, speak to *no* one—the union, your Managing Agent, no one. HURTSFOE gets wind of this, we're *all* in trouble. *(Hands him business-card from briefcase)*　When you're finished with the Committee, call here. Before ten tomorrow if you want to stop HURTSFOE. Speak only to the lady on the card, Mrs. Clara Gelber; tell her to reach a man called "Pop"—he's one of HURTSFOE's top people—tell her to inform him that the Carter matter has been resolved, this "Pop" fellow will take it from there.

DANFORTH　　*(reading from card)*　"Park East Real Estate Agency . . .

NAT   HURTSFOE's advisory group; smart people, good hearts, they negotiate with management. *(Hands him another card)* Here; if there's trouble tonight, call me— *(They both rise)* That's my club on Eighty-Sixth, ask for Dr. Engels, he'll contact me. *(Pats* DAN-FORTH'S *cheek)* Goodbye and good luck.

*(*DANFORTH *moves quickly towards the stone steps; stops, turns to them)*

DANFORTH   *(quietly)* Midge . . . Ben . . . I want you to know that this has been a very important conversation for me, for *many* reasons . . . a lot of primary thoughts . . .

NAT   I think it's been an important conversation for all of us. Goodbye.

DANFORTH   An important exchange of ideas, a . . . a sudden aware-ness of certain generational values that I—

NAT   I warn you, one more word and there'll be a citizen's arrest for crimes against the language.

DANFORTH   *(he smiles, shakes his head)* Fact is, certain areas, I *do* have trouble talking . . .

NAT   Also leaving. Go now, the phone! *(*DANFORTH *races briskly up the steps)* Quickly. Let me see those sneakers flash!

*(*DANFORTH *exits.* NAT *turns triumphantly towards* MIDGE, *his cane held high in the air like a sword of victory)*

MIDGE   *(he slumps on the bench)* Never; we ain't never gettin' away with this . . .

NAT   *(to himself, smiling)* Truth is, I always *did* want to be a lawyer . . . but years ago there were so many choices . . .

MIDGE   Black Battalion of *Bastogne?* . . . We ain't never gettin' away with this . . . Gonna catch *on* to us, only a matter of *time* now; find out you ain't no lawyer, find out there ain't no HURTSFOE—

NAT   You're better off than you were twenty minutes ago, right? You still have your job, don't you? A week, a month, by then I'll have a *better* idea, *another* plan. What's wrong with you? Why aren't you awed by this triumph? Why aren't you embracing me?

MIDGE   *(rising, angrily)* Was playin' that boy just *right* 'fore you opened your mouth. Had him goin' for extra Severance—catches on now, I lose it *all*. What I do to deserve you? What I *do*, Reissman—

NAT   Reissman is the name of my surgeon; eight years they trained his hands to take my wallet.

MIDGE   O.K., *Schwartz*man, you're Sam Schwartzman—

NAT   Not him either.

MIDGE   Then who the hell *are* you, Mister? Shit, if you ain't Hernando and you ain't Schwartzman, and you ain't Rappaport, then—

NAT   *(Softly, looking away)* Just now I was Ben Gold. I was Ben for a while . . . You use who you need for the occasion. An occasion arises and one chooses a suitable person to—

(During these last few lines GILLEY *has stepped forward from the shadows on the bridge above, at left, near the ledge where* LAURIE *has drifted off to sleep—a sudden sense of his presence has awakened her; frightened, she has swept up her bag and art supplies, raced across the bridge and exited at right.* GILLEY *is an Irish kid, about sixteen; an impassive, experienced, and almost unreadable face. The faded color of his jeans and jean-jacket and his careful, economical movements make him inconspicuous and, in a sense, part of the park; for all we know he may have been standing there in the shadows for an hour. He has a constant awareness of everything around him, the precision of a pro and the instincts of a street creature. We hear the distant sound of the Carousel Band-Organ playing "Queen City March," the last melody of the fading day. During the last fifteen minutes or so the pretty colors of the autumn afternoon have gradually given way to the dark shadows of early evening, the faint chatter of crickets and the lonely lights of the two lampposts on the bridge, reminding us of the isolated and near-empty section of the park we are in.* GILLEY *stands quite still now on the bridge, a silhouette beneath the lamplight, looking off at what must be the other benches along the lakeside, studying the few remaining people on them and their possessions, considering the possibilities.* NAT *has suddenly interrupted his last speech to look up at the Bridge)*

NAT   Who's that? There's no glow, the girl is gone.

*(*MIDGE *knows the all too familiar figure on the bridge and that it is the appointed "collection" time; he turns away, trying to look unconcerned)*

MIDGE   Nobody. That's nobody.

NAT   That's *him*, right? The punk.

MIDGE   Ain't *the* punk, just some punk.

NAT   That's our punk, isn't it?

MIDGE   Not *our* punk, not *our* punk; just *my* punk.

NAT   Excuse me, I have something to discuss with him—

*(He starts towards the Bridge—*MIDGE *grabs both of* NAT'S *arms and quite forcefully pulls him back—*GILLEY *starts, slowly, casually down the back stairs to the Tunnel, towards* MIDGE *and* NAT*)*

MIDGE   *(a strong grip on* NAT, *whispering urgently)* Now you listen here to *me*, No-Name. This kid, you run your mouth on him he finish you, then finish me sure. Sit down— *(Shoves* NAT *down on bench, sits next to him)* These kids is crazy; beat up old folks for *exercise*, boy. Sass this kid, he stomp us *good*— *(pointing to the off-stage benches)* and these folks here, while he's doin' it they gonna keep *score*, gonna watch like it's happenin' on the TV.

*(*GILLEY *appears in the darkened Tunnel, some distance behind them. He remains quite still, deep in the Tunnel, waiting)*

MIDGE   Toll on this bridge is three dollars and that bridge gonna take me home. *(Rises, taking his newspaper)* Call it a *day*, boy. See you sometime.

*(*MIDGE *starts into the Tunnel towards the waiting* GILLEY. *Silence for a moment)*

GILLEY   *(flatly)* Who's that?

MIDGE   Friend of mine.

GILLEY   Where's he live?

MIDGE   Dunno. Hangs out here; he—

GILLEY   *(moves down behind* NAT'S *bench, leans towards him; quietly)* Where you live?

NAT   First I'll tell you where I work. I work at the Nineteenth Precinct— *(Turns, holds out his hand)* Danforth; Captain Pete Danforth, Special Projects, I—

GILLEY   *(takes his hand; not shaking it, just holding it tightly)* Where you live?

NAT   Not far, but I'm—

GILLEY   Walk you home, y'know.

NAT   That won't be necessary, it's—

GILLEY   Cost you three.

NAT   Listen, son, I don't need—

GILLEY   Cost you four. Just went up to four, y'know. *(To both)* Saw this lady this morning. Dog-walker, y'know. Five, six dogs at a time. Give me an idea. Walk you both home. Terrific idea, huh? *(To* NAT*)* Terrific idea, right? *(Silence for a moment.* GILLEY *tightens his grip on* NAT'S *hand.* NAT *nods in agreement.* GILLEY *lets go of his hand; pats* NAT *gently on the head)* Right. Walk you both; four each.

MIDGE   But our deal was—

GILLEY   Four.

MIDGE   O.K.

GILLEY   Right. *(Starts into Tunnel)* O.K., boys; everybody walkin'; convoy movin' out. *(*MIDGE *walks dutifully behind* GILLEY. NAT *remains seated. A moment;* GILLEY *moves slowly back to* NAT'S *bench, stands behind him)* Hey, that's everybody, right? *(Silence for a moment.* NAT *hesitates; then picks up his briefcase and slowly, obediently rises, his head bowed.* GILLEY *nods his approval, turns, starts walking into the Tunnel;* MIDGE *following)* O. K.; nice and slow; movin' out, headin' home, boys . . .

*(*NAT *remains standing at the bench. This immobility is not a conscious decision on* NAT'S *part; he just finds himself, quite simply, unable to move)*

MIDGE   *(stops, turns to* NAT; *a frightened whisper)* Come on, *please, move . . . move,* Mister . . .

*(*GILLEY *stops in the Tunnel, aware that he is not being followed. He turns to* NAT; *starts quickly to the bench, shoving* MIDGE *out of his way as he moves towards* NAT. NAT *holds his hand up urgently,* GILLEY *stops just in front of him)*

NAT   *(quickly)* Take it easy, I don't fight with Irish kids. I know the same thing now that I knew sixty-five years ago: don't fight with an Irish kid. *(Points to him)* How did I know Irish? I hear; I know all the sounds. But better, I know the feelings. This is because sixty-five years ago I was you. Irish kids, Italian, Russian, we *all* stole. Then, like now, the city lives by Darwin; this means everybody's on somebody's menu— *(Passionately, moving closer to him)* Trouble is, you got the wrong supper here. Me and Midge, you're noshing on your own. We live in the streets and the parks, we're dead if we stay home; just like you, Gilley. You're angry. You should be. So am I. But the trouble's at the top, like always—the

Big Boys, the Fat Cats, the String-Pullers, the *top*—we're down
here with you, kid. You, me, Midge, we have the same enemy, we
have to stick together or we're finished. It's the only chance we
got.

(Silence for a moment)

GILLEY Five. Went up to five. Y'mouth just cost ya a dollar. *(NAT
does not respond.* GILLEY *holds out his hand)* O.K., that's five; in
advance, y'know.

NAT *(softly)* No. I can't do that. I won't do that. Gilley, please understand; we mustn't do this. *(Touching his jacket pocket)* I have twenty-two dollars; I would share it with you, gladly share. But not
like *this*; not us . . .

GILLEY Great. Gimme the twenty-two. *(Shaking his head:)* Y'mouth,
I'm tellin' ya. It's costin', y'know.

NAT *(quietly, sadly)* I'm . . . I'm very disappointed . . .

MIDGE *(whispering)* Give it to him.

NAT I can't do that, kid; not *all*; that's unreasonable. *(*GILLEY *reaches for* NAT'S *pocket,* NAT *shoves his hand sharply away)* I have limited funds. I can't do that.

GILLEY *(calmly takes hunting knife in fancy leather sheath from his belt;
unsheathes the knife, holding it down at his side)* Ask you once more.

MIDGE *(from Tunnel, trembling)* Please, *give* it to him, Mister . . .
please . . .

NAT Gilley, this is a mistake. Don't do this. *(*GILLEY *glances quickly
about the area to see if he is being observed, then holds up his knife; a
demonstration)* No, no knives, not for us. Not between us. We're
together—

*(*NAT *makes a sharp underhand move with his cane, hitting* GILLEY'S
wrist; GILLEY *drops the knife, holding his wrist in pain and surprise;*
GILLEY *looks at* MIDGE *as though to ask for aid with a misbehaving
child, then kneels down quickly to pick up his knife.* NAT, *more in fear
and frustration than courage, raises his cane in the air with both
hands, shouting—an angry, guttural, old battle cry—and strikes a
sharp blow on the back of the kneeling* GILLEY. GILLEY *cries out in
pain, rising, outraged, leaving his knife, slapping the cane out of*
NAT'S *hand—*NAT *steps back, helpless now;* GILLEY *grabs him by
both shoulders and swings him around fiercely, flinging him backward
with a powerful throw,* NAT *falling back against the stone ledge at the
edge of the lake, hitting the ledge sharply and then rolling off onto the*

path where he lies quite still, face down, away from us. GILLEY *glances about, grabs up the wallet from* NAT'S *coat, then moves quickly towards the Tunnel, shouting over his shoulder at* MIDGE)

GILLEY   Tell your friend the rules! You better tell you friend the rules, man—

(GILLEY *stops—looks back at the very still form of* NAT—*then races quickly off into the darkened Tunnel, forgetting his knife, disappearing into the shadows of the park.*

MIDGE *moves down towards* NAT *as quickly as possible, kneels next to him*)

MIDGE   *(quietly)* Hey . . . hey, Mister . . . ? *(Silence. He touches* NAT, *gently)* Come on now, wake up . . . wake up . . .

(NAT *remains quite still. Silence again.* MIDGE *rises to his feet, shouting out at the lake)*

MIDGE   Help! . . . Over here! . . . *(No response.* MIDGE *looks out across the lake, a near-blind old man staring into the darkness around him)* Look what we got here . . .

(Silence again; only the sound of the early evening crickets. The park grows darker, MIDGE'S *face barely visible now in the lamplight as . . .)*

THE CURTAIN FALLS

Above and previous page, Judd Hirsch and Cleavon Little

Right, Hirsch and Josh Pais

Opposite page, top, Hirsch, Little and Michael Tucker.

Bottom, Walter Matthau and Ossie Davis in the movie version

ACT TWO

SCENE: The same; three in the afternoon, the next day. Before the curtain rises we hear the Carousel Band-Organ playing "We All Scream For Ice Cream."

AT RISE: MIDGE *is alone on the path; he is seated at the far left end of the center bench, his newspaper unopened on his lap, looking straight ahead, unable to relax in the pleasant sunlight that shines on the bench. The Carousel Music continues distantly now; the melody drifts in and out with the gentle autumn breeze.* LAURIE *is in her usual position on the bridge, far above* MIDGE, *sketching dreamily.* MIDGE *continues looking solemnly out at the lake. A full minute passes.*

We begin to hear NAT'S *voice, off left, singing "Puttin' on the Ritz," approaching slowly.* MIDGE *looks left, then immediately opens his newspaper, holds it up to his bifocals, "reading."* NAT *enters Up Left, moving slowly down the path within an aluminum walker. The walker is a three-sided, four-legged device with three metal braces holding the sides together; his briefcase and cane are hooked over two of the braces; there is a three-inch gauze bandage above his right eye. Although* NAT *moves very slowly he manages to incorporate the walker into his natural elegance, using the walker rhythmically rather than haltingly, a steady ambulatory tempo to the bouncy beat of his song, as he approaches the bench.* MIDGE *is turned away with his newspaper, ignoring him completely.*

NAT *continues towards the bench, singing the song with great gusto, pausing momentarily to tap his walker on the path for rhythmic emphasis, then continuing to the bench, parking the walker next to it as he finishes the last line of the song.* NAT *sits carefully on the bench.* MIDGE *continues to read his newspaper, making no acknowledgment of* NAT'S *arrival.*

NAT   *(rubbing his hands together)* Well, that punk, we got him on the run now. *(He leans back comfortably)* Yessir, got him where we want him now. *(Jabbing the air)* Boom, on the arm I got him; boom on the back. Boom, boom, boom—

MIDGE   *(not looking up from paper)* Tell me somethin', Rocky; you plannin' to sit here on this bench? 'Cause if you *are*, I got to move to another spot.

NAT   I'm sure you were about to inquire about my health. *(Taps his hip)* Only a slight sprain, no breaks, no dislocations. I am an expert at falling down. I have a gift for it. The emergency room at Roosevelt was twenty dollars. Not a bad price for keeping the bandit at bay.

MIDGE   *(folding newspaper)* *You* movin' or am *I* movin'? Answer me.

NAT   I guarantee he will not return today. He wants the easy money, he doesn't want trouble—

MIDGE   *(puts on his hat)* O.K., leavin' now . . .

NAT   And if by some odd chance he *does* return, I feel we were close to an understanding. We must realize, you and I, that this boy is caught like us in the same dog eat dog trap—

MIDGE   *(he rises)* Goodbye; gonna leave you two dogs to talk it over. Movin' on now.

NAT   Wait, Carter—

MIDGE   *(leans close to him)* Can't see your face too-good; what I *can* see got Cemetery written all over it. So long for *good*, baby.

NAT   Sir, a friendship like ours is a rare—

MIDGE   Ain't no friendship. Never *was* no friendship. Don't even know your goddamn *name*.

NAT   Yesterday you helped a fallen comrade—

MIDGE   You was out *cold*, Mister. Waited for the ambulance to come, done my duty same's I would for *any* lame dog. Said to myself, that ain't gonna be *me* lyin' there. *(Takes* GILLEY'S *leather sheathed hunting knife from pocket)* See this item here? Kid run off without his weapon, see. He comin' back for it today sure. I come here to give it back to him, stay on that boy's *good* side. *(Starts down path towards stone ledge at far left)* O.K., waitin' over here so he sees you and me is no longer *associated*; which we *ain't*, got that? He comes, don't want you *talkin'* to me, *lookin'* at me, contactin' me any way whatever.

NAT   So; the Cossack leaves his sword and you return it.

MIDGE   You bet. *(Settles down on ledge)*

NAT   *(leans towards him)* You have had a taste of revolution and will not be able to return to subjection, to living in an occupied country!

MIDGE   Watch me.

*(*MIDGE *closes his eyes, puts his huge handkerchief over his face, curls up on ledge.*

*CLARA *enters on the stone steps at right; attractive, early forties, styl-*

ishly bohemian clothes; she is walking quickly, purposefully down the steps towards NAT'S *bench.* NAT *rises, using the bench for support, unaware of the approaching* CLARA, *pointing his cane at* MIDGE)

NAT   No, *no*, you must not pay this punk for your existence, to live in your own land!

MIDGE   *(from under the handkerchief)* Nap time now. You're talkin' to nobody.

NAT   Exactly! No one! Surrender to the oppressors and you are no one! (MIDGE *begins to snore quietly)* Sure; sleep! Sleep then, like any bum in the park—

CLARA   *(stopping on steps)* Excuse me . . .

NAT   *(still to* MIDGE*)* A *napper* . . .

CLARA   Excuse me, I hate to interrupt you when you're driving somebody crazy . . .

NAT   A napper and a groveler! Why did I waste my time?!

CLARA   *(seeing the walker, the bandage; concerned, frightened, moving towards bench)* God, what happened? . . . Are you all right?

NAT   Everything's fine; don't worry, don't worry . . .

CLARA   Stitches this time?

NAT   A scratch.

CLARA   Your hip?

NAT   A sprain, a sprain . . .

CLARA   Dad, what happened? Why didn't you *call* me? Another fight, right? You got into another fight, didn't you?

NAT   *(sits on small bench) What* fights? I don't fight.

CLARA   How about four weeks ago? How about attacking that poor butcher at Gristede's? What was that?

NAT   I didn't attack the butcher. I attacked the meat. That was because of the prices.

CLARA   He said you shoved all the meat off his display counter with your cane—

NAT   It was a demonstration—there were thirty people in the store, I was trying to rally them, the meat-shoving was an illustration—

CLARA   The meat hit the butcher and you threw out your hip. Also the chances of starting a commune on Seventy-Second and Broadway are very slim. What happened this time, Dad?

NAT   Well, a young boy—confused, disadvantaged, a victim of society—

CLARA   A mugger. *(She nods)* You fought with a mugger. *(Pacing anxiously behind center bench)* Of course, of course, it was the next step; my God . . .

NAT   We were talking, we reached an impasse—

CLARA   That's it. No more. I can't let this happen anymore. I let it go, I've been irresponsible. You have to be watched. I'm not letting you out of my sight, Dad.

NAT   Stop this, you're frightening me . . .

CLARA   Oh, *I'm* frightening *you*, huh? I live in terror—the phone will ring, the police, the hospital. My God. It was quiet for a month, but I should have known. This guy Danforth calls this morning and I know you're on the loose again—

NAT   Ah, good, he called—

CLARA   Oh, he *called* all right— *(Takes out message; reads)* "Tell HURTSFOE that the Carter matter is settled; I reached the Committee; Reissman said to call." . . . Jesus, HURTSFOE again; HURTSFOE's on the march again. I take it you're Reissman.

NAT   That was yesterday—

CLARA   And tomorrow who? And tomorrow *what?* I came to tell you it's the last *time!* No more calls—

NAT   You *covered*, didn't you?

CLARA   Yes, yes. Once again, once again. Christ, in one year I've been the headquarters for the Eighth Congressional District, CBS News, the Institute for Freudian Studies, and the United Consumers Protection Agency . . .

NAT   *(fondly)* Ah, yes, *UCPA* . . .

CLARA   *(sighs, nodding)* UCPA, UCPA . . . Look, Dad—

NAT   What's *happened* to you? My own daughter has forgotten what a principle is!

CLARA   What principle? There's no *principle* here. It's fraud. Personal, daily fraud. A one-man reign of terror and I'm the one who gets terrorized. Never knowing who the hell I'm supposed to be everytime some poor sucker calls my office. A *principle?* You mean when that panic-stricken Manager of the Fine Arts Theatre called thinking there was going to be a Congressional Investigation because he showed German movies? I *still* don't understand how you convinced him you were a congressman—

NAT   What, you never saw an elder statesman before?

CLARA   But there's no such *thing* as a Floating Congressional District—

NAT   It's *because* he didn't know that he deserved it! That and showing movies by ex-Nazis. These people think that nobody *notices*, Clara—

CLARA   No *more!* It's over! Today was my last cover, that's what I came to tell you. Little did I know you were also back in combat again. *(Sits on center bench, opposite him)* Searched this damn park for two hours— *(Pointing up right)* What happened? You're not giving speeches at the Bethesda Fountain anymore?

NAT   Why should I? So you can find me there? shut me up, embarrass me?

CLARA   It's *me*, huh? It's me who embarrasses *you*—

NAT   Exactly; hushing me like I was a babbling child, a—

CLARA   Embarrassment, let's talk about embarrassment, O. K.? Three weeks ago I come back to my office after lunch, they tell me my Parole Officer was looking for me.

NAT   *(bangs his cane on the ground)* Necessary retaliation! It was important that you see what it's like to be pursued, watched, guarded . . . *(Turns to her, quietly)* You *do* frighten me, Mrs. Gelber. You do frighten me, you know. I'm afraid of what you'll do out of what you think is love. Coming to the Fountain once a week—it's not stopping me from talking; that's not so bad. It's the test questions.

CLARA   I don't—

NAT   The test questions to see if I'm too old. *(Taps his head)* Checking on the arteries. "Do you remember what you did yesterday, Dad? . . . Tell me what you had for lunch today, Dad?" One wrong answer you'll wrap me in a deckchair and mail me to Florida; *two* mistakes you'll put me in a home for the forgettable. I know this. My greatest fear is that someday soon I will wake up silly, that time will take my brain and *you* will take me. That you will put me in a place, a home—or worse, *your* house. Siberia in Great Neck. Very little frightens me, as you know; just that. Only what you will do.

CLARA   Dad . . .

NAT   I don't answer the door when you come. That's why. I watch through the hole in the door and wait for you to go away. That's why I moved from the Fountain, Clara. And why next week you won't find me *here* either.

CLARA   *(after a moment)*   You don't understand; I . . . I care . . . Someone has to watch out for you. Jack doesn't care, or Ben or Carole. They don't even speak to you anymore.

NAT   Good; God bless them; lovely children. Lovely, distant children.

CLARA   This isn't fair, Dad; I don't deserve this . . .

NAT   Dad. Who is this "Dad" you refer to? When did *that* start? I'm a "Pop," a Pop or a Papa, like I always was. You say "Dad" I keep looking around for a gentleman with a pipe.

CLARA   O.K., why don't I just call you "Dr. Engels" then? *(Silence for a moment.* NAT *turns to her)* Did you really think you fooled me? Dr. Engels the therapist? Dr. Fred Engels from the Socialists' Club? Really now.

NAT   But why did you keep writing all those letters to him—?

CLARA   Normal conversation with you is hopeless. Seemed like the best way to reach you. I sent "Dr. Engels" twelve letters in two months, I said everything I felt.

NAT   Smart. Smart girl. Well, at least you're still smart . . . even though the passions are gone, even though the ideals have evaporated . . .

CLARA   Stop . . .

NAT   I remember when you believed that the world did *not* belong to the highest bidder . . .

CLARA   The old song, stop . . .

NAT   This, of course, was before you went into Park East Real Estate, before you gave up Marx and Lenin for Bergdoff and Goodman . . .

CLARA   Jesus, at least get a new set of words—

NAT   Look at you! Look what you've become! Queen of the Condominiums, peasant skirts for two hundred dollars, betrayer of your namesake—

CLARA   Goddamn *name*—

NAT   Clara Lemlich, who stood for something—

CLARA   You *gave* me the name; I had no *choice*—

NAT   Clara Lemlich, who stood for something and stood up for it . . .

CLARA   *(leans back on bench)* Ah, you're rolling now . . .

NAT   Cooper Union; November, Nineteen-Nine . . .

CLARA   You're only eight . . .

NAT   *(looking away)* I'm only eight, the Shirtwaist Makers are there, thousands of them . . .

CLARA   *(whispering)* You're standing in back with your father . . .

NAT   I'm standing in the back with my Father; he holds me up so I can see. A meeting has been called to protest conditions. Gompers speaks, and Mary Drier, Panken, and Myer London. All speak well and with passion, but none with the courage to call a general strike. All speak of the bosses who value property above life and profits above people, but all speak with caution . . .

CLARA   *(whispering)* Until suddenly . . .

NAT   Until suddenly from the back of the hall, just near us, rises a skinny girl, a teenager; she runs up onto the platform, this little girl, she runs up unafraid among the great ones; she shouts in Yiddish to the thousands, this girl, with the power of inspiration . . . this girl is Clara Lemlich. "I am a working girl, one of those striking against intolerable conditions. I am *tired* of listening to speakers! I offer a resolution that a general strike be called—*now!*" *(Softly)* A moment of shock . . . and then the crowd screams, feet pound the floor! The chairman, Feigenbaum, calls for a second; the thousands cry "second!" in one voice. Feigenbaum trembles, he shouts to the hall, "Do you mean this in good faith? Will you take the Jewish oath?" Three thousand hands are raised—my father is holding me up, his hands are not free. "Raise your hand, boy, raise your hand for us and I will say the oath"—my hand goes up; I feel his heart beating at my back as my father with the thousands chants the solemn oath: "If I turn traitor to the cause I now pledge, may this hand wither from the arm I raise!" Again there is silence in the hall . . .

CLARA   *(Softly; caught up in the story again, as always)* And then Feigenbaum shouts . . .

NAT   And Feigenbaum shouts— *(he raises his fist in the air)* a general strike has been called! *(A moment; then he lowers his fist)* Thirty-two years later, December, Forty-One, Roosevelt vows vengeance upon the Fascists, and the next day *you* are born with a powerful scream at Kings County Hospital—I say to your mother, "Ethel, sounds to me like Clara Lemlich." This is the name . . .

CLARA and **NAT** *(together)* And this is the passion you were born with . . .

CLARA *Finis.*

NAT *(turns to her)* And only forty-one years later you have turned into my own, personal K.G.B.

CLARA Go to hell.

NAT I can't; you'll follow me.

(She turns to him, sharply)

CLARA Clara, Clara—it's not a name, it's a curse. The Cause, the goddamn *Cause*—everybody else gets a two-wheeler when they're ten, I got "Das Kapital" in paperback. Sundays you sent me out for bagels and lox and the Weekend Daily Worker; I hide it in the bag so half of Flatbush Avenue doesn't point at me. Fights at school, kids avoiding me, daughter of the Reds. My friend Sally— my *only* friend—we're down in the street on a Saturday morning; she tells me she believes in God. I'm confused, I run upstairs to the Central Committee; "Pop, Sally Marcus says she believes in God. What should I tell her?" "Tell her she'll get over it," you say. I tell her, she tells her mother, and the next day I got *no*body on the block to play with; *alone* again, *alone*—

NAT *(leans towards her)* Unfair! This isn't *fair*. Later you believed in your *own* things and I loved you for it. You gave up on the Party, I respected you. The Civil Rights, the Anti-War; you marched, you demonstrated, you *spoke*—that was *you*, nobody *made* you, you loved it—

CLARA I *did* love it—

NAT You *changed*—

CLARA No, I just noticed that the world didn't.

NAT Ah, first it was me, then it was the world. It's nice to know who to blame. Ten *years*, what have you done?

CLARA What have I *done?* I got married and had two children and lived a life. I got smarter and fought in battles I figured I could win. That's what I've done.

NAT Lovely. And now, at last, everybody on the block plays with you, don't they? Yes, all the kids play with you now. You married Ricky the smiling Radiologist; he overcharged his way into a house in Great Neck where your children, as far as I can see, believe firmly in Cable Television. They'll fight to the death for it! And all the kids play with *them* too. It's the new utopia: everybody plays with everybody! My enemies, I keep up! My enemies, I don't forget; I cherish them like my friends, so I know what to *do*—

CLARA   And what's that? What the hell do you do? Lead raids on lambchops at Gristede's? Oh, God, it's all so easy for you, I almost envy you. You always know what side to be on because you fight old wars; old, old wars . . . *(At bench, leaning towards him)* The battle is *over*, Comrade; didn't you notice? Nothing's *happened*, nothing's changed! And the Masses, have you checked out your beloved Masses lately? They don't *give* a crap. *(He turns away)* Are you listening? *(Grips his arm urgently)* Are you *listening* to me? I have received your invitation to the Revolution and I send regrets. I'm busy. I've given up on the Twentieth Century in favor of getting through the week. I have decided to feel things where I can get to feel something *back*; got it?

NAT   I was wrong; you're not even smart anymore. So not much changed. So what? You think I don't know this? The proper response to the outrages is still to be outraged. To be out*raged!*

CLARA   *(her arms outstretched in mock supplication)* Forgive me, Father; I'm not on the barricades anymore! I haven't been arrested for ten years, I'm obviously worthless! If you were talking to me in *jail* right now, you'd be overjoyed—

NAT   Not overjoyed. *Pleased* maybe . . .

CLARA   Christ, I was the only kid at the Columbia riots whose father showed up to coach! I *still* don't believe it! There you are on the steps of the Administration Building, shouting at the cops, pointing at me— *(Imitating NAT)* Hey Cossacks, look at this one! You can't stop her! *Four* of you—it'll take *four* of you to put her in the wagon!

NAT   It took *six!*

CLARA   *(she suddenly starts to laugh)* My father, my riot manager; God, I still don't believe it . . . a night in the slammer, and you waiting for me in the street when I got out . . . champagne, you had *champagne* . . .

NAT   *(laughing with her)* It was a graduation. What parent doesn't show up for a graduation?

CLARA   Why the hell am I laughing?

NAT   Because it was funny.

CLARA   *(shaking her head)* Jesus, what am I going to do with you?

NAT *(quietly)* Hello, Rappaport . . . *(No response; he raises his voice)* Hello, Rappaport!

CLARA I'm not playing.

NAT Come on, we'll do the "don't slap me on the back" one. You remember.

CLARA *(turns away)* I don't.

NAT Hello, Rappaport!

CLARA Stop . . .

NAT Hello, Rappaport; how's the family?

CLARA *(after a moment, softly)* I'm not Rappaport.

NAT Hello, Rappaport; how's the shoe business?

CLARA *(smiling)* I'm not Rappaport.

NAT *(leans towards her, slaps her on the back)* Hello, Rappaport; how the hell are ya?

CLARA *(doing the routine)* I'm not Rappaport, and don't slap me on the back!

NAT Who are *you* to tell me how to say hello to Rappaport? *(They both laugh. Silence for a moment)*

CLARA *(turns to him; quietly)* Pop, I have to do something about you.

NAT No, you don't.

CLARA Pop—

NAT At least I'm "Pop" again—

CLARA You'll get killed. The next time you'll get killed. I dream about it.

NAT In general, you need better dreams—

CLARA I want you out of this neighborhood, I want you off the street. I want you safe. I'm determined.

NAT *(reaching for walker)* I have an appointment—

CLARA *(holds his arm, firmly)* O.K., we have three possibilities, three solutions. You'll have to accept one of them. First, there's living with me in Great Neck; you'll have your own room, your own separate—

NAT Rejected.

CLARA Second; Ricky has found a place, not far from us, Maple Hills Senior Residence. I've checked it out; it's the *best* of them— *(tak-*

ing Maple Hills book from handbag, showing pages) really attractive grounds, Pop; this open, sunny, recreation area—

NAT   Rejected.

CLARA   O. K . . . O.K., there's one more possibility; I'm not crazy about it, but I'm willing to try it for one month. You stay at your place, you do not hide from me, you make yourself available for visits by me or some member of the family once a week. You don't wander the streets, you don't hang around the park; you go out every afternoon to *this* place . . . *(More gently, taking brochure from handbag)* West End Senior Center; I was there this morning, Pop; this is a great place. Hot lunch at noon and then a full afternoon of activities . . .

NAT   *(puts on bifocals, holds brochure up to his eyes, reading)* "One o'clock: Dr. Gerald Spitzer will present a slide presentation and informative program on home health services; refreshments will be served. Two o'clock: Beginners Bridge with Rose Hagler. Three-fifteen: Arts and Crafts Corner supervised by Ginger Friedman . . . " *(He studies the brochure for a moment)* O.K. . . . we got three possibilities; we got exile in Great Neck, we got Devil's Island, and we got kindergarten. All rejected. *(Hands her back the brochure; rises from bench, opening the walker)* And now, if you'll excuse me . . .

(He starts moving down the path to the right with the walker. We begin to hear the distant sound of the Carousel as he continues down the path)

CLARA   All right, here it is: I'm taking legal action, Pop, I'm going to court. *(NAT stops on the path, his back to her. She remains on the bench)* I saw a lawyer a month ago after the Gristede Uprising; I'm prepared. Article Seventy-Eight of the Mental Hygiene Law, judicial declaration of incompetency, I'll get Ricky and me authorized as custodians. According to the lawyer I've got more than enough evidence to prove that you are both mentally and physically incapable of managing yourself or your affairs. In addition to a proven history of harrassment, impersonation, and assault. *(She turns away; quietly, firmly)* I look at that bandage, I . . . You can hardly see, and with that walker you're a sitting duck. I don't want you hurt, I don't want you dead. Please, don't force me to go to court. If you fight me, you'll lose. If you run away, I'll find you. I'm prepared to let you hate me for this.

(Silence for a moment)

NAT   You're not kidding.

CLARA I'm not.

(Silence again; only the sound of the distant, gentle, Carousel Music. He moves back to the bench, sits next to her)

NAT *(quietly)* Clara, I've got to tell you something. I put it in my papers, a letter for you when I died, you would have known then . . . *(Hesitates a moment, then proceeds gently)* Your mother and I, it was not the liveliest association, but there was great fondness between us. Whatever I tell you now, you must know that. August, Nineteen Thirty-Nine, I'm at the Young Workers' Club on Houston Street; you talked about dialectical materialism and you met girls. It's a Friday night, the day of the Hitler-Stalin Pact; Ribbentrop shakes hands with Molotov on the front page of the Journal-American and this woman bursts into tears. Everyone's arguing, discussing, but this woman sits there with her tears falling on the newspaper. This was Ethel, your mother. My heart was hers. Soon we are married; two years later you are born—and during the next ten years those other people. Fine. All is well. Then . . . then comes October, Fifty-Six . . . October Third . . .

(He lapses into silence, turns away)

CLARA Tell me. What is it?

NAT I met a girl. I fell in love.

CLARA You're human, Pop, it happens. There's no need to feel—

NAT I mean in *love*, Clara. For the first and only time in my life; boom.

CLARA Don't worry, it's not—

NAT Clara, she was a *girl*. Twenty-four; I was fifty-five.

CLARA *(riveted)* What happened? Where did you meet her?

NAT It was in the Grand Street Library, second floor reading-room. I'm at the main table, I look up, I see this lovely girl, Hannah, Hannah Pearlman; she's studying a grammar book. She looks up; she *smiles* at me. I can't speak. She goes back to her book. She has a sad look, someone alone. I see a girl, troubled, lost, marks on her hands from the needle-trades. She rises to leave. Someone should speak to her. Can it be me? Can I have the courage . . . ? *(Softly, with love)* I speak. I *speak* to her; and for hours our words come out, and for hours and days after that in her little room on Ludlow Street. It was the most perfect time. She tells me I have saved her from killing herself . . . I saved her just in time . . . just in time, Clara . . . she did not die, she did not die . . . *(Silence for a moment. Then he speaks briskly, as though awakening from a dream)*

Well, I'm married to Ethel, nothing can come of it. Four months, it's over. She goes to live in Israel, a new life. Six months later, a letter . . . there is a child . . .

CLARA My God . . .

NAT A girl . . . And then, every year or two a letter. Time goes by; I think often of the library and Ludlow Street. Then silence; there are no letters, never another. Three months ago there's a message for me at the Socialists' Club: Sergeant Pearlman will be here at five. Five o'clock, at the door, Sergeant Pearlman is a girl. In Israel, women, everybody's in the Army for two years. Well, Sergeant Pearlman . . .

CLARA Yes . . .

NAT Sergeant Pearlman is my daughter. Twenty-six, a face like her mother; a fine face, like a painting. She herself is an artist; she comes to this country to study at the Art Students' League and to find me. *(Silence for a moment)* Here's the point. She has decided to take care of me; to live with me. That's why I've told you all this, so you'll know. In December, we leave for Israel. This is where I will end my days. You see, there is nothing for you to worry about.

(Silence for a few moments)

CLARA *(quietly)* This is . . . this is a lot for me to take in, all at once. A lot of information . . .

NAT Not easy, but I'm glad I told you. Better you know now.

CLARA I want to meet her.

NAT You shall.

CLARA When?

NAT In two days. Friday. At the Socialists' Club, in the dining room, Friday at lunchtime. I'll bring sandwiches.

CLARA Good. *(After a moment; softly)* She'll . . . she'll take care of you.

NAT That's the point.

CLARA *(letting it all sink in)* Israel . . .

NAT Yes, Clara. *(She turns away, trying to cover her emotion. He touches her arm; gently)* Clara, don't be upset. I'll be fine. It's for the best, Clara . . .

(She rises briskly from the bench)

CLARA   Well, at last you've got a daughter who's a soldier.

NAT   Sit. Where are you going?

CLARA   *(checks watch)* My train. You know, the Siberian Express.

NAT   *(holds out his hand to her)* They got them every half-hour. Sit a minute.

CLARA   Got to go. See you Friday. *(She moves quickly towards the stone steps at right; near tears)*

NAT   Wait a minute. *(She goes quickly up the steps)* Hey, Rappaport! Hello, Rappaport! *(She exits)* Rappaport, what happened to you? You used to be a tall, fat guy; now you're a— *(She is gone. He shouts)* Rappaport! *(Silence for a moment. He speaks quietly)* Hey, Rappaport . . .

(Silence again. NAT *remains quite still on the bench; he strokes his beard nervously, sadly. He suddenly winces, as though aware for the first time of the pain in his hip; shifts position on the bench.* MIDGE, *still lying on the stone ledge at far left, lifts the handkerchief off his face)*

MIDGE   You made it up.

NAT   *(softly)* Of course.

MIDGE   You made it all up . . .

NAT   Go back to sleep.

MIDGE   Conned your own kid, that's a sin.

NAT   I did it to save a life. Mine.

MIDGE   *(sitting up on ledge)* You ain't a nice guy. 'Shamed I even sung a song with you.

NAT   You don't understand. Nursing homes danced in her head; desperate measures were required. *(Grips walker, rising forcefully from bench)* You; you would just go toddling off to Maple Hills.

MIDGE   Wouldn't hustle my own child to save my ass.

NAT   She's not mine anymore. She has become unfamiliar. *(Starts moving Up Left on path, in walker, as though to exit past* MIDGE *at ledge)*

MIDGE   Won't get away with it anyway. In two days, she'll—

NAT   *(continuing forcefully up path)* In two days I'll be in Seattle . . . Hong Kong, Vladivostok, Newark; I'll be where she can't get me.

MIDGE   Seattle, shit, you can't get down*town*, boy.

NAT   I'll be *gone, somewhere*. When she comes to the Club, I'll be *gone*—

MIDGE   *(angrily, blocking his path)* And what *she* do? Wait there all day, thinkin' you're dead? *(NAT stops, MIDGE pointing at him)* What kinda man *are* you? Smart talk and fancy notions, you don't *give* a damn!

NAT   A *letter*, I'll . . . I'll leave a letter for her . . . *(Silence for a moment; he sits on the small bench, upset, confused)* I'll send her a letter; I'll explain the necessity for . . . my behavior . . .

(He trails off into silence, exhausted, at a loss for words; he stares thoughtfully out at the lake)

MIDGE   *(suddenly looks up at bridge, whispering)* Gilley—

(We have seen THE COWBOY *enter Up Right on the bridge several moments earlier, strolling halfway across the bridge before* MIDGE *notices him; a tall, genial-looking tourist, about thirty-five, he wears an immaculate white Stetson, finely tailored buckskin jacket, and polished boots. He moves politely towards* LAURIE, *stopping a respectful distance from her, peering at the sketch she's been working on;* LAURIE *apparently unaware of him.* NAT, *lost in his own thoughts, continues to look out at the lake, unaware of* MIDGE *and the scene above him)*

MIDGE   *(softly, squinting up at them)* Ain't Gilley; too big . . .

COWBOY   *(smiling, pleasantly, a well-mannered western voice)* Well now, M'am, you sure got that lake just right. Fine work, I'd say. Looks just like—

LAURIE   *(not looking at him)* Fuck off, Cowboy.

COWBOY   *(cordially, tipping his Stetson as though returning her greeting)* Afternoon, M'am.

LAURIE   How did you find me?

COWBOY   Natural-born hunter, Miss Laurie. 'Specially rabbits.

LAURIE   Ever tell you how much I hate that bullshit drawl? *(Turns to him)* What is this, Halloween? You haven't been west of Jersey City.

COWBOY   Pure accident of birth, M'am. My soul's in Montana where the air is better.

LAURIE   *(abruptly hands him bank-envelope)* See ya later, Cowboy.

(She starts briskly, calmly, across bridge to right)

COWBOY   Well, thank you, M'am.

(Opens envelope, starts counting bills inside)

MIDGE   Sure don't *sound* like Ella Mae . . .

COWBOY   *(quietly)* Three hundred and twenty . . . ? *(LAURIE quickens her pace across the bridge, almost running)* Three hundred and twenty outa two *thousand*—

(LAURIE races towards the stone steps at right, THE COWBOY darts up left, disappearing. MIDGE quickly grabs NAT, breaking into his reverie, pulling him to his feet)

MIDGE   Come on now— *(Moving NAT into the safety of the shadows at the left of the bridge, whispering)* Bad business . . . bad park business here.

(LAURIE races breathlessly down the stone steps towards the Tunnel, an escape—but THE COWBOY suddenly emerges from the Tunnel, blocking her path)

COWBOY   *(calmly, evenly)* See the rabbit run. Dirty little rabbit. *(Grips her arms, thrusts her forward towards the bench; she bumps against the bench, dropping her sketchpad. He remains a few steps away; continuing quietly, evenly)* I live in a bad city. What's *happenin'* to this city? City fulla dirty little rabbits. Park fulla junkies, *unreliable, dis*honorable junkies . . .

LAURIE   That's all I could—

COWBOY   *(holding up the envelope)* Kept your nose filled and your head happy for a year and a half, and look what you do. Look what you do.

LAURIE   *(moving towards him)* Sorry, right now that's the best I—

(He slaps her hard across the face with the bank-envelope, jerking her head back; then he throws the envelope full of bills to the ground)

NAT   *(from shadows at far left)* What? What happened . . . ?

MIDGE   *(holding NAT's arm, whispering)* Shhhh . . . stay now.

COWBOY   *(calmly again)* You . . . you got to take me serious. 'Cause you don't take me serious, I don't get my money and you don't get older. *(A moment passes; then he moves past her at the bench, starting towards the Tunnel)* My cash. Tomorrow. Here. Six o'clock.

LAURIE   *(moving towards him)* Need more time . . . not enough time, I can't—

(In one quick, almost mechanical movement, he turns and hits her sharply in the face, as though correcting an error. She blinks, dizzy from the blow, sits down on the bench, trembling; there is blood on her

lip. NAT *takes a step forward in his walker, but* MIDGE *holds him firmly in the shadows)*

COWBOY   *(kneels next to her at the bench; quietly)* Mustn't say "can't," Miss Laurie. Don't say that. You are the little engine that can. I believe in you. *(Takes out his handkerchief, starts quite delicately, carefully, to dab the blood off her mouth)* This gets around, folks'll start thinkin' The Cowboy's got no teeth. Law and order ain't reached these parts; fellah like me got to protect himself, right? *(She nods)* My cash. Tomorrow. Here. Six o'clock. And don't try to hide from me, little rabbit. Don't do that. That would be a mistake. *(She nods. He rises, puts his handkerchief back in his pocket; shakes his head sadly)* Damn town. Damn town's turnin' us all to shit, ain't it? *(Turns, walks briskly into the darkened Tunnel, tipping his hat cordially as he exits)* Afternoon, M'am.

*(*LAURIE *kneels down on the ground, sobbing, retrieving the envelope and the scattered bills.* MIDGE *moves out of the shadows and quickly towards her,* NAT *moves slowly towards her in his walker.* MIDGE *reaches his hand out tentatively, tenderly touches her shoulder)*

MIDGE   You O.K., lady?

LAURIE   *(tears streaming down her face)* Great. Just great. *(She looks up at them)* Fellahs . . . how ya doin', fellahs?

MIDGE   Here . . . take this. *(Gently hands her his handkerchief; she accepts it, rising to sit on bench.* MIDGE *points in the direction of* THE COWBOY'S *exit)* That boy; he a dealer, or a shark?

LAURIE   Dealer. But he gave me credit.

MIDGE   Can you get the money? *(She shakes her head hopelessly. He nods)* Uh-huh. What I heard, lady, you best get outa town; fast and far.

LAURIE   I was just gettin' it together . . . straightening out, Mister . . . *(Shaking with sobs, opening sketchpad, showing him the pages)* Art school, I started art school, see . . .

MIDGE   *(softly, touching her shoulder)* Outa town, chil'; fast and far.

LAURIE   These guys, you don't get away; they got branch offices, man, they got chain stores . . .

NAT   She's right. *(Parks his walker next to the bench)* Other measures are called for. *(He sits next to her)* Tell me, Miss; two days from now, Friday, what are you doing for lunch on Friday?

LAURIE   *(quietly, trembling)* Friday . . . ? Jesus, looks like Friday I'll be in the hospital. Or dead maybe . . . or dead . . .

NAT (*his arm around her; gently, firmly*) No, you won't be in the hospital. I promise you. And you will not die . . . you will not die.

(*Blackout. In the darkness we hear the sound of the Carousel Band-Organ playing "The Sidewalks of New York"; the music building gradually louder in the darkness, reaching a peak and then slowly fading as the lights come up.*

It is six o'clock, the evening of the next day. MIDGE *and* NAT *are alone on the path, seated on the center bench.* NAT *wears dark sunglasses, a white silk scarf, and an old but stylish Homburg, his cane at his side, his walker folded and hidden behind the bench. He looks serious and elegant.* MIDGE *wears an old suit-jacket instead of his usual sweater, and a hat that he had once considered fashionable. The bridge lamp-posts are lit above; the dark shadows of early evening gather in the Tunnel and along the path.* MIDGE *glances anxiously up and down the path. He lights a cigarette, inhales, coughs. Silence for a few moments*)

NAT Time, please.

MIDGE (*takes out pocket-watch, holds it up against his bifocals*) Ten to six.

NAT Good. Say my name again.

MIDGE I got it, I got it; you keep—

NAT Say the name.

MIDGE Donatto.

NAT The whole name.

MIDGE Anthony Donatto.

NAT Better known as?

MIDGE (*impatiently*) Tony the Cane. O.K.? Now will ya—

NAT Tony the Cane Donatto. Good. O.K., *your* name.

MIDGE I—

NAT Your name.

MIDGE (*with a sigh of resignation*) Kansas City Jack.

NAT *Missouri* Jack, *Missouri* Jack. *See*, it's lucky I asked.

MIDGE Missouri Jack, Kansas City Jack, what the hell's the *difference?* He ain't even gonna ask me.

NAT It could come *up*. In these matters details are very important. Details is the whole game, believe me. What time is it?

MIDGE I just told—

NAT   Missouri Jack is better than Kansas City Jack. Has a sound to it. Music. I know these things. Details is everything. You should introduce yourself to him.

MIDGE   Nossir, *nossir;* do what I *said* I'd do and that's *it*. Don't even like doin' *that* much. Dicey deal here, say the least— *(Starts to cough, indicates cigarette)* Looka me, ain't had a cigarette thirty-two years, July; you got me smokin' again. *(Pointing at him)* O.K., promised that po' girl I'd help her out, but I ain't hangin' around here a second longer'n I have to. You a time-bomb, Mister, I hear you tickin'.

NAT   I ask you to look at the record, sir! I ask you to look at the *harm* I've done you! Gilley did not return yesterday as I predicted and he did not come today. No more payoffs; correct?

MIDGE   O.K., so far he—

NAT   And your job—has anybody there *mentioned* firing you since I dealt with Danforth? Do you still have your home?

MIDGE   Yeah, well, O.K., so far they—

NAT   And today a few minutes of your time to help the victim of Gene Autry; the woman requires our aid. He comes here, you go up to him, you say "excuse me, my boss wants to see you," you send him over to me and you're *done;* finished.

MIDGE   You bet; then I *split*, that's *it*. Go home, hear about it on the TV. *(Shaking his head mournfully)* Still don't see why you even need me to—

NAT   *Details, details;* gives him the feeling I've got a staff, an organization. It fills in the picture. Details are crucial. I know my business. What time is it? *(MIDGE sighs, takes out his pocket-watch.* NAT *turns, squinting into the Tunnel)* Never mind; he's here. On the button.

(MIDGE turns sharply as THE COWBOY *emerges from the darkened Tunnel.* NAT *adjusts his Homburg, crosses his legs, leans back comfortably, elegantly, on the bench.* THE COWBOY *walks down to the ledge at far left, glances about, then looks solemnly up at the bridge. After a few moments he sits down at the edge of the ledge, takes off his Stetson, starts cleaning it carefully with a small brush, waiting.* MIDGE *remains quite still on the bench, looking out at the lake. Silence for a few moments)*

NAT   *(whispering)* Now. *(MIDGE continues to look out at the lake.* NAT *whispers again)* Now, Carter.

(MIDGE rises, buttons his jacket, straightens his hat, preparing him-

self; then crosses to within six feet of THE COWBOY. THE COWBOY *is looking away from him, watching the path at left)*

MIDGE   *(barely audible)* Excuse me, my boss wants to see you. *(No response. He speaks a bit louder)* Excuse me, Mister . . . my boss wants to see you.

THE COWBOY   *(turns to* MIDGE*)* You talkin' to *me*, partner?

MIDGE   Yeah. *(Points behind him)* My boss over there, he wants to see you.

COWBOY   Your boss?

MIDGE   Yeah, I'm on his staff. He wants to see you.

COWBOY   Who the hell're you?

MIDGE   Me? I'm nobody. I'm on the staff.

THE COWBOY   *(leans towards him)* What do you want with me? Who are you?

MIDGE   I'm . . . I'm Missouri Jack.

COWBOY   Missouri Jack. Sounds familiar. You ever—

MIDGE   You don't know me. I'm nobody.

COWBOY   Nobody?

MIDGE   Yeah, definitely. Nobody at all; believe me. *(*THE COWBOY *shrugs, turns away)* Him, over there, he's somebody. He wants to see you.

COWBOY   I'm busy.

MIDGE   He's the boss. Donatto. Tony Donatto.

THE COWBOY   *(sharply)* Great. I'm *busy*.

(He leans back on the ledge, looking the other way, ignoring MIDGE, *watching the path)*

MIDGE   O.K. then, guess I'll be on my way. *(He turns, starts walking briskly towards the stone steps at far right)* Yeah, gotta be gettin' along now. Nice meetin' you, pleasure talkin' to you . . .

NAT   *(to* COWBOY, *loudly)* Hey, Tom Mix. *(*THE COWBOY *turns;* NAT *pats the bench)* You, Roy Rogers, over here.

COWBOY   What do *you* want?

NAT   I want not to shout. Come here. *(No response.* MIDGE *quickens his pace up the steps)* Laurie Douglas, two thousand dollars.

COWBOY   What—

NAT   You know the name? You know the sum? *(Pats bench)*   Here. We'll talk.

(THE COWBOY starts towards him. MIDGE stops in the shadows halfway up the steps, turns, curious, watching them at a safe distance. NAT will remain aloof behind his sunglasses, seldom facing THE COW-BOY, never raising his voice)

COWBOY   *(approaching bench)*   What *about* Laurie Douglas? Who are you?

NAT   I am Donatto. Sit.

COWBOY   Look, if that junkie bimbo thinks she can—

NAT   The junkie bimbo is my daughter. Sit.

COWBOY   She's got a father, huh? *(Sits)* Thought things like her just accumulated.

NAT   *(taking old silver case from jacket, removing small cigar)* Not that kind of father. Another kind of father. I have many daughters, many sons. In my family there are many children. I am Donatto.

(He lights the cigar. THE COWBOY studies him)

COWBOY   I never heard of—

NAT   On your level, probably not. *(Patting THE COWBOY's knee)* A lot of you new boys don't know. I fill you in. My people, we work out of Phoenix. We take commands from Nazzaro, Los Angeles; Capetti, New Orleans . . . *(No response; NAT leans towards him)* Capetti, New Orleans . . . *(turns to MIDGE)* Jack, he doesn't know Capetti, New Orleans. *(NAT chuckles heartily, MIDGE stares blankly back at him; NAT turns to THE COWBOY again)* Capetti will be amused by you. I am not. Capetti, many years ago, he gives us our name—I talk of the old days now, the good days—he calls us, me and Jack, "The Travel Agents." This is because we arrange for trips to the place of no return. You understand?

COWBOY   *(sharply, snapping his fingers)* Let's get *to* it, pal, there's some *bucks* owed me—

NAT   *(covers THE COWBOY's snapping fingers with his hand, gently)* Please don't do that, it upsets me. We will speak of your problem now. The girl, Laurie; I am not pleased with her. A two-grand marker for drugs, she brings shame on my house. She says she is slapped, threatened. I am unhappy with this. It is not for you to deal with her. She is of my family. Forget the girl; you never met her. Forget, Cowboy, or you yourself become a memory.

COWBOY *(smiles, leans back on bench)* You tryin' t'tell me that two old guys like you—

NAT Of course not. We don't touch people like you; we have *people* who touch people like you. I pick up a phone, you disappear. I make a call, they find you floating. Yes, we are old now, the Travel Agents; many years since we did our own work. In Fifty-Four, our last active year . . . *(turns to* MIDGE*)* How many floating, Jack? *(Silence,* MIDGE *stares blankly back at him)* He doesn't remember either. I think if we count Schwartzman, it was fourteen—

THE COWBOY *(leaning very close to him)* Don't like the sound of this, hoss; it does not ring right in the ear.

NAT Don't you understand? Missouri and me, we fly here personally from Phoenix last night to speak to you—

COWBOY If you just came in from Phoenix, what were you doing here yesterday?

NAT Yesterday? What're you—

COWBOY And the day before that. Seen you here two days runnin'.

NAT You . . . you are mistaken. *(*MIDGE *starts to retreat up the steps towards the exit)*

COWBOY *(lifts walker up from behind bench)* Had this with you yesterday. I got an antenna picks up all channels, Dad; helps me not to wake up dead.

NAT I advise you to call your people, check the name—

COWBOY Game's over, stop it—

NAT Call them now—

COWBOY Please don't continue this. I'm gettin' depressed—

NAT You are making a serious mistake, a very serious—

COWBOY *Please* don't do this— *(He throws the walker clattering to the ground) Hate* bein' played foolish; *hate* it. First she cons me, then she gets two old creeps to front for her. Don't *like* it. *(Pacing behind bench)* City gone rotten, shills like you, this Big Apple's just rottin' away . . . *(*NAT *starts to rise;* THE COWBOY *pulls him sharply back down onto the bench)* This is hurtin' me. Makin' me *feel* bad. *(Pulls off* NAT'S *sunglasses)* Who *are* you, man? *(Yanks off his Homburg)* What's the deal? Where is she?

NAT *(quietly)* A . . . a note was left with my attorney this morning. If I do not return by Seven, they will send people here. His card— *(Hands him business card)*

THE COWBOY *(crushing the card in his hand)* You're out of aces, friend. Where's she hidin'? Where's she at?

NAT   I am not at liberty to—

COWBOY   *(grips* NAT'*s scarf, pulls him close)* Run a street business. Lookin' bad on the street, girl's makin' me look like shit on the street. Got folks *laughin'* at me. *(Gives him one fierce shake)* You got to take me *serious* now. You got to tell me where she's *at.*

NAT   *(quietly, unable to make his mind work)* Allow me to introduce myself; I . . . I'm . . .

*(*THE COWBOY *pulls the scarf tighter around* NAT'S *neck, like a kind of noose, shaking him violently now, shouting)*

COWBOY   You in harm's way, Dad, you in harm's *way* now! Got to *tell* me, got to *tell* me! Gonna rock you till the *words* come out— *(Shaking him fiercely, continuously, rhythmically,* NAT *halfway off the bench now, almost falling to the ground)* Rock you, *rock* you, *rock* you—

MIDGE   *(taking a step down the stairs)* Leave him be! Leave him *be* now!

COWBOY   *(continues shaking* NAT*)* *Rock* you, *rock* you—

MIDGE   Leave the man be! Leave him go else I get a cop!

COWBOY   *(turns, still holding* NAT*)* Well now, it's Mr. Nobody . . .

MIDGE   *(retreating a step)* You . . . you go away, you leave him be else I get a cop. *(Pointing Up Right, trembling)* Cop right near—cop-car at the boathouse this hour, right near.

COWBOY   That case you don't *move,* little man, you stay right *there* . . .

*(*MIDGE *hesitates; then starts up the stairs)*

COWBOY   I ask you not to go, little man . . .

*(*MIDGE *continues up the stairs as quickly as he can;* THE COWBOY *lets go of* NAT*, letting him fall to the ground, starts towards the stairs)*

COWBOY   Askin' you to *stop,* buddy; stop right *there*—

*(*MIDGE *stops on the stairs, his back to* THE COWBOY. THE COWBOY *continues towards the base of the stairs;* MIDGE *turns, holding* GILLEY'S *unsheathed hunting knife high in the air; the large blade glistens.* THE COWBOY *stops; backs up a bit towards the Tunnel. The knife is shaking;* MIDGE *grips the handle with both hands to steady it)*

COWBOY   *(tips back his Stetson)* Well now, well now . . . what do we got here?

MIDGE   We got a crazy old man with a knife.

COWBOY   Crazy ol' man, you can't even see me.

MIDGE   *(still trembling)* See a blue shadow with a hat on it. Come close enough, I stick you. *(A step forward, thrusting knife)* I swear I stick you, boy.

(THE COWBOY starts retreating back towards the Tunnel; smiles, tips his hat, as though gracefully admitting defeat)

COWBOY   Afternoon, Jack.

(He turns as though exiting into the Tunnel; it would appear to MIDGE that THE COWBOY is leaving, but we can see that he has merely ducked into the shadows within the Tunnel, at right, where he waits for MIDGE. MIDGE continues towards the Tunnel, his courage and pride building, his knife raised high)

NAT   *(from the ground, whispering)* Get away, Carter . . . get away . . .

MIDGE   *(moving into Tunnel, shouting)* Now *you* the one goes away, *you* the one does the leavin', Cowboy; this here's *my* spot . . . *(Continuing into Tunnel, unaware that THE COWBOY is hidden just behind him in the shadows of the Tunnel Archway)* Mess with me, I peel you like an apple! Sliced Cowboy comin' up! Cowboy Salad to go—

(THE COWBOY moves suddenly out of the shadows behind MIDGE— we see the sharp, violent thrust of THE COWBOY'S hand as he grabs MIDGE'S shoulder—

Blackout; we hear the sudden loud, pulsing rhythm of the Carousel Band-Organ playing "Springtime in the Rockies." The powerful sound of the Band-Organ continues in the darkness for a few moments, and then the red-orange colors of autumn gradually light up the sky behind the bridge, leaving the downstage area in darkness and the bridge and the Archway in stark silhouette. Leaves fall against the red-orange sky; the Carousel Music continuing powerfully for several moments and then slowly fading into the distant, more delicate melody of "The Queen City March" as the rest of the lights come up.

It is twelve days later; a cloudy autumn morning, eleven o'clock. NAT is alone on the path, seated at the far left end of the bench. He wears his bifocals, a thick woolen scarf, and a faded winter coat; his walker is folded at his side, his briefcase nowhere in sight. He remains quite still, staring rather listlessly out at the lake; from time to time he shiv-

ers slightly in the October breeze, holds the scarf up closer about his neck. He seems fragile, older—or rather he seems to be his own age, very much like any old man whiling away his morning on a park bench. Several moments pass. A few autumn leaves drift lazily down onto the path. Silence except for the now quite distant and gentle sound of the Carousel Music. After a while NAT *reaches into his jacket pocket, takes out the West End Senior Center brochure, holds it up to his bifocals, studying it. Several more moments pass.*

We see MIDGE *appear in the darkened Tunnel; he is moving slowly and carefully through the Tunnel with the aid of a "quad-cane"—a cane with four aluminum rubber-tipped legs at its base. It takes him several moments to reach the bench; he crosses in front of* NAT, *pointedly ignoring him, sits at the far right end of the bench, opens his copy of* "The Sporting News", *starts to read. The Carousel Music fades out. Silence for a few moments.* NAT *turns, leans towards* MIDGE)

MIDGE   *(quietly)* Don't say a word.

NAT   *(after a moment)* I was only—

MIDGE   Not a word, please.

(Silence again. MIDGE *continues to read his newspaper)*

NAT   I was only going to say that, quite frankly, I have missed you, Carter.

MIDGE   O.K., now you said it.

NAT   *(after a moment)* I would also like to express my delight at your safe return from the hospital. I only regret that you did not allow me into your room to visit you.

MIDGE   Ain't lettin' *you* in there—shit, tell 'em you're a doctor, start loppin' off pieces of my foot. Had twelve beautiful days an' nights without you.

NAT   Quite right. I don't blame you.

MIDGE   Told 'em, don't let him in what*ever* he says—he tell you he the head of the hospital, tell you he invented *novocaine*, you don't let him in.

NAT   I certainly don't blame you. The fact is I've stopped doing that.

MIDGE   Yeah, *sure*—

NAT   It's true. Since the Cowboy—an episode during which, may I say, you behaved magnificently; not since General Custer has there been such behavior—since that time I have been only myself. That Friday, Clara comes lunchtime to the Socialists' Club; I tell her the truth. She comes, there are tears in her eyes,

I decide to tell her the truth. I will admit I was helped in this decision by the fact that the girl, Laurie, did not show up. *(He turns away, quietly)* I could have covered, another story, my heart wasn't in it. My mouth, a dangerous mouth; it makes you Missouri Jack and almost kills you; makes an Israeli family and breaks my daughter's heart. I have retired my mouth.

MIDGE   *(still looking away, bitterly)* Yeah, well, long's we talkin' *mouth* damage, boy—lawyer for the Tenants' Committee found out there ain't no HURTSFOE; I'm outa my *job* now. Yeah, movin' me and the Erie City out in four weeks. No extra Severance neither. Danforth come to the hospital to tell me personal; bring me a basket of fruit. Now 'stead of my Christmas cash I got six fancy pears wrapped in silver paper.

NAT   I . . . I deeply regret—

MIDGE   'Sides which, look what you done to Laurie. How you expect her to show up? Said you'd help her with that Cowboy; now she's in worse trouble than ever. *(Bangs his quad-cane on the ground)* 'Sides which, there ain't one good hip left on this bench now. And long's we keepin' score here, what happened to Gilley? Tell me the truth; Gilley's *back*, ain't he?

NAT   *(after a moment)* Yes. *(Quietly)* He charges six dollars now.

MIDGE   So seems to me you pretty much come up O for Five on the whole series here.

NAT   Please, I assure you, my wounds require no further salt . . .

MIDGE   'Nother thing—I ain't no General Custer. Way I heard it, the General got wiped out. Well, not *this* boy. Shit, wasn't for a lucky left jab I near blew that Cowboy away. *(Takes a small piece of buckskin fringe from his pocket)* See this? Small piece of that Cowboy is what it is. His jacket, anyways. Near took a good slice outa that boy, 'fore he dropped me. *(Leans back on bench, smiling)* Know what I seen in the hospital every night, fronta my bed? I seen that Cowboy's eyes, them scared eyes, them big chicken eyes when my weapon come out. That was one, surprised, frozen-solid, near-shitless Cowboy. Dude didn't know *what* happened. Dude figured he had me on the ropes, out come my weapon and he turn *stone*. Lord, even eyes like mine I seen *his* eyes, they got *that* big lookin' at me. Yeah, yeah, he seen *me*, all right, he *seen* me; gonna be a while 'fore he mess with *this* alley cat again. *(Studying the piece of buckskin)* Must be a way to frame a thing like this . . .

(Silence; then the distant Carousel Band-Organ starts playing it's

first song of the day, "Sidewalks of New York"; NAT looks up, realizing what time it must be)

NAT   *(starts to rise, using bench for support)* Unfortunately, I must leave now . . .

MIDGE   *(turns to him, smiles)* Best news I heard all day.

NAT   I am expected at the Senior Center at noon. The day begins at noon there. I must be prompt; Clara checks up. *(Unfolding the walker)* Also weekends in Great Neck. I am seldom in the park anymore.

MIDGE   *(returns to his newspaper)* News is gettin' better and better . . .

NAT   *(steps inside of walker, his hands on the rails)* The hospital said you just got out, I came today on the chance of seeing you. I felt I owed you an apology; also the truth. My name is Nat Moyer; this is my actual name. I was a few years with the Fur Workers' Union, this was true, but when Ben Gold lost power they let me go. I was then for forty-one years a waiter at Deitz's Dairy Restaurant on Houston Street; that's all, a waiter. I was retired at age seventy-three; they said they would have kept me on except I talked too much, annoyed the customers. I presently reside, and have for some time, at the Amsterdam Hotel; here my main occupation is learning more things about tuna fish than God ever intended. In other words, whatever has been said previously, I was, and am now, no one. No one at all. This is the truth. Goodbye and good luck to you and your knife. *(He starts moving slowly down the path with his walker towards the exit at left)* Better get going to the Center. At Twelve, guest speaker Jerome Cooper will lecture on "Timely Issues for the Aging"; refreshments will be served to anyone who's alive at the end . . .

MIDGE   *(quietly, shaking his head)* Shit, man, you *still* can't tell the truth.

NAT   *(continues moving away)* That was the truth.

MIDGE   Damn it, tell me the truth.

NAT   I *told* you the truth. That's what I was, that's *all*—

MIDGE   *(angrily, slapping the bench)* No, you wasn't a waiter. What was you really?

NAT   I was a waiter . . .

MIDGE   *(shouting angrily)* You wasn't just a waiter, you was *more* than that! Tell me the truth, damn it—

NAT   *(he stops on the path; shouts)* I was a *waiter*, that's *it!* *(Silence for a moment; then he continues down the path on his walker. He stops after a few steps; silence for several moments. Then, quietly:)* Except, of course, for a brief time in the motion picture industry.

MIDGE   You mean the movies?

NAT   Well, *you* call it the movies; *we* call it the motion picture industry.

MIDGE   What kinda job you have there?

NAT   A job? What I did you couldn't call a job. You see, I was, briefly, a mogul.

MIDGE   Mogul; yeah, I hearda that. Ain't that some kinda Rabbi or somethin'?

NAT   In a manner of speaking, yes. *(Moving towards* MIDGE *at bench)* A sort of motion picture rabbi, you might say. One who leads, instructs, inspires; that's a mogul. It's the early Fifties, Blacklisting, the Red Scare, terror reigns, the industry is frozen. Nobody can make a move. It's colleague against colleague, brother against brother. I had written a few articles for the papers, some theories on the subject. Suddenly, they call me, they fly me there—boom, I'm a mogul. *(Sitting on bench)* The industry needs answers. What should I do?

MIDGE   *(leans towards him, intently)* What *did* you do?

NAT   Well, that's a long story . . . a long and complicated story . . .

(He crosses his legs, leans back on the bench, about to launch into his story, the Carousel Music building loudly as . . .)

THE CURTAIN FALLS

CONVERSATIONS
WITH
MY FATHER

CONVERSATIONS WITH MY FATHER

T he curtain goes up and suddenly we are in a saloon burnished with
memories of New York past. There is a wonderfully baroque jukebox
and small tables and framed photographs of Benny Leonard and Barney
Ross. Over the bar there's a giant moose head and a photograph of an ebul-
lient F.D.R. American flags are everywhere. And a Yiddish song is playing.
"Rumania, Rumania, Rumania ... Geven amol a land a zise, a sheyne ..."

We are suddenly in the world of Herb Gardner's luminous play,
Conversations With My Father, and we have been transported back to the
New York that all of us have left behind. This is a play about a father and
his sons, about the nature of being Jewish, about survival and disaster. But
it's not at all narrow; by being specific, it's also universal. As a result, this
layered, beautifully crafted play is about all those fathers who came to New
York from terrible places, and all the sons who had to learn the sometimes
dark and dreadful lessons about becoming Americans.

"Here's what we got going for us, kid," says Eddie Goldberg to his
two-year-old son, Charlie, who sits mute in a stroller. Eddie drops a nickel
in the jukebox. "We got America."

He plays Paul Whiteman's version of "America the Beautiful," but
this moment isn't hokey; it's ironical. Particularly as Eddie Goldberg talks
to the child about his dream of moving from Canal Street to the dubious
glories of Uptown:

"Now there's only two ways a Jew *gets* Uptown; wanna get outa
here, kid, you gotta *punch* your way out or *think* your way out. You're
Jewish, you gotta be smarter than everybody else; or cuter or faster or funnier. Or tougher. Because basically, they want to kill you; this is true maybe
thirty, thirty-five hundred years now and is not likely to change next
Tuesday. It's not they don't want you in Moscow, or Kiev, or Lodz, or Jersey
City: it's the earth, they don't want you on the *earth* is the problem; so the
trick is to become necessary. If they need you they don't kill you. Naturally,
they're gonna hate you for needing you, but that beats they don't need you
and they kill you, got it?" To which, in a moment, the Yiddish actor
Zaretsky (who does a twelve-minute version of *The Dybbuk*) looks up from
his newspaper and says: "Itzik, the only Jew in this room being persecuted
is two years old."

That line gets a big laugh, and the play is full of laughter. Eddie is funny; his wife tells jokes; and irony suffuses the narrative. The play is a classic example of the way the funniest men are also the most serious. This is not a tract about anti-Semitism; it's an entertainment, a drama of wit and intelligence that gets to your head by way of the belly. Eddie teaches his son to go to the body in street fights; Gardner does the same.

At one point, Eddie gives his two-year-old son the basic advice for survival in America and uses a sentence that chilled me: "Don't take shit from nobody." That was also the basic advice given to me in Brooklyn a half-century ago by my Irish-immigrant father. The same exact phrase. My father, who also had F.D.R. on the kitchen wall, would have loved Eddie Goldberg's saloon. And Eddie Goldberg too — even after he changed his name to Ross, in honor of the welterweight fighter and opponent of Jimmy McLarnin.

And as an Irish immigrant, he'd have understood the issues of the play. Like Brian Friel's *Dancing at Lughnasa*, Gardner's play is also about language: words, names, the lost language of Old Country myths. Long before the Jews surrendered Yiddish for English, the Irish language was slain by the Brits. The Irish Anglicized their names too. And every child of the Irish diaspora will understand what happens when Goldberg becomes Ross; Itzik becomes Eddie; his wife, Gusta, becomes Gloria. In the end, you are what you are. And even while cursing God, Eddie remains triumphantly Jewish.

Gardner's own father ran a saloon down by the old Police Headquarters on Centre Street, and the place, the emotions and many of the events are autobiographical. "But it's a collage," he said. "Some of my father, parts of two uncles ..." Gardner grew up in Brooklyn, he remembers clearly the mini-pogrom that hit New York on election night in 1944, when the children of the American Right roamed the neighborhoods in search of Jews, whom they blamed for the war. "That happened," he said. "I was there."

Those events figure in the play. But they are not used to attack the idea of America; they are part of a larger affirmation. In this, his greatest play, Herb Gardner reminds us once again of the truth of Faulkner's line, that we love in spite of, not because.

— PETE HAMILL
New York City

I was first introduced to the plays of Herb Gardner in the late seventies by a mutual friend, the director Gene Saks. Gene and I were on a pre-Broadway tour of my play *How the Other Half Loves* when we spent many late nights together cowering in out-of-town hotel rooms desperately trying to fend off producers' "improvements" to the script and production. Gene and I had both started out as actors and, during those anxious pre-Broadway times, we exchanged the standard disaster stories in which theatre people delight. (But when did you ever hear a good theatre anecdote start, "I was in this terribly successful show ..."?) Amongst these was a classic one of Gene's when he appeared as a child-hating children's entertainer, Chuckles the Chipmunk, in Herb's play, *A Thousand Clowns*. On the Broadway first night Gene nervously waited in the wings for two long acts, laden down with a dozen or so vital props but finally when his cue came contrived to go on empty handed.

When I escaped back to England (The Times knocking us to the canvas on a technical KO) I got hold of a copy of *Clowns* and in 1984, as part of a US mini-season, I directed it along with Simon's *Last of the Red Hot Lovers* and Gurney's *The Dining Room* at my home theatre in Scarborough, North Yorkshire. The season came and went, we had a lot of laughs doing it, life went on and I never got to meet Herb in person though we had some very entertaining phone conversations.

It was nearly ten years later, in 1993, that he mailed me a copy of *Conversations With My Father*. Actually, I think he'd sent it less with a view to my directing it than as a request for help from a fellow author, since he was having difficulty getting a production in the UK. It was, he explained, different from *Clowns*, being a rather personal play. Reading it, I considered that to be the understatement of the decade. It was an intensely personal play. A funny, moving portrait of a Jewish immigrant family growing up in New York through a depression and a world war, managing somehow to overcome racial prejudice, cultural upheaval and social change. In particular, I was captivated by the central character, Eddie, who to my mind is as richly drawn as any contemporary dramatic figure I have come across. Based, of course, on Herb's own father, we were very lucky in the Scarborough production to have Judd Hirsch, the original creator, reproduce his electrifying performance as Eddie in our tiny 300 seat theatre in the round, and then at The Old Vic in London.

During the production, I once asked Herb how he came by the title. At the age of seventeen, it seems, Herb had come into his father's bar ("The Golden Door" of the play, actually "The Silver Gate" in life) early one morning to break the news to him that he had decided not to go to college. His father's reaction was immediate and clear; he proceeded to wreck the bar, overturning tables, hurling bar-stools, smashing glasses. Exhausted finally, he sat on the one remaining stool among the wreckage — the bar now looking very much like Berlin in nineteen forty-five. There was a long silence. "Well," he declared calmly, "I think that was a very good conversation."

— ALAN AYCKBOURN
London, England

Conversations With My Father was originally presented by the Seattle Repertory Theatre in April 1991.

The play was subsequently presented by James Walsh at the Royale Theatre in New York City on March 28, 1992. The cast was:

CHARLIE	Tony Shalhoub
JOSH	Tony Gillan
EDDIE	Judd Hirsch
GUSTA	Gordana Rashovich
ZARETSKY	David Margulies
YOUNG JOEY	Jason Biggs
HANNAH DI BLINDEH	Marilyn Sokol
NICK	William Biff McGuire
FINNEY THE BOOK	Peter Gerety
JIMMY SCALSO	John Procaccino
BLUE	Richard E. Council
YOUNG CHARLIE	David Krumholtz
JOEY	Tony Gillan

Directed by Daniel Sullivan
Setting by Tony Walton
Costumes by Robert Wojewodski
Lighting by Pat Collins

CHARACTERS

CHARLIE

JOSH

EDDIE

GUSTA

ZARETSKY

JOEY, age 10

HANNAH DI BLINDEH

NICK

FINNEY THE BOOK

JIMMY SCALSO

BLUE

CHARLIE, age 11-13

JOEY, age 17

The Homeland Tavern—also known as Eddie Goldberg's Golden Door Tavern, The Flamingo Lounge, and The Twin Forties Cafe— on Canal Street, near Broadway, in Lower Manhattan.

ACT I: Scene 1: June 25, 1976, early evening.

Scene 2: July 4, 1936, early morning.

ACT II: Scene 1: July 3, 1944, early morning.

Scene 2: About seven that evening.

Scene 3: August 8, 1945, early morning.

Scene 4: October 15, 1965, early morning.

Scene 5: About eight weeks later, early morning.

Scene 6: June 25, 1976, early evening.

ACT ONE

Scene: The interior of The Homeland Tavern on Canal Street near Broadway in Lower Manhattan, June 25, 1976. Although the place is obviously very old, some attempt had been made at one time to give it an Old Tavern style in addition. The original patterned-tin ceiling is there, the pillared walls, the scarred oak bar, the leaded-glass cabinets, the smoked mirror behind the bar, the high-backed wooden booths with their cracked leather seats, the battered and lumbering ceiling fans; but someone has tried to go Old one better here, a kind of Ye Olde Tavern look—a large, dusty Moose head has been placed above the mirror, its huge eyes staring into the room; an imitation antique Revolutionary War musket and powder horn hang on the wall over one of the booths, and over three others are a long-handled fake-copper frying pan, a commander's sword in a rusty scabbard, and a cheaply framed reproduction of "Washington Crossing the Delaware"; a large copy of the Declaration of Independence, with an imitation-parchment-scroll effect and a legend at the bottom saying "A Gift for You from Daitch's Beer," hangs on the back wall next to the pay phone, its text covered with phone numbers; a battle-scarred Old Glory print is tacked up over the yellow "Golden Door" of the entrance and a dozen copies of old oil lamps have been placed about the room with naked light bulbs stuck in them. But the genuinely old stuff is in disrepair—absent panes in the glass panels, missing slats in the booths, gaps in the ceiling design, blades gone from the fans, moth-holes in the Moose-hide, dents in the pillars, the thick heating and water pipes acned by age and too many paint jobs—and the fake old stuff is just too clearly fake and second hand, so the final effect of the place is inescapably shabby. Somehow, though, there is still something warm, colorful, and neighborhood-friendly about the place; you'd want to hang around in it.

The bar runs along the left wall and the four booths run along the right, a few tables and chairs at center. The entrance is down left at the end of the bar, and on the wall behind the bar is a very large but not very good oil painting of four men playing poker and smoking cigars, one of them wearing a green eyeshade. Dozens of photographs of Boxers and Performers—the ones of Benny Leonard, Barney Ross, and Eddie Cantor are autographed—have been taped up around the mirror, as has the December 6, 1933, front page of "The New York Times" heralding the end of Prohibition; a large photo of Franklin D. Roosevelt, a cigarette holder clenched in his broad smile, hangs in a fancy frame over the cash register. Against the wall up center is a glowing red, yellow, and orange Wurlitzer Jukebox, Model 800, a beauty; to its left a door with a small circular window opens into the tiny bar-kitchen, and to its right a stairway leads up to the door of the Apartment over the bar where a family once lived.

At Rise: Before the curtain goes up we hear the zesty, full-spirited voice of Aaron Lebedeff, backed by a wailing Klezmer Band, singing the beginning of an old Yiddish Music Hall song called "Rumania, Rumania"; an invitation to the joys of food, wine, romance, friendship, dancing, and more food. The song speaks of Rumania but it could be telling us about Odessa, Budapest, Warsaw, Lodz, Brody, the places of an older and better world that may never have existed but certainly should have.

LEBEDEFF'S VOICE

> "Rumania, Rumania, Rumania . . .
> Geven amol a land a zise, a sheyne,
> Ah, Rumania, Rumania, Rumania,
> Geven amol a land a zise, a fayne,
> Dort tsu voyen iz a fargenign,
> Vos dos harts glust kentsu krign,
> A Mamaligele, a Pastramile, a Karnatsele,
> Un a glezele vayn, aaaaaaaah . . . !"

(Lebedeff's Voice and the bouncing Klezmer Band continue as the curtain goes up and we see that the Music is coming from the Jukebox; its pulsing colors and the glow from the open Apartment door at the top of the stairs are the only real light in the bar at first. It is early evening, June 25, 1976; no one onstage, the upended chairs on the tables and the dim, dust-filled light tell us that the place has been closed for a while. The Music continues in the empty bar for a few moments)

LEBEDEFF'S VOICE

> "Ay, in Rumania iz doch git,
> Fun kayn dayges veyst men nit,
> Vayn trinkt men iberal—
> M'farbayst mit Kashtoval.
> Hey, digi digi dam, digi digi digi dam . . . "

(A sudden rattle of keys in the entrance door and Charlie, early forties, casually dressed, enters briskly, crosses immediately to the stairs leading to the Apartment door, shouts up)

CHARLIE   *(trying to be heard above the Music)* Josh!   *(Opens Jukebox, turns off the Music, tries again)*   Josh!

JOSH'S VOICE   Yeah?

CHARLIE   It's five-thirty. *(He shifts his keys from hand to hand, glancing about the bar, waiting for Josh; he clearly doesn't want to stay in the place any longer than he has to. He looks up at the Moose for a moment, then raises his hand in farewell)*   Well, Morris . . . goodbye and good luck.

(Josh, about twenty, appears in the Apartment doorway carrying an old folded Baby-Stroller, an antique samovar, some faded documents, a few dusty framed photographs)

JOSH   Who're you talking to, Dad?

CHARLIE   Morris. Morris the Moose. We haven't had a really good talk since I was twelve. Find some things you want?

JOSH   *(coming down the stairs)* Great stuff, Dad, great stuff up there. History, history. Grandma's closet, just the *closet*, it was like her own Smith*sonian* in there. *(Putting objects on table)* You sure you don't want *any* of this? *(Opens Stroller, places it near bar)* Look at this; perfect.

CHARLIE   Seems a little small for me, Josh. *(Reaches briskly behind bar for bottle of cold Russian vodka, knowing exactly where to find it, fills shot-glass)*

JOSH   Dad, believe me—some of the stuff upstairs, you really ought to take a look before I pack it up. Some extraordinary *things*, Dad—wonderful brown photographs full of people looking like *us*—some great old books, Russian, Yiddish—

CHARLIE   *(briskly)* It's all yours, kid. Whatever you can fit in your place. And anything down here; including Morris. Only the basic fixtures are included in the sale.

JOSH   *(not listening, absorbed in documents)* Perfect, this is perfect, one of Grandpa's bar signs— *(reads from faded posterboard)* "V.J. Day Special, the Atomic Cocktail, One Dollar, If the First Blast Don't Get You, the Fallout Will."

CHARLIE   *(impatiently, checking watch, pointing upstairs)* Josh, it's getting late; pick what you want and let's go.

JOSH   *(reads from old document)* "Declaration of Intention to Become a Citizen" . . . *Your* Grandpa, listen . . . "I, Solomon Leib Goldberg, hereby renounce my allegiance to the Czar of All the Russias, and declare my intention to—"

CHARLIE   *(cutting him off)* Got the station wagon right out front; pack it up, let's move.

JOSH   I don't get it; only a month since Grandma died, why does the place have to be sold so fast?

CHARLIE   Leave a bar closed too long it loses its value. Customers drift away. That's how it works. Deal's almost set. *(Points upstairs)* Come on, Josh, let's—

JOSH   I don't get it, I just don't get it . . . *(Going up stairs)* What difference would another *week* make? What's the hurry, what's the *hurry* here, man . . . ? *(He exits into Apartment. Charlie sits at bar; then looks up at Moose)*

CHARLIE   He wants to know what's the hurry here, Morris.

(Silence for a moment, Charlie lost in thought; the Jukebox glowing brighter as we hear the sudden sound of a full Chorus and Marching Band doing a thunderous rendition of "Columbia, the Gem of the Ocean")

CHORUS and **BAND**   *(from Jukebox)*

"Three cheers for the red, white and blue,
Three cheers for the red, white and blue,
The Army and Navy forever,
Three cheers for the red, white and blue . . ."

(All stage lights, one section after the other, coming up full now in strict cadence to the trumpets, drums and Chorus: the many fake oil lamps, the overheads, the bar-lights, the dawn-light from the street, all coming up in tempo to reveal an image of rampant patriotism only dimly perceived in earlier shadow—red, white and blue crepe bunting hung across the full length of the bar-mirror and on the back of each booth, and several dozen small American flags on gold-painted sticks placed everywhere about the room; the trumpets building, the ceiling fans spinning, as Eddie Goldberg, a man in his early forties who moves like an ex-boxer, bursts out of the Kitchen, a swath of bunting across his shoulders, a batch of foot-high flags in one hand and an individual flag in the other, waving them all to the Music. July Fourth, 1936, and Eddie Goldberg have arrived suddenly and uninvited— Charlie turning slowly from the bar to watch him. Eddie wears a fine white shirt, black bow-tie, sharp black pants and noticeably polished shoes—an outfit better suited to an Uptown cocktail lounge than to this Canal Street gin-mill. He parks the batch of flags on a nearby table, drapes the bunting with a grand flourish across the Stroller, sticks the individual flag onto the hood—all these movements in strict time to the powerful March Music that continues to blare out of the Jukebox, his spirits rising with the soaring finale of the record, circling the Stroller once and finishing with a fancy salute to the Kid within,

kneeling next to the Stroller as the record comes to a trumpet-blast-ing, cymbal-crashing end)

CHORUS and BAND   *(continued)*

"When borne by the red, white and blue,
When borne by the red, white and blue,
Thy banners make tyranny tremble,
When borne by the red, white and blue!"

EDDIE   *(he points to the Moose)*   Moose. See? See the nice Moose? Moose, that's an easy one. An "M" at the beginning, "MMMM," and then "OOOO"; Moose. Mmmmooooose. See the pretty Moose? Just look at the Moose. Moose. *(He waits. Silence from the Stroller)*   Forget the Moose. We'll wait on the Moose. "Duckie." Hey, how about "duckie"? You had "duckie" last Saturday, you had it down cold. "Duckie." *(Reaches under Stroller, takes out wood-en duck, presents duck)*   Here ya go, here ya go; duckie. *Here's* the duckie. Look at that duckie; helluva duckie, hah? Hah? *(Hides the duck behind his back)*   Where's the duckie? You want the duckie? Ask me for the duckie. Say "duckie." *(Silence for a moment; he leans against the bar)*   You lost it. You lost "duckie." You had it and you lost it. Now we're losin' what we *had*, we're goin' *back*wards, Charlie. *(Starts to pace in front of bar)*   Kid, you're gonna be two; we gotta get movin' here. Goddamn *two*, kid. I mean, your broth-er Joey—your age—we had a goddamn conver*sationalist* in there! *(Silence for a moment)*   Charlie, Charlie, you got any idea how much heartache you're givin' us with this issue, with this god-damn vow of *silence* here? Six words in two years and now *gornisht*, not even a "Mama" or a "Papa." *(Grabs the batch of flags, starts placing one on each table about the room; quietly, controlling himself)*   Frankly, I'm concerned about your mother. Granted, the woman is not exactly a hundred percent in the Brains Department her*self*, also a little on the wacky side, also she don't hear a goddamn word anybody says so why should you want to talk to her in the first place—nevertheless, on this issue, my heart goes out to the woman. She got a kid who don't do shit. She goes to Rutgers Square every morning with the other mothers, they sit on the long bench there—in every stroller, right down the line, we got talkin', we got singin', we got tricks; in *your* stroller we got *gor-nisht*. We got a kid who don't make an *effort*, a boy who don't *extend* himself. *(Leaning down close to Stroller)*   That's the *trouble* with you, you don't *extend* yourself. You never did. You don't *now*, you never *did*, and you never *will*. *(Suddenly, urgently, whispering)*   Come on, kid, gimme something, what's it *to* ya? I open for busi-ness in an hour, every morning the regulars come in, you *stare* at them; I tell 'em you're sick, I cover for you. It's July Fourth, a special occasion, be an American, make an effort. *(Grabs the duck off the bar, leans down to the Stroller with it)* Come on: "duckie," just a "duckie," one "duckie" would be a Mitzvah ... *(Silence from the Stroller; then the beginnings of a sound, barely audible at first; Eddie leans forward, smiling hopefully)* What's that? What ... ? *(The sound grows louder, but there is no discernible word, and finally what we hear quite clearly is pure baby-babble, something like "ba-bap, ba-bap, ba-bap ... ")* Oh, shut up. Just *shut* up, will ya! If that's how you're gonna talk, then shut ya goddamn *trap!*

(Eddie turns sharply and throws the wooden duck violently across the room—it smashes against the farthest down right booth, barely missing Charlie, who has been seated in the booth, watching. Charlie turns, startled, as the pieces of the duck clatter to the floor. Eddie strides angrily over to the bar and then behind it, turning his back to the Stroller, starts to clean glasses from the sink and slap them onto a shelf as the baby-babble continues)

EDDIE   *(shouting)* The conversation is *over*, kid!

(The baby-babble stops abruptly. Silence for a moment)

CHARLIE   *(to Audience; calmly, cordially)* Duck Number Sixteen; other casualties this year include four torn Teddy bears and a twisted metal frog. *(Rising from booth, moving down towards us)* "Gornisht"—in case it wasn't clear to you—means "nothing." "Gornisht *with* gornisht" being less than nothing. The only thing less than that is "bupkes," which is beans, and less than that is "bupkes mit beblach," which is beans with more beans. In Yiddish, the only thing less than nothing is the existence of something so worthless that the presence of nothing becomes more obvious. Which brings me to the story of my life ... *(Shrugs, smiling)* Sorry; I can't resist a straight-line, even one of my own. I just—I hear them coming. I am often criticized for this. Oh, but they are everywhere and always irresistible: there are people who are straight-lines—both my ex-wives, for example, and all of my accountants—days, sometimes entire years, whole cities like Newark and Cleveland—"What did you do in Newark last weekend? I dreamt of Cleveland"—and some lifetimes, whole lifetimes like my father's, are set-ups for punch-lines. *(Moving towards Stroller)* That's me in the stroller there and, as you can hear, I *did* finally learn to talk—last year I even started using the word "duck" without bursting into tears— *(We hear the sudden sound of the Kid crying; he leans down to Stroller, whispers gently)* Don't worry, kid . . . in just a few years they'll be telling you you talk too much.

EDDIE   (*shouting*) Gloria! (*Remains with his back to Stroller, continues briskly cleaning glasses*) Gloria, the kid! Change the kid! (*The Kid is instantly quieter, comforted by the sound of his father's voice even though he's shouting*) Gloria, the kid! Time to change him! (*Then, louder*) For another kid! (*Turns towards stairway*) Gloria, why don't you *answer* me?!

GUSTA'S VOICE   (*from upstairs, a strong Russian accent*) Because I only been Gloria two and a half weeks . . . and I was Gusta for thirty-eight years; I'm waiting to recognize.

EDDIE   I thought you liked the name.

GUSTA'S VOICE   I liked it till I heard it hollered. Meanwhile, your wife, Gloria, she's got a rusty sink to clean.

EDDIE   Hey, what about the *kid* here? I gotta get the bar open!

GUSTA'S VOICE   (*graciously*) A shaynim dank, mit eyn toches ken men nit zayn oyf tsvey simches.

CHARLIE   (*to Audience*) Roughly, that's "Thank you, but with one rear-end I can't go to two parties."

EDDIE   English! English! Say it in *English*, for Chrissakes!

GUSTA'S VOICE   You can't say it in English, Eddie, it don't do the job.

CHARLIE   She's right, of course, English don't do the job. Sure, you can say "Rise and shine!," but is that as good as "Shlof gicher, me darf der kishen," which means "Sleep faster, we need your pillow"? Does "You can't take it with you" serve the moment better than "Tachtrich macht me on keshenes," which means "They don't put pockets in shrouds"? Can there be a greater scoundrel than a paskudnyak, a more screwed-up life than one that is ongepatshket? Why go into battle with a punch, a jab, a sock and a swing when you could be armed with a klop, a frosk, a zetz and a chamalia? Can poor, undernourished English turn an answer into a question, a proposition into a conclusion, a sigh into an opera? No. No, it just don't do the job, Pop. (*Eddie flips a switch, lighting up the freshly painted entrance to the bar*) Behold . . . the Golden Door— (*taking in the bar with a sweep of his hand*)—and here, "Eddie Goldberg's Golden Door Tavern" . . . formerly "Cap'n Ed's Place," "The Café Edward," "Eduardo's Cantina," and "Frisco Eddie's Famous Bar and Grill"; living above it are Gloria and Eddie, formerly Gusta and Itzik, their sons Charlie and Joey, formerly Chaim and Jussel— (*a sweep of his hand up*

towards the Apartment doorway as Zaretsky enters) and our boarder,
Professor Anton Zaretsky— *(No matter how quietly or subtly, it is
impossible for this old actor to come into a room without making an
entrance—this same theatrical glow is true of his departures—proceeding purposefully down the stairway to the bar now, carrying his seventy years like an award, his unseasonably long, felt-collared coat draped
capelike over his shoulders, his thin cigarette held elegantly, Russian-
style, between his thumb and forefinger)* —formerly of Odessa's
Marinsky Theatre and the Second Avenue Yiddish Classic Art
Players; now, in leaner times, appearing solo and at club meetings
as *all* of the Second Avenue Yiddish Classic Art Players, some
ascribing this to the Depression and others to the inconvenience
of having to work on a stage cluttered by other actors.

*(As Zaretsky arrives at the bar, Eddie, without turning to him, and
clearly enacting the ritual of many mornings, briskly pours half a
tumbler of straight vodka, places it behind himself on the bar, still
without turning, and quickly resumes his busy preparations. Zaretsky,
with a sweep of his arm and a sharp flick of his wrist, downs the vodka
in one efficient swallow; he places the empty tumbler with a snap on
the bar, pauses a moment—then lets go with a truly hair-raising,
shattering, siren-like scream of pain. The scream, obviously part of the
ritual, is in no way acknowledged by Charlie, the Kid in the Stroller,
Eddie—who continues with his back to Zaretsky—or Zaretsky himself. Silence again for a moment or two)*

ZARETSKY *(elegant Russian accent, to Kid in Stroller and Eddie)* Chaim,
Itzik, God had two great ideas: beautiful women, and how to
drink a potato.

*(He crosses briskly to his usual table at center, opens his newspaper—
one of several Yiddish journals he carries with him along with an old
carpetbag-style valise—and sits deep into his chair and a world of his
own, encircled by his morning vodka and "The Jewish Daily
Forward"; all this as Charlie moves towards the stairway, looks up at
Apartment, continues talking)*

CHARLIE   Very important distinction between living behind your
store and living *above* it—two years ago we'd made the big move
from "living in back" on Rivington to "living over" on Canal;
surely goodness and mercy and the Big Bucks would soon be following us.

ZARETSKY   *(not looking up from paper)* For those interested, from
today's "Jewish Daily Forward," an item: "Yesterday morning in
Geneva, Stefan Lux, a forty-eight-year-old Jewish journalist from
Prague, stood up in the midst of a League of Nations meeting,

pulled an automatic pistol from his briefcase, shouted 'Avenol, Avenol,' and shot himself in the chest. In his briefcase a letter to Secretary General Joseph Avenol stating that he has killed himself publicly to awaken the League's conscience to the plight of the Jews in the Reich." *(Silence; waits for response, then turns page)* I thank you all for your attention.

EDDIE   *(slaps the bar with his towel)* O.K., Charlie, I know what's *up*, I know what you're *doin'* . . . *(Turns to Stroller; smiling)* And I *like* it! *(Approaching Stroller with diaper and towel)* You're *my kid* and you're not gonna say what you gotta say till you're damn good and *ready*. So I say *this* to you—don't let nobody push you around, and I include *myself* in that remark; got it? Because I would be tickled pink if the first goddamn sentence you ever said was: "Charlie Goldberg don't take shit from *nobody!*" *(Taking dirty diaper out of Stroller)* O.K., now I see you got a hold of your dick there. This don't bother me, be my guest. There's many schools of thought on grabbing your dick, pro and con. Me, I'm pro. I say, go to it, it's *your dick*. What you hope for is that someday some kind person out there will be as interested in it as you are. What you got a hold of there is optimism itself, what you got there in your hand is blind hope, which is the best kind. *(Grips edge of Stroller)* Everybody says to me, "Hey, four bars into the toilet, *enough*, *forget* it, Eddie—a steady job tendin' *bar*, Eddie, maybe managin' a class place"—I say, "I don't work for *nobody*, baby, this ain't no employee's personality; I sweat, but I sweat for my *own*." *(Deposits slug in Jukebox, making selection)* And I ain't talking about no gin-mill, kid, I ain't talkin' about saloons and stand-up bars— I'm talkin' about what we got *here*, Charlie . . . I'm talkin' about America . . . *(From the Jukebox we begin to hear a full Chorus and Orchestra doing a gorgeous rendition of "America, the Beautiful," all strings and harps and lovely echoing voices)* We give 'em *America*, Charlie— *(Takes in the place with a sweep of his hand as the Music fills the room)* We give 'em a Moose, we give 'em George Washington, we give 'em the red-white-and-blue, and mostly we give 'em, bar none, the greatest American invention of the last ten years—*Cocktails!* *(He flips a switch, illuminating the entire bar area, the mirror glows, a long strip of bulbs running the length of the shelf at the base of the mirror lights up the row of several dozen exotically colored cocktail-mix bottles; he points at the Stroller)* O.K., *Canal* Street, y'say—that's not a cocktail *clientele* out there, these are people who would suck after-shave lotion out of a wet washcloth— *(Advancing on Stroller as Music builds)* *Nossir!* The trick here, all ya gotta remember, is nobody's equal but everybody *wants* to be—downtown slobs lookin' for uptown class, goddamn Greenhorns lookin' to turn Yankee—New York style American Cocktails, Charlie! We liquor up these low-life nickel-dimers just long enough to bankroll an Uptown lounge—

CHORUS and **ORCHESTRA** *(a Soprano solo rising delicately as Eddie kneels next to Stroller)*

" . . . Thine alabaster cities gleam,
Undimmed by human tears . . . "

EDDIE *Yessir,* that's where we're *goin',* you and me; I'm lookin' Uptown, kid, Madison, Lex—I got a *plan,* see, I'm *thinkin'—* *(Rising with the lush Soprano)* because there's only two ways a Jew *gets* Uptown; wanna get outa here, kid, you gotta *punch* your way out or *think* your way out. You're Jewish you gotta be smarter than everybody else; or cuter or faster or funnier. Or tougher. Because, basically, they want to kill you; this is true maybe thirty, thirty-five hundred years now and is not likely to change next Tuesday. It's not they don't want you in Moscow, or Kiev, or Lodz, or Jersey City: it's the earth, they don't want you on the *earth* is the problem; so the trick is to become necessary. If they need you they don't kill you. Naturally, they're gonna hate you for needing you, but that beats they don't need you and they kill you. Got it? *(His arms spread wide in conclusion)* This, kid . . . is the whole story.

CHORUS and **ORCHESTRA** *(Full Chorus and Strings as the Music comes to a lush finale)*

" . . . From sea to shining sea!"

ZARETSKY *(not looking up from newspaper)* Itzik, the only Jew in this room being persecuted is two years old.

EDDIE You, Actor; quiet.

ZARETSKY Fortunately, he understands very few of your dangerously misguided words, Itzik.

EDDIE *Eddie,* goddamnit, *Eddie!*

ZARETSKY Please, enough; I am not feeling very vigorous this morning. You have kept an entire household awake all night with your terrible noises.

EDDIE Terrible *noises?* I'm up all night doin' a complete refurbish on the place, single-handed, top to bottom; I don't hear no comment. *(Continuing work behind bar)* Guy *lives* here should show an interest.

ZARETSKY   *(he puts down his paper; looks about, nodding thoughtfully)* Ah, yes. Ah, yes . . . Tell me, Eddie; what period are you attempting to capture here?

EDDIE   Early American.

ZARETSKY   I see. How early?

EDDIE   Revolutionary *War*, shmuck. From now on this place, it's always gonna be the Fourth of July here. How about that Moose?

ZARETSKY   *(leans back, studying it)* Ah, yes; the Moose.

EDDIE   How's it look to ya?

ZARETSKY   Shocked. Completely shocked to be here. One minute he's trotting freely through the sweet green forest—next thing he knows he's staring out at a third-rate saloon on Canal Street; forever. Yes, shocked and dismayed to be here, in Early America. As am I, *Eddie. (He lifts up his newspaper)*

EDDIE   *(turns sharply from bar)* Greenhorn! Greenhorn bullshit! You came here a Grinneh, you *stayed* a Grinneh. *Grinneh*—you were *then*, you are *now*, and you always *will* be! *(Leans towards him)* I *hear* ya, what kinda *noise* is that? "I don't feel wery wigorous"— what *is* that? Ya don't have to *do* that, ya *know* ya don't, you could get *rid* of that. I come here after *you* did, listen to me. Check the patter. I read Winchell, I go to the movies, I know the score—

(During these last few moments, Gusta has entered from the Apartment above and stopped about halfway down the stairs, her attention caught by the Moose head; small, perpetually busy, near forty, she carries two large pots of just-cooked food, each about a third of her size)

GUSTA   Eddie, there's an animal on the wall.

EDDIE   It's a Moose.

GUSTA   All right, I'll believe you; it's a Moose. Why is it on the wall?

EDDIE   For one thing, it's a Moose *head*—

GUSTA   Believe me, I didn't think the rest of it was sticking out into Canal Street.

CHARLIE   Hey . . . she's actually *funny* . . . *(To Eddie) Laugh*, will ya?

GUSTA   *(crossing quickly to Kitchen)* My favorite, personally, was "Cap'n Ed's Place"; I liked those waves you painted on the mirror, and your sailor hat, *that* was a beauty.

EDDIE   Captain's hat, it was a *Captain's* hat— *(Quietly, to Stroller)* Why do I talk to her? Why? *Tell* me. Do *you* know?

GUSTA *(chuckling, setting pots down on stove)* Meanwhile, I see so far nobody showed up for the Revolution.

EDDIE Because we ain't *open* yet! *Eight* o'clock, that's the law, I stick to the rules. *(Points to framed Roosevelt photo)* Like F.D.R. says, in that way he's got—"It is by strict adherence to the rules that we shall avoid descent to the former evils of the saloon."

GUSTA *(indicates F.D.R. photo)* Look at that smile, the man him*self* is half-drunk mosta the time. Your Roosevelt, he says, "There is nothing to fear but fear itself." What, that's not *enough?*

EDDIE Not another *word*—not another word against the man in my place!

GUSTA *(approaching Stroller with bit of food on stirring spoon, singing softly, an old Yiddish lullaby)*

> "Oif'n pripitchok, brent a faieril,
> Un in shtub iz heys,
> Un der rebe lerent kleyne kinderlach
> Dem alef beys . . ."

CHARLIE *(at Kitchen, inhaling the memory)* That food . . . Brisket Tzimmes, Lokshen Kugel . . .

GUSTA *(sitting next to Stroller, gently)*

> "Zetje kinderlach, gedenktje taiere,
> Voseer lerent daw . . . "

(Zaretsky starts to hum along with her)

> "Zogtje noch amol, un take noch amol,
> Kometz alef aw . . . "

EDDIE Hey, you people want lullabies, what the hell's wrong with "Rock-a-bye Baby"? A good, solid, American hit—

GUSTA *(softly, reaching spoon into Stroller)*

> "Zogtje noch amol, un take noch amol,
> Kometz alef aw . . . "

CHARLIE *(softly, kneeling near her)* She's young . . . she's so young . . .

GUSTA *(smiling sweetly)* Now sing along with me, darling; just "Alef aw" . . . *(Singing, Charlie behind her urging the Kid to respond)* "Kometz alef aw . . . alef aw . . ." *(No response; she shrugs)* A shtik fleysh mit oygen. *(Goes back to Kitchen)*

CHARLIE My mother has just referred to me as "a piece of meat with two eyes."

EDDIE   That's why the kid don't talk, he don't know what *language* to speak!

GUSTA   *(laughing to herself, stacking dishes on bar)*   Eddie, Ethel called me with two good ones this morning—I mean, *good* ones—

EDDIE   Not now, Gloria. Gimme the Specials.   *(Turns to blackboard over bar marked "Today's Specials," picks up chalk)*

GUSTA   So this old Jewish mama, lonely, a widow—her fancy son can't be bothered, sends her a parrot to keep her company—

EDDIE   The *Specials*, Gloria—

GUSTA   This is a five-hundred-dollar parrot, speaks six languages, including Russian and Yiddish—

EDDIE   The pots, the pots, what's in the *pots?!*

GUSTA   A week goes by, he don't hear from her, calls up, "Mama, did you get the parrot?" "Yes," she says, "thank you, Sonny; *delicious.*" *(Breaks up, laughing happily, turns heat down under pots)*   Eddie, you want the Specials?

EDDIE   *(to Stroller)*   Come on, Charlie, *tell* me, why do I . . . ? Yeah.

GUSTA   O.K., in the big pot, Brisket Tzimmes with honey, carrot, sweet potato, a dash raisins.

EDDIE   *(writing in bold letters on blackboard)*   "Mulligan Stew."

GUSTA   *(removing apron)*   Next to it, still simmering, we got Lokshen Kugel with apple, cinnamon, raisin, a sprinkle nuts.

EDDIE   *(thinks a minute, then writes)*   "Hot Apple Pie."

CHARLIE   *(whispering)*   No, Pop . . . no . . .

GUSTA   *(taking school notebook from shelf near phone)*   Now I go to Mr. Katz. Don't forget, in a half-hour, you'll turn me off the Lokshen please.

EDDIE   Twelve *years*—twelve years of English with Mr. Katz you're still sayin' "turn me off the Lokshen"!

GUSTA   *(going to entrance door)*   It's not just English at the Alliance, we *discuss* things; politics, *Jewish* things.

EDDIE   Goddamn *Commie*, that Katz; he's open Washington's Birthday, *Lincoln's, now* he's teaching on July Fourth!

GUSTA   He's not a Communist; he's only an Anarchist.

EDDIE   What's the difference?

GUSTA   Louder, and fewer holidays.   *(Breaks up again, laughing, opens* *door, waves to Stroller)* Bye-bye, Charlie, when Mama comes back we chapn a bisl luft in droysen, yes?

CHARLIE *(to Audience)* "Catch a bit of air outside."

EDDIE *English*, for Chrissakes, *English*—

GUSTA *(as she exits, laughing)* "Delicious," she says, "delicious" . . .

EDDIE *(shouting at door)* English— *(Turning sharply to Zaretsky)* English! The *two* of ya, the *mouth* on ya, kid's all screwed up, thinks he's livin' in Odessa; meanwhile ya give my *joint* a bad feel. Goddamn Jewish *news*papers all over the place—what're we, advertisin' for *rabbis* here? *(Points to Jukebox)* Goodness of my heart I put some Jew Music on the Box for ya—all I ask ya don't play it business hours or in fronta my kids. Next thing I know Jack says you're playin' "Rumania" straight through his *shift* last night. The two of ya, I swear, you're discouragin' the proper clientele here, and that's the fact of the matter. Jews don't drink; this is a law of nature, a law of nature and of commerce. *(He slaps the bar with finality; then resumes his work. Silence for a moment)*

ZARETSKY *(singing, from behind his newspaper, a thick brogue)*

"Oh, Dan-ny Boy,
The pipes, the pipes are callin' . . . "

EDDIE *(leans forward on bar)* Damn *right*, Mister—damn *right* that's who drinks! You can't sell shoes to people who ain't got no *feet*, pal!

ZARETSKY *(singing)*

"From glen to glen . . . "

EDDIE Hey, far *he* it! Far be it from me to discuss makin' a living! *(Coming out from behind bar)* What's that foreign mouth been *gettin'* you, Zaretsky? A once-a-month shot in the Mountains puttin' retired Yiddlach to sleep with old Sholem Aleichem stories? *Pushkin* for the Literatniks? What? When's the last time you saw somebody in a Yiddish theater under a hundred who wasn't dragged there by his Zayde? Read the handwritin' on the goddamn *marquee*, amigo; it's *over*. Gotta give 'em what they *want*, see. That's the Promised Land, pal—find out what they want and *promise* it to them. *(Takes frozen vodka from under bar)* Yessir— *(Pouring half-glass; to Stroller)* A toast to that, Charlie!

CHARLIE Pop never drank—except to propose a toast, and that toast was always to the same thing . . .

EDDIE *(holding glass aloft, towards front door)* The new place,

Charlie . . . to today, the Openin' Day . . . I lift my lamp beside the Golden Door; bring me your tired, your poor, your drinkers, your winos, your alkies, your—

ZARETSKY   *(lowers his newspaper)* I knew a man once, Itzik Goldberg, with the colors of Odessa and the spirit of a Jew, and I saw this man turn white before my eyes, white as milk—Grade A, pasteurized, homogenized, American *milk!*

EDDIE   *(softly, to Stroller)* Very sad, Charlie; a dyin' man with a dead language and no place to go. *(Downs vodka, turns sharply, shouting)* Check me out, Actor—current cash problems I gotta *tolerate* your crap—soon as this place hits you're out on the *street,* inside a year you're sleepin' in *sinks,* baby; this is a *warning!* *(Slaps glass down)*

ZARETSKY   *(shouting, fiercely)* And a warning to *you,* sir; I shall no longer countenance these threats!

CHARLIE   This exchange, a holler more or less, took place every day, except Sunday, at approximately Seven-Fifteen A.M. After which, they would usually— *(Sees his father pouring another vodka; Charlie is suddenly anxious)* Oh, shit, another one . . .

EDDIE   *(downs second vodka; then, quietly, to Stroller)* Hey, y'know, anything you got to say to me, nobody's gonna know, it's all strictly confidential. *(Takes small red ball from Stroller, tosses it back in pleasantly)* There ya go, pick up the ball and give it back to Papa. *(Silence)* Pick it up . . . *(A sudden, frightened whisper escapes him)* Oh, kid, don't be dumb . . . you're not gonna turn out to be dumb, are ya? *(Pause)* Those eyes; don't look at me like that, Charlie . . . *(Sits on chair next to Stroller, gazing into it)* You got your grandpa's sweet face, see . . . exactly, to the letter; the soft eyes and the gentle, gentle smile, and it scares the shit outa me. His head in the Talmud and his foot in the grave, the guy come here and got creamed, kid. Not you, Charlie; I'm gonna do good here, but you're gonna do better. There's two kinda guys come off the boat: the Go-Getters and the Ground-Kissers. Your grandpa, though a better soul never walked the earth, was to all intents and purposes, a putz; a darling man and a born Ground-Kisser. In *Hamburg,* in the harbor, we ain't even *sailed* yet and the kissing begins: he kisses the gangplank, he kisses the doorway, he kisses the scummy goddamn *steer*age *floor* of the S.S. Pennland. Nine hundred miles we walk to get to the boat, just him and me, I gotta handle all the bribes. Ten years *old,* I gotta grease my way across the Russian Empire, he don't know how. *Fine* points, this is all he ever knew: *fine* points. *My* grandpa, one o' them solid-steel rabbis, gives Pop a sweet send-off back in Odessa: "Have a good trip, Solomon," he says; "eat kosher or die." So twenty-six days on the boat Pop eats little pieces of bread they give ya with kosher stamps on 'em and a coupla prayed-on potatoes; *I'm* scroungin' everything in sight to stay alive. *Fine* points! Pop loses thirty pounds, *he's* a wreck but the *lips,* the lips are in great shape, the lips are working! New York harbor, he's kissin' the deck, he's blowin' kisses to Lady Liberty, he's kissin' the *barge* that takes us to Ellis Island. On the mainland, forget it, the situation is turnin' pornographic. Twenty-eight blocks to his brother on Rivington—some people took a trolley, *we* went by lip. On Grand Street I come over to him, this little rail of a man, I say, "Get off your knees, Pop; stand up, everybody's *lookin',* what the hell're ya doin'?" Looks at me, his eyes are sweet and wet, he says, "It's God's will that we come here, Itzik. I show my love for his inten- tions . . . " *Fine* points! *(Suddenly rises, bangs his fist on the table next to him, showing the effects of his vodka)* Goddamn *fine* points . . . *(Gradually turning towards Zaretsky, who remains behind his newspaper)* Opens a joint here on Rivington: Solomon's Tavern. The man is closed Friday night and Saturday by God's law and Sunday by New York's—the income is brought by Elijah every Passover. Comes Prohibition, he sticks to the letter; coffee, soda, three-two beer and no booze—every joint in the neighborhood's got teapots fulla gin and bourbon in coffee cups, we're scratchin' for nickels and lovin' God's intentions. A summer night, late, they come to sell him bootleg: two little Ginzos and this big Mick hench with eyes that died. "Oh, *no,*" says Papa the Putz, "not *me.* Against the *law,*" he says—he's *educatin'* these yo-yo meat grinders, right?—he says he's callin' the cops and the Feds and he's goin' to all the local congregations to talk his fellow Jews outa buyin' or sellin' bootleg. "Do it and you're a dead Yid," says the hench. Pop don't get the message—no, he's got his *own* message now—in a week he hits every landsman's bar he can find, he's tellin' 'em they gotta respect where God has sent them; gets to five, six shuls that week, *three* on Saturday, he's givin' goddamn public *speeches* in Rutgers Square! A five-foot-six, hundred-and- twenty-pound Jew has selected Nineteen Twenty-One in America as the perfect time to be anti-gangster! What the *hell* did he think was gonna protect him? The *cops?* His *God?* By Sunday morning he is, of course, dead in Cortlandt Alley over here with his skull smashed in. They hustle me over there at Seven A.M. to say if it's him; I know before I get there. When they turn him over I don't look—it's not the bashed-in head I'm afraid of; I'm afraid I'll see from his lips that with the last breath he was kissing the dust in Cortlandt Alley. *(Moving briskly up to bar)* The *perfection* of it—his Jewish God had his soul and America had his heart, he died a devout and patriotic *putz! (Reflexively splashes vodka into glass, downs it in a gulp, slaps glass onto bar. A moment; he chuckles)* So he don't get thrown outa heaven, he gives two bucks to this place, the Sons of Moses, to guarantee his soul gets prayed for; for two dollars they send me a card every year for the rest of my *life* to remind me to light Pop's Yahrzeit candle and do the Kaddish for him; I can't get halfway through the prayer without sayin' "Go to hell, Pop." I look at the card, I see the alley. And wherever I live, the card comes. Wherever you go, they find you, those Sons of Moses. The putz won't leave me be. He wouldn't shut up *then* and he won't shut up now . . . he won't shut up . . . he won't shut up . . . he won't shut *up*—

(In one sudden, very swift movement, he kicks over the bar-table next to him, its contents clattering to the floor; Charlie, taken completely by surprise, leaps to his feet in his booth as the round table rolls part-way across the bar-room floor. Eddie, quite still, watches the table roll to a stop. Silence for a moment. Zaretsky lowers his newspaper)

ZARETSKY   *(raising his glass, proudly)* To Solomon Goldberg . . . who I saw speak in Rutgers Square against drinking and crime to an audience of drunks and criminals. Completely foolish and absolutely thrilling. We need a million Jews like him. *(Downs shot, turns sharply)* You came to the Melting Pot, sir, and *melted* . . . melted *away*. *(Slaps glass down)*

EDDIE   *(turns to Zaretsky; quietly)* Whatsa matter, you *forget*, pal? *(Moving slowly towards Zaretsky's table)* Wasn't that *you* I seen runnin' bare-ass down Dalnitzkaya Street—a dozen Rooski Goys and a coupla Greek Orthodox with goddamn *sabers* right behind, lookin' to slice somethin' Jewish off ya? Only thirty years ago, you were no kid *then*, moving pretty good considerin'. Did they catch ya, pal? What'd they slice off ya, Zaretsky? Your memory? They held my grandpa down under his favorite acacia tree and pulled his beard out—his beard, a rabbi's honor—they're tearin' it outa his face a chunk at a time, him screamin' in this garden behind his shul, they grabbed us *all* there that Saturday comin' outa morning prayers. This chubby one is whirlin' a saber over his head, faster and faster till it whistles—I know this guy, I seen him waitin' tables at the Café Fankoni—"Im takin' your skull-cap off," he says to my brother Heshy; one whistlin' swing, he slices it off along with the top of Heshy's skull, scalpin' him. Heshy's very proud of this yarmulkeh, he's Bar Mitzvah a month before and wears it the entire Shabes—he's got his hands on his head, the blood is runnin' through his fingers, he's already dead, he still runs around the garden like a chicken for maybe thirty seconds before he drops, hollerin' "Voo iz mine yarmulkeh? . . . Voo iz mine yarmulkeh?" The kid is more afraid of not being Jewish than not being alive. *(At Zaretsky's table, leaning towards him)* My mother, they cut her ears off; her ears, go figure it, what was Jewish about *them?* Regardless, she bled to death in the garden before it got dark, ranting like a child by then, really nuts. The guy's caftan flies open, the one doin' the job on Ma, I see an Odessa police uniform underneath, this is just a regular beat cop from Primorsky Boulevard, and the waiter too, just another person; but they were all screaming, these guys—louder than my family even—and their women too, watching, screaming, "Molodyets!" "Natchinai!" "good man," "go to it," like ladies I seen at ringside, only happier, all screaming with their men in that garden, all happy to find the bad guys. *(Sits opposite Zaretsky)* This Cossack's holdin' me down, he's makin' me watch while they do the ear-job on Ma. "Watch, Zhid, watch! Worse to watch than to die!" He holds me, he's got my arms, it feels like I'm drowning. Since then, nobody holds me down, Zaretsky, nobody. I don't even like hugs. *(Grips Zaretsky's wrist, urgently)* The October Pogrom, how could you forget? Livin' with us two *years* now, you don't even *mention* it. You wanna run around bein' Mister Jewish—that's *your* lookout—but you leave me and my kids *out* of it. *(Rises, moving briskly to bar)* I got my own deal with God, see; Joey does a few hours a week o' Hebrew School, just enough to make the Bar Mitzvah shot—same with Charlie—I hit the shul Rosh Hashana, maybe Yom Kippur, and sometimes Fridays Gloria does the candle routine; and that's *it.* You treat God like you treat *any* dangerous loony—keep him calm and stay on his *good* side. Meanwhile . . . *(Takes folded legal document from cash register, smiling proudly)* Today, today the Jew lid comes off my boys. *(Striding back to Zaretsky's table, opening document with a flourish)* Check it out, Anton, you're the first to know— *(Reads from document)* "Southern District Court, State of New York, the Honorable Alfred Gladstone, presiding. Application approved, this Third day of July, of the year Nineteen Hundred and Thirty-Six; Change of Family Name—" *(Holding document aloft)* Yessir; so long, Goldberg; as of One P.M. yesterday you been livin' here with the *Ross* family—outside, take note, the sign says "Eddie Ross' Golden Door"; shit, I just say it out *loud,* I get a shiver. *(Sits next to Zaretsky, pointing to photos over bar)* "Ross," yessir—honor o' Barney "One-Punch" Ross and Mr. Franklin Delano Roosevelt, friend of the Jews, God bless 'im. *(Leans towards*

Zaretsky) Goldberg sat down with ya, pal . . . *(Slaps table, stands up)* but Ross rises. *(Striding briskly up towards bar)* And he's got business to do!

ZARETSKY   *(after a moment, quietly)* You didn't mention the feathers . . . *(Eddie stops, turns to him; Zaretsky remains at his table, looking away)* All the goose-feathers, Itzik. Three days exactly, the perfect pogrom; and on the fourth day, in the morning, a terrible silence and feathers everywhere, a carpet of goose-feathers on every street. The Jews of the Moldavanka, even the poorest of them, had goose-feather mattresses and pillows; and this made the Christians somehow very angry. So from every home they dragged out mattresses, pillows, ripped them open and threw the feathers in the streets; thousands of mattresses, millions of feathers, feathers everywhere and so white and the blood so red on them, and the sky so very blue as only could be in Odessa by the sea. All beautiful and horrible like a deadly snow had fallen in the night. This is what I remember. In the big synagogue on Catherine Street they had broken even the highest windows, and these windows stared like blinded eyes over the Moldavanka. And below there are feathers in all the acacia trees on Catherine Street, white feathers in the branches, as though they had bloomed again in October, as though the trees too had gone mad. And crazier still that morning, waddling down the street towards me, an enormous fat man, like from the circus, laughing. I watch him, silent like a balloon on the soft feathers, into one empty Jewish house and then another he goes, growing fatter as he comes, and now closer I see the face of the Greek, Poldaris, from the tobacco shop, and he is wearing one atop the other the suits and cloaks of dead Jews. No, Mr. Ross, they didn't catch me, and no, I didn't forget; this morning even, the fat Poldaris follows me still, laughing, waiting for my clothes. *(Turns to Eddie)* A picture remains—a picture more disturbing even than the one of Eddie Cantor in black-face you have hung in my room. That first night I am hiding in the loft above the horses in the Fire Station and I see on the street below me young Grillspoon kneeling in the feathers before his house, his hands clasped heavenward, like so. He pleads for his life to be spared by five members of the Holy Brotherhood who stand about him—this group has sworn vengeance on those who tortured their Savior upon the cross, Grillspoon obviously amongst them, and each carries a shovel for this purpose. Now, a Jew does not kneel when he prays, nor does he clasp his hands, and it becomes clear that poor Grillspoon is imitating the manner of Christian prayer, hoping to remind them of themselves. The actor in me sees that this man is fiercely auditioning for the role of Christian for them—and these men for the moment stand aside from him, leaning on their shovels as they watch his performance. Presently, however, they proceed to rather efficiently beat him to death with their shovels. Talk about bad reviews, eh? *(Rises, takes a step towards Eddie)* Unfortunately, you have decided that the only way to become somebody in this country is first to become no one at all. You are kneeling in your goose-feathers, Mr. Ross. *You*, you who profess to be such a violent Anti-Kneeler.

EDDIE   Go to hell, Actor. *(Turns away sharply, starts briskly stacking glasses behind the bar)*

ZARETSKY   *(moving steadily towards Eddie)* For God's *sake*, Itzik, they had to *take* your grandfather's beard and your brother's yarmulkeh—but what is yours you will *give* away; and like poor Grillspoon you will reap the disaster of a second-rate Christian imitation. And as a pro*fessional*, I *swear* to you, Itzik— *(bangs his fist on the bar)* you are *definitely wrong for the part!*

(Eddie wheels about sharply, about to speak—but Joey Goldberg bursts in from the Apartment above, speaking as he enters, cutting Eddie off; a tough-looking ten-year old, he bounds down the stairs, his Hebrew School books tied with a belt and slung over his shoulder, heading directly for his morning task—a tray of "set-ups" on the bar)

JOEY   Hey, sorry I'm late, Pop—

ZARETSKY   Jussel! A guten tog, Jussel!

JOEY   A guten tog, Professor! Vos harst du fun der Rialto!

EDDIE   *(anguished, slapping bar)* My God, they got *him* doin' it now too . . .

CHARLIE   *(fondly)* Hey, Joey . . .

JOEY   *(passing Stroller)* How ya doin', kid?

CHARLIE   *(to Audience)* Besides me, Joey loved only two things in this world: the New York Giants and the Yiddish Theatre; for my brother had witnessed two miracles in his life   Carl Hubbell's screwball, and Mr. Zaretsky's King Lear.

JOEY   *(carrying set-ups to center table, spotting valise)*   Hey, Mr. Zaretsky . . . we got the *satchel* . . .

ZARETSKY   Yes, Jussel— *(grandly lifting valise)* today a journey to Detroit, in Michigan, there presenting my solo concert—"Pieces of Gold from the Golden Years."

EDDIE   Hey, Joey, I got the *Moose* up, see—

JOEY   *(a quick glance at it)* Yeah, great— *(To Zaretsky, fascinated)* "Pieces Of Gold" . . . what's the lineup on that one?

ZARETSKY   *(opening valise)* The Program, as follows—

EDDIE   Joey, the *set*-ups—

ZARETSKY   *(his arms outstretched, setting the scene)* A simple light— possibly blue—reveals a humble satchel, and within— *(Joey and Charlie, their arms outstretched, saying the words with him)*—a world of Yiddish Theatre!

EDDIE   The *set*-ups, Joey—

(Joey continuing absently, sporadically, to place set-ups on tables, his gaze fixed on Zaretsky's performance)

ZARETSKY   *(takes tarnished gold crown from valise, placing it on his head)* To begin—

JOEY   The old guy with the daughters!

ZARETSKY   Der Kenig Lear, of course! *(Drops crown into valise)* Three minutes: an appetizer. And then— *(removes a battered plaster skull; studies it, fondly)* "Zuch in vey, umglicklickeh Yorick . . . ich hub im gut gekennt, Horatio . . . " *(Briskly exchanging skull for an ornate dagger; a thoughtful gaze, whispering)* "Tzu zein, oder nicht tzu zein . . . dus is die fragge . . . " *(Replacing dagger with a small, knotted rope)* The bonds of Sidney Carton, the shadow of the guillotine . . . *(Looks up; softly)* "Es is a fiel, fiel besera zach vus ich tu yetst, vus ich hub amol getune . . . " *(Swiftly replacing rope with the fur hat of a Cossack general)* The "Kiddush HaShem" of Sholem Asch, sweeping drama of seventeenth-century Cossack pogroms; condensed. *(Drops Cossack hat into valise)* When they have recovered— *(Places yarmulkeh delicately on his head; directs this at Eddie, busy behind bar)* Sholem Aleichem's "Hard To Be A Jew" . . . humor and sudden shadows. *(Removes yarmulkeh; his arms outstretched, grandly)* In conclusion, of course, my twelve-minute version of "The Dybbuk," all in crimson light if equipment available; I play all parts . . . including title role. *(A moment; then he bows his head as though before a huge Jewish Audience in a grand hall; he speaks quietly)* I hear the applause . . . *(He looks out)* I see their faces, so familiar . . . and once again I have eluded the fat Poldaris. He shall not have my clothes. *(Silence for a moment; then he picks up his valise, striding briskly to the front door)* Give up my Yiddish Theatre? No, Itzik, I don't think so. Yes, overblown, out of date, soon to disappear. But then, so am I. *(Turns at door)*

I go now to the tailor, Zellick, who repairs my robes for Lear. Good morning to you, Jussel; and good morning to you, Mr. Ross, and, of course, my regards to your wife, Betsy.

(Zaretsky exits; Eddie instantly intensifies his work behind the bar; Joey not moving, looking off at front door, still in awe)

EDDIE   *Fake*-o, Joey, I'm tellin' ya—fake-o four-flushin' phony. Man don't make no sense, any manner, shape or form.

JOEY   You should see the way he does that *Dybbuk* guy, Pop, he really—

EDDIE   Joey, the set-ups—what happened to the goddamn *set*-ups here! And the *mail*, kid, ya *forgot* it yesterday.

JOEY   *(picks up books)* Gonna be late for Hebrew, Pop, it's almost Eight—

EDDIE   Then ya shouldn'ta hung around watchin' Cary Grant so long.

JOEY   Ten to Eight, Pop, gotta get goin'—

EDDIE   Bring in the *mail* first, you got obligations here, Mister.

JOEY   *(puts books down)* O.K., O.K. . . . *(Passing Stroller)* He say anything today?

EDDIE   All quiet on the western front.

JOEY   *(looking into Stroller)* Don't worry about him, Pop; look at the eyes, he's gettin' *everything*. *(As he exits)* He's smart, this kid; very smart, like me.

EDDIE   And modest *too*, I bet. *(Alone now; he pauses for a moment, then goes to the Stroller, peers in thoughtfully)* Everything?

CHARLIE   Every word, Pop.

EDDIE   *(leans forward)* Hey, what the hell're ya *doin*'? This ain't no time to go to *sleep*. You just got *up*, for God's sake— *(Shaking the Stroller)* Let's show a little *courtesy* here, a little common goddamn *courtesy*. *(Stops)* Out. He's *out*. I either got Calvin Coolidge with his dick in his fist or he's *out!*

JOEY   *(entering, thoughtfully, with stack of mail)* Pop, the sign outside, it says "Ross" on it . . .

EDDIE   That's our new name, you're gonna love it; honor o' Barney himself. *(Takes mail, starts going through it)*

JOEY   You mean not just for the place, but actually our new name?

EDDIE   All done; legit and legal, kid, Al Gladstone presidin'— *(Takes envelope from mail)* Son of a bitch, the Sons of Moses, Pop's Yahrzeit again . . .

JOEY   So my name is Joe Ross? That's my name now? Joe Ross? Very . . . brief, that name.

EDDIE   *(studying blue card from envelope)* Fifteen *years*, they find me every time, it's the Royal Mounted Rabbis . . .

JOEY,   Joe Ross; it starts—it's *over.*

EDDIE   Hey, *Hebrew* school—

JOEY   *(suddenly alarmed)* Jeez, went right outa my *mind*— *(Grabs Hebrew texts, races for door, slapping yarmulkeh on his head)*

EDDIE   *Wait* a minute— *(Points to yarmulkeh)* Where ya goin' with *that* on your head? What're ya, crazy? Ya gonna go eight blocks through Little Italy and Irishtown, passin' right through god-damn *Polack* Street, with *that* on your head? How many times I gotta tell ya, kid—that is *not* an outdoor garment. That is an indoor garment *only.* Why don't ya wear a sign on your head says, "Please come kick the shit outa me"? You put it on in Hebrew School, where it belongs.

JOEY   Pop, I don't—

EDDIE   I'm tellin' ya *once* more—stow the yammy, kid. *Stow* it.

JOEY   *(whips yarmulkeh off, shoves it in pocket)* O.K., O.K. *(Starts towards door)* I just don't see why I gotta be ashamed.

EDDIE   I'm not askin' ya to be ashamed. I'm askin' ya to be smart. *(Sees something in mail as Joey opens door; sharply)* Hold it—

JOEY   Gotta go, Pop—

EDDIE   *Hold* it right there—

JOEY   Pop, this Tannenbaum, he's a killer—

EDDIE   *(looking down at mail; solemnly)* I got information here says you ain't *seein'* Tannenbaum this morning. I got information here says you ain't even headed for Hebrew School right now. *(Silence for a moment. Joey remains in doorway)* C'mere, we gotta talk.

JOEY   *(approaching cautiously, keeping at a safe distance)* Hey . . . no whackin', Pop . . .

EDDIE   I got this note here; says— *(Takes small piece of cardboard from mail, reads)* "Dear Sheenie Bastard. Back of Carmine's, Remind you, Jewshit Joe, Eight O'Clock A.M., Be there. Going to make Hamburger out of Goldberger—S.D." Bastard is spelled here B-A-S-T-I-D; this and the humorous remarks I figure the fine mind of the wop, DeSapio. *(After a moment, looks up, slaps bar)* And I wanna tell ya *good* luck, *glad* you're goin', you're gonna *nail* 'im, you're gonna *finish* 'im, you're gonna murder 'im—

JOEY   Wait a minute—it's O.K.? Really?

EDDIE   —and here'a couple pointers how to do so.

JOEY   Pointers? *Pointers?* . . . I need a *shot*gun, Pop; DeSapio's near twice my size, fourteen years *old*—

EDDIE   Hey, far *be* it! Far be it from me to give pointers—a guy got twenty-six bouts under his belt, *twelve* professional—

JOEY   Yeah, but this DeSapio, he really *hates* me, this kid; he hated me the minute he *saw* me. He says we killed Christ, us Jews.

EDDIE   They was *all* Jews there, kid, everybody; Christ, His mother, His whole crowd—you tell him there was a buncha Romans there too, makes him *directly related* to the guys done the actual hit!

JOEY   I *told* him that, Pop—that's when he *whacked* me.

EDDIE   And I bet you whacked him back, which is appropriate; *no* shit from *no*body, ya stuck to your *guns*, kid—

JOEY   So why're we hidin' then? How come we're "Ross" all of a sudden? *(With an edge)* Or maybe Ross is just our *out*door name, and Goldberg's still our indoor name.

EDDIE   *Hey*—

JOEY   I don't *get* it, this mean we're not Jewish anymore?

EDDIE   Of *course* we're still Jewish; we're just not gonna push it.

JOEY   *(checking watch)* Jeez—three minutes to Eight, Pop, takes five to get there, he's gonna think I'm chicken— *(Starts towards door)*

EDDIE   *One* minute for two pointers; let 'im wait, he'll get anxious—

JOEY   He's *not anxious*, Pop, I promise ya—

EDDIE   Now, these pointers is based on my observations o' your natural talents: the bounce, the eye, the smarts—

JOEY   *(protesting)* Pop—

EDDIE   C'mon, I seen ya take out Itchy Halloran with one shot in fronta the Texaco station; who're we *kiddin'* here? Hey, I was O.K., but *you* got potential I *never* had.

JOEY   But Itchy Halloran's *my height*, DeSapio's twice my *size*—

EDDIE   *(ignoring him)* O.K., first blow; your instinct is go for the belly, right?

JOEY   *Instinct?* His belly is as high as I can *reach,* Pop—

EDDIE   Wrong: first blow, forget the belly. Pointer Number One— ya listenin'?

JOEY   Yeah.

EDDIE   *(demonstrating, precisely)* Considerin' the size, you gotta rock this boy *early* . . . gotta take the first one up from the *ground, vertical,* so your full body-weight's in the shot. Now, start of the fight, right away, *imm*ediate, you hunk *down,* move outa range; then *he's* gotta come to *you*—and you meet him with a right fist up *off the ground;* picture a spot in the middle of his chin and aim for it— *(demonstrates blow; Joey copies)* then comes the important part—

JOEY   What's that?

EDDIE   Jump back.

JOEY   Jump back?

EDDIE   Yeah, ya jump back so when he falls he don't hurt ya.

JOEY   When he *falls? Murder,* he's gonna murder me. Pop, Pop, this is an *execution* I'm goin' to here! I'm only goin' so I won't be ashamed!

EDDIE   There's only one thing you gotta watch out for—

JOEY   *Death,* I gotta watch out for *death*—

EDDIE   Not death . . . but there could be some damage. Could turn out to be more than one guy there, you're gettin' ganged up on, somethin' *special*—this *happens,* kid—O.K., we got a weapon here— *(takes framed photo of Boxer from wall)* we got a weapon here, guaranteed. *(Hands photo to Joey)* What's it say there?

JOEY   *(reading)* "Anybody gives *you* trouble, give *me* trouble. I love you. Love, Vince."

EDDIE   O.K.; June Four, Nineteen Twenty-One, I come into the ring against Vince DiGangi, they bill him "The Ghetto Gorilla"—a shrimp with a mustache, nothin', I figure an easy win. Five *seconds* into Round One comes a *chamalia* from this little Eye-tie—I'm out, I'm on the canvas, your Pop is *furniture,* Joey. I open one eye, *there's* DiGangi on his knees next to me, he's got me in his arms, he's huggin' me, he's kissin' my face, he loves me. I give him his first big win, his first knockout. I *made* him, he says, he's gonna love me forever. And he *does.* That's the nice thing about these Telanas, they love ya or they hate ya, but it's forever; so, *remember*— *(leans towards him)* things get outa hand, you got a group situation, somethin'—you holler "DiGangi è mio fratello, *chiamalo!*" *(Grips his shoulder)* "DiGangi è mio fratello, *chiamalo!*" Say it.

JOEY   "DiGangi è mio fratello, chi . . . amalo!"

EDDIE   That's "DiGangi's my brother, *call* him!" *(Softly, awestruck, imitating their response)* Whoa . . . "DiGangi" 's the magic word down there, biggest hit since Columbus, lotta power with the mob. Perhaps you noticed, Big Vito don't come around here pushin' protection, whatever. This is the result of *one* word from Mr. Vincent DiGangi. *(Pats Joey's hand)* Very heavy ticket there, kid, you don't want to use it unless the straits is completely dire. *(Slaps bar)* O.K., ya got all that?

JOEY   *(starting towards front door without much spirit)* Yeah; take the first one up from the ground, jump back, and tell 'em about DiGangi if I still got a mouth left. *(As he passes Stroller; softly, sighing)* Well . . . here I go, Charlie.

CHARLIE   *(speaking on behalf of the silent child)* So long, Joey. Murder 'im.

(Joey stops at door; brushes off his shirt, stands up straighter, taller—then puts on his yarmulkeh)

EDDIE   What're ya doin' *that* for?

JOEY   This'll drive 'im crazy. *(Flings open door, darts off into street, racing past Hannah Di Blindeh and Nick, a matching pair of ragged, aging alcoholics who have been standing in the threshold; they are early-morning drinkers who have clearly been waiting at the door for the bar to open, anxious for their first shot of the day. We hear Joey's voice as he races down the street)* They're here, Pop.

EDDIE   *(looks up)* Ah . . . Fred and Ginger. *(Checks pocket watch)* Eight o'clock; on the button. Dance right in, kids.

CHARLIE   *(gradually remembering, as they enter)* Jesus, it's *them* . . . Of course, of course . . . no day could begin without them . . .

(Hannah, near sixty, Russian, and obviously sightless, wears faded, oddly elegant, overly mended clothing that may have been fashionable thirty years earlier. Nick's bushy white beard and matted hair make it hard to read his age, anywhere between early fifties and late sixties depending on the time of day; he has a soiled, ill-fitting suit and shirt, what had once been a tie, a noticeably red nose, and a clear case of the pre-first-drink shakes. During the minute or so of Charlie's next speech, Hannah, Nick and Eddie will go through the very specific steps of their morning ritual. Before they reach their assigned bar-stools,

Eddie will have dropped a piece of lemon peel into a stemmed glass, filled it halfway with cold vodka and placed it in front of one stool, then snapped a neat row of three shotglasses down in front of the other, briskly filling each with straight bourbon. With due courtliness, Nick will escort Hannah to the bar, pull out her stool for her, not sit till she is seated; then she will finish her vodka in three separate delicate sips, saying "Lomir lebn un lachn" before each, while in exactly the same tempo, Nick says "You bet" in response to each of her toasts and downs his row of bourbon shots, his shakes vanishing with the contents of the third glass, Hannah finally sighing "Nit do gedacht" as she sets her empty glass down to end the first round; all this beginning and ending with the following speech, Charlie thoughtful, remembering, as he talks to us)

CHARLIE   Hannah . . . Hannah Di Blindeh—meaning Hannah The Blind One; I used to think Di Blindeh was her last name—and Nick; I didn't know his last name, a problem he often shared with me till his third shot of bourbon—

HANNAH   Lomir lebn un lachn—

NICK   You bet—

CHARLIE   Called "Nick" because, by his sixth shot, he believed—or would like *you* to believe, I was never sure which—that he was, in fact, Santa Claus; you can see the resemblance. In any case, this was an identity preferable to that of forcibly retired police sergeant; it seems that, in celebration of Repeal Day, Nick had managed to shoot out all the street-lamps in front of the Twenty-Second Precinct. He carried this famous Smith and Wesson with him every day to Pop's bar, which allowed them *both* to think of him as a kind of guard-bouncer for the place—God knows if he could still *aim* the damn thing, but Pop loved the street-lamp story and never charged him for a drink. Pop never charged Hannah for a drink either—

HANNAH   Lomir lebn un lachn—

CHARLIE   That's "May we live and laugh."

NICK   You bet—

CHARLIE   She'd been blinded somehow on the second day of the October Pogrom; Hannah didn't remember what she saw that second day, but what she heard still woke her up every morning like an alarm clock—

HANNAH   Lomir lebn un lachn—

CHARLIE   The noise didn't go away till she finished her first vodka.

HANNAH *(sets her glass down)* Nit do gedacht.

CHARLIE "May it never happen here."

NICK *(sets down his third shot-glass)* You bet.

HANNAH *(same Russian accent as Gusta, as she "looks" about)* Something different here, Itzik. I got a feeling . . . no more "Frisco Eddie's."

EDDIE Right; I love ya, Hannah—it took *you* to notice.

HANNAH "Frisco Eddie's"—gone. This includes the Chuck-a-luck wheel, Eddie?

NICK Yeah; he's got a kinda . . . museum here now.

HANNAH A shame; I *liked* that Chuck-a-luck wheel. But a museum, that's unusual. This could be something. The child, Eddie; he speaks yet?

EDDIE Well, fact is—

HANNAH *(fondly)* Vet meshiach geboyrn vern mit a tog shpeter.

CHARLIE "So the Messiah will be born a day later."

NICK You bet.

HANNAH Gentlemen—today's Number: I am considering seriously, at this time, betting Number Seven-Seven-Six; this in honor of Our Founding Fathers. Comments, please.

NICK Seven-Seven-Six it *is;* a fine thought, Hannah.

HANNAH Next, we make the horse selections. You have brought the sheet, Nick?

NICK *(takes Racing Form from pocket)* At the ready, darlin'.

HANNAH Excellent. *(As Nick escorts her to their table)* Until such day, which is likely never, they make a Braille Racing Form, you and me is buddies, Nick.

NICK Longer than that, sweetheart, longer than that . . .

(Finney the Book suddenly bursts into the room—a tight, tiny bundle of forty-five-year-old Irish nerves under a battered Fedora, he heads straight for his special upstage booth near the wall-phone. Usually anxious, depressed and fidgety, he seems in particularly bad shape today; the sound of Nineteen-Thirties Irish New York and the look of Greek tragedy)

EDDIE Hey, Finney!

NICK Mornin', Finn'.

CHARLIE *(fondly, as Finney enters booth)*   Ah, Finney . . . our

Bookmaker In Residence; Finney The Book arrives at his office, ready to take bets on the Daily Number, and an occasional horse—early today but tragic as ever, having given up on the Irish Rebellion twenty years ago for a cause with even worse odds . . .

FINNEY *(slumps in booth)* Oh, me friends . . . me friends . . . Nick, Eddie, Hannah . . . truly the Tsouris is on me this day!

HANNAH Finney, darling . . . what *is* it?

FINNEY What is it? What is it, y' say? It's the bloody July *Fourth*, is what it is! Every bloody Greenhorn from here to the river bettin' Seven-Seven-Six, every bloody Guinea, Mick, Jew and China-boy bettin' the Independence! *(Rising solemnly in his booth)* "Finney, Finney," I say to m'self the dawn of every Fourth. "Finney, m'boy, stay in your *bed* this cursed and twisted day!"—and *fool* that I am, *obliged* as I am t'me regulars, I hit the bloody *street!* It's me damned code of *honor* does me in! *(Shoves his hands deep into the pockets of his baggy suit-jacket—we hear now the jingle and rustle of hundreds of quarters in one and hundreds of singles in the other)* Four *hundred*—four hundred *easy* on Seven-Seven-Six and the mornin' still new yet! Seven-Seven-Six comes in, me entire Mishpocheh's eatin' *toast* for a year! *(Suddenly aware of the dozens of American flags about him)* And what have ya got *here*, Eddie, me bloody *funeral* arrangements?! My God, man, the only thing missin's a bloody fife and drum to march me to me grave!

NICK *(pointing to phone)* Well, you'd best start layin' off some bets then, Thomas—

FINNEY Every damn Book in the *city's* tryin' to lay off the same bloody number, boy! Tom Finney, what's to *become* of ya? Finney, Finney . . . *(Suddenly turns to Eddie)* And while we're on it, Edward—even I do survive this day—I can't be givin' ya no more twenty for' the use o' me booth; it's ten at best, here on.

EDDIE What *is* this, *lep*rechaun humor? *(To Hannah and Nick)* Man's kiddin' me, right?—his own booth, his own personal *booth* Nine till Post Time, *choice* location—

FINNEY Edward, Edward, all me fondness, ya know damn well I'm bringin' in more pony-people who drink than you're bringin' in drinkers who'll wager— *(Indicates Stroller)* Eight-to-one the boy don't say a word till Christmas. *(Heads briskly to phone)*

EDDIE The new *place*, I'm *tellin'* ya, it's all gonna turn around—

FINNEY *(grabs phone)* Better start layin' off now or I'm surely gornisht in the mornin'. *(Dialing anxiously)* Home of the bloody *brave* . . .

HANNAH *(handing quarter out towards him)* Finney, darling . . . twenty-five cents on number Seven-Seven-Seven. May you live and be well.

FINNEY *(takes coin)* Blessin's on ya— *(Into phone)* Ah, now, is that me sweet Bernie there, the Saint Bernard himself? Finney here, and wonderin' would you care to take two hundred on— *(to the dead phone in his hand)* Star-Spangled bloody Banner . . . *(Dialing again)* Finney, Finney, you're sendin' an S.O.S. to a fleet o' sinkin' ships . . .

(He will continue, quietly, to call several more "Banks" through this next scene; the following dialogue between Nick and Hannah will happen at the same time as his call to Bernie)

NICK *(opens Racing Form)* Where ya want to start: Belmont, Thistledown, Arlington Park . . . ?

HANNAH I say Thistledown; why not?

NICK Thistledown it *is* then. O.K., first race we got Dancin' Lady, four-year-old filly, Harvest Moon by Wild Time, carryin' one fifteen . . .

(They will continue, quietly and with great concentration, to pick horses for the next several minutes   both Finney's call to Bernie and their above dialogue happening at the same time as the entrance of two new customers: Blue, followed a few moments later by Jimmy Scalso. Blue is large, Irish, about fifty, slow-moving, powerful, seeming at all times vaguely amused either by something that happened some time ago or something that might happen soon)

BLUE *(taps bar)* You got Johnny Red?

EDDIE *(pouring drink)* Like the choice; *I* got it. *(Snaps it on bar)* Now *you* got it.

(Jimmy Scalso enters a few moments later, sleekly Italian, just thirty, wiry, a smiler, wearing the kind of carefully tailored silk suit that demands a silver crucifix on a chain about his neck; he speaks and moves rapidly and surely but is still somehow auditioning for a role he hasn't gotten yet. Scalso steps jauntily up to the bar, sits on a stool near Nick and Hannah; Blue takes his drink to a distant table, opens his newspaper)

SCALSO You got Daitch on tap, fellah?

EDDIE   I got it; like the choice. *(Working tap-spigot)* *I* got it— *(Places full mug on bar)* Now *you* got it.

SCALSO   New place, huh? I see the sign outside, "Opening Day." *(Eddie nods pleasantly)* I like the feel. Lotta wood; none of that chrome shit, shiny shit. And the lights: not dark, just . . . soft; like it's always, what? Evening here. *(Pause; sips his beer)* So here we are, the *both* of us, huh?—workin' on a holiday. Ain't been on a vacation, when?—three, no four, *four* years ago. Four years ago, February. I take the wife and the kid to Miami. O.K., sand, sun, surf; *one* day, it's *over* for me, enough. I'm the kinda guy—

NICK   *(to Scalso, quietly)* Do you know who I am?

SCALSO   *(ignoring him like the barfly he is)* —kinda guy I am, I don't get the *point* of a vacation. You go, you come back, there you *are* again. I'm the kinda guy, I gotta be movin', workin'.

HANNAH   Give him a hint, Nick.

NICK   I give you a hint; "Ho, ho, ho."

SCALSO   They say, what?—"don't mix business with pleasure," right? Well, business *is* my pleasure, what can I tell ya? Second day in Miami, second *day*, I'm goin' crazy, I wanna get *outa* there.

NICK   *(speaking confidentially, to Scalso)* You better watch out . . . you better not cry; better not pout, I'm tellin' you why . . .

SCALSO   Here in town, I'm up, a cup of coffee, a little juice, I'm outa the house—I can't *wait* to go to work. Saturday, *Sun*day, I don't *give* a shit. The wife says to me, "Jimmy, Sunday, we'll go to the park; you, me, the kid, we row a boat." I says to her, "Baby, I hate that shit, I'm *not* that kinda *guy*." She says—

EDDIE   *(leans towards him, quietly)* Would you do something for me?

SCALSO   What?

EDDIE   Shut the hell up.

SCALSO   Huh?

EDDIE   Shut your goddamn face. Zip it up. Can it. Button the ruby-reds. Silencio. Got it?

SCALSO   Hey, Mister, what the hell kinda—?

EDDIE   You're boring. I can't stand it. It's killin' me. That Moose up there, he's dead, it don't bother him. Me, while you're talkin' I got individual brain cells up here dyin' one at a time. Two minutes with you, I'm sayin' Kaddish for my brain. Shut up and drink your beer.

NICK   *(confidentially, to Scalso)* I'm makin' a list . . . and checkin' it twice, gonna find out who's naughty and nice . . .

SCALSO   How come ya got a guy here half off his *nut*, and *I'm* the one ya—?

EDDIE   Because who he *thinks* he is is a hundred times more interestin' than who you *are*. You ain't just borin', buddy, you're a goddamn *pioneer* in the field.

SCALSO   Hey, I come in here for a beer, a little conversation, I don't expect a guy to—

EDDIE   You think the price of a beer you own *one minute* of my time? *(Leans close to him; calmly)* O.K., I got two things I want ya to do for me. The first thing I want ya to do is go away, and the next thing I want ya to do is never come back. That's two things; can ya remember that?

SCALSO   *(slaps bar)* Place is open to the public, I got a right to sit here and drink my beer. Who you *oughta* be throwin' out is these two *drunks* here—

EDDIE   I got a private club here, pal. I got my own rules. You just had a free beer; goodbye.

SCALSO   This ain't no private club.

EDDIE   *(indicating bar-room)* Right, this ain't no private club; but this— *(takes billy-club out from under bar; grips it firmly)* this is a private club. It's called the Billy Club. Billy is the president. He wants you to leave.

(Hannah raises her head, listening; Blue looks up from his newspaper; Finney turns from the phone, watching, tensely twisting his hat)

SCALSO   *(after a moment)* Ya mean you're willin' to beat the shit outa some guy just because ya think he's *borin'?*

EDDIE   *(taps the club)* Right; self-*defense*, pal.

(Scalso suddenly starts to laugh, slapping the bar, enjoying himself)

BLUE   *(puts his drink down)* Come on, Jimmy; tell him, we got a long day comin'.

SCALSO   Hey, Blue, Blue, I like this guy, I like this guy . . . *I like this guy!* (Still laughing; Eddie regarding him stonily, tightening grip on club) You are *great*, Goldberg . . . you are *some*thin', baby . . . "A private *club*, the *Billy* Club" . . . great, great . . .

BLUE   *(rising from table, impatient with him)* Enough now; we got alotta *work* here, boy.

SCALSO   *(still chuckling)*   Absolutely right, babe. Goldberg . . . Goldberg, Goldberg, *Goldberg;* you are cute, you are some cute Jew, you are the cutest Jew I ever saw. And tough; I never seen such a tough Jew, I include the Williamsburg Boys. *(Eddie, his club at the ready, waiting him out)* I'm Jimmy Scalso; maybe you don't hear, various internal problems, Vito had an appointment with the Hudson River, which he kept, Seranno gimme alla his Stops; bye-bye, Big Vito—bon jour, Jimmy. *(Eddie, absorbing this, lowers club to his side)* Y'know, I seen ya box, barkeep, Stauch's Arena, I'm sixteen—hey, Blue, this was *some*thin', The East Side Savage against Ah Soong, The Fightin' Chinaman—

BLUE   Move it along, boy; move it *along,* will ya?

SCALSO   Absolutely right, babe. O.K., business, Goldberg; Vito's got fifty-four Stops, fifty-three is solid—some reason he lets one of 'em slide; yours. I'm checkin' the books, ya got no cigarette machine here, ya don't got our *Defense* System, you got a Box should be doin' two and a half a month, you're doin' seventy. *Our* records, selected *hits, thirty* top tunes a month—you take only two. *(Points to Jukebox)* Blue, what's he *got* on there? *(Slaps himself on the head)*   Shit, where's my goddamn *manners*—Mr. Goldberg, this is Blue, for Blue-Jaw McCann; called such because the man could shave five times a day, he's still got a jaw turns gunmetal blue by evenin', same color as the fine weapon he carries. A man, in his prime, done hench for Amato, Scalisi, Carafano . . .

(Scalso pauses a moment, letting this sink in. Eddie puts his club down on the bar. Scalso nods, acknowledging Eddie's good sense)

BLUE   *(checking the Jukebox)*   All right, he's got eight here by a fella, Leba—Leba—

HANNAH   *Lebedeff.* Aaron Lebedeff, the Maurice Che*valier* of the Jewish Stage—

BLUE   Then there's a couple, a fella, Zatz, half-a-dozen Eddie Cantor, somebody Ukelele Ike, Jolson, Kate Smith, The U.S. Army Band, Irish Eyes—

SCALSO   *(his head in his hands)*   Stop, stop, stop, *night*mare, it's a *night*mare! Somebody *wake* me, I'm *dreamin'!* Goldberg, Goldberg, you're takin' the joie outa my goddamn *vie* here! *(Looks up mournfully, shouting)*   Whatta ya think ya *got* here, Goldberg, a *Victrola?* This is a *Box,* this is *our* goddamn *Box* here, *income, income.* Weird foreign shit, hundred-year-old *losers,* and mosta the plays is your own *slugs!* Where's the *hits,* where's— *(Stops himself; quietly)*   O.K., everybody calm down. A new day, a new dollar, right? *(Pacing, to Blue)* No Butts, no Defense, shit on the Box; Vito musta been crazy . . .

FINNEY *(whispering)* Tell him, Eddie; DiGangi . . .

EDDIE *(whispering, sharply)* Shut up.

SCALSO *(pleasantly, a man bestowing gifts)* O.K., new deal, we start fresh—my true belief: everybody's happy. Goldberg, item one, comes tomorrow, A.M., cigarette machine—fifiy-fifty split; Butts come certain sources, the price is hilarious. Item two: Angelo Defense System—I hear ya screamin' "Protection racket, ugly Italian behavior, get me outa here!" *(Softly, almost misty-eyed)* My reply: au *contraire*, my darlin' Hebrew, a Wop and a Yid is one heart beatin' here. "Angelo Defense System" meanin' defense against every greasy hand wants *in* your satchel! The cops *alone*, whatta ya pay Christmas? Also Inspectors: Fire, Garbage, whatever—the Angel flies in. Figure what you save, one monthly shot to the Angel; words fail. *(Crossing up to Jukebox)* The Box; tomorrow, A.M., my people come, *out* goes the goddamn funeral music, the Memory Lane Losers, the Hollerin' Hebes—*in* comes forty selected hits; once-a-week collection. Finney here, business as usual; already under the wing, a Defense System who I'm affiliated. *Finale:* same split like Vito on the Box, *plus* you got a one G advance from me on your end, good will, get acquainted, my pocket to yours, this very day. *(Strides back down to bar, takes neatly folded wad of hundreds from jacket, places it on bar in front of the silent Eddie, sits on stool opposite him; then flatly, evenly)* Now, some banana-nut reason, this deal don't appeal; need I mention, things happen. The Angel come down, fly away with the Liquor License, twenty, thirty days, outa business. Things break, toilets don't work, beer deliveries slow down— *(Suddenly smacks himself on the forehead)* What the hell am I talkin'!? I gotta tell The East Side Savage birds-and-bees basics? You know the story. Gimme the Brocheh, baby; we go in peace. Whatta ya say?

(Silence; he waits for Eddie's answer as does everyone else in the barroom. A thoughtful moment, then Eddie picks up the wad of bills)

EDDIE *(turns to Hannah, quietly)* Hannah, how about you take Charlie into the kitchen, give him a little something to eat. Brisket's on your right, some Lokshen on the left. *(Hannah, with some help from Nick, wheels the Stroller into the Kitchen and exits as Eddie turns to Scalso, continuing pleasantly)* Fact of the matter, you first come in here, I figure you are definitely not with the Salvation Army; and this guy here, the bulge in the right jacket-pocket is probably not his Holy Bible, I say to myself. *(Blue chuckles softly, Scalso smiles)* I do *not* know you are a Seranno boy, got alla Vito's Stops now. *(He shrugs apologetically)* Not knowin' this, I do the club thing for ya, kinda demonstrate my attitude and feelings how I run my place. *(A beat; then he tosses the wad of bills into Scalso's lap)* Which remains the exact same. You're boring me to death, Ginzo. *(Continues calmly)* I want your nose and your ass, and everything you got in between, *outa* my business. I don't want your cigarette machine, your records, your advice, and I want your goddamn Angel off my shoulder. I give you the same deal I give Vito on the Box, and that's *it*. And now I want you and your over-the-hill hench outa my joint instantaneous. Goodbye and good luck. *(He picks up the club, raps it sharply on the bar like a gavel)* Conversation over; end of conversation.

(Scalso remains quite still, Blue takes a small step forward from the Jukebox, Charlie rises tensely in his booth, Finney is wringing his Fedora like a wet bathing suit)

HANNAH'S VOICE   *(softly, from Kitchen)* Pogrom . . . pogrom . . . pogrom . . . pogrom . . .

SCALSO   *(points to his silver crucifix; quietly)* This here J.C., my Pop give it to me; remind me of Our Savior, but mostly, he says, to do things peaceful before I do 'em hard; this has been my approach with you here. But you know what comes to me, I listen to you? Sooner or later, tough or chicken, lucky, unlucky, Jews is Jews. Ain't this the way, Blue? Ain't this the way? Goddamn *guests* in this country, they are—they're here ten minutes, they're tellin' ya how to *run* the place . . . *(He puts his hand on Eddie's arm)* I pride myself, makin' friends with you Jews—but sooner or later, every *one* of ya—

(Eddie reaches forward, gets a firm grip on Scalso's crucifix and chain and pulls him across the bar with it, holding him firmly down on the bar)

EDDIE   You was holdin' my arm . . .

SCALSO   *(struggling)* Hey, my J.C., my J.C.—

EDDIE   You know us Jews, we can't keep our hands off the guy.

SCALSO   *Blue, Blue . . .*

(Blue thrusts his hand into his gun-pocket, Nick turns to him; Finney races up stairs, hovering in Apartment doorway)

EDDIE   *(retaining firm grip on Scalso)* Here's the situation: Mr. Blue, whatever you got in mind right now, a fact for ya: Nick here, an ex-cop, got two friends with him, Mr. Smith and Mr. Wesson;

there's some say his aim ain't what it used to be, but a target your size he's bound to put a hole in it somewheres; 'sides which, he don't care if he kills ya, he thinks Donder an' Blitzen gonna take the rap for him anyway. *(Lets go of Scalso, holds his billy-club high in the air; all in the room frozen)* Scalso, any part of you makes a move on me, I bust it with Billy. This is the situation, both of ya. Stay and make a move; or go. *(Moving up to Jukebox, watching them carefully)* Meantime, while you're makin' up your mind, I got a need to hear one o' those Hollerin' Hebes; gonna play one of my records on my Box here . . . *(Quickly deposits slug, makes selection; turns to face them, his club at the ready)* My personal suggestion, we go for a safe and sane Fourth.

(Eddie's eyes dart from Scalso to Blue, Finney grips the edge of the Apartment doorway; Blue, his hand firmly in his gun-pocket, looks over at Nick, sizing him up. Nick, still standing at the far end of the bar, slips his hand into the holster under his jacket, holds it there)

NICK   *(quietly, to Blue)* I see you when you're sleepin', I know when you're awake; I know if you've been bad or good, so be good for goodness sake . . .

FINNEY   *(whispering urgently to Eddie)* Just tell 'em about DiGangi; we stop all this, Eddie—

EDDIE   *(quietly)* Don't need him, I got it under control. This is mine.

(Suddenly, from the Jukebox, we begin to hear Aaron Lebedeff's rousing rendition of "In Odessa" and its irresistibly danceable Klezmer Band backup; Lebedeff sings a dream of the old Moldavanka, inviting us to return to a world of swirling skirts, endless dancing, grand times till dawn in the shoreline cafés of the Black Sea and, of course, the food that was served there. Nick, Scalso, Finney, Blue and Charlie remaining quite still, the pulsing beat of the Klezmer Band filling the silence of this tense moment, Eddie starting to snap the fingers of his left hand to the beat, the billy-club still held high in his right, Music continuing to build through the scene)

LEBEDEFF'S VOICE:

> "In Ades, in Ades, af der Moldavanke,
> Tantst men dort a Palanez, mit a sheyn tsiganke . . . "

(Scalso rises suddenly from his barstool, going to center of room, forceful, commanding, on top of it again)

SCALSO   *(shouting, pointing fiercely at Eddie)* The man *marked* me, Blue; he put a *mark* on me! *(Blue takes a step forward; Scalso clenches his fists, ready to spring)* O.K., school's in *session* now, barkeep;

lesson time; Professor Blue and me, we gonna *teach* you something . . .

JOEY'S VOICE *(shouting, from street)* Pop! Hey, *Pop!*

(Zaretsky suddenly bursts through the front door, his arm around a somewhat battered, bloody-nosed, but very proud Joey. A man who knows how to make an entrance, Zaretsky speaks immediately as he comes through the door, using the threshold as his stage; the Group remains frozen)

ZARETSKY No, not since David and Goliath have I seen such! Yes, the child bleeds, but wait till you see what this *DeSapio* looks like—

JOEY He went *down*, Pop, he went *down*— *(Indicating his bloody nose)* I mean, later he got *up*, but there was—

ZARETSKY Please, Jussel, allow me—I come upon this child, familiar to me at a distance; opposing him, I tell you, a veritable *Visigoth* of a boy, he— *(His voice trails off; he becomes aware of the stillness in the room)* I feel that I do not have the full attention of this group.

EDDIE *(quickly, quietly)* Congratulations, kid. Go to Sussman's, pick up the bread order. Now.

JOEY Pop, I gotta tell ya—

EDDIE *Suss*man's. *Now.*

JOEY Christ's sake, Pop—

EDDIE *Now!*

JOEY *(as he reluctantly exits)* Christ's sake . . .

(Zaretsky sees the billy-club in Eddie's hand, glances at the unfamiliar figures of Scalso and Blue; Eddie remaining quite still, snapping his fingers as the Music continues, swaying slightly to the beat)

EDDIE Anton, we got a situation here.

SCALSO *(grips Blue's arm, urgently)* Now, Blue, *now*; place is fillin' up. Look, Blue, man wants to dance; help him dance, Blue—the feet, go for the feet. I want to see the man *dance*, make him dance, make him *nervous* . . .

BLUE *(after a moment; his eyes fixed on Eddie)* Nervous? You ain't gonna make *this* boy nervous. This boy don't *get* nervous; which is what's gonna kill him one fine day. *(Pulls his empty hand sharply out of his gun-pocket, his gaze never leaving Nick and Eddie)* Now *today*, Jimmy, here's how the cards lay down: what you got here is an ol' shithouse and a crazy Jew. Two and a half on this Box, boy?

You give this Jew Bing Crosby in person, you give him Guy Lombardo appearin' nightly, he don't pull in more'n a hundred. Now, tell me, Jimmy-Boy, you want me to go shoot Santa Claus for a hundred-dollar Box?

SCALSO *(urgently, commanding)* We gotta leave a *mark*, Blue, on *some-*body, on *something*. Fifty-four Stops, this news travels; there gotta be consequences here, Blue, things *happened* here—

BLUE *Consequences?* This Jew don't know consequences and don't care. Look at his eyes, Jimmy. He just wants to kill you, boy; don't care if he dies the next minute, and don't care who dies with him. Make it a rule, Jimmy-Boy, you don't want to get into a fight, weapon or no, with a man ain't lookin' to live. *(He turns, walks briskly towards front door)*

SCALSO *(not moving, rubbing neck-burn)* Things *happened* here, Blue—

BLUE Seranno ain't gonna give a cobbler's crap about this place—fifty-three Stops to *cover*, Jimmy-Boy, let's go.

SCALSO *(silence for a moment; then, striding angrily towards Blue)* Hey, hey—how about you leave off callin' me "Jimmy-Boy," huh? How about we quit that shit, right?

BLUE *(patting Scalso's shoulder)* In the old Saint Pat's, y'know, over on Prince, we used t'make you Guineas have mass in the basement. Biggest mistake we ever made was lettin' you boys up on the first floor. *(He exits. Scalso remains in doorway, turns towards Eddie)*

SCALSO *(pointing, fiercely)* O.K., now here's somethin' for *you* and *Billy* and the entire fuckin' *club*—

(But the Lebedeff Music has built to an irresistible Freylekeh rhythm—irresistible, that is, to any triumphant Jew in the room—and Eddie, holding the billy-club over his head with both hands, begins to spin around the center table to the beat)

EDDIE Hey, Jimmy-Boy, you wanted to see the man dance . . . he's dancin' . . . *(Takes his handkerchief out of his pocket, extends it towards Zaretsky, a gesture of invitation as old as the Music he dances to)* Hey, Actor, Actor . . . come, come, this Ginzo loves dancin' . . .

(Zaretsky joins Eddie in perhaps the only thing they can ever agree upon, the pleasure of dancing to an old Lebedeff tune; Zaretsky takes the other end of the handkerchief and, the handkerchief held taut between them over their heads, they dance aggressively towards Scalso, their feet stomping to the beat, Scalso backing away towards the door.

Joey suddenly bursts through the door just behind Scalso, shouting at his back)

JOEY   DiGangi! DiGangi è mio fratello! Chiamalo! Chiamalo!

SCALSO   *(surrounded by two dancing Jews and a screaming child; he shouts)* Buncha crazy Hebes here . . . !

(Scalso exits into the street. Zaretsky and Eddie triumphant, Zaretsky swirling to the Music, Eddie beating out the rhythm fiercely with his club, Finney and Nick clapping to the beat, Joey's arms in the air, shouting)

JOEY   It *works*, Pop! The *DiGangi* number; it works! It works!

EDDIE   Of *course* it works!

JOEY   *(proudly) Comes* to me, Pop, comes to me these guys don't *look* right, see—

EDDIE   Nobody messes with the Ross boys!

JOEY   Who?

EDDIE   Ross! Ross! Joey *Ross*—the kid who beat DeSapio!

JOEY   But I didn't *win*, Pop—

EDDIE   *(prowling the room with his club, his tension unreleased by Scalso's defeat) Sure* you won, kid, we only got winners here, *winners . . .*

ZARETSKY   *(points a challenging finger)* So then, Itzik, I have seen you rise from your knees—something of your spirit has been touched today!

EDDIE   *(fiercely)* Only thing got touched was my goddamn *arm*, Actor.

HANNAH   *(leaning out of kitchen)* So, the coast, I am assuming, is clear?

EDDIE   Everything under control here, babe.

HANNAH   *(standing in kitchen doorway)* Gentlemen . . . I got big news . . .

ZARETSKY   What, Hannah?

HANNAH   Gentlemen . . . *the child has spoken!*

(The Group cheers, but Eddie cuts sharply through them)

EDDIE   *What?* What did he say . . . ?

(All fix on Hannah expectantly as Nick guides her down into the room)

HANNAH   Two statements, clear like a bell; The first, very nice, he touches my hand, he says, "Papa." *(All but Eddie responding happily; he remains silent, quite still)* The second statement, a little embarrassing to repeat . . .

EDDIE *What*, Hannah . . . ?

HANNAH A couple seconds later, he's got my hand again, this time a firm grip, he says—clear like a bell, I tell you—"No shit from nobody!"

(Zaretsky applauds lustily, shouting "Bravo," Nick and Finney cheer loudly, waving their hats, Joey leaps joyously in the air yelling "Hey, Champ"; Eddie remains silent, striding sharply away from the cheering Group, his club held tight in his fist)

EDDIE *(shouting, fiercely, above the Group)* And no *exceptions* . . . ! *(Raising club violently over his head)* No *exceptions* . . . nobody . . . ! *(smashing club down on center table)* nobody . . . !

(The Group turns to him, startled, quite still, as Eddie continues, out of control now, wildly, striking a chair, another table, killing them like Cossacks, shouting with each blow)

EDDIE . . . nobody . . . nobody . . . *(Striking Charlie's booth, Charlie rising to his feet, riveted)* Nobody! . . . *(Eddie freezes with this last shout, his club held high in the air, ready to strike another blow as . . .)*

THE CURTAIN FALLS

Marc Bryan-Brown

Judd Hirsch
with, *top*,
Tony Gillan,
middle,
William Biff
McGuire,
Marilyn
Sokol, Peter
Gerety, and
bottom, John
Procaccino

ACT TWO

Before the curtain rises we hear a full Chorus and Marching Band moving up into a thunderous, rousing, next-to-last stanza of "Columbia, the Gem of the Ocean."

CHORUS

"Three cheers for the red, white and blue,
 Three cheers for the red, white and blue,
 The Army and Navy forever,
 Three cheers for the red, white and blue . . . "

At Rise: The blaring trumpets rise in pitch to herald the final stanza as the curtain goes up. Charlie alone in the darkened bar—the dim, early evening light of the Present—seated exactly where he was at the beginning of the play, at the far end of the bar near the glowing Jukebox, listening thoughtfully to the triumphant conclusion of the Music to which Eddie first burst into the room.

CHORUS

"Three cheers for the red, white and blue,
 Three cheers for the red, white and blue,
 Thy banners make tyranny tremble,
 Three cheers for the red, white and blue . . . "

A cymbal-crashing, drum-rolling finale; Charlie continues to look into the colors of the now silent Jukebox for a moment or two, then turns to us.

CHARLIE   *(indicating Moose)*   Well—as Morris will tell you—the Golden Door Tavern did *not* get us Uptown; nor did Eddie Ross' Silver Horseshoe, the Empire State Sports Club, or even Ed Ross' Riverview, mostly because we didn't have one. *(Inserting slug in Jukebox, making selection)* But then came the summer of Forty-Four, the heyday of Café Society and, of course, its pulsating heart—Sherman Billingsley's Stork Club. *(With a sweeping gesture towards bar)*   Eddie's response was swift and glorious: Ladies and Gentleman, July Third, Nineteen Forty-Four . . . the Opening Day of the Flamingo Lounge.

(A huge pink and crimson plaster-and-glass chandelier in the shape of a flamingo in flight—its spread wings, thrust-back legs and proudly arched head framed by several dozen glowing pink light bulbs—descends through the ceiling over the bar as we begin to hear the catchy bongo and trumpet Calypso intro to the Andrews Sisters' recording of "Rum and Coca-Cola" coming from the Jukebox)

ANDREWS SISTERS

> "Out on Mandenella Beach,
> G.I. romance with native peach,
> All day long make tropic love,
> Next day sit in hot sun and cool off, drinkin'
> Rum and Coca-Cola . . . "

(Music continuing, building, as lights come up full; it's exactly eight years later, about 7 A.M. on Monday, July 3, 1944, and we see that the bar-room has gone through a transition from general Early American to general Tropical Caribbean, the dominant theme, as always, being Gin-Mill Shabby. The Early American stuff remains but joining it now are coconut-shell candle holders and plastic pineapples on each table, crepe-paper leis hung about on hooks, an incandescent tropical sunset painting over the Jukebox, brightly illustrated placards announcing various rum-punch drinks and their "Reasonable Introductory Prices" tacked up on the walls, running across the bottom of the mirror a red and white banner reading "Welcome to the Flamingo! Opening Day!" and over the door a painting of a flamingo with just the word "Lounge" under it. Eddie's usual Fourth of July bunting across the top of the mirror and small flags along the bar are in evidence, though the flags have not yet been put on the tables and booths. In addition, it is the summer of the Fifth Annual "Miss Daitch" Contest and a string of six small posters, featuring a smiling head-shot and brief bio of each Contestant, hangs across the right wall just above the booths; beneath these a bright banner states the Daitch Beer slogan: "There Is a Difference and the Difference Is Daitch"; below that: "Vote Here for Miss Daitch, 1944," and next to the far right booth a ballot-box and a stack of ballots. All this revealed as the Music and Charlie continue)

CHARLIE   And tonight . . . the Victory Party, in honor of what we're all sure will be Joey's twenty-eighth straight win since he got his Amateur Card . . . *(as Joey, almost eighteen now, enters from the Kitchen with a tray of plastic pineapples, places them on tables, his boxer's authority and the tiptoe bounce of his walk distinctly similar to his father's)* . . . twenty-three knockouts, six in the first three rounds, and four decisions. Got his A.A.U. card at fourteen—two years before the legal age—by using Vince DiGangi's son Peter's Baptism Certificate, so he's earned a very big reputation over the last four years for somebody called Pistol Pete DiGangi. *(Joey turns, heading up to bar, the back of his jacket emblazoned with a "Pistol Pete" logo)* I, of course, was known as the only kid ever to be knocked down by Cock-Eye Celestini—he being several years my junior, an infant really, and visually disabled—

EDDIE   *(bursts in from the Kitchen, delighted, waving a folded newspaper)*
Hey, ya see the ad in the "Mirror" this morning?—ya see that?—
top of the *Card* tonight, Joey, top of the *Card.* "Bazooka-Boy"
Kilbane, *nobody*—goddamn *Main Event* even *with* this Mick bozo!
This is because ya made a goddamn *name* for yourself, kid! *(He
moves over to Joey, the two of them sparring, jabbing, ducking, weav-
ing about amidst the tables now, clearly a morning ritual, as Eddie continues)* Let me tell ya about Kilbane's weak spot—his *body;* his
entire body. Tonight's *pointer?* Bring some stamps with ya and
mail the putz home! *(Indicates radio as their sparring continues)*
*Broad*cast—broadcast over the goddamn *air*waves tonight, Speed
Spector him*self* doin' the Blow-by-Blow; *Spector.* Closin' the place
up soon as the fights start, nobody in here unless by special invite;
victory party, champagne, the works. I'd be at ringside, per usual,
but I gotta hear this comin' outa the *Philco,* kid, I *gotta.* After,
Spector always does an On-the-Spot with the Main Event
Winner; gotta *hear* it, right? *(As their sparring ends, Eddie—clearly outboxed and happily exhausted by Joey—returning to set up bar)* By
the way, durin' the On-the-Spot, ya wanna drop a mention there's
a new class place openin' on Canal, the Flamingo Lounge, this is
optional— *(Suddenly slaps his head)* Will you shut ya *trap,* Eddie?!
This is *your* night, kid—don't *mention* me—what the hell am I
talkin' about?! Would somebody *please* tell me to shut *up?!*

ZARETSKY   *(entering from Apartment)* All right; shut up. *(Moving
down to his usual table, folding back page of newspaper)* For all assem-
bled, I have here a certain item . . .

EDDIE: Shit, the Jew News . . .

ZARETSKY: Gentlemen, we have here on page twelve of "The New
York Times", amidst ads for Stern's Department Store and a
Jewelry Consultant, an item, five sentences in length, which
reports to us that four hundred thousand Hungarian Jews have
thus far perished in the German death camps of Poland as of June
Seventeenth; and further, that three hundred and fifty thousand
more are presently being deported to Poland where they are
expected to be put to death by July Twenty-Fourth. *This* on page
twelve; however— *(turns to first page)* we find here on the front
page of this same journal, a bold headline concerning today's
holiday traffic; I quote: "Rail and Bus Travel Will Set New July
Fourth Peak." *(Neatly folding paper)* I offer these items, fellow
residents, for the news itself, also an insight into the ironic editorial policies of America's most prominent daily journal; owned,
incidentally, by Jews.

(Joey has moved down to Zaretsky's table, clearly absorbed, as always, by Zaretsky's "Jew News")

JOEY   *(quietly, studying newspaper)*   Jesus, the next three weeks . . . that's three hundred and fifty thousand in the next three *weeks* . . .

EDDIE   *(turns sharply from his work behind the bar)*   Come on, Actor, the *truth*—what's it *say* there? That's another one o' those "Informed Sources *say*," "Foreign Authorities *tell* us" goddamn stories, ain't it? If it's true, where's the *pictures?!* How come I never seen it in "Life" magazine? How come I never seen it in the "March of *Time*," they got *every*thing! *Winchell* even! How come *Roosevelt* don't mention—if F.D.R. *believed* all that he'd be doin' somethin' about it this *minute, guaranteed!*

ZARETSKY   *(rising at his table)*   Itzik, you are a foolish tender of *bars! Election* year, he's *got* your vote already, he will not stir the *pot!* He will be silent, your Golden Goy. He listens, he hears the old and horrible songs—he knows that nobody believes the Jews are dying, only that somehow Jews are making millions from the war and want it. He will be quiet, Itzik, as quiet now as the Jews of page twelve!

EDDIE   *(shouting)*   Do ya *mind*, Zaretsky? Do ya *mind* if we just let the guy go and win the goddamn *war?* Is that *O.K.* with you? The man knows what he's *doin'*, pal—he does *now*, he always *did*, and he always *will*. Meanwhile, you breathe one *word* of that crazy shit durin' Joey's party and you're gonna see *my* twelve-minute version of "The Dybbuk"!

ZARETSKY   *(slams his fist on the table)*   I *refuse*—I refuse, sir, to have a conversation of this nature with a man who has just spent the morning putting light bulbs in a huge pink bird! *(Turns to Joey, suddenly pleasant, cordial; one of those instant transitions of which this old actor is very fond)*   I am off then to the home of the Widow Rosewald, who, among other favors, now repairs my robes for Lear, and kindly tolerates the aging process, both hers and mine. And, of course, my best with the Bazooka tonight. Bonne chance, Jussel, Joey, Goldberg, Ross, DiGangi— *(patting his cheek)* whoever you are. *(Striding to the front door)*   Don't worry, Itzik; tonight I shall sit quietly and cheer appropriately. In future, also, you will have less concern of my Jew News . . . as there are fewer and fewer Jews, there will be less and less news. *(He exits abruptly)*

(Silence for a moment; Eddie continues busily setting up behind the

bar, Joey studies the newspaper article, Charlie absorbed, watching all this from near the Jukebox and not his usual booth)

JOEY *(quietly)* I think it's all true, Pop.

EDDIE *(distracted)* What?

JOEY What Mr. Zaretsky's tellin' us, Pop, I think it's all true. It's *gotta* be—I mean, look at all the shit that's goin' on *here*.

EDDIE Here is business as usual; maybe a little worse this summer.

JOEY A little *worse* this summer?— *(Moving down towards him)* Pop, *Brooklyn*, they hit two cemeteries in one *week*. You been on Rivington lately?—Jewish stars with Swastikas painted over 'em, they're poppin' up on the walls like Lucky *Strike* ads. The Gladiators, the Avengers—*Boys'* clubs, they call 'em—they're on the prowl every night beatin' the crap outa Hebrew School kids. Grabbed a kid comin' outa Beth-El Saturday, ripped off his shirt and painted "Jew" on his chest, like maybe he *forgot*—you *hearin'* any of this, Pop?

EDDIE *(busily stacking glasses, his back to Joey)* It's not I ain't hearin' ya, kid; it's I *heard* it all already; been goin' on since before you was born. But this stuff *Zaretsky's* talkin' about—not even in the old Moldavanka was there ever such.

JOEY But if it's true—

EDDIE If it's true then Uncle Nick's got his *sleigh* parked outside! It's all too crazy, kid, I'm tellin' ya. *(Turns to him)* Now lemme *alone*, will ya—I gotta *open* here in twenty minutes! *(Joey moving thoughtfully up towards phone, Eddie glancing about)* Shit, he ain't done the *set*-ups yet— *(Shouting)* Charlie! Charlie, where are ya?! Charlie!

(Charlie hears his name, tenses, looks up)

YOUNG CHARLIE'S VOICE *(from Apartment above)* I'm in the studio, writing.

EDDIE The studio. Is that the same as the toilet?

YOUNG CHARLIE'S VOICE Sometimes.

EDDIE *(shouting)* Charlie, *move* it, *now*, *pronto*, *down* here!

YOUNG CHARLIE *(entering from apartment)* I'm coming, I'm in transit . . .

(Young Charlie, about eleven, concerned, thoughtful, and many worlds away, slouches down the stairs carrying a stack of loose-leaf pages and several pens; Eddie leans towards him confidentially)

EDDIE Charlie, I got this problem; see, until your book comes out and you become a millionaire, I figured I'd still run my little business here . . . *(shouting)* so how about ya do the goddamn *set*-ups and help me *open* the place! The set-ups and the *mail*, Mister, you got obligations!

YOUNG CHARLIE *(quietly getting tray of set-ups from bar)* I got the mail already, it's by the register.

(Eddie exits, briskly, to work in Kitchen as Young Charlie begins to go rather distractedly about the task of placing set-ups on two or three tables; Charlie watches him silently, intently, for a few moments, then . . .)

CHARLIE Jesus, they were right, I *didn't* pick up my feet. *(Leans towards him)* The shuffling, what's with the *shuf*fling here? Straighten up, will ya? C'mon, Charlie, what happened to "No shit from nobody"?

YOUNG CHARLIE   *(a forlorn sigh, whispering)* Oh-boy-oh-boy-oh-boy . . .

CHARLIE I don't get it, in all the albums I'm always *smiling* . . . *(Nods thoughtfully)* Yeah, but that's because they kept saying "smile" . . . *(Following, close to him, gently)* Don't worry, kid, you're gettin' out. *Outa* here. Sooner than you think. What is it, money? You need money? Bucks, Charlie, *bucks*, the bucks are on their *way* . . . Oh, if I could just give you a coupla dollars, hand you a twenty, right now; a kinda loan, a . . . *(During the above, Young Charlie will have deposited several slugs in the Jukebox, punched the same key several times and crossed over to the "Vote Here for Miss Daitch, 1944" display where he is now clearly entranced, as always, by the face of Miss Daitch Contestant Number Two, Peggy Parsons, and the biography beneath it; we begin to hear the Helen Forrest-Dick Haymes recording of "Long Ago and Far Away" from the Jukebox, their voices drifting dreamily in the empty bar)* Oh, my God . . . Peggy Parsons . . . *that's* it . . . *(Turns to us, as it all comes back)* The Miss Daitch Contest of Forty-Four, our bar has been selected as one of the officially designated polling places in the neighborhood . . . *(Softly, from memory, as Young Charlie studies bio)* "Pretty, perky, pert Peggy Parsons, or 'Peggo' as she prefers to be called, plans to pursue an acting career in motion pictures . . . " Peggo, Peggo . . . To say that I had a crush on Peggy Parsons would be to say that Mao Tse-Tung had a crush on Communism; only the beginning of July and I had already cast over six hundred ballots in the Greater New York area. *(Young Charlie sits in Charlie's usual booth, starts fervently re-writing whatever is on his loose-leaf pages, all of it clearly*

inspired by occasional glances at Peggy; the Music swells, filling the bar)
Yeah, go with it, Charlie, this is it, it doesn't get better than
this . . . *(Sits next to him in booth, leans close)* Very important: love,
Charlie, love does *not* make the world go round, *looking* for it
does; this is important . . . Also very important, Charlie, in about
ten years you're gonna meet a girl at the Museum of Modern Art,
in front of the "Guernica"—let this painting be a *warning* to
you—don't go out with this girl, don't even *talk* to this girl, by all
means do *not marry this girl*—

JOEY   Hey, Charlie— *(Hangs up phone, comes down towards booth)*
Been settin' up tickets for the guys, everybody tells me—

YOUNG CHARLIE   *(points to pages in Joey's pocket)* Did you read it?

JOEY   Charlie, *listen*, word's out, the Avengers, the Gladiators, they're
gonna be roamin' tonight, like Memorial Day, or maybe like the
Jew Hunt on Pell Street—whatever, I don't want you walkin' over
to Rutgers Arena by yourself tonight. Gonna work out with
Bimmy, then I come *back* for ya—are you listening?

YOUNG CHARLIE   Yeah, after Bimmy's I go with you. Did you *read* it?

JOEY   Sometimes, I tell ya, it's like you're not *present* here—

YOUNG CHARLIE   *(rising in booth)* Did you read the *letter*, fa Chrissake!

JOEY   I *read* the letter, I *read* the goddamn letter! It's completely nuts
and wacko. Also hopeless and dumb.

YOUNG CHARLIE   If you got a criticism, tell me.

JOEY   Charlie, number one: I don't *get* it— *(Indicating the Miss Daitch
photos)* These girls, they all got the same *smile*, the same *eyes*, the
same *nose*— *(Pointing)* C'mon, tell me, what's the difference
between Peggy Parsons . . . and "Lovely, lively Laurie Lipton"
here?

YOUNG CHARLIE   The difference? The *diff*erence? Why am I discussing this with a boxer?

JOEY   I got to go to Bimmy's—

YOUNG CHARLIE   *(holds up loose-leaf pages)* Thirty seconds, Joey—the
revised version; I changed key words.

JOEY   *(leans against booth)* Twenty.

YOUNG CHARLIE   *(reads from pages)* "Mr. Samuel Goldwyn, Metro-
Goldwyn-Mayer Studios. Dear Sam: Enclosed please find photo
of Peggy Parsons. I think you will agree that this is the outstanding exquisiteness of a Motion Picture Star. You may reach her by
the Daitch's Beer distribution place in your area is my belief. If

Motion Picture employment is a result you may wish to say to her who recommended her eventually. She or yourself can reach me by post at the Flamingo Apartments, Six Eighty-One Canal Street, New York City. In closing I think of you first-hand instead of Darryl or David because of your nation of origin Poland which is right near my father's original nation Russia. Yours truly, C. E. Ross." *(Young Charlie does not look up from the letter, so concerned is he about his brother's response. Joey, sensing this, sits opposite him in the booth)*

JOEY   To begin with, that's an exceptionally well-put, well-written letter, Charlie . . .

YOUNG CHARLIE   I know what you're thinkin', but *wild things* happen out there, Joey; they're findin' stars in *drug*stores, *ele*vators—

JOEY   Right, and I'm sure the feeling you have for this Peggy is—

YOUNG CHARLIE   Peggo, she prefers to be called Peggo—

JOEY   Peggo, right—is genuine. So let's follow this through for a moment. Say, thousand-to-one shot, but Goldwyn, somebody in his office, sees the picture, say he gets a hold of her; say she's grateful, comes down here to Canal Street to see you, right?

YOUNG CHARLIE   Right, right.

JOEY   And you're eleven.

YOUNG CHARLIE   Joey, I'm *aware* that there's an age problem; I will *deal* with it.

JOEY   *(after a moment, quietly)* Tell ya, sometimes, the similarities, you and Pop, it scares the shit outa me, kid.

YOUNG CHARLIE   *(studying letter)* Maybe "Dear Sam" 's too familiar; maybe "Dear Samuel" or "Mr. Goldwyn," huh?

JOEY   *(pats his shoulder)* Right; that'll do it. *(Rises, starts briskly towards front door)* Gotta get to Bimmy, I ain't worked out since the Chocolate Chopper. *(As Eddie enters, returning from work in Kitchen to go to stack of mail behind bar)* See ya before the fight, Pop; comin' back to pick up Charlie.

EDDIE   *(looks up from mail)* Hey, this kid tonight—an easy win, but the Bazooka's got a little weight on ya and I don't like his left—so go for the kill *early*; the *kill*, Joey. Remember, the boy is *nothin'*; he is *now*, he always *was*—

JOEY   *(as he exits into street)* —and he always *will* be!

CHARLIE   *(to us, from booth)* Brother, brotherly, brotherhood: dyna-mite, powerhouse words, you could take them up off the ground like a punch; they meant—and still, now, at this moment, mean—Joey. However, take note, the only time Pop talks to me is when his prince is unavailable . . .

EDDIE *(behind bar, studying a letter)* Charlie, the *set*-ups, what happened? *(Young Charlie leaves booth to continue his task)* You can stick the flags in the pineapples, O.K.? *(Young Charlie carries flags and tray of set-ups to center table; Eddie, still looking down at the letter, speaks quietly, solemnly)* Charles . . .

(Young Charlie freezes at table)

CHARLIE "Charles," in this household, is my criminal name.

EDDIE Charles . . . I'm lookin' at a letter here from the Star of David School, Rabbi Rubin.

YOUNG CHARLIE These flags, Pop, they don't fit into the pineapples . . .

EDDIE *(still looking down at letter, calmly)* This is *some* letter, this letter. It's got my undivided attention.

YOUNG CHARLIE Hebrew's been over a week now, Pop; it don't start again till—

EDDIE *(continuing calmly)* Turns out it's been over for *you* a very long time now. About eight months, according to this letter. Also according to this letter there's been a lot of *other* letters. Says here, Rubin, "I had assumed from your past responses to my inquiries regarding Charles' religious training . . ." Turns out Rubin's been writin' to me, and I been *answerin'* him on this matter seven months now. Hey, I even got compliments on "the grace and wisdom of my remarks," says here. He *especially* likes the graciousness how I keep payin' him anyway even though you ain't goin' there no more.

YOUNG CHARLIE Pop, how about we—

EDDIE *(still calmly, folding letter)* Convenient for ya, you bein' the one gets the mail. Musta got distracted today, huh? Yeah. Bugsy Siegel don't get distracted, Frank Costello don't get distracted; Dillinger got distracted *once* . . . and now he's dead.

YOUNG CHARLIE *(moving towards bar)* Pop, I gotta tell ya—

EDDIE Charlie, look at my hands. Are ya lookin' at my hands?

YOUNG CHARLIE Yeah.

EDDIE What I'm doin' here is I'm holdin' onto the edge of the bar because if I let go I'm gonna beat the crap outa ya.

YOUNG CHARLIE Here's what—

EDDIE I'm here loadin' up shickers so you can hang out with God, twenty a month to the Star of David, hard cash, and you ain't even *there*. *(Quietly, in awe)* While I'm *sayin'* it, I don't believe it. I don't believe that you're standin' there in front of me alive, I didn't kill you yet.

YOUNG CHARLIE It was *wrong*, the whole *thing*, I *know*, but lemme—

EDDIE My hands, they're lettin' go of the bar— *(Suddenly moving out from behind bar towards Young Charlie, Young Charlie backing up fearfully across the room, his hands raised, urgently)*

YOUNG CHARLIE I gotta tell ya *one* thing, Pop, *one thing!*

EDDIE *(after a moment)* One thing.

YOUNG CHARLIE *(keeping his distance; fervently)* That place; you don't know what it *is* there, the Star of David. It's a terrible place. It's not even a Temple or anything. It's just this ratty place on Houston Street. This ratty room on the second floor of a building, two Rabbis in a room makin' a buck. Pop, I swear, God isn't there like you think.

EDDIE He's *there*, kid. Take my word for it—

YOUNG CHARLIE Over Pedro and Olga's *Dance* Studio? Two ratty guys with bad breath who throw chalk at your head and slam books on your hand every time you miss a trick? I mean real angry guys with bugs in their beards; sometimes they just kick you in the ass on general principles.

EDDIE Yeah, that's God all right; I'd know Him anywhere.

YOUNG CHARLIE That ain't God, those guys—

EDDIE Sure they ain't, I know that; but they're *connected*. That's the whole thing in life: *connections*, kid. *(Relaxes slightly, leans towards him)* First thing, right off, I guarantee you, there's a God. You got that?

YOUNG CHARLIE I'm with you on that. We only disagree on where He's located.

EDDIE Hebrew School, He's located *there*; so you go back there. Sit. *(Young Charlie sits obediently at center table; Eddie sits opposite him)* Because there's times—you're in trouble, you're really sick, and especially when you die, just before you die—you'll be glad you stayed in touch. That's the payoff. There's gonna be a time, guaranteed, you'll be grateful I made ya go; but the main thing is if ya don't go back I'm gonna kill ya.

YOUNG CHARLIE   I don't get it, Pop. Ma lights the candles Friday, starts the prayer, ya say, "Cut the shit and let's eat"; ya *never* go to Temple anymore, the *bar* was open last Rosh Hashana, ya—

(Eddie suddenly grabs Young Charlie by the collar of his shirt with one hand and pulls him halfway across the table)

EDDIE   I stay in *touch*, Criminal! Look, you're makin' me grit my teeth! My goddamn *bridge* is crackin'! I stay in *touch*, Putzolla! Twenty a month to Rubin and the bandits so you should learn the worda the Torah and the worda God—

YOUNG CHARLIE   I can't breathe, Pop—

EDDIE   That's two shifts a month I'm puttin' out for God here exclusive, same like I done with Joey! Are you breathing?

YOUNG CHARLIE   *No—*

EDDIE   Then *breathe—* *(Lets him go)* And I got married by a Rabbi, under God, twenty-five years and I stick! How *come* I stick? A woman, we all realize, is at this time a wacky person, nearly deaf; also a rough mouth don't encourage my endeavors whatever. *(Silence for a moment)* This is currently. But there was occasions otherwise. *(Glances up at Apartment door, then leans towards Young Charlie; quietly)* You hearda the expression "raven-haired"? O.K., there's some girls got hair they call "midnight black," very beautiful, but it got no light in it, see. "Raven-hair" is like the bird, glossy, light come *out* of it, got its own light comin' out—this is what she had. First time I seen her she's runnin' down these steps to the beach, this hair is down to her ass, flyin' behind her like wings, her arms is out like she's gonna hug the entire Black Sea, laughin' . . . *(Slaps the table)* And then, Sonny-Boy, minutes, *minutes*—I swear to you, minutes after the Rabbi pronounced us the lights went out in her hair like somebody turned off a switch; and the mouth began. Continuing in this manner until she became the totally wacky deaf person we know in our home at this time; she is at this *moment* upstairs, stirring a pot, getting wackier and deafer. But I *stick!* *(Slaps the table again)* That's my point, kid: I *stick.* Because there'll be a night one day when the heart attack comes and somebody'll have to call Dr. Schwartzman and the ambulance. And who will do it? The Wacky Ravenhead! In five minutes she covers a fifty-year bet! Why? Because I put my money on a good woman. Wacky and deaf; but good. There's a lot of people got this kind of arrangement. It's called a Coronary Marriage. And when you find a better reason for people staying together, let me know. Love? forget it. Who are they kidding? It won't be there when you get home and it won't call Dr. Schwartzman for you. *(Leans closer)* Same with God. I *stick*. I stick and so will you. Because all God's gotta do is come through *once* to make Him worth your time. Maybe twice. Just one big deal and once when you die so you ain't scared shitless. *(Picks up letter)* O.K., you hang in with Rubin till the Bar Mitzvah shot. Whatta we talkin' about?—a coupla years, tops, it's *over;* you're joined up with *my* Pop and *his* Pop and *his* and all the Pops back forever—you're covered, it's set, I done my job; then ya do whatever the hell ya want. *(Holds out his hand)* Deal? *(A moment, then Young Charlie shakes his hand; Eddie rises, starts briskly back towards bar)* C'mon, let's seal it. *(Young Charlie follows him, Eddie goes behind bar)* Mine's vodka. What'll ya have?

YOUNG CHARLIE   *(sits opposite him, elbows on bar)* Let's see . . . you got lemon juice and seltzer?

EDDIE   Like the choice; *I* got it—   *(A spritz, a splash, places it on bar)* Now *you* got it. *(Pouring his vodka)* Yeah, good; I think this was a good conversation.

YOUNG CHARLIE   Me too . . . I mean it ain't exactly Andy Hardy and the Judge, but it's somethin'. *(He laughs at his own joke; soon Eddie laughs too, joining him, they "click" glasses)* Boy, Pop, you're right—

EDDIE   *(still laughing)*   Sure I'm right—

YOUNG CHARLIE   *(still laughing)* I mean about Mom, she sure is *some* wacky *deaf* person; I mean, she—

(A sudden, resounding smack in the face from Eddie sends Young Charlie reeling off his bar-stool, knocking him to the floor. Charlie, in his booth, holds his cheek, feeling the impact)

EDDIE   *(shouting)*   You will not mock your mother! Even in jest!

YOUNG CHARLIE   *(half-mumbling, still on his knees, his head still ringing, shocked and hurt at once)* Hell with you, *hell* with you, don't make no sense . . .

EDDIE   *(comes out from behind bar, thundering, pointing down at him)* What's *that?* What do I hear?! Gypsies! Gypsies! The Gypsies brought ya! This can't be mine!

YOUNG CHARLIE   *(scrambling to his feet, screaming)* Oh, I wish to God they *had!* I wish to God the Gypsies brought me! I don't wanna be from *you!* *(Darting from table to table as Eddie stalks him, the boy gradually rising to full, wailing, arm-flailing rage)* Nothin' fits together, nothin' ya *say!* Goddamn switch*eroo* alla time! *Her? Her? You! You're* the crazy one, *you're* the deaf one, *you're* the one nobody can talk to! *(Whacking pineapples off of tables, wildly,* *screaming, pointing fiercely at Eddie)* Loser! Loser! Goddamn *loser!* You're a goddamn crazy *loser* in a goddamn loser *shit*house here!

(Eddie suddenly snaps, a moment of pure madness, races towards him, grabbing a chair, raising it over his head, clearly about to smash it down on Young Charlie; Young Charlie drops to the ground, his arms over his head, Eddie lost in rage, all his enemies below him)

EDDIE   *(roaring) You people . . .* !

(Eddie freezes, about to strike, looks down, sees that it's Young Charlie; he slowly lowers the chair, trembling with rage, looking at it, realizing for a moment what he was about to do, shaken, quite still; he tosses the chair to the ground)

YOUNG CHARLIE   *(rises, unaware of what's happening to his father)* Come on, great, let's see ya do the one thing ya *can* do . . . *(Shouting, his fists raised, holding his ground)* No. No more hitting this year. This is *it* . . . Come on, come on, Pop . . . just one more move, I'm the perfect height; just one more move and I kick you in the balls so hard ya don't straighten up for a *month* . . . *(Full power now)* One more move and it's right in the balls—right in the *balls*, Pop, I swear to God!

EDDIE   Swear to who?!

YOUNG CHARLIE   God! I swear to God!

EDDIE   *(after a moment, quietly)* See how He comes in handy? *(A pause; then, still a bit shaken, covering)* Well, I . . . I believe I've made my point. Sometimes ya gotta illustrate, y'know . . . for the full clarity of the thing. *(Sound of Gusta approaching from the Apartment above, humming a few phrases of "In Odessa," Eddie heading briskly back to bar, pulling himself together)* Now you'll excuse me, I gotta open in five minutes. First day of the Flamingo Lounge.

(Eddie takes a quick shot of the vodka he left on the bar, erasing the episode, returning to work as Gusta enters from the Apartment carrying her usual two large pots of just-cooked food, humming brightly, Young Charlie eventually retreating slowly, thoughtfully to his booth and his loose-leaf pages.)

GUSTA   *(placing pots on Kitchen stove)* Today we got the usuals, Eddie—Mulligan Stew, Cottage Fries, General Patton's Pancakes, D-Day Dumplings—

EDDIE   General Patton's Pancakes, I forget—

GUSTA   Potato Latkes—

EDDIE   Potato Latkes, right—

GUSTA   *(bringing plate of food to Young Charlie's booth)* Upstairs, simmering, I got for Joey's party tonight—it's just us, Eddie, I'll use maiden names—Kasha-Varnishkes, also Holishkes with honey and raisin.

EDDIE   Great, Gloria, great—

GUSTA   *(starts back towards Kitchen)* Joey's boxing-fight, I'll be upstairs; you'll inform me at knockout time, I bring down the food.

EDDIE   Don't worry, this guy won't *touch* him, Gloria—

GUSTA   This is how it is with me: I can't watch, so I can't listen either; it hurts.

EDDIE   *(approaching her at Kitchen doorway; quietly)* Hey, for the party tonight, how about ya take the pins outa y'hair . . . let it, y'know, free.

GUSTA   I let it free it goes in the soup.

EDDIE   I mean, just loose, y'know, like flowin'.

GUSTA   Who's gonna *see*, Finney, Nick—?

EDDIE   *Me, I'll* see it—

GUSTA   *(suddenly)* Eddie, there's a bird on the ceiling.

EDDIE   It's a *flamingo.*

GUSTA   All right, I'll believe you; it's a flamingo. Why is it on the ceiling?

EDDIE   Gonna be like a *symbol* for us, Gloria, for the place; like I was tellin' Joey: Borden's got a cow, Billingsley's got a stork, Firestone—

GUSTA   How much did the dopey bird cost?

EDDIE   It just so happens this hand-made, hand-crafted, sixty-eight-light Flamingo Chandelier is the only one of its kind in the world.

GUSTA   Two is hard to imagine. *(She goes to Kitchen stove; Eddie continues, high with "Opening Day" fever)*

EDDIE   Gloria, I'm talkin' to Joey this mornin', somethin' *come* to me—somethin' for the *place*, somethin' we never *tried* before—a *word, one* word, a magic word's gonna make all the difference!

GUSTA   Fire.

EDDIE   Advertising!

GUSTA We'll burn it down and get the insurance. The Moose *alone* puts us in clover. *(Exits deep into Kitchen, out of sight)*

EDDIE *Advertising!* Advertising, kiddo! *(Exits into Kitchen, pursuing her, inspired; we hear his voice from inside, his enthusiasm building)* I'm talkin' about a small ad, classy, in there with the Clubs, Gloria—just a picture of a flamingo, one word: *"Lounge,"* under it; under that "Six Eighty-One Canal"—like everybody *knows* already, like it's *in*, Gloria—

CHARLIE *(during above, rising from booth, moving towards Kitchen)* Leave her alone, Pop, leave her *alone*, it's never gonna *happen*—

EDDIE'S VOICE Guy comes in here regular, works for the "Journal-American," runs a heavy tab, I trade him on the *space*, kid—

CHARLIE *(during above, louder and louder)* —stop, we're never going Uptown; stop, *stop* driving us *crazy* with it, Eddie—this *bar*, this goddamn *bar!*

YOUNG CHARLIE *(at booth, writing, as Eddie's voice continues)* "Dear Mr. Zanuck . . . it would not be perfectly candid of me if I did not frankly admit and advise you that I have just previously contacted Sam on this exact matter . . . "

CHARLIE *(turns, anguished, caught between the two of them)* My God, you're just as crazy as *he* is . . .

YOUNG CHARLIE *(writing, his confidence building)* " . . . I refer to the enclosed Peggy Parsons. We live in a competitive industry, Darryl, and I do not wish to keep this woman in a basket . . . "

(We begin to hear the sound of about Twenty Teen-aged Boys' Voices, quite distantly at first, far down the street outside, singing happily, with great gusto; the sound of the Voices and their song growing louder and louder, reaching a peak as we hear them pass the front door, then fading out as they continue along Canal Street; Young Charlie completely oblivious to this sound as he continues to write his letter; Charlie gradually caught by the sound of the Boys' Voices, the song drawing him slowly down to the front door as the passing Voices reach their peak; all lights dimming far down now except for the remaining full light on Charlie at the front door, his face mirroring his almost forgotten but now vividly remembered helplessness and fear at the sound of the Boys' Voices and their song)

TWENTY BOY'S VOICES *(to the tune of the Marine Corps Hymn)*

"On the shores of Coney Island
While the guns of freedom roar,
The Sheenies eat their Matzo Balls

And make money off the war,
While we Christian saps go fight the Japs,
In the uniforms they've made.
And they'll sell us Kosher hot dogs
For our victory parade.
So it's onward into battle
They will send us Christian slobs,
When the war is done and victory won,
All the Jews will have our jobs."

(Sound of laughter, a crash of glass, then cheering as the Boys' Voices fade into the night)

CHARLIE *(shouts towards the fading Voices)* If Joey was here . . . if Joey was here you'd never get away with it!

(The Boys' Voices are quickly obliterated by the sudden sound of a Cheering Crowd, raucous and enthusiastic, and the machine-gun voice of Ringside sportscaster Speed Spector blasting out the blow-by-blow of a fight in progress, the tiny yellow light of the Philco radio dial popping on in the darkness and then glowing brighter as the Cheering Crowd, Spector's Voice and all the barlights come up full to reveal that night's Party and the Party Guests: Hannah, Nick and Finney, gathered about the radio, Eddie entering from the Kitchen holding two champagne bottles aloft on a tray full of fancy glasses, a silk vest added to his usual Uptown Bartender's white shirt and black bow-tie, Zaretsky entering somewhat later from the Apartment above wearing an old but splendid smoking-jacket and cravat for the occasion; Charlie remaining at front door looking off towards street, Young Charlie no longer onstage)

SPECTOR'S VOICE *(from Philco, breathless, one long sentence)* . . . toe to toe and here they go fourth round another *fight* friends *first* three bouts waltz-time dancin' *darlings* number *four* we got a slammin' *slug*fest here Killer Kalish and Homicide Hennesy tradin' solid *body* shots insteada *party* favors here tonight forty-five seconds into frame *four . . . (Charlie being gradually pulled away from the front door by the much pleasanter memory of Spector's Voice)* . . . carryin' it to Kalish lightnin' *left* rockin' *right* a stick a stick a jab a hook hook hook roundhouse *right* Killer's outa *business . . .*

CHARLIE *(to us, as Spector and Cheering Crowd continue)* Well, they didn't call him Speed Spector for nothin', did they? And tonight we waited for *that voice* to talk about *my* brother. First, however, would be the usual pre-Main Event interview with Big Mike Baskin of Big Mike Baskin's Broadway Boys' and Men's Clothes, sponsor of the Tuesday Night Amateurs. We, of course, all knew him as the former Manny Buffalino of Buffalino's Grand Street Garments who gave a silver-plated watch to each of the winners . . . and a terrible headache to Pop.

SPECTOR'S VOICE   . . . whatta ya think about that whoppin' big *win*, Big Mike?

BIG MIKE'S VOICE   Spid, dis boy, alla tonight win' gonna get a sil'-plate wash froma Big Mike. Now, he don' like dis wash, he can hocka dis wash for fifteen doll'—

EDDIE   *(entering with champagne)* Can't stand the *mouth* on that greaseball— *(Turns radio volume way down; they all protest)* Don't worry, Joey's bout ain't on for five minutes anyways—goddamn Steerage *Green*horn; twenty-six locations, man's sittin' on a coupla mil—*nobody* knows what the hell he's *talkin'* about! What's his *angle*, how's he *do* it—?

FINNEY   *(as Zaretsky enters, slapping Zaretsky on back)* Evenin', Mr. Z.; how's Show Business?

ZARETSKY   Mr. Finney; Abbott and *Costello* are in Show Business, Amos and even *Andy* are in Show Business, Franklin Delano *Roosevelt* is in Show Business—

FINNEY   *(pinching Zaretsky's cheek)* Lost me bearin's, darlin', it's the joy of the night—

EDDIE   *(placing bottles on center table)* I say sixty seconds into Round One this champagne is pourin' and Gloria's down with the goodies!

HANNAH   And Nick wears the *shirt* tonight.

EDDIE   Great . . .

FINNEY   The shirt, of course . . .

HANNAH   The occasion demanded.

ZARETSKY   This then is a shirt of some significance, I assume.

NICK   Oh, ya might say. Ya might well say, Mr. Zaretsky. *(Opening old jacket to reveal a faded yellow shirt instead of his usual faded white shirt; there are dark brown stains on the shoulder and collar)* For this then is the blood of Barney Ross, spilled the night he lost the World Welterweight to Armstrong, the greatest Losin' Win I ever saw.

EDDIE   Greatest Losin' Win in the history of the fight game.

FINNEY   Easy.

NICK   Second *row* we are, the four of us; May Thirty-One, Nineteen

Thirty-Eight, Round Five, his legs said goodbye to the man, never to return in what was t'be the last bout o' Barney's life. Ref Donovan's beggin' Ross to let 'im stop the thing—"No," Barney says, through the blood in his mouth, "I'm the Champ, he'll have to beat me in the *ring* and *not* on a stool in m'corner!" There then come ten rounds of a horror ya never want to see again, but proud ya saw the once for the grandness that was in it, the crowd is quiet and many look away, but at the end the cheers is for Barney who lost his title and won his pride. *(Looking about at his friends)* Which is why we call it, the four of us . . .

NICK, EDDIE, FINNEY . . . the Greatest Losin' Win we ever saw!

HANNAH   In my case, heard.

FINNEY   It was in the Twelfth Barney's blood hit the shirt—

HANNAH   A thundering right from Armstrong, yes—

EDDIE   Ya *get* it, Actor—ya see why me and my boys are called *Ross* now?

FINNEY   *(suddenly turns to radio)* My God, the *fight*—

EDDIE   Oh, *shit*— *(He dashes to the radio, quickly turns up volume)*

(We hear the sound of the Cheering Crowd as Eddie turns the volume up full, the sound building louder and louder as the Crowd chants rhythmically; Charlie sits solemnly in his booth, nodding, remembering it all too well)

THE CROWD   Chicken *Pete* . . . Chicken *Pete* . . . Chicken *Pete* . . .

HANNAH   *(confused, frightened)* Chicken Pete, Nick? . . .

SPECTOR'S VOICE   *(shouting above the chanting Crowd)* . . . Listen to *that*, Fans! *New* one on Old *Speed* here; got a Referee, one fighter, whole crowd, packed Arena—*one* thing missing: the *other* fighter! Pistol Pete is *not* in that ring, *not* in the locker room, *no*-where to be found, friends . . .

(All in bar-room stunned at first; Eddie, the others, not moving, riveted by the information as it comes out of the radio; the sound of the chanting Crowd building, filling the room)

SPECTOR'S VOICE   . . . Ref Gordon tells me Pistol Pete's not in the *building*, no *message*, no *word*; *sounds* like the best explanation of this one's comin' from the crowd itself . . .

THE CROWD   *(louder and louder)*   . . . Chicken *Pete* . . . Chicken *Pete* . . . Chicken *Pete* . . .

FINNEY   *(bewildered, staring into radio)* He didn't *show*, Joey didn't *show* . . .

(The sound of stomping and clapping joins the rhythmic chant of the Crowd now as Eddie moves slowly out from behind the bar, carefully controlling his fear and confusion)

EDDIE   *(quietly, evenly)* He's hurt, he's hurt . . . out *cold;* he'd have to be out *cold* to stay away from that bout . . . he's hurt . . . *(Moving towards phone)* Bimmy's, maybe somebody at Bimmy's, somebody knows . . .

ZARETSKY   He leaves with Chaim for the Arena, this is an hour ago . . .

FINNEY   I heard them Avenger boys was gatherin' on Pell . . .

HANNAH   Nit do gedacht . . .

NICK   *(rising from stool)* I go to the Precinct, get some of the fellahs . . .

EDDIE   *(picking up phone)* Yeah, yeah . . .

THE CROWD   *(building to peak now)* . . . Chicken *Pete* . . . Chicken *Pete* . . . Chicken *Pete* . . .

(The front door bursts open and Joey rushes in, followed by Young Charlie; though somewhat shaken, there is something decisive, resolved in Joey as he stands tensely at the center of the room, his "Pistol Pete" jacket gripped in his hand; Young Charlie, clearly bewildered by the evening's events, stays close to his brother)

HANNAH   *(trembling)* Jussel, Jussel . . . ?

JOEY   *(gently)* Everything's fine, Hannah.

EDDIE   *(starts towards him; quietly)* Thank God, you're O.K . . . you're O.K . . .

JOEY   I'm not O.K. *(Races behind the bar towards the sound of the chanting Crowd, snaps off the radio; the room is silent)* I will be.

EDDIE   The *fight*, kid, the *fight* . . . what the hell *happened* . . . ?

JOEY   *(slaps his jacket onto the bar, grabs up vodka bottle and shot-glass)* No more fights. No more fights, Pop. Not here. *(Fills his shot-glass, downs it)*

EDDIE   Not *here?* Not *here?* What the hell does *that* mean? I need some *explainin'* here, kid, I gotta—

ZARETSKY   Let him *speak*, Itzik.

JOEY   *(quietly)* Pop, this mornin', workin' out with Bimmy—

EDDIE   *Tonight*, kid, I wanna know about *tonight*—

JOEY   *(continuing, firmly)* This mornin', workin' out with Bimmy, we're skippin', we're sparrin', my mind ain't there, Pop. I'm doin' math. Three hundred and fifty thousand Jews in twenty-one days, comes out seventeen thousand five hundred a day, *this* day, today—

EDDIE   A buncha crazy *stories*, Joey, I told ya— *(Wheeling on Zaretsky)* *You*, it's you and your goddamn *bull*shit—

JOEY   *(moving towards him)* Please, ya gotta be quiet, Pop. That's maybe two thousand just while I'm workin' out. Seventeen thousand five hundred a day. No, it's impossible, I figure; Pop's *right*, it's nuts. I keep punchin' the bag. I come back to pick up Charlie, we're headin' over, not Seven yet; then I hear people hollerin', I look up, I see it. Top of the "Forward" Buildin', tallest damn buildin' around here, there's the "Jewish Daily Forward" sign, y'know, big, maybe thirty feet high and wide as the buildin', electric bulbs, ya can see it even deep into Brooklyn, *forever*, Pop. What they did is they took out the right bulbs, exactly the right bulbs, gotta be hundreds of 'em, so instead of "Jewish Daily Forward" the sign says: "Jew Is For War"; it's goddamn blazin' over the city, Pop, and Charlie and me start runnin' towards it, we're still maybe eight blocks away, we're passin' alotta people and kids on Canal, pointin' up, laughin', some cheerin', "Son of a *bitch*, son of a *bitch*, we fight the *war* and the Jews get *rich*," a guy grabs my arm, smilin', musta seen me box, guy my age, he says, "Pete, Pete, let's go get us some Yids, Pete!" and I know that second for sure they are doin' seventeen thousand five hundred a day, somewhere, seventeen thousand five hundred a day and I'm a guy spends his time boppin' kids for a silver-plated watch from Big Mike, hockable for fifteen dollars; right now I wouldn't hock me for a dime. Point is, I'm goin' in, Pop. I'm gettin' into this war and I need your help, now. *(Eddie is silent)* Army don't register me till next month, then it could be a year, more, before they call me. *Navy*, Pop, Navy's the game; they take ya at seventeen with a parent's consent. Eight A.M. tomorrow I'm at Ninety Church, I pick up the consent form, you fill it out, sign it, ten days later Boot Camp at Lake Geneva, September I'm in it, Pop. Korvette, Destroyer, Sub-chaser, whatever, *in* the goddamn thing.

EDDIE   *(after a moment)* Your mother will never—

JOEY   I just need you, Pop. One parent. One signature. *(Silence for a moment)* Do me a favor; take a look outside. Just turn left and look at the sky.

(During Joey's story, Hannah has moved instinctively closer to Nick, holding his arm; Zaretsky rises)

ZARETSKY   Come then, Itzik.

(Eddie turns towards the door; Zaretsky crosses to the door, exits into street, followed after a moment by Eddie and then Finney; Nick starts to go but Hannah whispers fearfully to him)

HANNAH   Stay with me, Nick. They'll look, they'll describe.

NICK   *(embracing her)*   Sure, darlin', sure . . .

(Silence for a few moments; Charlie, in his booth, watching the two boys)

YOUNG CHARLIE   You didn't tell me that part . . . about goin' in. You didn't mention that.

JOEY   It come to me, Charlie.

YOUNG CHARLIE   *(urgently)*   Lotta guys to fight *here*, y'know, the Avengers, the Gladiators; ya don't have to go all the way to *Europe*, ya—

(Eddie enters, crosses slowly to bar, sits on stool; he is followed by Finney, and then Zaretsky who remains at doorway looking out into street)

FINNEY   *(to Hannah and Nick)*   Hangin' over town like a second bloody moon, it is.

EDDIE   *(after a moment, slapping bar)*   Get me the goddamn paper, I sign it *now*. Go down to Ninety Church Street, wake the Putzes *up*, bring me the form and I sign it now. All I ask, kid, you're over there, you kill a couple for your Pop, *personally. (Starts towards Joey; fiercely)* Kill 'em, Joey, *kill* 'em. *Show* 'em, kid, show 'em how a Jew fights.

JOEY   *(grabs Eddie's fist, holds it proudly in the air)*   And in this corner, wearin' the green trunks—The East Side Savage!

(All cheering, patting Joey on the back, except for Zaretsky and the two Charlies)

YOUNG CHARLIE   *(looking anxiously from one to the other)*   Everybody goin' so *fast* here, so *fast*—

NICK   Try to get home for Christmas, kid—

YOUNG CHARLIE   They got *reasons*, y'know, why they don't take guys till they're eighteen, they got—

JOEY   *(turns to Zaretsky, who has remained silent at front door)* You're *with* me, aren't ya?

ZARETSKY   *(after a moment)* Yes . . . *yes*, were I your age— *(Joey rushes forward, embraces him)*

EDDIE   *(holding champagne bottle aloft, rallying the Group)* Hey, hey, hey—we still got a *party* goin' here—a *better* one—goddamn Warrior's *send-off* we got here! *(Pops cork at center table as all gather round, except for Young Charlie who moves slowly over to his usual booth, sits near Charlie)* First-class Frog juice we got here—*I* got it— *(Pouring for Joey first)* Now *you* got it, kid— *(As he pours for the others)* Hey, this ain't just Bazooka Kil*bane* goin' down—I'm talkin' about the whole goddamn Nazi-Nip *War* Machine here! *(Raising his glass)* To the Winnah and still Cham*peen!*

HANNAH   *(raising her glass)* So what's wrong with the Bounding Main?

NICK   *(raising his glass)* Right! To the Navy!

FINNEY   *(raising his glass)* To the Navy and Victory!

ALL   *(loudly, raising glasses)* The Navy and Victory!

(They click glasses just as Gusta enters from the Apartment above carrying a large tray of Party-food; starts down stairs, confused, seeing Joey amongst the Group)

GUSTA   The boxing-fight, Joey, you won already? Nobody informed me. *(They all turn to her, their six glasses held aloft, poised; she stops near Joey)* Ah, no marks; good. O.K., Party-treats— *(Goes briskly to down left table, a distance from the Group, starts taking dishes from tray, placing them on table, her back to them; they all remain quite still, watching her)* First, of course, basics: we got Kasha-Varnishkes, we got Holishkes, special for Mr. Zaretsky we got Kartoffel Chremsel with a touch apple . . .

HANNAH   *(quietly)* Eddie signs a paper, Gusta, Joey goes to war.

GUSTA   *(a pause; then she continues briskly)* We got Lokshen Kugel, we got a little Brisket Tzimmes with honey, special for Charlie we got Cheese Blintzes, a side sour cream . . .

JOEY   *(softly, moving towards her)* Ma, did you hear that, Ma . . . ?

GUSTA   And special for Finney and Nick—why not, I was in the mood—we got Mamaligele Rumanye with a smash strawberry.

JOEY   Ma . . .

GUSTA   *(a moment; she turns to him)* I hear everything, Sonny. You got some good news for me? *(Looks over at the Group)* I hear it all.

It's just that twenty years ago I started making selections. *(Walking slowly towards the Group)* You see, if I listened, I would want to speak. And who would hear me? Who would hear me? Who would *hear* me?

(She slaps Eddie hard across the face. A beat; we hear the sudden sound of a full Marching Band and a Male Chorus doing a blasting, drum-rolling, lusty-voiced rendition of "Anchors Aweigh" as all lights fade quickly down on the frozen Party Group and the still figures of Gusta and Eddie, Music continuing at full Volume)

MALE CHORUS

> "Anchors aweigh, my boys,
> Anchors aweigh,
> Farewell to college joys,
> We sail at break of day, day, day, day . . . "

(During Charlie's next speech the pulsing Jukebox lights will come up again and with them the half-light in which we will see only Eddie and Young Charlie remaining onstage and making those changes in the bar-room that would have occurred during the thirteen months till the next scene begins: Eddie solemnly draping a length of black ribbon about the frame of the grinning F.D.R. photo, then proudly hanging a map of the Pacific Theatre of War over the Jukebox, happily placing several blue and white Service Stars about the room, including one over Joey's boxing photo, finally exiting into Kitchen; Young Charlie will take down the Miss Daitch Display—being careful to keep the Peggy Parsons photo which he stores, among other treasures, in the hollow seat of the booth he and Charlie usually use. Charlie will have moved down towards us only a moment after the blackout on the Party Scene, humming a few phrases of "Anchors Aweigh" along with the Jukebox, then speaking immediately to us during the action described above)

CHARLIE   Joey called the shot exactly: September, he was in it—desperately trying to promote his way onto a Convoy-Korvette in the European Theatre, he ended up on a Destroyer in the Pacific and, as Joey pointed out, the only dangerous German he ever got to face was our dentist, Dr. Plaut—but he was *in* it; and, finishing ten weeks of Gunnery School in four, he became quickly known aboard the Destroyer Campbell as "The King Of The Twin-Forties"—double-mounted antiaircraft machine-guns in a swiveling steel bucket operated by a Gunner and an Ammo Man— *(Here replicated by Young Charlie holding two broom handles atop a spinning bar-stool)* Yes, Joey was proud and brave and good and strong—but mostly, he was *gone*. *(Young Charlie puts on the "Pistol*

Pete" jacket Joey left on the bar, his posture noticeably straightening) He was gone and *I* was here, the house was mine. I was it: star of the show, Top of the Card, the Main Event. Civilians look for job openings in wartime . . . and there was an opening here for Prince.

(Charlie turns to center as lights come up on Young Charlie alone onstage, seated comfortably on bar-stool, his feet up, legs crossed at the ankle, on bar, gazing critically at the huge painting of the Four Poker Players over the bar-mirror. Sound of Harry Truman's Voice fading up with the lights as "Anchors Aweigh" record ends on Jukebox)

TRUMAN'S VOICE   . . . on Hiroshima, a military base. We won the race of discovery against the Germans. We have used it in order to shorten the agony of war, in order to save the lives of thousands and thousands of young Americans. We shall *continue* to use it until we completely destroy Japan's power to make war . . .

EDDIE   *(bursts in from Kitchen)* The Atomic Cocktail, Charlie! *(Holds aloft two large containers of freshly mixed cocktails) Two* kindsa rum, light *and* dark, shot o' grenadine—pineapple juice and coconut cream, give a kinda Tropical-Pacific feel. *(Sets containers and handmade placard on bar)* Whatta ya think, kid?

YOUNG CHARLIE   *(still looking at Poker Picture, thoughtfully)* That's a terrible painting, Pop.

EDDIE   *(reads from placard—he's illustrated it with a classic mushroom-cloud Hiroshima photo from a newspaper)* "Atomic Cocktail—One Dollar—If the First Blast Don't Get You, the Fallout Will." How about that, Charlie?

YOUNG CHARLIE   *(squints at Poker Picture)* Not only poorly painted, but look at all the *room* it takes up.

EDDIE   What?

YOUNG CHARLIE   This painting here, Pop; it's no good.

EDDIE   What're ya talkin' about? This here's a handpainted oil picture, seven feet by *six*, fits *exact* over the mirror. This is an original by goddamn Lazlo *Shim*kin; run up a big tab, gimme the picture on a trade-off. Got any idea what this thing's *worth* today?

YOUNG CHARLIE   Nothin', Pop.

EDDIE   Listen, Putz, this picture been sittin' up there since a year before you was *born*. You seen it every day o' ya *life*—all of a sudden it's no *good?*

YOUNG CHARLIE   Yes; strange, isn't it?

EDDIE *(quietly)* I gotta open the bar in twenty minutes; otherwise I would immediately take the picture out in the alley and burn it. Only thing I can suggest to you in the meantime, Charlie, is that you *spend the rest of your goddamn life lookin' the other way! (Leaning towards him)* Gypsies! Gypsies! The *Gypsies* left ya at my doorstep! *This* can't be *mine!* Before this personally autographed Lazlo *Shim*kin picture goes, *you* go. *(Points) Feet* off the bar, and finish the set-ups.

ZARETSKY *(entering from Apartment above)* Ah, I sense artistic differences in the air.

YOUNG CHARLIE *(starts working on set-ups)* 'Morning, Mr. Zaretsky.

ZARETSKY Chaim, you have not yet, I trust, fetched the mail? *(Young Charlie shakes his head)* Good then, it shall be my task. I expect today a cable from Buenos Aires, in Argentina, where still exist two hundred thousand speakers of Yiddish, there confirming my appearance, a full three weeks of concerts; my first since the War. *(Starts towards front door)*

YOUNG CHARLIE *(impressed as always)* Hey, Argen*tina* . . . Great.

EDDIE *(stacking glasses)* Three weeks without ya, Anton; breaks my goddamn heart. Don't worry, babe, we'll keep y'room *just* the way ya left it.

ZARETSKY Unfortunately. *(Opens front door)* A room in which, for twelve years, sunlight has appeared almost entirely by metaphor. *(Exits into street. Silence for a moment)*

EDDIE *(his back to Young Charlie, busily stacking glasses)* O.K., just for laughs, Putz, what's so ugly about that picture?

YOUNG CHARLIE For one thing, the light, Pop . . . *(Eddie squints at the painting)* It's all like . . . flat, see. It's like the light is coming from *every*where, y'know, so it's not really—

EDDIE Yeah, right, O.K., good this come up. This stuff about where the light's comin' from, also these here poems and stories you been writin'. Take a for-instance— *(takes folded piece of loose-leaf paper from cash-register)* this poem ya give me Father's Day.

YOUNG CHARLIE Did ya like it? Ya never mentioned—

EDDIE Sure, sure. *(Hands it to him, sits at their usual center table)* Do y'Pop a favor, O.K.? You read this to me, then I'm gonna ask ya a question. *(Young Charlie hesitates for a moment)* Go ahead.

(Young Charlie starts to read as Zaretsky returns with the mail, places all but a few pieces on bar, listens attentively to poem)

YOUNG CHARLIE *(reading)* O.K. . . . "Father of the Flamingo; by C. E. Ross: . . . He leadeth them beside distilled waters, he restoreth their credit; and if they be Mick Shickers, he maketh them to lie down in dark gutters. And yea, though I may walk through the valley of the shadow of Little Italy, I shall fear no Goy or evil sound, 'cause my Pop has taught me how to bring one up from the ground."

ZARETSKY *(applauding)* Bravo, Chaim; bravo! *(He exits upstairs, continuing to nod his approval for the work of a fellow artist)*

EDDIE O.K., very nice. *(Leaning forward, pleasantly)* O.K., now all I'm askin' is a truthful answer: who helped ya out with that?

YOUNG CHARLIE Nobody, Pop. I mean, it's a Twenty-Third Psalm take-off, so I got help from the *Bible*—

EDDIE I *know* that, *besides* that—the thing, the *ideas* in there, how it come together there—you tellin' me nobody helped ya out on that, the *Actor*, nobody?

YOUNG CHARLIE Nobody, Pop.

EDDIE *(he pauses, then indicates the chair opposite him; Young Charlie sits)* O.K., there's times certain Jewish words is unavoidable, I give ya two: Narrishkeit and Luftmensh. Narrishkeit is stuff *beyond* foolish—like what?—your mother givin' English lessons, this would be Narrish-work. Now this Narrishkeit is generally put out by Luftmensh—meanin', literal, *guys* who live on the *air*—from which we get the term "no visible goddamn means of support." Poem-writers, story-writers, picture-painters, we got *alotta* 'em come in here; what ya got is mainly y'Fairies, y'Bust-Outs and y'Souseniks—a blue *moon*, ya get a sober straight-shooter, breaks even. *(Slaps the table)* Now, I'm lookin' at this poem two months now, besides takin' note, numerous situations, how you *present* y'self, kid—first-class, flat-out *amazin'*, this poem. *(Young Charlie smiles happily, Eddie taps his son's head)* It's goddamn Niagara *Falls* in there—now all we gotta do is point it the right way so ya can turn on a coupla *light* bulbs with it. The *answer?* Head like yours, ya know it already, don't ya?

YOUNG CHARLIE *(confused but flattered)* No; I don't, Pop.

EDDIE I speak, of course, of the Legal Profession! Brain like that, how you get them words together, I'm talkin' *Up*town, Charlie, I'm talkin' about the firm o' Ross, Ross, *Some*body and *Some*body; you're gonna be walkin' through places the dollars stick to your *shoes*, y'can't *kick* the bucks off. Hey, looka the experience you got already, huh?— *(rises, arms wide, delightedly struck by the perfect* *illustration)* —twelve years now you been pleadin' cases before the bar!

(Eddie laughs happily at his joke, slapping the bar, Young Charlie laughing with him, their laughter building with the sharing of the joke, Charlie joining them)

CHARLIE   *(chuckling)* Not bad, not bad; one for *you*, Pop . . . *(Suddenly frightened, remembering; he shouts)* Now—it was *now*—

(We hear Gusta scream from upstairs—a long, wrenching, mournful wail, like the siren of a passing ambulance—even at this distance, a stairway and a closed door between them, the sound permeates the bar-room. Then silence; Eddie and Young Charlie frozen for a moment, then both racing towards the bottom of the stairs. Before they can reach the first step, though, Zaretsky enters at the top of the stairs from the Apartment above, closing the door quietly behind himself. Eddie and Young Charlie remain quite still, several feet from the stairs; Zaretsky takes a step or two down towards them)

ZARETSKY   The telegram I opened was not for me, Itzik. It is for you and Gusta. Jussel is dead. He was killed two days ago. The first telegram says only *(he reads)* "The Secretary of War desires me to express his deep regret that your son, Petty Officer Second-Class Joseph Ross, was killed in action in defense of his country on August Sixth, Nineteen Forty-Five." *(A moment)* Gusta stays upstairs; she requests to be alone for a while. *(Eddie and Young Charlie remain standing quite still at the bottom of the stairs, their backs to us, not a tremor, their emotions unreadable)* There is more; shall I go on? *(Eddie nods)* Enclosed also, a cable, this from Captain Nordheim of the Destroyer Campbell. He begins: "The fanatical suicide attack which caused the death of your son . . . "

(Charlie, downstage, continuing the cable from memory now as Zaretsky continues reading, inaudibly, on the stairs behind him)

CHARLIE   " . . . is tragically consistent with the desperate actions of our enemy at this time of their imminent surrender. On the morning of August Sixth a force of eight Zeros descended upon the St. Louis and the Campbell at one-minute intervals; the Sixth and Seventh of these craft being destroyed by Petty Officer Ross from his Forward Forty-Millimeter position, the Eighth now aimed directly for his battle-station. With ample time to leave his position for safety, your son, to his undying honor, remained at his weapon, as determined to destroy the target as was the target to destroy his battle-station. As recommended and reviewed by myself and the Secretary of the Navy, it has been deemed appropriate to recognize his selfless valor by awarding the Navy Cross to Petty Officer Second-Class Joseph Ross. In addition, I have respected your son's prior request to be buried at sea, the Kaddish being read by an Ensign Sidney Berman for the name of Jussel Solomon Goldberg, also by the same request."

(Starting with the first line of the above speech, the action will begin to move forward in time behind Charlie to the evening of the next day, the first of the seven days of Shiva, the family's mourning period— daylight giving way to night outside and near-darkness in the bar as Charlie speaks, Zaretsky slowly folding the cable, putting on a yarmulkeh, and then joining Young Charlie behind the bar where they drape a large piece of black cloth over the long bar-mirror; their movements—and those of the others during this transition—are deliberate, trancelike, ritualized, as though to the beat of inaudible music. During the draping of the mirror, Gusta will have entered from the Apartment, her head covered with a dark shawl, carrying a tray of pastries and Eddie's black suit-jacket; she places the tray on the center table, drapes the jacket over a chair next to it, then places a piece of black cloth over Joey's Navy photograph above the Jukebox as Eddie, who has remained quite still at center, slowly puts on his jacket, then sits at center table, blankly, looking off, as though in a dream. Young Charlie comes up behind Eddie, delicately places a yarmulkeh on his father's head and then one on his own as Nick, Hannah, and then Finney come quietly through the front door, wearing dark clothes, each bearing a box of pastry, moving slowly, silently, through the half-light of the bar-room; Gusta embracing Hannah, the two women holding onto each other for a few moments before Nick leads Hannah gently away to their table and Gusta sits at the Center table near Eddie. After saying the last few words of the memorized Nordheim cable, Charlie pauses a moment, then turns to look at Eddie who remains quite frozen, listless, on his chair. Hannah and Nick at their usual table now, holding hands, Finney in the shadows of his booth, his head bowed. Charlie moves close to Young Charlie and Zaretsky now. The old man and the boy, having lit the seven-day memorial candle and placed it on the far left table, sit near its glow, leaning towards each other in quiet conversation)

CHARLIE I'd never said the Mourner's Kaddish before; I knew what the Hebrew words meant—but suddenly that morning in the synagogue it made no sense to me; here in this ancient, ancient prayer for the dead was not a reference, not a phrase . . . not a word about death.

ZARETSKY *(leans towards Young Charlie, answering his question)* It's not *about* death, Chaim; we have here a prayer about faith only, absolute faith in God and his wisdom. *(Closes his eyes)* Listen, the music of it, "Yisgaddal v'yiskaddash shmey rabboh . . ." You praise God, "B'rich Hu": "blessed be He; blessed, praised, glorified, exalted . . ."

EDDIE *(quietly, almost to himself, still looking off)* It's like the Mafia, Charlie . . . It's like talkin' to a Mafia Chief after he does a hit, ya kiss the Capo's ass so he don't knock *you* off too: "Hey, God, what a great idea, killin' Joey Ross. Throwin' my cousin Sunny under a garbage truck—I thought *that* was great—but havin' some nutso Nip drop Joey, this is you at the top of your *form*, baby . . . " *(Gusta rises slowly, staring down at him)* Oh, yeah, magnified and sanctified be *you*, Don Giuseppe . . . *(Gusta turns sharply, walks quickly to the stairs and exits into the Apartment; Eddie barely glancing at her, continuing louder now, all in bar turning to him)* Hey, Charlie, that's *it* for Hebrew School. Over and *out*, kid. I hear ya go *near* the goddamn place I bust ya in the chops... *(Rises, pulls off his yarmulkeh, then yanks off Young Charlie's)* Hell with the Bar Mitzvah; I'm takin' ya to Norfolk Street and gettin' ya *laid* that day . . . *(As Eddie continues, louder, his rage growing, we begin to hear Gusta singing the old Yiddish lullaby we heard in Act One, distantly, gently, from upstairs)*

GUSTA'S VOICE *(singing)*
"Oif'n pripitchok,
Brent a faierel,
Un in shtub iz heys . . . "
(Continuing softly through the scene . . .)

EDDIE . . . Three years Joey put in, the prayers, the bullshit, the Bar Mitzvah shot, the goddamn criminal *con* of the whole thing. I *knew* it— *(Shouting, striding fiercely to bar, tearing black cloth off of mirror)* I *told* ya, I knew it all *along* it was a sucker's game! You *watch* me, alla you, *tonight* I go to Beth-*El*, I go to the *East Window* because this is where God's supposed t'hear ya better—and I tell 'im, I tell the Killer Bastard—get *this*, God, I ain't a *Jew* no more! *Over*, pal! Fifty years of bein' a Jew Loser; over, baby! *Take* 'em, take the *resta* them, they're *yours*—*you* chose 'em, *you* got 'em—

YOUNG CHARLIE *(quietly)* Shut up . . .

EDDIE —every God-fearin', *death*-fearin', scared-*shit*less *Jew*-creep is *yours*—but not *Eddie*, not—

YOUNG CHARLIE Shut up, will ya? *(He rises)* You really gonna blame this on *God*, Pop? Really? This is what you *wanted*, Pop: Mr. America, the toughest Jew in the Navy, and you got it; only he's dead. Every *letter*, *twice* on the phone with him I heard ya—"Kill, kill, *kill* 'em, kid!" Same as you screamed at ringside. And you want *God* to take the blame for this? *(Pointing fiercely, tears in his eyes)* All for *you*, Pop, the Ring, the Twin-Forties, he was fightin' for *you.* "Kill 'em, kid! *Get* 'em!" No, Pop, no, not *God*, not God—you, it was *you*, it was *you*, Pop. *(He races quickly up the stairs, crying, exits into Apartment, slamming the door behind him)*

(Silence for a moment, even Gusta's distant singing has stopped. Eddie goes quickly up the stairs to the door)

EDDIE   Listen to me, kid; ya got it all wrong, I straighten it out for ya . . . *(He tries to open the door, but it has clearly been locked from the inside; he leans closer, raises his voice a bit, trying to talk to Young Charlie through the door)* Listen to me, Charlie; it's just my wacky Pop, see. Just my wacky Pop all over again. *Fine* points; it's the goddamn *fine* points, kid— *(Louder, almost cracking, his rage holds him together)* He *knows* this Nip Fruitcake is comin' right *for* 'im, but he stays there behind his gun, because he thinks he's *supposed* to! It's my Pop all over again, pal—fine points; goddamn fine points! Wacky, the *both* o' them . . . *wacky* . . . *(Silence. He tries the knob again)* Come on, kid; open up. *(One bang on the door; sternly, evenly)* Hey, Charlie; open up. *(Silence)* Let's move it, Charlie; let me in. *(Starts banging more forcefully on door)* Let me in, Charlie; let me *in* there. *(Now wildly, fiercely, pleading with his son, pounding with all his strength, the door shaking from his blows)* Charlie, Charlie, let me *in*, let me *in!* *(Both fists together now, pounding rhythmically, shouting with each blow)* Let me *in*, let me *in*, let me *in* . . .

(He continues banging on the door, his shouting almost like a chant now; Nick and Finney rise as though to come to his aid; Zaretsky remains on his wooden box, his head bowed, intoning loudly above the din)

ZARETSKY   "Yisgaddal v'yiskaddash shmey rabboh . . ."

(A sudden silence, a sharp drop in light, they are all quite still, frozen silhouettes in the dim remaining glow; Charlie alone in a small spotlight at right, caught by the moment)

CHARLIE   *(turns to us; softly, a plea)* I didn't mean it, I just . . . I mean, I was *twelve* at the time, very upset, a *kid* . . . I was just . . . ya know what I mean?

(The sudden sound of Lyndon Johnson Voice fills the stage, his echoing drawl offering the promise of the Great Society as Eddie, Zaretsky, Hannah, Nick and Finney exit into the shadows of the bar, the Flamingo Chandelier rising into the darkness above it, Charlie moving slowly down center as this part of his past disappears behind him)

JOHNSON'S VOICE   Is our world gone? We say farewell. Is a new world coming? We welcome it. And we bend it to the hopes of Man . . .

CHARLIE   *(turns to us, brightening)* Amazingly . . . amazingly, life went back to normal after Joey died—Pop quickly resumed living at the top of his voice and the edge of his nerves, battling with Zaretsky in the mornings and me in the afternoons and re-naming the bar "Big Ed's Club Canal." My next bout with Pop—oh, there were a few minor exhibition matches about leaving home at seventeen, not going to Law School, not visiting often enough—but our next real bout was more than twenty years later. October Fifteenth, Sixty-Five; I remember exactly because it was the morning the Vatican Council announced that the Jews were no longer responsible for the death of Christ . . . *(As he continues, an older Gusta, her raven hair streaked with gray, enters from the Kitchen in the dim half-light behind him, carrying a tray; she will move briskly from table to table as he speaks, clearing away the many plastic pineapples and coconut shells, eventually disappearing back into the Kitchen)* By then I had become one of the blue-moon Luftmenshen who had *made* it in the Narrishkeit business. This, starting at the age of twenty-*three*, by knockin' out almost one novel a year. The most familiar to you, from the early Sixties, would be "Over at Izzy's Place," the first of the "Izzy" books, eight and still counting, three best-sellers by then, vast areas of virgin forest consumed by paperback sales, undisputed Middleweight Champ at thirty-four, I had become . . . unavoidable. And so had Izzy. Izzy, tough but warm, blunt yet wise, the impossible and eccentric Bleecker Street tavern-keeper who won not only your heart in the final chapter, but the Mayor's Special Cultural Award that year for "embodying the essential charm and excitement of New York's ethnic street life." *(Shakes his head, smiling)* Unavoidable, that is, to everyone but Pop. Hard to take it personally, he never read anything longer than Winchell's column or the Blow-by-Blows in the Trib. We were down to maybe four or five visits a year by then—the first half of each being consumed with how long it'd been since the last one and the second half with contractual arrangements for the next—and we didn't meet at the usual family weddings and Bar Mitzvahs because Pop would never again enter a synagogue or any place that resembled one . . . *(Lights coming up slowly on the bar as he continues; Gusta, who has returned from the Kitchen, sits alone now at the center table, business-like, in charge, wearing glasses, checking a stack of bills, as Charlie moves about her in the empty bar-room indicating the places where The Regulars once sat)* Hannah was gone by then, and Nick too; I never did learn their last names. Finney—old, but sharp as ever—smelled O.T.B. and Legal Lottery in the wind and was now taking Temperature-Humidity Index bets at a Kosher Delicatessen in Boca Raton. Mr. Zaretsky died in January of Sixty-One, just a week before his ninety-third birthday, during the closing moments of a concert for the Y.M.H.A. of St. Louis, in Missouri, performing his twelve-minute version of "The Dybbuk"; passing away in crimson light, playing all parts . . . including title role. *(Moving down behind Gusta's chair as she continues busily checking bills)* I called Mom every Sunday to hear her two jokes of the week, but this last call was different— Pop'd had a mild heart attack in Sixty-Four from which he'd quickly recovered, but now she said something had "gone wrong with the health"; I asked for more details but she was already into her second joke by then— *(Sound of Eddie laughing loudly from the Kitchen as though at what Charlie has just said; morning light starts to stream in from outside as Gusta rises with her stack of bills, exits briskly up the stairs into Apartment)* —so I came down early the next morning to check it out myself, and found him, as always, in better shape than I was . . . *(Eddie enters from the Kitchen chuckling happily at something on the front page of "The New York World-Telegram"; Eddie, though twenty years older, seems spry enough as he walks down towards the far right booth, sharply opening the paper to read the rest of the front-page story that amuses him so much; the front page faces us now and we see a huge banner headline which states: "Vatican Absolves Jews Of Crucifixion Blame." Charlie turns to him)* Pop . . .

EDDIE   *(glances up from paper, pleasantly)* Hey . . . it's *him*. *(Returns to paper)* How ya doin', kid?

CHARLIE   Fine, fine; I'm—

EDDIE   How'd ya get in?

CHARLIE   I got my key. Listen, Pop, I was . . . uh . . . in the neighborhood, stopped by . . .

EDDIE   *(sits in booth, still reading paper)* In the neighborhood?

CHARLIE   Yeah, right . . . *(Approaches booth, indicating headline)* Well, I see you've gotten the big news, Pop.

EDDIE   Winchell had it two days ago. Just sent the Pope off a telegram on the matter; here's a copy. *(Hands him piece of note paper)*

CHARLIE   *(reading)* I don't think they just hand telegrams to the Pope directly, Pop; especially ones that say, "Thanks a lot, you Greaseball Putz."

EDDIE   Well, let's see, must be what?—four, five months now since you last—

CHARLIE   Let's skip that one this time, O.K.? Mom tells me we got a health problem here.

EDDIE   *(slaps table, laughing)* I don't believe it. I don't *believe* it. Six *months* ago I say I'm not feelin' so good, she decides to hear it *now*. That listening thing she does—I'm tellin' ya, kid, it's wacki- er than ever—the woman hears less and less every week and what she *does* get comes to her entirely by *carrier*-pigeon. *(Charlie smiles; Eddie rises from booth)* Old news, kid, I'm fine now; looka me. *(Demonstrates a boxing combination)* Looka me, huh? Also the place is a hit, Charlie; just happened the last few months. Hey, not *giant*, but a hit. *(Chuckles, pointing upstairs)* She did it; the Wacky One. Turns out, right near here, starts out a whole new neighborhood, "HoHo"—

CHARLIE   That's "SoHo"—

EDDIE   *(with a sly wink)* I'm tellin' ya, kid, *Ho*Ho—wall-to-wall Luftmensh, blocks and *blocks* of 'em, doin' nothin' but Narrishkeit, and they got these *galleries* here, hustlin' the Narr for 'em; *bucks*, Charlie, bucks like ya wouldn't believe—and all from this Narrishkeit done by these Luftmensh livin' in these Lufts around here.

CHARLIE   Lofts, Pop.

EDDIE   And the *rent* for these Lufts—I'm talkin' *Vegas* money, Charlie. Anyways, maybe five months ago, a coupla these Narrishkeit Hustlers come in here, they're havin' some o' the Mulligan Stew—they go *crazy* for it—

CHARLIE   I don't blame them—

EDDIE   Next thing I know we got a goddamn *army* o' these Narrishkeit people with the fancy Lufts comin' here, they're gob- blin' up everything in sight, they love the stuff and they love Mama—under the original *names*, the Varnishkes, the Holishkes—they come in strangers, they go out grandchildren. I put up a new sign outside, musta seen it, "The Homeland"—I up the prices a little, we're a *hit*; not a cha*malia*, but we're doin' O.K. Your Mom done it. *(Sits at center table)*

CHARLIE   She mentioned something about hiring a waitress, but I had no idea— *(sits opposite him)* this is *great*, Pop.

EDDIE   Yeah; so how *you* doin'?

CHARLIE   Well, I'm workin' on a new—

EDDIE   Hey, I seen ya on the T.V. last week.

CHARLIE   Oh?

EDDIE   Yeah, you was gettin' some prize for somethin', the Mayor was there.

CHARLIE   Right.

EDDIE   Yeah, I seen ya on the T.V. You come in old.

CHARLIE   Old?

EDDIE   Yeah; I mean, you're a young fellah, but on T.V. you come in old.

CHARLIE   Pop, do you happen to recall *which* prize it was and *what* I got it for?

EDDIE   It was one o' them "Dizzy" books.

CHARLIE   "Izzy," Pop, "*Izzy*"—

EDDIE   Maybe it was the tuxedo.

CHARLIE   The tuxedo?

EDDIE   That made you come in old. Yeah, that's what it was.

CHARLIE   O.K., Pop, I'm glad you're feeling well, and I'm delighted about the place. *(Rising to leave)* Now I gotta—

EDDIE   O.K.; give my regards to . . . to . . . uh . . .

CHARLIE   Allison.

EDDIE   What happened to Sally?

CHARLIE   We were divorced three years ago. As you well know.

EDDIE   *(hits his head)* Of course. Of course. Hard to keep track, alla them—

CHARLIE   Pop, I've only been married twice, Sally and *Karen*—

EDDIE   Better catch up; that puts you two behind Rita Hayworth. So what's with this . . . uh . . . ?

CHARLIE   Allison. You've had dinner with her twice. Last time for three hours. She told you she was editing a book that proved Roosevelt did nothing for the Jews during the War. You broke two plates and walked out. She thought you were cute.

EDDIE   *(after a moment)* Shit, *marry* that one.

CHARLIE   *(starts towards door)* O.K., I really gotta—

EDDIE   Right; hugs to Sarah and Josh—hey, Josh; where's my Josh? Been a coupla *months* now—

CHARLIE   He was hanging around here entirely too much, Pop, it was—

EDDIE   We talk things *over,* we *discuss* things—

CHARLIE   Pop, he's the only ten-year-old at Dalton who drinks his milk out of a shot-glass.

EDDIE   *(laughs happily)* A *pisser,* that kid; goddamn *pisser*—

CHARLIE   *(opens door)* Right; see ya around—

EDDIE   *(quietly)* O.K., them books, I read one. *(Charlie turns at door, his hand on knob)* Well, not *read;* I give it a skim. The first one. *(Chuckling)* That's some *sweet*heart, that guy. Who *is* that guy? The bartender with the two sons, comes from Russia; who *is* that sweetie? Got *all* sweeties in there, y'sweet blind lady, y'sweet ex-cop, y'sweet bookie—*three* pages, I got an attack o' diabetes.

CHARLIE   Pop, if I told the truth they'd send a *lynch*-mob down here for ya.

EDDIE   Always glad to see new customers, kid. This guy in the book, supposed to be a Jewish guy, right? What kinda Jew is that? Don't sound like no Jew *I* ever heard. Could be anything—Italian, Irish, some kinda Chink even. *(Turns to newspaper)* Well, what the hell, regardless, I wanna wish ya good luck with them "Dizzy" books.

CHARLIE   Izzy! *(Closes door, turns to him)* Izzy, Izzy, Izzy. As you know damn *well.* O.K., that's it. No more, Pop, that was *it.* I am never playing this fucking game again; it's *over. (Moving towards him)* Izzy? You don't like him? Not Jewish enough for ya? He's *your* Jew, Pop, you made him up. He's *your* Jew, and so am I; no history, no memory, the only thing I'm linked to is a chain of bookstores. Vos *vilst* du?—that's Yiddish, Pop; it means "What do you *want?*" God bothered you, we got rid of him. Hugging bothers you, we do not touch. Here I am, Pop, just what the Rabbi ordered; only now you don't like it; now you don't want it. Vos vilst du, Goldberg? *(Leans towards him at table)* That prize you don't know the *name* of for the books you never read —I won it, Pop, *me,* the *air*-person, I *did* it— *(bangs fist on table, shouting)* — right here at this bar, everything you *asked* for. I am an honest-to-God, red-white-and-blue, *American fucking millionaire.* A *mil,* Pop, a *mil,* a *bundle!* And I never sleep, only in moving vehicles, I hail a cab to take a nap; I work, I work, there's like a fire in me and I don't know where it is so I cannot put it out. And the fire is you. I *did* it, Pop. I won. K.O. in the first *round*. Vos *vilst* du, Papa? Vos *vilst* du fun mir? What do you fucking *want?*

(Silence for a moment. Eddie remains quite still)

EDDIE   *(quietly)* You shouldn't use "fuck" in a sentence, Charlie, you never put it in the right place. You don't blow good, kid, never did; ya don't have the knack. Another item: I listen to ya, I don't like the scorin' on this bout. How about *I* get credit for all the hits and *you* get the credit for bein' a nervous nut. *(Rises from chair, his old energy)* What're you, Goddamn Zorro the Avenger? What? You lookin' to come back here with your empties and get a refund? I didn't *order* this item, you ain't a *cake* I baked. I wasn't just your Pop, or Joey's neither, I'm Eddie; for this I take all blame or commendations. Nothin' else. I lived in *my* time, now you gotta live in *yours*, pal, and you can't send me the goddamn bill. Give it *up*, kid, give it the hell *up*. Give yourself a rest, you'll waste your life tryin' to catch me, you'll find y'self twenty years from now runnin' around a cemetery tryin' to put a stake through my heart. Sure I screwed up; now it's *your* turn. Yeah, let's see what *you* do when you look at Sarah or Josh and see *your* Pop's eyes peekin' out at ya; or worse, your *own*. Let's see what ya *do*, kid. *(Turns, starts towards bar)* Meanwhile, currently, I admit I give ya a hard time—but, frankly, I never liked Rich Kids. *(He stops, stands quite still; speaks briskly)* O.K., conversation over. End of conversation. See ya around; goodbye— *(Grips back of chair, staggers, as though about to faint, whispering)* Shit, here we go again . . . *(He suddenly falls to the ground, the chair clattering down with him)*

CHARLIE   *(rushing to him, breathless)* Pop, Jesus . . . Pop . . .

EDDIE   *(almost immediately, sitting up)* It's O.K., it's O.K., get me a vodka . . .

CHARLIE   *(helping him up)* Pop, I thought you—

EDDIE   *Vodka*, get me a vodka— *(Charlie races behind the bar; Eddie, standing now but still a bit unsteady, leans on the table for a moment)* O.K., O.K. now. Comes, then it goes. *(Walking slowly to bar)* Comes, then it goes. Fine now. Perfect. *(Charlie, behind bar, quickly pouring a glass of vodka, handing it out to him—but Eddie grabs the bottle and takes a long swig directly from it)* Excellent. Excellent. *(Sets bottle down on bar, renewed. Silence for a moment)* O.K., I conned ya, Charlie . . . I got this heart thing; special disease named for some Goy, Smithfield. Your Mother says right off, "How come you got Smithfield's Disease and he don't got yours?"

Don't care how old the joke is, what the occasion, she tells it. Turns out that wasn't no heart attack last year, it was this *Smithfield* number. The valve closes up, you keep fallin' asleep, fallin' over— *(Pulls wheelchair out from behind far end of bar)* I'm supposed to sit in this thing alot because I keep droppin' alla time. What kills you is these Embies—

CHARLIE *(quietly)* I think that's . . . that's Embolus, Pop . . .

EDDIE *(moving wheelchair down left)* Right. Anyways you can shoot off these Embies anytime. They go all over the joint. Musta shot one off four weeks ago, I'm all screwed up, I go in for these tests—turns out I'm the proud owner of a new, fully automatic *Smithfield*. Knocks you off in like six months or maybe next Tuesday. *So— (sits down in wheelchair)* good ya stopped by, we do a wrap-up shot, I got a *job* for ya—

CHARLIE *(sits next to wheelchair)* The doctors, they're *sure?*—I mean, I can get you—

EDDIE   Minute I get the news I got only one item concerns me, see; I go down to Barney's Tattoo Parlor on Mott, take care of it right off, goddamn relief. Looka here— *(Rolls up both sleeves, Charlie comes closer to look at the two tattoos)* One says "Pistol Pete," see, nice gun picture there, and this one here—

CHARLIE *(reading elaborate red and blue tattoo on Eddie's left arm; confused)* "King Of The Twin-Forties." I don't—

EDDIE *(triumphantly)* Hebrew *law*, Charlie—one of the oldest—you can't get buried in *any* Jewish Cemetery if you got tattoos! Twenty *years*, kid, I ain't had to be no kinda *Jew* at *all*—coulda ended up gettin' *Kaddished*-over, full-out ceremony, then gettin' stuck in some sacred Jew-ground with a buncha Yiddlach for *eternity!* *(Quietly, glancing upstairs)* She ain't to be trusted on this issue; since Joey, the woman is a goddamn religious *fanatic*—candles, prayers, every weird little holiday— *(Leans towards Charlie, grips his arm)* So, here's the job, Charlie—*anything* goes wrong, I want your personal guarantee—

CHARLIE   Of course, Pop—

EDDIE *(hands him card from wallet)* Here's where ya put me, kid; place in Queens, no religions whatever, no Gods of any type.

CHARLIE   It's done.

EDDIE   Because the woman, I'm tellin' ya, she's got her eye on this spot in Brooklyn where they planted the Actor. Woman thinks dyin' is movin' to the *suburbs*, wants us all *together* there—me, her,

Ethel, and *Zaretsky!* Can ya *picture* it, Charlie?—me and Zaretsky, goddamn *room*mates *forever!* Wouldn't get a minute's rest. 'Specially *now*, what I know *now* . . . *(He looks away. Silence for a moment)*

CHARLIE   *What?* What do you know now?

EDDIE   *(pause; a deep breath, plunges in)*   O.K.—*day* before he goes to St. Louis, the man gets a flash he's gonna kick it, makes out a will. Man is ninety-goddamn-*three*, he's first makin' out a will. Brings a lawyer over here, *also* about a hundred and eight, Ruskin, used to do all his business when he had the New Marinsky on Houston, wants me and Finney to witness, sign the will. I look it over, I see two things—first, I'm not in it; second, whatever he's got is goin' to the State of Israel . . . whatever he's *got* bein' one million, five hundred thousand dollars and change. A mil and a half, Charlie; the man was sittin' on a *mil* and a *half*. And this Ruskin almost as rich; *Ruskin*, with an accent on 'im made Zaretsky sound like George M. *Cohan!* They sell this Marinsky dump for bupkes back in Twenty-Eight; they parlay the bupkes into a fortune, they was good at *business*, *American business*, and the rest he got from them goddamn *concerts*, Charlie! *(A pause; he rubs the arm of the wheelchair)* I made Finney promise to zip it; I never told you, Gusta, nobody . . .

CHARLIE   Hey, far as me and Joey were concerned, you were always the *boss* here; wouldn't've made any difference—

EDDIE   A mil and a *half*, Charlie—he's livin' in that little room, takin' shit from me—

CHARLIE   He *loved* it here, Pop—he even liked fightin' with *you*, he—

(Charlie stops in mid-sentence, aware that Eddie has started to nod off to sleep . . . Eddie suddenly hits the arm of his wheelchair, forcing himself awake)

EDDIE   *(outraged)* A *millionaire*, Charlie! Workin' in a loser language! He did everything *wrong*—and he was a hit! Can you make sense of this, Charlie? *Zaretsky*, why *him*—why *him* and not *me*? And, you'll forgive me—I wish ya all the best— *(gripping Charlie's arm)* but why *you*, ya little Putz, you with your goddamn *Narri*shkeit— why *you*, and not me? Why? *(Starting to become drowsy again)* Surrounded by goddamn millionaires here . . . Can you make *sense* of this . . . the Bucks, what happened? The Big Bucks, why did they avoid me? Wherever I was, the Bucks never came, and when I went to where the Bucks were they flew away like pigeons . . . like pigeons in the park . . . *(His head nodding forward,* *drifting off)* Got this dream alla time I'm at Ellis Island, only I'm the age I'm now. Old days, you had a disease, they wouldn't let ya in. They mark on your coat with chalk, "E" for eye, "L" for lung, and they send ya back. In the dream, I got an "H" for heart and they won't let me in . . . they won't let me in, Joey . . . *(He falls deeply asleep in the wheelchair. Silence. Charlie leans anxiously towards him)*

CHARLIE   Pop . . . ? *(Touches his arm gently)* Pop . . . ? *(Silence again. Charlie rises, carefully turning the wheelchair around so that Eddie's sleep is not disturbed by the morning light that comes in from the front door. Eddie remains with his back to us; during this next scene we will not see his face except perhaps for brief glimpses of his profile. Charlie speaking to us as he turns the chair)* Six weeks later one o' them Embies shot off into the left side of Pop's brain, paralyzing his right arm and leg and taking away his ability to speak. *(Opening small side table on arm of wheelchair, placing pad and pencil on it)* Two weeks back from the hospital he had somehow taught himself to write almost legibly with his left hand—according to this terrific Speech Therapy lady I went to, this meant he could eventually be trained to speak again. But all he was able to produce were these unintelligible, childlike noises, and he refused to see anyone, no less try to *speak* to anyone, including Gusta. He closed "The Homeland" down and sat here. Ten days, like this. On the eleventh day, armed with some hints from the Speech Therapist, I came down to take a shot. *(To Eddie)* Delighted to see me, huh? *(Eddie shakes his head angrily)* And you're thinkin' what's the sense of trying to learn how to speak again because you figure you *can't*, also why torture yourself if you ain't gonna live that much longer *anyway*, right? *(Eddie points with his left hand as though to say "You got it," then does a powerful "Go away" gesture)* Right. And there's these clear pictures in your head of all the words you want to say and your mouth just won't do the job, right? *(Eddie does not respond. Then, after a moment, he nods "Yes")* O.K., now I don't know *how* this works or *why* this works, but there's a thing you're capable of right now called "Automatic Speech." As impossible as it must feel to you, you are capable, right now, of saying, distinctly as *ever,* certain automatic phrases—ends of songs, if I do the first part, a piece of a prayer, something. And, thing is, you hear yourself *do* that and that'll get you to want to work at the whole talkin'-shot again, see. *(Eddie scribbles something on the pad on the arm of his wheelchair, hands pad to Charlie)* "Go *away.* Stay away." Pop, I gotta try the number here. C'mon, gimme a chance . . . *(Charlie leans forward, singing softly)* "Oh beautiful for spacious skies . . . " *(Pause, no response. Charlie tries again)* "Oh beautiful for spacious skies, for amber . . . " *(Silence for a few moments; then very suddenly, sharply)* You got some ice-cold Daitch on tap, fel-lah?

EDDIE   *(suddenly)* I got it, now *you* . . . got it. *(Eddie realizes what he has just done. Charlie smiles. Silence for a moment; Eddie appears to be chuckling softly)*

CHARLIE   Well, now. Shall we proceed, sir? *(Silence for a moment. Eddie turns away; then looks at Charlie; he nods)* O.K., now we got some pictures here . . . *(Takes a stack of eight-by-eleven-inch cards out of an envelope)* Objects, people, animals, O.K.? Double item here, see; there's a picture of the thing and then the word for it printed underneath. You go for either one—word or picture, and *say* what it is. Be patient with yourself on this, O.K.? *(Eddie nods)* O.K.; animals and birds. *(Looks through cards, stops at one; smiles)* Yeah, here's a good beginning . . . *(He turns the card around; it is a full-color illustration of a duck)* "Duck." We'll start with "Duck."

(Eddie does not move, there is a long silence. Then Eddie, rather force-fully, raises his left arm, the middle finger of his hand jabbing upward, giving Charlie "The Finger." Eddie continues to hold his hand up firmly; the lights come down, one single light remaining on "The Finger")

CHARLIE   *(turns to us)* Well, there it is, my last image of my father: his memorial, his obelisk, his Washington Monument. *(He moves across towards his booth at far right, the light gradually dimming down on "The Finger" during his next speech; only a small spotlight on Charlie, the rest of the stage in near-darkness)* He died about seven months later; by then he was talking, even hollering, and terror-izing his third Speech Therapist. *(We hear the distant sound of a Cantor singing a phrase of the Kaddish, rising then fading, as the bare-ly visible shape of the older Gusta comes out of the Kitchen; she rolls the wheelchair off into the shadows as Charlie continues)* Bicentennial's next week, two hundred years since America was born and, two days later, ten years since Pop died. I wish I could tell you that he won my heart in the final chapter, but he did not. I light his Yahrzeit candle every year, though, and say the prayer; I figured Mom would appreciate it. *(After a moment)* It's a month now since *she* died, joking as she closed her act. "I'm thinking of becoming a Catholic," she says, that last night. "And why's that, Ma?" I say, feeding her the straight-line like a good son— *(With Gusta's accent)* "Well, Sonny, I figure better one of *them* goes than one of us." *(Takes keys from jacket)* I miss her, of course; but I will not miss this place. *(A beat)* Pop got his wish, of course; I buried him in this aggressively non-sectarian joint called Hamilton Oaks out in Queens. However, one of the reasons I never forget his Yahrzeit is that every year, a week before the Sixth . . . *(he takes the familiar blue and white card out of his jacket)* this card comes from the Sons of Moses to remind me. For fifty bucks he got them to find me for the *rest of my life*. Los Angeles, *London*, the Virgin fucking *Islands*, they *find* me, those Sons of Moses . . .

(The sudden lights of the Present—the early evening light of the beginning of the play—come up in the barroom as Charlie holds the card up and crushes it fiercely in his hand; he tosses the mangled card on the floor and strides angrily towards the bar; the old Stroller once again down left, his rage building as he slams noisily about behind the bar looking for his glass and vodka bottle)

CHARLIE   The old switcheroo—the old switcheroo every time! Never made any *sense, never*—his *head*, his *head*, it was *Steeple*chase up there, the goddamn *Roller*-coaster— *(Bangs his fist on the bar)* None of it, nothing he said, *none* of it fit together—*none* of it—*still* doesn't—son of a bitch—

JOSH   *(entering briskly from the Apartment above, carrying two cartons; brightly)* Dad . . . Dad, I've been thinking, how about—why don't we *keep* this place and just get somebody to *run* it for us; y'know, a manager, we'll find a good manager. We *keep* it, Dad, we keep it just the way it *is*; I'll help out, weekends, every summer, maybe even—

CHARLIE   *(fiercely, wildly, shouting)* I *told* you, we're *selling* it, we're selling it, you don't *listen*—

JOSH   *(startled)* I just—I just thought maybe we could—

CHARLIE   *(he smashes his fist on the bar, coming quickly out from behind bar towards Josh)* It's *gone*, over, outa *my* life, outa *yours*, over, over— *(Charlie, blindly, violently, his fist raised, advancing on Josh, Josh backing fearfully away across the room)* —you don't *listen*, you *never* did—you don't *now*, you never *did*, and you never *will*—

(Josh is trapped against one of the booths, startled, frozen. Charlie stops, stands quite still, trembling with his own rage; then gradually begins to focus on his son's frightened eyes; he lowers his fist)

CHARLIE   *(lost, whispering)* Josh . . . sorry, I was . . .

(Josh backs away towards the front door, warily, as though from a stranger)

JOSH   *(softly)* You get yourself together, O.K . . . ? I'll wait in the car, O.K . . . ?

CHARLIE   Josh, I'm sorry . . . I was . . . see, I was . . .

JOSH   You get yourself together, I'll be in the car . . .

CHARLIE   *(moving towards him, his hand up)* Josh, what happened, let me explain . . .

(But Josh has gone out into the street with his cartons, the door closing behind him. Charlie stands exhausted at the center of the room, looking at the door; silence for several moments. He turns, looks about at the bar for a moment, sees the crumpled Sons of Moses card on the floor; he picks it up, studies it thoughtfully, then starts straightening it out as he walks slowly towards the bar. We begin to hear the violin introduction to Aaron Lebedeff recording of "Rumania" from the Jukebox, and then Lebedeff's rousing voice)

LEBEDEFF'S VOICE

"Rumania, Rumania, Rumania . . .
Geven amol a land a zise, a sheyne . . . "

(As Charlie reaches the bar and sits on one of the stools; the old bar-lights fade quickly up, the colorful lights of the Thirties and Forties, and Eddie enters briskly from the Kitchen, the younger Eddie with his fine white shirt, black bow-tie and sharp black pants; Eddie goes directly behind the bar, takes a glass and a bottle from the shelf, pours with his usual flourish and sets a drink down next to Charlie; Charlie looking down at the card as the Lebedeff Music fills the room, Eddie leaning forward with his hands on the bar, looking at the front door, waiting for customers, as . . .)

THE CURTAIN FALLS

Screenplay

Dustin Hoffman and Shel Silverstein with Dr. Hook

WHO IS HARRY KELLERMAN AND WHY IS HE SAYING THOSE TERRIBLE THINGS ABOUT ME?

Who Is Harry Kellerman And Why Is He Saying Those Terrible Things About Me?

I wish I could do the role of George Solloway today. I needed more experience, maturity, years than I had at the time to understand what Herb was talking about. But what a screenplay he wrote! Some of the scenes are now, thirty years later, still echoing in the corners of my memory. Especially the scenes with Barbara Harris as Allison; simply said, they're very special, replete with abundantly insightful dialogue of men-women relationships. And Barbara's performance is up there with the best of them. I'm proud to have been part of this film, perceptively directed by Ulu Grosbard, and with those incredibly talented members of the cast: Barbara, Gabe Dell, Jack Warden, David Burns, Dom De Luise, Rose Gregorio, Regina Baff, and of course Shel Silverstein. Finally, I'm doubly proud to have been part of Herb's original, brilliant assault on the madness of success.

— DUSTIN HOFFMAN
Los Angeles, California

JUDITH CRIST
(*New York Magazine*, June 28, 1971)

"Time ... it's not a thief. It's much sneakier. It's an embezzler up nights juggling the books so you don't notice anything's missing." So says Barbara Harris as Allison in Herb Gardner's *Who Is Harry Kellerman And Why Is He Saying Those Terrible Things About Me?*, a remarkable film in construction, content and performance.

Here is Dustin Hoffman's Georgie, the 40-plus hero of *Harry Kellerman* who is a top songwriter, rich, divorced, miserable — and as ready for the "cookie jar" as any of our contemporaries who have devoted "Fifty-two thousand, five hundred and sixty dollars plus cab-fares" and seven years to analysis. We go through one of Georgie's sleepless nights with him, filled with panic calls to and/or visits with his psychiatrist (Jack Warden in a marvelous series of impersonations), his accountant (Dom De Luise, beautifully puzzled by having to like the man whose books he fixes), his father (David Burns in an eloquent memorial performance as a loving man facing the end of living) and various buddies, and bulging with flashback bits of biography that present us with his first love, his wife, his parents and the girl (Barbara Harris at her poignant perfect) who might be his salvation if only Kellerman doesn't bad-mouth him to her.

Herb Gardner's original screenplay — and his first movie work since *A Thousand Clowns* in 1965 — has echoes of *The Goodbye People*, his 1960 Broadway play, in its concern with life and death, with the guess-who-died-today syndrome of the old, the sudden realization of time passing by the not-so-young. Georgie has come to see his children as "goddam clocks," because he still feels as if he's eighteen; his dream is of "a new life and a day without fear." Miss Harris's Allison turns thirty-four but is "prepared for twenty-two." It's only Georgie's father who knows that one doesn't expand the business in the face of dying; one does the tasks of the day.

Gardner is a humanistic wit and one of the most literate writers around; he knows his milieu and his little people in big places. Through Hoffman and Miss Harris and all his characters he touches the pulse of life with shrewd perceptions. The film is a throbbing creation, a work of remarkable style, beautiful rhythms and an engrossing pace.

Opposite top, Barbara Harris and Dustin Hoffman

Left, Dustin as Georgie in Midtown Tunnel

Above, Producer/Writer Herb Gardner with Jack
Warden and Dustin Hoffman

CAST

GEORGIE	Dustin Hoffman
ALLISON	Barbara Harris
DR. MOSES	Jack Warden
LEON	David Burns
MARGOT	Betty Walker
GLORIA	Rose Gregorio
SID	Gabe Dell
IRWIN	Dom De Luise
SUSAN	Amy Levitt
MARTY	Joe Sicari
HALLORAN	Ed Zimmermann
CHOMSKY	Joseph Elic
NEWSDEALER	Rudy Bond
SALLY	Candy Azzara
SAMANTHA	Robyn Millan
LEMUEL	James Hall
RUTHIE	Regina Baff
CAPT. LOVE	Shel Silverstein

CREDITS

PRODUCER/DIRECTOR	Ulu Grosbard
PRODUCER/WRITER	Herb Gardner
ASSOCIATE PRODUCER	Fred C. Caruso
DIRECTOR OF PHOTOGRAPHY	Victor J. Kemper
MUSIC AND LYRICS	Shel Silverstein
MUSICAL DIRECTOR	Ron Hafkine
CAMERA OPERATOR	Edward Brown
1ST ASSISTANT DIRECTOR	Peter Scoppa
2ND ASSISTANT DIRECTOR	Larry Albucher
LOCATION COORDINATOR	Robert Barth
SCRIPT SUPERVISOR	Sid Gecker
PRODUCTION DESIGNER	Harry Horner
SET DECORATOR	Leif Pederssen
SOUND	Jack C. Jacobsen
COSTUME DESIGNER	Anna Hill Johnstone
MAKEUP	Dick Smith
HAIR	Bill Farley
EDITOR	Barry Malkin
ASSOCIATE EDITOR	Craig McCay
PRODUCTION SECRETARY	Lois Kramer
PRODUCER'S SECRETARY	Liz Bleiweiss
UNIT PUBLICIST	Ted Albert

*A grizzled face against a pre-dawn sky; the unshaven face hums mournful-
ly. Included in the shot are the frets of a guitar. A hand-rolled cigarette rests
on the pegs, its smoke curling up past the face. The face is sunburned beneath
a battered cowboy hat and the blueblack sky beyond it is wide and open. The
man hums quietly, almost to himself, his voice and guitar-strum are distinctly Western . . .*
*After several moments of soft humming he begins to sing the words of the
song . . .*

GEORGIE

> "This is the last mornin' . . . "

Camera pulls back as the song continues, revealing GEORGIE SOLOWAY; *he
is sitting in a deck chair on the lush terrace of his vast Fifth Avenue duplex;
he wears a monogrammed velour bathrobe, silk pajamas, and cowboy boots.
Tiny lights outline a black-and-white striped awning, black marble letters
over terrace doorway read: "Soloway Productions: Horizons Unlimited,"
icy-white sculpture rests on severe black pedestals, a jukebox stands amongst
them like one more piece of sculpture . . .*

GEORGIE   (cont)

> " . . . that I wake up in this dirty city
> Lookin' for the sunshine
> As the buildings black the skies . . .
> This is the last mornin'
> That I wash in rusty water
> Try to shave a face
> That I don't even recognize
> I'm goin' home . . . "

We see GEORGIE'S *apartment on top of the General Motors Building at
Fifty-ninth and Fifth; we see the huge white building, the tiny lights at its
roof where* GEORGIE *lives, the pre-dawn skyline and river beyond, but*
GEORGIE'S *voice stays close, intimate, whispering mournfully into our
ears . . .*

GEORGIE   (cont)

> " . . . down the hallways rats are skitterin'
> I can smell the garbage rottin'
> Hear the children cryin'
> In apartments down below . . .
> This is the last mornin'
> That I'm gonna have t'listen to it
> I'm goin' home . . . "

*Now the G.M. Building towers above us, a block of ice thrust into the sky;
we turn slowly and then move across the deserted expanse of Fifth Avenue,
dawn light hinting at edges of skyline, moving through gusts of steam which*

rise from manholes, movement matching the slow guitar-strum and GEORGIE'S *gentle, tired voice* . . .

GEORGIE

" . . . This is the last mornin'
That I try to breathe the heavy air
Fight the crowds, avoid the traffic
Watch the world turn gray
This is the last mornin'
That I drink my coffee standin' up
Smile and speak to strangers
Who just turn and walk away . . .

We continue across Fifth, discovering a Calypso Street Band asleep amongst their instruments beneath the huge statue of General Sherman, his fierce stallion led by a bronze angel of peace. The Street Band consists of three colorfully dressed black musicians who sleep gracefully entwined in their instruments, a collection of wash basins, garbage-can covers, and oil drums. Camera moving up to outstretched angel's hand and then above it into sky as we cut to:

Aerial view of Manhattan, pre-dawn; we pass through smog and threatening clouds, a dark and forbidding city slides by below us . . .

GEORGIE

" . . . and I'm so tired of tryin' t'stand against it
all alone . . . "

We are looking straight down from GEORGIE'S *terrace, fifty floors to the street, the building plunges down below us.*

GEORGIE

" . . . this is the last mornin'
That I'm gonna try to fight it
I'm goin' home . . . "

Terrace ledge; GEORGIE *close to us, writing on small piece of paper; resting paper on ledge. Behind him, from the pulsing light of the jukebox, we hear a* ROCK GROUP *pick up the song where* GEORGIE *left off* . . .

ROCK GROUP *(O.S.)*

" . . . home, home,
I'm goin' home . . . "

GEORGIE
(as he writes)

There was a time when I was planning to live
forever, but I have found it necessary to
change those plans . . .
    (hesitates; writes again)
Yours very truly, George Raymond Soloway . . .

He nods, satisfied with his note, puts pencil in pocket, takes roll of Scotch tape from same pocket; coolly, carefully tapes note to awning-support at edge of terrace ledge . . .

We move closer as he climbs up on the ledge, stands at the very edge, gripping awning-support to steady himself . . .

ROCK GROUP *(O.S.)*
" . . . down below the subway's screamin'
As I lie here halfway dreamin'
Lookin' at the ceilin' wonderin' where
The dream went wrong . . .

GEORGIE *lets go of awning-support; looks down. He takes a deep breath, closes his eyes, leans forward . . .*

ROCK GROUP *(O.S.)*
" . . . this is the last mornin'
That I'm gonna have t'think about it . . .
I'm goin' home . . .

Sound of high wind, rattling of suicide note taped to awning-support.
GEORGIE *glances sideways at note, then returns to jumping attitude.*
He glances at the note again . . .
Takes pencil from pocket, leans toward awning-support, scratches out a word, writes in another word above it; nods, satisfied with revision, puts pencil back in pocket; returns to jumping posture.
A moment . . . then he turns toward the note again, takes out pencil, adds a sentence to the bottom of the note, crosses it out, adds another sentence; shakes his head, still not satisfied.
He is standing at the very edge of the terrace ledge now, becoming more and more absorbed in the rewriting of the note; finally sitting at the edge of the ledge, his feet dangling over the edge, his legs crossed, resting the note on his knees, writing with great concentration, nodding his head, mumbling new phrases . . .
He holds the note up to study it.
A gust of wind takes the note from between his fingers; it flutters up several inches out of reach; he stands to grab for it . . .
We pull sharply back as note glides away from him; he lunges for it, loses his balance, and falls forward off the ledge.

GEORGIE
(whispering)
Son-of-a-bitch . . .

GEORGIE *falls sharply down, his face flashing past us in horror, shock; his arms outstretched, grabbing at the air as he descends . . .*

ROCK GROUP *(O.S.)*
"This is the last mornin'

That I'm gonna have t'think about it . . .
I'm goin' home . . . "

GEORGIE'S *sharp drop suddenly slows to a gliding, floating, easy drift; a fall in slow motion that matches the wandering rhythm of the off-screen singing and guitar-strum, as the title appears:*

WHO IS HARRY KELLERMAN AND WHY IS HE SAYING THOSE TERRIBLE THINGS ABOUT ME?

Credits continue through GEORGIE'S *descent; his figure falling slowly, slowly past the words, arms and legs outstretched, gliding, spinning, swimming down, his cowboy hat floating beside him . . . He is smiling, relaxed, at peace . . . catching the suicide note as it floats down next to him; takes out pencil, perfecting the note as he falls . . .*
He floats gracefully down toward us, the song continuing gently through his downward ballet . . .

                    ROCK GROUP   *(cont)*
" . . . this is the last mornin'
That I'm gonna try t'fight it . . .
I'm goin' home . . .
Home, I'm goin' home
Home, home . . . "

We follow GEORGIE *down through the last screen credit and into:*

His analyst's office.
GEORGIE *lands feet-first on his analyst's couch, bounces back up, trampoline-style, lands again, settles back on couch.* DR. SOLOMON F. MOSES, *a kindly Viennese in his late fifties, sits in an armchair at the head of the couch. Having observed* GEORGIE'S *arrival, he takes a few careful notes, considers them thoughtfully, then turns to* GEORGIE.

                    DR. MOSES
Mr. Soloway, we cannot entirely rule out the
possibility, at this point, that you are a bird.

                    GEORGIE
A what . . . ?

                    DR. MOSES
A bird, Mr. Soloway. A winged, flying, bird.

                    GEORGIE
What kind of a bird . . . ?

DR. MOSES

A loony-bird, Mr. Soloway. A crazy, nutsy, loony-bird—

A blast of sunlight and traffic noise as GEORGIE *sits up in beach chair on terrace, guitar in his arms, late afternoon. Shakes his head, rubs his stubbled face, frightened; then urgently punches out number on speaker-phone. Guttural buzzing from speaker, then—*

DR. MOSES' VOICE

Hello, yes? Dr. Moses here.

GEORGIE

Doc-baby . . .

DR. MOSES' VOICE

Hello, yes?

GEORGIE

Hey, Mandrake, it's me . . .

DR. MOSES' VOICE

Hello . . . ?

GEORGIE

It's me, Georgie, your highest-paying crazy-head . . .

DR. MOSES' VOICE

Yes, hello, Mr. Soloway. How are you?

GEORGIE

Seven years and you don't know how I am yet. Beautiful.

Traveling with GEORGIE *into main room and then up stairs . . .*

DR. MOSES' VOICE

Mr. Soloway, you have not appeared for your last
five sessions . . .

GEORGIE
(strums, sings, going up stairs)
"...yeah, one more ride
World of sunshine waitin' for you
On the other side . . . "

DR. MOSES' VOICE

Mr. Soloway—

GEORGIE

M'new hit, doc, number eight on the Singles
Chart and climbin' like a son-of-a-bitch—

Entering bedroom; speaker over full-length mirror . . .

DR. MOSES' VOICE

Mr. Soloway—

> GEORGIE

—thirty-eight thousand in the last quarterly ASCAP
earnings period, second highest composer's royalty in the . . .

He sees his rumpled, sleepless form in the mirror . . .

> DR. MOSES' VOICE

That is not what you called to tell me about . . . is it,
Mr. Soloway?

> GEORGIE
> *(quietly)*

Dr. Oz. . . . Six nights. No sleep. Looka my face.
> *(steps closer to mirror)*

Inside is worse. Midgets in there, havin' a picnic,
chompin' on m'brains. Sleep. Wear my pajamas all
day just in case it comes, like party clothes in case of
an invitation . . .

*He grabs old sweatshirt and workpants, dressing on his way downstairs and
across main room, tossing bathrobe and pajamas at random along the
way . . .*

> DR. MOSES' VOICE
> *(speaker; base of stairs)*

No sleep at all, Mr. Soloway?

> GEORGIE

Some. Not good. Close my eyes and I'm jumpin' offa
everything; roofs, ledges, bridges, trains, planes . . .
gotta see ya right away, honey . . .

> DR. MOSES' VOICE
> *(speaker over fireplace)*

Mr. Soloway, your regular appointment is—

> GEORGIE

My marbles, doc; they are spilling. They are rolling
out onto the floor and behind the refrigerator
where you can't get at them anymore . . .

> DR. MOSES' VOICE

Very well, Mr. Soloway; can you be here immediately?

> GEORGIE
> *(heads for spiral staircase)*

Beautiful. I'm buyin' you Vienna for your birthday.

*"Click" from speaker as he heads downstairs, carrying guitar in case; hums
melody of "We're Off to See the Wizard" . . .*

> MARTY'S VOICE
> *(from below)*

He's here! I got 'em! Georgie!

We are traveling downstairs toward MARTY *and* LEMUEL *at reception desk.* MARTY *dressed in white leather, ascot, sunglasses.* LEMUEL, *drooping mustache, tattered country clothes, guitar and sandals, stares transfixed at wood-paneled wall. Above the reception desk, marble black letters read "Horizons Unlimited: Publishing, Recording."* MARILYN, *the receptionist, shrugs helplessly at* GEORGIE.

> GEORGIE

Marty, go away.

> MARTY

This is it, Georgie. You'll flip out. The voice. The heart breaks.

> LEMUEL
> *(to wall)*

Beautiful . . .

> GEORGIE

What's happening?

> MARILYN

Moses and the Ten Commandments, Studio A; Captain Love, Studio B; Doctor Hook and the Medicine Show, Studio C . . .

We move briskly with GEORGIE *down hallway,* MARTY *and* LEMUEL *in pursuit, dialogue mixed with blasts of sound and action as we pass open office doorways and blinking lights of studios, flashes of "Last Morning" and "One More Ride" heard in passing . . .*

> MARTY

Georgie . . .

> GEORGIE

Marty, I told ya to stay outa here with your acid-head, freak-out—

> MARTY

Georgie, look, look; you're offending my boy—

> GEORGIE

How can I offend him when he don't know he's here?

> LEMUEL
> *(to white carpet)*
Beautiful, beautiful . . .

> MARTY

Bayou country. Untouched. Purity. Hundred percent. Breaks the heart. Great group name. We put shades on him. Ya got one blind mouse. We get two other mice, whaddya got?

GEORGIE *steps into elevator.* MARTY *follows, pulling* LEMUEL *after him.*

                    MARTY   *(cont)*
    Three Blind Mice. You get it? Beautiful.

Elevator; as it descends, GEORGIE *punching out number on speaker phone
next to control panel.*

                    MARTY
    O.K. Make one demo album you got eighty percent
    of the boy.

                    LEMUEL
              (to roof of elevator)
    Beautiful . . .

                    MARTY
    O.K. Three Blind Mice. Forget it. Mistake. I hate it.
    We put a dress on him. Call him "It." . . .

              VOICE FROM SPEAKER
    Yessir.

                    GEORGIE
    Chomsky, the car, quick, goin' to see the Wizard.

                    MARTY
    It's not a chick, it's not a cat, what is it? It's *"It."* . . .

Doors open, GEORGIE *steps out, humming softly . . . Sudden sound of wailing siren—*

Hands of huge clock in lobby: exactly five P.M.*—*

Factory whistle screams—

Alarm bell jangles—

*Street clock, Sixtieth and Fifth; we move down to the Calypso Street Band,
the same three men seen earlier, gathered beneath the clock with their
instruments. They hit a downbeat; a sudden, gleeful, mad, frenzied gesture
as their instruments explode with sound—*

*Bank of elevators in empty G.M. lobby; doors gasp open, crowds gush forth
toward us—offscreen sound of Calypso Street Band; tin cans, cowbells, oil
drums, banging, throbbing, thwanging, rattling music continues through
scene, building in volume and intensity as sequence progresses—*

Crowds stampede toward us to exit doors.

GEORGIE *is caught up in lobby rush, beneath dazzling chandelier;* MARTY
and LEMUEL *in pursuit—*

MARTY
(*screaming as he is swallowed in crowd*)
Eighty-five, Georgie, eighty-five percent of the
boyyyyyyy . . .

Calypso Street Band; music building—

GEORGIE *seeking refuge next to marble column in front of G.M. Building
as crowds crush past, jagged scrawl on column demands "Drop the Bomb."*

Crush of businessmen with attaché cases shoves past GEORGIE, *knocking guitar case from his hand;* GEORGIE *horrified as his precious possession goes
thwanging across the marble plaza through legs of crowd—
Horns, sirens, whistles, motors, Street Band building in intensity—*

*Street Band, delighted; one of them holding out garbage-can cover into
which coins are thrown, clanking in—*

GEORGIE *scrambling through legs of crowd for lost guitar—*

Scurrying legs of crowd tramping guitar case—

Angry FLOWER VENDOR *shoving roses at center of hurrying crowd, screaming "Take! Take! Beauties! Beauties!"—*

Scurrying feet trampling guitar case; GEORGIE *swoops up guitar in his
arms like a baby, group galloping for bus butters past him—
Traffic roar and Street Band building—*

Hotel Doorman blowing whistle for—

Old Woman screaming for—

People racing, shouting for—
"Taxi! Taxi! Taxi! Taxi!"
Street Band DRUMMER *beating out tempo as chant continues
for—*
"Taxi! Taxi! Taxi! Taxi!"

GEORGIE
Chomsky! Chomsky! Where the hell—

*We are darting desperately, scanning blurred rushes of traffic for his car,
moaning buses, screeching cabs—
Suddenly, a smiling face of* GEORGIE *on the cover of "Time" magazine,
beneath it the legend "Soloway: Voice of the People?" We move back to see
five copies, one above the other in display on corner newsstand.*

GEORGIE *grabs magazine off display, a lifeline in the storm, Street Band music builds through scene . . .*

> NEWSDEALER
> *(a grim face in the shadows of the stand)*
> That's fifty cents.

GEORGIE *ignores him, leafing through pages, looking for himself.*

> NEWSDEALER   *(cont)*
> You're blocking the stand, pest. I'm losing business.

> GEORGIE
> Sir, I—you won't believe this—I never carry any
> money on me, but I—

> NEWSDEALER
> *(peering out of stand at him)*
> I believe you. Gimme the book back.

> GEORGIE
> Trust me—I'll give you the money later—ten dollars—
> *(desperately, showing cover)*
> Look, this is me, Georgie Soloway, I live right up
> there, on top of the General Motors Building.

> NEWSDEALER
> Good. I live on the chandelier in Radio City Music Hall.
> Gimme the book back, I'll call a cop!

> GEORGIE
> Please, I gotta have this—

> NEWSDEALER
> *(hysterical)*
> Look what he's doing to me! Rush hour, I'm losing
> business! Look!
> *(reaches out of stand, grabs GEORGIE'S arm)*
> I'll get the cops on you! Pest! Pest! Rotten hippie!

GEORGIE *wrenches himself free, races off into crowd with magazine.* NEWSDEALER *comes out of stand, a rotten old man with a visored cap, huge money-changer clinking like a tambourine under his belly; he charges after* GEORGIE, *waving metal paperweight . . .*

> NEWSDEALER   *(cont)*
> The book! The book! Bandit! Hippie! Gimme the book!

GEORGIE *runs, looking about wildly for his car—*

The Calypso Street Band quickens tempo as though aware of the chase.

NEWSDEALER *in screaming pursuit.*

GEORGIE *running.*
Sound of shattering thunderclap.

The screen turns gray.

Intercuts of GEORGIE *running and the shards of life that slash past him become swifter, spiraling; we rush past—*

Two men fighting for an umbrella in a trash basket.

Woman trying to shatter bus door when it closes in her face.

Sherman's bronze angel, arm outstretched, wanting a cab.

Flashing "Off-Duty" lights, madly chattering meters.

Girl using her huge model's bag to beat out two men for a cab.

People looking up at threatening sky, panic, shouting "Taxi! Taxi!"

Soldiers lunging with fixed bayonets in Fifth Avenue War monument, seen in glimpses between charging traffic.

Expensive shoes rushing on wet streets.

Street Band reaching a peak of rattling, banging, joyous frenzy.

GEORGIE *running, slips on wet pavement, we move down to him amongst rushing feet . . .*

NEWSDEALER *running toward us, almost upon us—*
Street Band and traffic noise reach their peak—

GEORGIE *scrambling to his feet, turns to:*

A Cadillac fender flashing into view, CHOMSKY *in driver's seat looking disdainfully down at his kneeling employer . . .*

CLOSE ON GEORGIE *as, half-crouching, he grabs guitar case, opens car door, stumbles forward, lying on the deep leather back seat of the limousine; saved.*
STREET BAND *music at peak and then—*
Sudden silence . . . only the faint ticking of an old and gentle clock . . .

Camera back to reveal that GEORGIE *is actually on the couch in* DR. MOSES' *office; late afternoon sunlight falls gently on the carpet.* DR. MOSES *sits a few*

feet away at his desk, hands folded, smiling with polite dignity. Several seconds pass . . .
GEORGIE *sits up at edge of couch, smiles pleasantly at the doctor.*
The distant clock ticks.
Finally . . .

GEORGIE

Hello . . .

> *(no reply. A slight wave of GEORGIE'S hand)*

Hi . . .
> *(no reply)*

How're ya feelin', doc?
> *(no reply)*

Good.
> *(picks up guitar case)*

Almost lost m'ax today . . . m'sweet ole ax . . .
> *(takes guitar out of case; touches it tenderly)*

Lotta good sounds . . . lotta heavy sounds come
outa this ax . . .
> *(strums; checking for damage)*

Sixty-one songs this year . . . not countin' two peace
marches, a cigarette commercial, four Christmas
ballads, the new Air Force Hymn, and a cancer jingle . . .
> *(quietly touching guitar)*

And a lotta songs left in this ax, right? . . . right, doc?

No reply. MOSES *listens thoughtfully.* GEORGIE *takes* "Time" *magazine from pocket, tosses it proudly on* MOSES' *desk.*

GEORGIE *(cont)*

Hey, looka that . . . Voice of the people . . .

No reply. MOSES *hardly glances at it.*

GEORGIE *(cont)*

How d'ya like that . . . ? Songs of love, Solly; can't
love anybody this year without usin' Georgie's
words. Everybody bangin' to Georgie's beat; finger
on the pulse, eye on the sparrow, everybody lovin'
Soloway-style . . .
> *(still no reply; his words hang in the air)*

Chrissakes, doc, nearly killed myself gettin' ya that
magazine; least ya could do is—

DR. MOSES

Mr. Soloway, you referred earlier on the telephone to an
emergency, a crisis—

GEORGIE

Mr. Soloway; chrissakes, seven years and you're still callin'
me Mr. Soloway. Aren't we buddies yet?

DR. MOSES

Fine, then. Tell me what's wrong, George.

GEORGIE

Good. There's this fella wants to kill me, Sol.
(goes to desk)
A fella that I don't know who it is. I mean, you're not a
paranoid if everybody really *does hate* you, right?
(sits at edge of desk)
Now we've established that I'm ready to be loved. I
mean, it's *years* gettin' me ready for that number. And
I'm really ready to love and commit myself to another
human being now, because I've learned to love myself
and forgive my self for how rotten I am. That's where
we are at now; that is the scene, right?

DR. MOSES

That's not exactly—

GEORGIE

I mean it cost me fifty-two thousand, four hundred
and sixty dollars, not counting cab fares and a lotta
years, so you could sell me back to myself. And
now I am supposed to be straight on this love thing . . .
and now . . . an *outside force* . . . a big gun from outa town,
a *person*, is screwing it up . . . ya got that?

DR. MOSES

George, I believe that we have several times discussed
the value placed upon the sums you exchange for my
professional services. You—

GEORGIE

Didn't mean to mention the money again, sorry—

DR. MOSES

—become in the exchange of value, obligated to your
own therapy by the fact of its cost—

GEORGIE

Doctor, Darling, Sweetness, forget it, that's—

DR. MOSES

If, however, you find it—

GEORGIE

Hush now . . .
(leans toward him; whispering)
Hush now, Dr. Ladybug, one of your children
is burning . . .

Sudden sound of rattling, banging Street Band. We move past GEORGIE *to window and skyline . . .*

GEORGIE
Started six days ago, Sol . . .

Skyline turning pink with dawn as chinning bar cuts horizontally across the screen.

   Two hands grab it and begin to pull up the man they belong to; he has his back to us, wears an exercise outfit, and appears to be hanging in midair over the skyline. He chants in rhythm with his pullups; we recognize the voice as GEORGIE'S.

GEORGIE
(chinning up)

In-
   (down)
vincible
   (up)
Un-
   (down)
daunted.

Phone rings; Street Band sound cuts out. He swings forward to speaker suspended from terrace awning, kicks "on" switch.

GEORGIE   *(cont)*
Yeah? Hello? Yeah?

SALLY'S VOICE
Hello, it's Sally.

GEORGIE
Sally, darlin' . . .
   (chinning up)
crazy . . .
   (down)
about you . . .

SALLY'S VOICE
Georgie, you sound out of breath . . .

GEORGIE
Exercise . . .
   (up)
Live . . .
   (down)
forever . . .
   (up)
Hey, sun's comin' up soon, darlin' . . .
   (down)
Come on over and watch the—

SALLY'S VOICE

Georgie, I just now had a terrible experience. Guy
calls me up. Says he's a friend of yours. Says you have
a wife, three children, several social diseases, and just
got out of Payne Whitney Clinic, where they put you
for behaving in a violent manner.

GEORGIE *drops to his feet. He looks into the webbed center of the speaker as
though it had eyes.*

GEORGIE

Who? Who said that? My God.

SALLY'S VOICE

Says his name is Harry Kellerman.

GEORGIE

I don't even . . . not even a familiar name.

SALLY'S VOICE

Is it true?

GEORGIE

My God. None. None of it. Who did he say he was to me?

SALLY'S VOICE

A friend. An ex-friend of yours. Says that's all you have
is ex-friends because of how sooner or later you behave
in a violent manner. He seemed to know you very well.

GEORGIE

My God. Who would do that to me?

SALLY'S VOICE

Somebody who hates you.

GEORGIE

My God. Who is Harry Kellerman?

SALLY'S VOICE

Somebody who hates you. Maybe you behaved toward
him in a violent manner.

GEORGIE
(softly; very close to speaker)
Darling Sally. Sweetness. Warmness. How long have
you been seeing me? Two months—

SALLY'S VOICE

Three weeks.

GEORGIE

Three weeks, hasn't it been great?

> SALLY'S VOICE

Yes, sure, Georgie.

> GEORGIE

Loveliness. Goodness. Golden corn muffin. Don't
let this throw you. Do ya trust me?

> SALLY'S VOICE

Yes, sure, Georgie.

> GEORGIE

Then ace it outa your head . . .
> *(touching speaker tenderly)*
Candystore, Nesselrode, please; forget Harry
What's-his-name.

> SALLY'S VOICE

Kellerman. Said his conscience was bothering him
and he had to tell me. Warn me. Georgie, why should
somebody call me like that at four-thirty in the
morning, Georgie?

> GEORGIE

I'll kill him . . .

> SALLY'S VOICE

Georgie . . .

> GEORGIE

I'll find him and I'll kill him . . .

> SALLY'S VOICE

Georgie, you sound like you are about to behave in
a violent manner.

> GEORGIE

Sally . . .

> SALLY'S VOICE

Thing is, Georgie, it's five A.M., I have to get up for
work soon. I only called to tell you . . .

> GEORGIE
> *(moving quickly to speaker)*
Sally, wait a minute . . .

> SALLY'S VOICE

It's very late, I have to go now . . .

> GEORGIE

Sally, wait . . .

> SALLY'S VOICE

It's actually very late . . .

GEORGIE
See ya at Sid's tonight . . .

SALLY'S VOICE
Tonight, actually, I better just get to sleep early tonight . . .

GEORGIE
Hey, Sally—

SALLY'S VOICE
It's very late now—

GEORGIE
Sally, you know me—

SALLY'S VOICE
I don't really know you, Georgie, I've only slept with you . . .

GEORGIE
(grabs speaker in both hands)
Sally, Cuteness, wait—

Speaker "clicks" loudly in his hands.
Speaker webbing; silence.
He slowly lets go of speaker; a moment, then he leaps up onto chinning bar.

GEORGIE
(chinning up and down)
Un-daunted . . . In-domitable . . . In . . .
    (he cannot lift himself, straining)
In . . . in . . . in . . .

He drops one arm. Hangs limply, one-handed, from the bar, dead weight; spinning slightly; he whispers.

GEORGIE
vincible . . .

He looks down to see: Himself lying on couch in DR. MOSES' *office. We move slowly down to him as he speaks . . .*

GEORGIE
Oh, Dr. Cute-person, do you read me? Irony, man,
do you dig the irony here? For years, I can't see a girl
more than once, twice, tops thrice, before splitting.
Unable to sustain with a lady a relationship.
    (sits up)
So now maybe I'm really ready to sustain and the
Mad Bomber, Attila the telephone, is calling up every
broad I boff and spreading the rotten on me . . .
    (rises, comes to desk)
Six days, Sol . . . six days and he's cost me at least four
chicks, two recording contracts, and a genuine English
butler. Single-handed, the guy's layin' the Black

Plague on me, givin' me the bad mouth all over town—Who would hate me so much? Whaddya think, doc? What should I—

Sudden sound of Big Band fanfare.
DR. MOSES *sits calmly at his desk, his hands folded, singing in the voice of Ray Charles; the Rayettes and a full band back him up offscreen.*

> DR. MOSES
> *(singing)*
"Don't tell me yo' troubles
I got troubles of my own
Don't tell me yo' troubles
Jus' leave me alone . . .
Go on home,
Tell it to a friend . . . "

> GEORGIE

Hey, Moses . . . hey, Moses, knock it off

> DR. MOSES
> *(singing)*
"Oh ya say yo' sweet love left ya,
Well whaddya think about me?
I got the same ol' heartbreaks
The same ol' miseries . . . "

> GEORGIE
> *(shouting)*
Doc, cut it out, will ya—?!

Music stops abruptly.

> DR. MOSES

What is it, George . . .

GEORGIE *is silent. He sits at the edge of the desk.*

> DR. MOSES   *(cont)*

Tell me what is wrong, George . . .

> GEORGIE

Doc, it is Cookie-jar time. It is time to put me in the Cookie jar.

> DR. MOSES

Cookie jar . . . ?

> GEORGIE

I mean the New York State Cookie jar, buster. Doc, certain things . . . certain things have been happening. Doc, I see a lotta shows that aren't listed. I mean they are not in the *T.V. Guide*, Sol . . . Last coupla nights, I get aholda Chomsky, we drive around in my limo . . .

figure if I'm movin' I can sleep, see . . .
    (pacing in front of desk)
Started thinkin' about King Lear last night. Old cat
in the forest, flippin' out . . . Shakespeare's a winner,
man . . . those sonnets, I tell
ya, the right music and they'd all be in the top ten . . .
King Lear, alone in the forest, see . . . he looks up at
the sky, he says . . . "Oh, God, let me not be mad . . . "
    (turns to MOSES; *quietly)*
Doc, I gotta know, am I gettin' crazy . . . ? Help me;
help me, oh Wizard, for I lie busted in the Yellow
Brick Road . . .

No reply; DR. MOSES *watches thoughtfully.*

GEORGIE   (cont)

Chrissakes, *say* something, will ya?! Isn't this your
table? I want service!

DR. MOSES

Calmly, George. It is clearly the Kellerman problem,
and the resulting lack of sleep. Your dreams seek other
stages on which to play. Our attempt here, of course,
must be to embrace reality, to welcome it, to—

GEORGIE

Why should I do anything for reality; it never done
nothin' for *me* . . .

DR. MOSES
(gesturing to clock)

We shall have to continue tomorrow, George—

GEORGIE

Not tomorrow, *now*—

DR. MOSES

George, I have waiting outside another patient—

GEORGIE
(sits on couch)

Not yet. Gimme another hour. I'll buy off your next
nut. Stick with me today and there's an extra grand
in it for ya—

CLOSE ON *a taxi meter attached to the head of the couch; angle widens to
reveal* DR. MOSES *in leather jacket and driver's cap; he pushes down the
metal flag, and the meter begins to tick: snickety-snick, snickety-snick . . .*

DR. MOSES

Forty-five cents for the first mile, ten cents for
each additional quarter mile; inquire for special
out-of-town rates . . .

CLOSE ON GEORGIE, *meter ticking offscreen; he shakes his head, rises from couch as angle widens to reveal* DR. MOSES, *who approaches him with prescription blank.*

> **DR. MOSES**
> I have here a prescription for sleeping pills, George;
> it is essential tonight that you—

> **GEORGIE**
> Pills. Pills. I come to you in flames, and you treat me
> for sunburn.
> *(picks up guitar case, grabs magazine off desk)*
> Who the hell needs you anyway? All I need is my
> songs—you and your goddamn pills—
> *(GEORGIE heads for door . . .)*
> I've *had* it, Moses, we're *finished.* Sweetheart, the
> Viennese Waltz is over . . .

> **SCREAMING AUDIENCE**   *(O.S.)*
> Peace, *now!* Peace, *now!* Peace, *now!*

We move down to a packed audience at the Fillmore East screaming . . .
We zoom into a light show, bursting purple amoebas, exploding flowers, at center the words "CAPTAIN LOVE."

> **SCREAMING AUDIENCE**   *(cont)*
> Love, *now!* Love *now!* Love, *now!* . . .

Spotlight at right as CAPTAIN LOVE *himself ambles toward microphone, raunchy clothes, beard and sandals, followed by four similarly dressed* SIDE-MEN.
CAPTAIN LOVE *holds up one lazy finger. The roaring crowd is instantly silent, not a breath.*
CAPTAIN LOVE *nods to* SIDEMEN *and the stage suddenly explodes with thwanging, pounding electric guitars—*

> **CAPTAIN LOVE**   *(singing)*
> "Now Bunky told Lucille, go walkin' out in the rain
> And don't come back till ya bring me somethin'
> .To put inside my vein
> One more ride
> Lucille, your man wants one more ride
> World of sunshine waitin' for me
> On the other side . . . "

GEORGIE *stands in aisle at back of theater, whispering . . .*

> **GEORGIE**
> Number four on the Rock Chart, climbin' like an eagle . . .

> **CAPTAIN LOVE**
> " . . . Then Lucille made him a little bit o'gumbo

And put it in the pot
She ground some glass up in there too
So he'd forget her not
On his last ride . . . "

GEORGIE *mouthing words to his song, tapping out beat on guitar case.*

CAPTAIN LOVE
" . . . World of sunshine waitin' for him
On the other side . . .
. . . Well, doctor, doctor, doctor, doctor
I'm sure I'm about to die
If you can't help me live a little longer
Won't you help me go out high
One more ride . . . "

CAPTAIN LOVE *stops, points to back of theater . . .*

CAPTAIN LOVE
Chillen', look who we got here, we got Soloway, his
own self—

Spotlight swings onto GEORGIE'S *face and the crowd cheers. He nods awkwardly . . .*

CAPTAIN LOVE
Come swing yo' ax, chile, c'mon . . .

GEORGIE
(quietly, shrugging)
Not a performer, I . . . just write the songs, I . . .

CAPTAIN LOVE
Chillen', whatta we want—?

SCREAMING AUDIENCE
Solowayyyyyy!

CAPTAIN LOVE
An' when we wan' him?

SCREAMING AUDIENCE
Nowwwwwwww . . . !

GEORGIE *moves forward hesitantly at first, then, guitar case held aloft, trots down the aisle to the screaming sound of—*

Soloway, nowwwwwwwww . . . !

GEORGIE *comes up onstage, spotlights flaring into our eyes,* SIDEMEN *singing;* CAPTAIN LOVE *and* GEORGIE *lean close to each other, whispering . . .*

GEORGIE
Bernie, how ya doin' . . . ?

CAPTAIN LOVE

Twenty-three hundred paid admissions at sixty
percent, Georgie . . .
(joins SIDEMEN, *singing)*
"Doctor, all I ask is one more ride
 World of sunshine waitin' for me
 On the other side . . . "
(whispering)
C'mon, Georgie, go . . .
(singing)
" . . . Now Bunky's in a pine box
 In the buryin' yard
 Lucille walks the streets, she's lookin' good
 But lookin' hard . . .

GEORGIE *closes his eyes, listening, picking up the beat . . .*

CAPTAIN LOVE

"for one more ride . . . "

He begins to join them, softly . . .

CAPTAIN LOVE and GEORGIE

"Mister, would you like one more ride
 World of sunshine waitin' for you
 On the other side . . . "

GEORGIE *smiles, slowly enjoying his guitar, the sound of their voices . . . he
begins to wail the song with them, ecstatic in the flaring spotlight . . .*

GEORGIE and CAPTAIN LOVE

"Hey, did this really happen
 Or was it all a dream
 Look down deep inside yourself
 You're gonna hear somebody scream
 For one more ride . . . "

Dissolve through GEORGIE'S *face to a distant* GEORGIE *playing harmonica,
crossing Fifth toward G.M. Building, two* A.M., *voices continue, O.S. . . .*

"Everybody wants just one more . . .
 Yeah, one more, one more, one more. Yeah, yeah,
 one more, one more . . . "

Dazzling chandelier in G.M. lobby; we move down to SUSAN. *She is seated
on the shimmering hood of a display Cadillac at center of lobby, dressed
entirely in lavender, including a lavender radio on a shoulder strap which
softly throbs rock music. Wailing* VOICES *fading under . . .*

" . . . one more, one more, one more . . . "

SUSAN

Georgie, I would like to know what is happening . . .

GEORGIE *at entrance; they are a great distance from each other, their voices echoing across the bright marble lobby.*

> SUSAN   *(cont)*
>
> I've been waiting two hours . . . Georgie, this is hostile behavior . . .

> GEORGIE
>
> Baby . . .

> SUSAN
>
> Like you could consider my goddamn dignity . . .

> GEORGIE
>
> Baby . . .

> SUSAN
>
> Like you always call after midnight, and I always come over . . . but I don't want you to think you can just always . . .

He rushes toward her, takes her hands, slides her off the Cadillac into his arms . . .

> SUSAN
>
> Oh, Georgie . . .

> GEORGIE
> *(mystified, trying to remember her)*
>
> Baby . . .

> SUSAN
>
> Georgie, it's been so long . . .

> GEORGIE
> *(a sudden inspiration)*
>
> Oregon seven, six, three, seven, one—Susan
> *(holds her face in his hands)*
> Susan, do ya still love me?

> SUSAN
>
> I . . . yes, I do, Georgie .

> GEORGIE
> *(takes her hand, leading her briskly to escalator)*
> C'mon, we'll drink to that . . .

> SUSAN
>
> Thing is, Georgie . . . do you . . . like do you love—

> GEORGIE
>
> I'll get you a drink on the top of the world . . .

> SUSAN
>
> Georgie, I am concerned about our relationship . . .
> *(she stops at base of escalator)*
> Georgie . . . do you think I'm dumb?

GEORGIE

Whaddya mean . . . ?

SUSAN

Do you go around . . . like do you go around telling people that you think I'm dumb . . . ? This fella called me, he said—

GEORGIE

Kellerman—

SUSAN

—you told him I was dumb and like the only reason you see me is to—

GEORGIE
(grips her arm tightly)

I'll kill him—

SUSAN

Is it true, Georgie; is that what you say to people—?

GEORGIE

I'll find him and I'll kill him—

SUSAN

I . . . I think I better go now . . .

GEORGIE
(still holding her arm, steps onto escalator)

Susan, wait, c'mon . . .

SUSAN
(frees herself, starts across lobby)

This has not been a pleasant evening . . .

GEORGIE
(escalator starts to carry him up)

Hey, Susan . . . don't leave . . .

SUSAN
(at door)

And don't call me so late anymore . . .

GEORGIE
(trying to come down escalator)

Don't leave, not tonight; I need you here . . .

SUSAN
(turns radio up, blasting rock)

Like . . . uh . . . like goodbye, Georgie . . .

GEORGIE
(still fighting escalator)
See, the people I call after twelve, those are the important people . . .

She is gone. He stops fighting, escalator carries him up . . .

GEORGIE
In the wee hours, Susan; in the small, enormous, hours . . .

GEORGIE *tapping out staccato rhythm on guitar case, singing softly; escalator carrying him up and away from us . . .*

GEORGIE
"Who, who, who is Harry Kellerman . . .
Who would do such a thing to his fellerman . . .?
yeah, five chicks
And he gave 'em all a jingle . . . "

GEORGIE, *in elevator, now rising . . .*

GEORGIE
" . . . he wants me alone
And he wants me single . . . "

GEORGIE *out of elevator and down fiftieth-floor hallway, passing many past and present photographs of a smiling* GEORGIE, *framed gold records, etc., tapping out rhythm on case, singing softly . . .*

" . . . hey, the last to go have gone
Even ol' Oregon,
Alone up here in heaven
And even old Oregon-seven
Has split . . . "

A flash bulb flares out screen, GEORGIE *turns to:*
PHOTOGRAPHER *darting about at other end of hallway, sound of cheap dance band, laughter, shouting . . .*

PHOTOGRAPHER
Everybody, *please* — closer together—

GEORGIE *is joined by young* GLORIA *in wedding dress, and then by his mother,* MARGOT, *and his father,* LEON; *all smiling, all posing, bulbs flashing through scene....*

GLORIA
(whispering)
Is it what you want, Georgie . . . ?

GEORGIE
Whaddya mean? What?

GLORIA
Being married, Georgie . . .

GEORGIE
Sure. Perfect. Forever, Gloria . . .

GLORIA
Forever, Georgie . . . our whole lives . . . till the day we die . .

Framed photograph of scene we have just witnessed, GEORGIE *is twenty-three years old, wearing a tuxedo; sound of staccato tapping on guitar case. Angle widens to include the older* GEORGIE, *leaning against wall next to photograph, guitar case in his arms, tapping out rhythm, humming "One More Ride," softly . . .*

Sound of distant piano music from upstairs, same melody but now in the form of a simple, beginner's piano duet . . .

He goes down hallway and starts up spiral staircase, following the piano music; his mother's voice singing . . .

MARGOT   *(O.S.)*
"Happy, dancing fingers
  Skipping o'er the keys . . . "

We are moving slowly across the main room to MARGOT *and an eight-year-old* GEORGIE, *seated with their backs to us, against skyline.*

MARGOT   *(O.S.)*
"...lightly as a butterfly
 Gently as the breeze
 One more time
 Let us do our lesson one more time . . . "
    (as they continue to play)
The melody's in the left, George . . . the left, son,
don't be afraid . . .

We are next to her on the piano bench . . .

MARGOT
" . . . Music is a mountain
 Let us see how high we all can climb . . . "

Sudden, harsh piano chords on cut to:

GEORGIE, *on piano bench hitting chords of "One More Ride," fiercely using the chords to bring himself to reality; rises, moving anxiously amongst instruments in music alcove, looking for distraction, a few whacks at his bongo drums, a quick run on his vibraphone, short riff on one of his harmonicas, anxiously grabs up remote-control TV unit, clicking it on expectantly, sitting down to watch. The set greets him with a blank, white, hissing screen. He begins to click from channel to channel and is greeted by one blind white eye after the other . . .*

GEORGIE
(softly, seducing his beloved)
C'mon . . . c'mon; TV, baby . . . anything . . . the
Star-Spangled Banner, anything . . .

Sound of crashing wave . . .
Sound of calliope music, noisy crowds . . .
GEORGIE *turns to look up at the top of the stairs—*

We are looking up old wooden stairs to the Coney Island Boardwalk. A young
GIRL *appears at the top of the stairs wearing Forties-style swimsuit running*
down the stairs toward us, her hand outstretched toward us . . .

The GIRL *laughs, grabs the hand of eighteen-year-old* GEORGIE, *running*
with him down the crowded beach, running away from us through the
crowds, hopping over sunbathers, dodging vendors, circling around ballplay-
ers, garbage cans, etc . . .

GEORGIE   *(O.S.)*
Hey, doc; Ruthie Tresh. Pretty, pretty Ruthie Tresh.
Red hair and lime-green sweaters. A candy store of a girl . . .
(strumming banjo, quietly, slow tempo, remembering
the words)
" . . .I'm singin' goodbye to goodbye,
Farewell to farewell,
This time I'm stayin' right here with ya
Don't ya worry
'Cause I never would kid ya . . . "

The two young figures running further and further away from us . . .

GEORGIE   *(O.S.)*
" . . . goodbye to travelin' with sorrow
Hello to see ya tomorrow . . . "

RUTHIE *and* GEORGIE *running under boardwalk, rippling through the*
striped shadows, guitar continues under...

GEORGIE   *(O.S.)*
I used to have the cleanest sneakers in the neighborhood . . .
I was eighteen and I knew how to live forever . . .

RUTHIE *standing naked in shadows next to battered upright piano in young*
GEORGIE'S *first apartment; dawn light falls in stripes across the one bare*
room. Near the piano is an ancient convertible couch-bed which is supposed
to fold out in sections across the floor; the third section is, at the moment,
refusing to fold out. GEORGIE *is out of sight, under the bed, trying to fix it.*
They speak in whispers . . .

RUTHIE
Georgie . . . ?

GEORGIE

Yes . . .

RUTHIE

Georgie, where are you? I can't see you.

GEORGIE

I am under the couch.

RUTHIE

Oh.

GEORGIE

I'm right under the couch here.

RUTHIE

Georgie . . . ?

GEORGIE

Yes . . . ?

RUTHIE

Why are you under the couch?

GEORGIE

Yes, I want to explain to you about that. There's this unfortunate thing that happened. See, this couch, Ruthie, this is a fold-out couch.

RUTHIE

Oh.

GEORGIE

And it won't fold out. That's the unfortunate thing.

RUTHIE

Oh.

GEORGIE

So what I'm doing is I'm trying to fix it. That's why I'm under it.

A rattling of metal from under the couch.

GEORGIE

Ruthie . . . You O.K.?

RUTHIE

Yes, fine. Well, actually I'm cold.

GEORGIE

Oh. Look, there's a blanket on the couch.

RUTHIE

Fine.

(*wraps blanket around herself; sits on piano bench on the other side of the room*)

Thank you. That's fine now.

Rattling, banging, from under the couch.

RUTHIE

How's it going?

GEORGIE

Well, it seems to be something with the spring.
You O.K.?

RUTHIE

Yes. It's just I was scared for a moment because when
I came out of the bathroom nobody was here. For a
second I thought you'd gone away.

GEORGIE

I didn't go away. I'm right here. There's just
something wrong with the spring. I'm really very
sorry about this. This is a very unfortunate thing.
This never happened before. It usually just folds out.

RUTHIE

Oh.

GEORGIE

It usually just folds right out.

RUTHIE

Have you folded it out a lot?

GEORGIE

Huh?

RUTHIE

The couch. I mean, have there been a lot of people
here who you fold it out for?

GEORGIE

Well, y'know, I mean—

RUTHIE

Listen, that's all right—

GEORGIE

Well, y'know, people come and I fold it out—

RUTHIE

That's all right—

GEORGIE

That's the way it goes—

RUTHIE

Of course.

A large piece of ceiling plaster crashes on the floor between them.

RUTHIE

Georgie, the ceiling is coming down.

GEORGIE

Oh.

RUTHIE

Big chunks of it.

Second piece of plaster smashes down.

RUTHIE

That was another one.

GEORGIE

I'm really very sorry about this. This never happened before.

RUTHIE

Here comes another one.

Crash of plaster.

RUTHIE

It's really coming down a lot, Georgie.

GEORGIE

Well, I better fix this first. And then I'll come out and look at the ceiling.

RUTHIE

O.K. But it's really coming down.
    (puts blanket over her head for protection)
Georgie, really a lot of people? Girls. I mean;
many, many?

GEORGIE

Well, y'know, life—

RUTHIE

I'm sorry. I have no right to ask. I was hoping not many, many. Just some.

Crash of plaster.

RUTHIE

Oh, God. It's really coming down. Plaster everywhere and I've never made love to anybody before.

GEORGIE

Nobody?

RUTHIE

No, not anybody and now the ceiling is coming down and the couch won't fold out and I'll get pregnant.

GEORGIE

Oh.

RUTHIE

A piece of the ceiling will fall on my head and I will
be dead.

(she begins to cry)

GEORGIE

Ruthie . . . Ruthie, the reason why this couch doesn't
fold out is because I never folded it out before; for
anybody. I've only slept on it alone, unfolded. Alone
and unfolded. I want you to know that.

(pause)

Ruthie, if this lovemaking thing is so terrific, then
how come I fixed this couch five minutes ago and I
am still lying here under it with my old socks?

A crash of plaster on the floor.

RUTHIE

Georgie . . .

Crash of plaster; then another.

RUTHIE

Georgie, can I come under there with you? Because I
think the ceiling is going to kill me.

GEORGIE

Yes, of course.

*She hobbles across the room wrapped in the blanket; disappears under the
couch. We hear their whispered voices.*

GEORGIE

Hello.

RUTHIE

Hello.

GEORGIE

Ruthie, I love you.

RUTHIE

You don't have to.

GEORGIE

I know I don't have to. But I do.

RUTHIE

That's good. Because I love you too, Georgie.

GEORGIE

Forever, Ruthie, always . . .

RUTHIE

Yes, Georgie, forever, always . . .

A crash of plaster.

RUTHIE

Hold me, Georgie . . .

A crash of plaster, then another, then several pieces at once.

RUTHIE

Hold me, Georgie, hold me . . . the sky is falling, the sky is falling . . .

Dissolve through falling plaster to oncoming subway train in tunnel beneath the city; silence, except for upbeat guitar strum and young GEORGIE *singing happily . . .*

GEORGIE'S VOICE

"I'm singin'
Goodbye to goodbye
Farewell to farewell
This time I'm stayin' right here with ya
Don't ya worry 'cause I never would kid ya . . ."

GEORGIE *and* RUTHIE *at far end of empty subway car.* RUTHIE *is stretched out on one long seat;* GEORGIE *is sitting up, strumming his old guitar; three* A.M. *on a summer night; gently whirring ceiling fans and* GEORGIE'S *quiet voice . . .*

GEORGIE

" . . . goodbye to travelin' with sorrow,
Hello to see ya tomorrow,
Singin' m'leave you never,
Singin' m'sweet forever
Song . . .
Forever . . . forever . . . "

RUTHIE

I love your songs. They make me cry.

GEORGIE

Ruthie; just you, and writin' my songs. That's all I need in the world. Jesus, school; I haven't shown up for a month.

Continues humming melody . . .

RUTHIE

Neither has my period.

The humming stops.

RUTHIE

Well, I thought I better tell you.

GEORGIE

Don't worry, honey.

RUTHIE

What does that mean?

GEORGIE

Don't worry about a thing, honey.

RUTHIE

What does that mean?

Young GEORGIE *smiles reassuringly . . .*

GEORGIE'S VOICE

And the fact is, Dr. Moses, I had no idea what it meant
at all . . .

Young GEORGIE *looks down at:*
The table in his parents' kitchen, 1948; a security still-life; checkered oil-
cloth, bowl of fruit, old and pleasant coffeepot on tile trivet, chattering toast-
er; well-polished napkin holder; some small account ledgers, eggs, bagels,
bialies, and permanence.

GEORGIE'S VOICE

There was nothing else to do but go directly to my
parents' kitchen table . . . where all decisions have
been made since the beginning of my life, since
the beginning of time . . . where it is not insane to
believe that, over a second helping of pot roast,
the Magna Carta was signed . . .

His parents, LEON *and* MARGOT SOLOWAY, *are busily eating breakfast and*
reading newspapers. We will not see young GEORGIE *in this sequence; they*
will look at us when they talk to him.

GEORGIE

Here they are, doctor. Here they are as they have
always been . . .

LEON

Oh, boy. Harry Truman makes me nervous. Oh, boy.

MARGOT
(looks up at us from newspaper)
Georgie. Danny Ackerman.

GEORGIE

Who?

MARGOT

Leon. Danny Ackerman.

LEON

Who?

MARGOT

Danny Ackerman. His heart. Poof.

LEON

Who?

GEORGIE

Here is Leon Soloway . . .

As LEON *begins elaborate ritual of preparing and lighting cigar* . . .

GEORGIE

On the floor below us is his restaurant, "Leon's Ports
of Call; Food from Far and Near," seven-twenty-four
Ocean Avenue, where occupancy by more than
forty-two people is dangerous, unlawful, and
highly unlikely . . . Look at his eyes. He is dreaming
of a larger restaurant. This is twenty years ago.
He is still dreaming . . .

LEON *picks up newspaper,* "The Brooklyn Eagle"; *shaking his head* . . .

GEORGIE

Soon he will try to talk to me. He has had trouble
talking to me, since the day he noticed I was taller
than he was. You will notice that he talks directly
to my chest, which is where my head used to be when
I was twelve . . .

LEON *leans toward us, poking newspaper* . . .

LEON

Georgie, look at this. Scarlotti's Café. Neptune
Avenue. My competition. Forty tables. Can you
imagine, Georgie? Can you imagine what they take
in there, one night, a place like that?

MARGOT

Danny Ackerman. You know, Leon. From the
Democratic Club.

LEON

Oh, yeah. What about him?

MARGOT
(*pokes newspaper*)

On his way to the airport yesterday. Poof. In the taxi
cab. No warning. Perfect health in a taxicab. His heart
on the way to Cleveland, Ohio, on business.

LEON

Danny Ackerman. I don't believe it.

MARGOT

A life is here; a life is over.

GEORGIE
(very quietly, as they remain buried in newspapers)
Pop . . . Ma . . . there are certain decisions . . . which I
have reached . . . about N.Y.U. and being a musicologist . . .

LEON

Danny Ackerman. We just saw him.

MARGOT

Sure. At the beach. Running in place.

LEON

Running. Jumping. Swimming.

GEORGIE
(very quietly)
. . . and about this girl, and writing songs and . . .

MARGOT

A young man. He couldn't have been more than what?

LEON

Sixty-four. Sixty-five, tops. He was—

GEORGIE
(loudly)
Pop . . . Ma . . . !

They both turn toward us. He proceeds quietly . . .

GEORGIE

I'll tell you why I came home this morning . . .

LEON

To eat.

MARGOT

No, Leon, it's his birthday. For what other occasion would
he leave his garret where God knows what's going on?

LEON

His birthday? Happy birthday, Georgie.

MARGOT

Nineteen years old and playing an out-of-tune piano in
a nightclub where God knows—

GEORGIE

It's not a nightclub, it's a kind of restaurant, see, it's—

MARGOT

An out-of-tune piano is a sin to the ears. Happy
birthday, Georgie.

LEON

Nineteen years old. Look at the face on that kid.
The intelligence in the eyes, Margot. Those are
not nineteen-year-old eyes, Margot.

GEORGIE

There's something I wish to discuss with you both,
frankly... First, about school—

The phone rings, MARGOT *leaves kitchen to answer it.*

LEON

Georgie, what about school? What's up?

GEORGIE

Well, I wanted to tell you both together . . .

MARGOT
(on phone)

Hello, Blanche . . .

LEON

Tell me; I got to go to the restaurant.

MARGOT

Blanche. Danny Ackerman.

LEON

What is it, Georgie?

MARGOT

Danny Ackerman. You know, from the Democratic Club.

LEON

You need some money?

GEORGIE

No. No money, Pop.

MARGOT

His heart, Blanche, on the way to Cleveland, Ohio . . .

LEON

Well, what is it, Georgie?

GEORGIE

Some things, some things . . .

LEON

Well, what is it? You got somebody pregnant, you quit
school, what?

GEORGIE

Yes.

LEON

Yes what? What yes?

GEORGIE

Both.

LEON

Both what?

GEORGIE

Both of what you just said.

LEON

What did I just say, what . . . ? Oh. Oh boy. You quit school *and* somebody's pregnant?

GEORGIE

Right.

LEON

Oh boy.

GEORGIE

Well, I want to—

LEON

Don't tell your mother. She won't understand.

GEORGIE

So I'm—

LEON

Somebody you want to get married to?

GEORGIE

Well, I was thinking—

LEON

You don't have to. I know a doctor. New Jersey. I'll fix it.

GEORGIE

Really?

LEON

Both waitresses at the restaurant. They run a shuttle, practically, to New Jersey.

GEORGIE

Thing is, Pop, I was thinking maybe—

LEON

You tell your mother, I'll kill you. She won't understand. She lives with your Aunt Blanche on Mars. Your sister Phyllis had an abortion her last year at Hunter College.

GEORGIE

I didn't know that. *Phyllis.*

LEON

Yup. You tell your mother, I'll kill you.

GEORGIE

Phyllis?

LEON

What about school? You don't want to be a whaddyacallit?

GEORGIE

Musicologist. Definitely not.

LEON

What would you like better?

GEORGIE

Song writing, maybe, I—

LEON

We're having dinner at Phyllis' Sunday night. You look funny at your sister, I'll kill you.

GEORGIE

I won't.

LEON

Here comes your mother . . . come tonight, after, the dinner rush; we'll work it out.

MARGOT

Leon. Blanche wants to talk to you.

LEON *leaves kitchen.* MARGOT *sits opposite us, leans toward us; very quietly.*

MARGOT

Georgie, I told Blanche to keep him on the phone. You got a girl pregnant, right?

GEORGIE

Well—

MARGOT

Oh, boy. Garrets and nightclubs. Well, I know a doctor in New Jersey. Don't worry.

GEORGIE

Really?

MARGOT

He was good enough for Phyllis. Don't worry.

GEORGIE

Phyllis?

MARGOT

You tell your father, I'll break your neck. He doesn't know the world outside that restaurant.

GEORGIE

O.K.

MARGOT

When he leaves for work, we'll talk. Arrangements.
(she smiles, warmly)
You're young, Georgie; don't worry . . . Don't worry,
you'll be free.

Sound of clattering roller-coaster, calliope . . . cut to:

RUTHIE*; table in crowded, noisy snack bar on Coney Island Boardwalk; twilight. She is looking directly at us, holding half an egg-salad sandwich in her
hand. She watches us for several moments; then—*

GEORGIE

You O.K., Ruthie?

RUTHIE

Yeah. It's just I thought we'd get married, Georgie.

GEORGIE

Yeah, me too. But, see, with school and everything . . .

RUTHIE

O.K.

GEORGIE

Thing is, when I finish school—

RUTHIE

Do you love me, Georgie?

GEORGIE

Sure I do. Now, don't worry, there's a doctor—

RUTHIE

That's O.K., I told my sister. She got me this doctor in
New Jersey.

GEORGIE

Oh.

RUTHIE
(puts sandwich down)
I gotta go home now. I told my sister I'd be home by
ten. She worries a lot now.

GEORGIE

Oh.

*She rises, we follow her down the row of busy tables to where the snack bar
opens onto the boardwalk. She turns to us, begins to back away from us down
the busy boardwalk .*

RUTHIE

I'll be in New Jersey a coupla days, Georgie .

GEORGIE

Uh-huh.

RUTHIE

Will ya wait for me, Georgie?

GEORGIE

Sure.

RUTHIE

Georgie, sometimes I think . . .

GEORGIE

I can't hear you, Ruthie.

RUTHIE

I think sometimes you never got out from under that
couch.

*She turns, walks away from us down the wide, busy boardwalk . . . We hear
a guitar downbeat, then the older* GEORGIE *quietly, half-humming . . .*

GEORGIE'S VOICE

"Hey, I'm singin'
 Goodbye to goodbye
 Farewell to farewell
 This time I'm stayin' right here with ya
 Don't ya worry 'cause I never would kid ya . . .
 Hey, goodbye to travelin' with sorrow
 Hello to see ya tomorrow . . .

*Coney Island skyline; night; including Ferris wheel, roller coaster, a mass of
lights and noise.*

GEORGIE'S VOICE

"Singin' m'sweet forever
 Singin' m'leave ya never
 Singin' m'sweet forever song . . ."

As old guitar continues under.

GEORGIE'S VOICE

Hey, Ruthie Tresh. Red hair and lime-green sweaters.
A candy store of a girl. Heard she got married to a
neurologist and lives in Forest Hills . . . where the
sky never falls.

DR. MOSES' VOICE

This is a machine speaking to you . . .

Cut from Coney Island skyline to skyline through GEORGIE'S *window.*

DR. MOSES' VOICE

. . . when you hear the machine go "beep-beep," you
will please leave your name, your telephone
number, and your message . . .

GEORGIE *is seated, as before, on bottom step of stairway, holding the old gui-*
tar; speaker-phone opposite.

DR. MOSES' VOICE

. . . "beep-beep" . . .

GEORGIE

Beep-beep. Right. Gotcha. Doc, that's the clearest
thing you've said to me in seven years—

MARTY'S VOICE

(shouting; sound of tapping on glass)
Georgie! Georgie-*baby!* We're here! We love you!

Glass enclosure around spiral staircase; MARTY *and* LEMUEL *within it.*
MARTY *shouts happily, waving legal documents,* LEMUEL *stares transfixed*
at pane of glass.

MARTY   *(cont)*

Oh, Georgie-baby! We're here! We love you! Right, Lemuel?

LEMUEL

Love .

GEORGIE

How'd you get in here ?

MARTY

On the wings of joy, Georgie, the wings of joy and happiness!

LEMUEL

Joy, happiness.

GEORGIE *goes to staircase, his anger building* . . .

GEORGIE

What the hell're you doing here?!

MARTY

You said to come, Georgie. Your production manager
called me—said you wanted to talk about a demo
with my boy—

LEMUEL

Love.

MARTY

—then he called the doorman, told him to—

GEORGIE

What production manager?

                              MARTY
Kellerman, he said, Harry Kell—

                              GEORGIE
Marty, go away . . .

                              MARTY
Now these contracts are very rough, but I'm sure we can—

                              GEORGIE
Away, Marty . . . go away . . .

                              MARTY
Georgie-baby—
          (*something in* GEORGIE'S *eyes makes him begin to retreat*
          backward down the stairs, shaking his head)
Humiliation. Hundred percent.

                              GEORGIE
Away, Marty, *now!*

LEMUEL, *unaware of any trouble, has stayed at the top of the stairs, smiling*
benignly at GEORGIE. MARTY *grabs his arm, pulls him down the stairs after*
him . . .

                              MARTY
Come on, Lemuel . . . he doesn't like white singers ;
it's not your fault.
          (*shouts up*)
White is beautiful!

                              LEMUEL
Beautiful, peace . . .

                              MARTY
Goddamn racist!

                              LEMUEL
Peace . . .

                              GEORGIE
          (*raises old guitar, shouting*)
Marty, get outta here—!

                              MARTY
          (*very quietly, pointing up*)
Look at you. Look at you, Soloway. You're crazy . . .
          (*as they go down hallway toward elevator*)
He told me about you. You're crazy . . .

Smoked mirror over fireplace; GEORGIE *sees himself holding guitar over his*
head . . . frightened by his own violent image . . . suddenly drops guitar as if
it were burning his hand . . .

DR. MOSES' VOICE
(speaker on terrace)
This is a machine speaking to you . . . you will please
leave your name, your phone number, and your message . . .

GEORGIE
(softly)
Listen, doc . . . *my* machine wants to meet *your*
machine ; think we can work something out?

GEORGIE *in terrace doorway, punches "off" button on speaker; his fingers
trotting nervously on speaker buttons . . .*

GEORGIE   *(cont)*
Who's around? Who's up? Who do I know?
   (punching out number on terrace speaker-phone)
—m'old buddy, yeah, yeah . . .

VOICE FROM SPEAKER
Yallow! Midtown!

GEORGIE
Hey, Midtown Drugs . . . How the hell *are* ya,
Midtown Drugs?

VOICE FROM SPEAKER
Oh; Mr. Soloway . . .

GEORGIE
Yeah. Send me up an overdose of anything.

VOICE FROM SPEAKER
What'll it be tonight, Mr. Soloway?

GEORGIE
The reason for living, some bubblebath and a comb.

VOICE FROM SPEAKER
Mr. Soloway, we're kinda busy here, if there's nothin'
I can send you, I—

GEORGIE
Matter of fact, I need a shave. I could use some shaving
equipment.

VOICE FROM SPEAKER
Fine. What'll it be? Blades, razor, cream—

GEORGIE
First thing I'm gonna need is a face. You can't shave
without a face.

GEORGIE *closes his eyes against a sudden blast of sunlight.*

GEORGIE
Midtown, send me a face . . .

An infant cries . . .

A penthouse terrace of the past, ten years earlier. A dazzling Sunday afternoon. Sunday church bells chime, we see his two children opposite; LEONARD, *six months old in playpen next to picnic table, five-year-old* PAUL *seated at table, leaning toward playpen with baby bottle, Central Park in background.*

GEORGIE'S VOICE
(singing softly, working on song lyrics)

"Free . . . free as the sun in the . . .
Free as a bird in the . . .

CLOSE ON GEORGIE: *shaved and younger in same beach chair, guitar propped on his knees, music paper resting on guitar, writing, squinting with great concentration; steals a note of music from church bells.*

GEORGIE

" . . .free as a bird flyin' high . . .
 Free as a cloud in the sky . . . "
　　(stops singing)
Gloria, come out on the terrace. The sun is shining.
It's terrific.

GLORIA'S VOICE

I'm reading the papers, Georgie.

GEORGIE
(singing softly)

" . . . free as me rollin' by . . .
 In my Pontiac . . . new Pontiac . . .
 New Pontiac . . . "
　　(stops singing)
What's the connection between reading the papers and
not coming out on the terrace, Gloria?

GLORIA'S VOICE

I'm just reading the papers, Georgie.

GEORGIE
(singing)

"Free as a bird flyin' high . . . "
　　(quietly)
I would like to know what's the point of us having
this big, beautiful terrace with sun pouring onto it
if you're never going to use it, Gloria.

GLORIA'S VOICE

I *use* the terrace, Georgie.

GEORGIE

In all the time we've been here you've never been out
on the terrace. Will you tell me why is that?

We move back to kids; LEONARD, *two years old now in highchair at picnic table, banging spoon; seven-year-old* PAUL *at picnic table, eating sandwich, reading picture book.*

GLORIA'S VOICE
Just because we have a terrace is no reason that I have to feel obligated to the terrace to be out on it all the time.

GEORGIE
I am not asking you to *sleep* on the terrace or live on the terrace, Gloria. I am just asking you to come out and read the papers with me on it.
(sings anxiously)
" . . . free as the clouds in the sky . . . "
(silence; then . . .)
Gloria, I am going to ask you once more to come out on this terrace. Because I know that you will *love* and *enjoy* being on this terrace. You could probably get a nice tan. And then I am going to drop the subject.
(singing quietly)
" . . .free as me rollin' by . . . "

We move back to the now five-year-old LEONARD *and ten-year-old* PAUL, *messily eating ice cream at picnic table.*

GEORGIE
It would really be a peaceful way to spend the afternoon, Gloria; believe me . . .
(hums nervously for a moment)
Gloria, please come out on the terrace. There's iced coffee out here for you . . .

GLORIA *standing behind him in terrace doorway. They are bathed in sunlight . . .*

GLORIA
O.K. Here I am.

GEORGIE
(not turning to her)
Oh. Good You want some iced coffee?

GLORIA
No thank you. Did you marry me because I was pregnant?

GEORGIE
Huh?

GLORIA
I was just in there and I started to cry on the newspapers and I wondered if you married me because I was pregnant.

GEORGIE
Chrissakes, that was ten years ago . . .

GLORIA

Twelve. Did you?

GEORGIE

Twelve years ago and you're just asking me now?

GLORIA

I always meant to ask you.

GEORGIE

Chrissakes, Gloria . . . why, all of a sudden, *now* . . .

GLORIA

Because last night when you made love to me
you called me Sandra and two months ago you
called me Jan; and since your making love to me
is a rare enough occasion I wish you would at least
get my name straight. Because you were in
California on business for at least six months this
year and when you are here your eyes never look
into mine and suddenly just before I noticed that I
was crying all over the magazine section and I
wondered if you married me because I was pregnant.

GEORGIE

I married you because I loved you, Gloria.

GLORIA

And now?

GEORGIE

And now I got this problem. It's not you . . . I got this
problem about time . . .

GLORIA

I was sitting in there thinking about when you were
playing piano at the El Bambino. I was waiting on
tables a *year* before you noticed me . . .

GEORGIE

. . . see, it's like this house is full of time . . . time
keeps goin' by . . . I keep thinkin', how come I got
two kids and I'm only eighteen years old . . .

GLORIA

. . . one night we're closing up and I found you asleep
on the piano bench so I covered you up with a
checkered tablecloth . . .

GEORGIE

. . . it's nothin' personal, see . . . but our kids, these
goddamn kids, they keep tickin' at me like clocks . . .

GLORIA

... when you woke up you said "Who are you?" And I said, "Gloria DeCecco, I've been watching you sleep ... "

GEORGIE

... like goddamn *clocks*, those kids ... I get terrified ...

GLORIA

That was twelve years ago and sometimes at night I still watch you sleep. Forever, you said, forever and always. So when you were away last month I went to speak to Arnie; I mean, I had to talk about this to somebody. You know how he is when he listens, good old Arnie, he keeps puffin' on that cigar. I talked all night. And then I slept with him. I don't understand how I could do that, Georgie. I started thinking I was crazy. I mean, I love being married. I love you. I even like laundry ... What do you think, Georgie? Do you think I'm crazy?
    (pause)
Did you hear what I told you?

GEORGIE

Sure.

Church bells begin to chime nearby.

GEORGIE

You want some iced coffee, Gloria?

GLORIA

No thanks.

GEORGIE

What would you like?

GLORIA

A divorce.

Sudden blast of bullfight music as we cut to: a close-up of an old bronze plaque which reads, "Juarez, Mexico. Liberty and Justice." The music is "The Great Manolete; La Virgen de la Macarena," trumpets, flourishes, and a solid marching beat as we move back past a sleeping Mexican peasant sprawled on the Courthouse steps holding a dead chicken; twelve just-divorced people march down the steps in a strict column of two, led by a sweaty, white-suited, Mexican lawyer.

LAWYER
    (shouting)
Follow me, boys an' girls ...

GEORGIE *is marching shoulder to shoulder with a bouncy, short, sixty-year-old man. Church bells chime nearby.*

> **GEORGIE**
> That was fast.

> **BOUNCY MAN**
> Short and sweet. Wowie, baby.

> **GEORGIE**
> Just a couple seconds . . .

> **BOUNCY MAN**
> Wowie, baby.

> **GEORGIE**
> Listen, are these things really legal . . . it's hard to believe . . .
> *(holds up divorce certificate, full of huge purple*
> *seals and flourishes)*
> I mean, is this any good? Damn thing looks like
> a stage prop.

> **BOUNCY MAN**
> Sure it's good; you betcha, baby. That's it. Wowie . . .

As the music builds and they march away from us . . .

> **BOUNCY MAN**
> . . . they stamp the old seal on there, kid, and it's over
> for good. That's it, baby, forever . . . always . . . you're
> free . . .

Sudden silence.
Sound of distant traffic, a night wind.

CLOSE ON GEORGIE: *the present, on beach chair; opens his eyes.*

At the other end of the terrace, LEONARD *and* PAUL, *ages ten and fifteen, playing chess in the dark, at picnic table.*

GEORGIE, *rising quickly to go toward them . . .*

He stands on the empty terrace, alone, his hands on the glassy surface of the table; Fifth Avenue church bells chime distantly . . .

> **GEORGIE**
> Free . . .

A moment; then he puts on cowboy hat, quickly punching out number on speaker-phone. Then we move with GEORGIE *into the main room as a cold, nasal voice bleats on from all the speakers.*

> **VOICE FROM SPEAKERS**
> Hello. Good morning. Five-seven-o-two.

> **GEORGIE**
> Hello, Answering Service. What's the answer?

VOICE FROM SPEAKERS
Hello; five-seven-o-two; good morning.

GEORGIE
(going up stairs)
It's Mr. Soloway; any messages, darlin'?

VOICE FROM SPEAKERS
Mr. Soloway, Box F-18, good morning, F-18 . . .

He nods "good morning."

VOICE FROM SPEAKERS
You have a message on July Third from a Mr. Kellerman . . .

He freezes, midstairs.

VOICE FROM SPEAKERS
He says, "have a safe and sane Fourth; love, Harry . . . "
(silence for a moment)
There is nothing else for you, F-18.

GEORGIE
Sure there is . . . somebody *else* must've called, look
again, darlin'—

VOICE FROM SPEAKERS
There is no point in looking again . . . There is nothing
for you, F-18.

DR. MOSES' VOICE
Merry Christmas. Ho, ho.

GEORGIE *turns to:*

DR. MOSES, *standing in front of the fireplace dressed as Santa Claus, a sack
of toys over his shoulder. With the exception of his Viennese accent he is a
total Santa, red-nosed, round, and white-bearded.*

DR. MOSES
Merry Christmas, nutsy-person. Ho, ho.

GEORGIE
Dr. Moses . . . why're you dressed like that? That's crazy.

DR. MOSES
You with the cowboy hat, you're calling *me* crazy?
(opening sack)
O.K., Charley; what do you want for Christmas?

GEORGIE
But it's only July . . .

DR. MOSES
Sure. July. Christmas. Why not? Boy, you are *some*
crazy-person, Charley.

GEORGIE

Georgie. My name is Georgie.

DR. MOSES

Your name is Charley and Christmas is in July, Wacko.

GEORGIE

But, Dr. Moses—

DR. MOSES

Don't argue with me what's crazy, Charley. I know crazy. And you're crazy. I got now hanging around with me eight fellas who think they're *reindeers*; so I got no time for you, fruitcake. Busy, busy, busy; everyplace craziness. So, quick; what do you want for Christmas, Charley?

GEORGIE

I'd like a new life and a day without fear.

DR. MOSES

Oh, that's a shame. I got you a choo-choo train.

GEORGIE

But I don't want—

DR. MOSES

Wise up, Charley; take the choo-choo.

GEORGIE

But I want . . . I want . . .

DR. MOSES

O.K., Charley, that's it for you—
(*hoists sack onto shoulder*)
No more presents . . .
(*turns toward fireplace*)

GEORGIE *starts quickly down stairs toward him* . . .

GEORGIE

Wait, wait . . .

DR. MOSES

No more presents, booby . . .

We follow GEORGIE *to empty fireplace* . . .

SID'S VOICE
(*from far below on street*)
Georgie's moth-er . . . Georgie's moth-er . . . can Georgie come out and play . . . ?

GEORGIE *smiles, relieved to hear his old friend's voice; as we cut to:*
SID *and* SAMANTHA, *in front of G.M. Building; we are behind them look-*

ing up to top of building which towers above us into night clouds. SID *is hollering up through a megaphone. Next to him is* SAMANTHA, *a very young, blankly beautiful girl with a hair style that is infinitely more complicated than her face; she is wearing a curly fun fur, and fun earrings and a fun hair-style, and is not having any fun.*

SAMANTHA
Sidney, what are we doing here?

SID
We are visiting m'buddy, George. It is George's
visiting hour.
        (hollering up through megaphone)
Come on down, Georgie ... come on down into the
world ...
        (turns to her)
And now, Samantha—

SAMANTHA
What are we going to do now, Sidney?

SID
The grown-ups are going to talk and you're going home.

SAMANTHA
Sidney, you promised—

SID
I lie a lot.

SAMANTHA
You said—

SID
Never listen to what I say.
        (handing her some money)
Now tuck yourself into a taxi; I have to talk to Georgie.

SAMANTHA
He's the one who wrote "Last Mornin'"; I'd like to meet—

SID
A taxi, Samantha; those are the yellow cars with the
lights on top.

SAMANTHA
But, Sidney—

SID
Samantha, you are very good at arriving, but you
leave badly. Now, be a good girl and I'll take you to
Thailand for the weekend.
        (as a cab passes)
Taxi!

(cab screeches to a halt)
It's New York and there are no dragons left to slay, so
I shot you a taxi.
(gallantly kisses her hand; she departs)
Good night and good morning; we leave for
Thailand Friday.

SIDNEY *smiles at* SAMANTHA'S *departure* . . .

SID
(through megaphone)
Samantha darling . . . you're leaving beautifully . . .
departure; excellent . . .

GEORGIE *joins him as taxi goes off.*

SID   *(cont)*
Oh, Georgie; a dum-dum, a ding-dong; her head
belongs in a crackerjack box and her ass in the
Louvre . . . Where is it, tell me, where is the right
combination . . . ? I shall have to screw every
attractive girl in the Greater Metropolitan Area. A
dirty job, Georgie, but somebody's got to do it.
(turns to him)
Lovely outfit, Georgie. You look terrible.

We follow them from G.M. Building entrance to corner.

GEORGIE
Jesus, Sid, I'm glad to see ya, gotta talk to ya . . .

SID
Came as soon as I got your message.

GEORGIE
Message—?

SID
Yeah, emergency, crash drive, red alert—

GEORGIE
Right, yeah . . . see, this Kellerman thing, it's gettin'
worse . . .

SID
(his arm around him)
Don't worry, man. I figure he's doin' ya a service,
knockin' off the losers. Time you put together a
new stable anyway.

GEORGIE
No sleep, Sid, no sleep . . . better try callin' my doc again—

SID

You and that doc. The docs're takin' over the world.
Blessed are the docs for they shall inherit the meek.
I know what you need—
    (opens ancient address book)
We must turn for inspiration to the Good Book . . .

GEORGIE

Ain't gonna help, Sid, I—

SID
    (flipping pages)
O.K., we got Susan Sometime. Sometime Susan never fails—

GEORGIE

She split, Sid, she—

SID

Stoney Joanic. Stoney Joanie's on the scene again—

GEORGIE

Not tonight, Sid, I—

SID

Wait a minute; Ping-Pong Julie; tall; nutsy eyes . . .

No response. SID *grabs his arm, and we travel with them as they walk down
the middle of deserted Fifth Avenue.*

SID

O.K., down to business; the audition, chick from the
audition, you score there?

GEORGIE
    (smiles warmly)
Allison . . . hey, y'know Sid, she's really—

SID

Give you the word on Allison. Chick's a grabber. I see
it in her eye. She lies in wait for the walking wounded
and grabs off the strays.

GEORGIE

But you don't know her, Sid; this one's different, she's—

SID

Chick's a grabber and I tell you true.

GEORGIE

But tonight I been thinkin', Sid . . . about gettin' older,
about how much time I got comin'—

SID

Listen to me— How many hits we wrote tgether?

How many? Twenty-two, babe. Twenty-two golden
beauties. Three this year alone—
(*gesturing to desolate, empty avenue*)
City's *ours* and we're still young. *Young*, Georgio;
Allisons and Allisons to go; do not make the funeral
arrangements until you are dead. I seen these Allisons
operate. It's Robespierre, man, it's the Reign of Terror.
She's lookin' to cop a basket fulla heads.

GEORGIE

Sid, if they're mostly losers, how ya gonna know when
the winner shows up, when—

SID

I am Baron von Richthofen; I am flying over enemy
territory. When I go down it will be an ace who
gets me. Meanwhile I shall not be strafed by bluebirds.
I will not go down in flames for a flamingo.

GEORGIE

I dunno, Sid, I—

SID

Hey, speaking of planes, what happened to the
flying Tuesday? You were gonna give me a call—

GEORGIE

Oh. Well, see, we—Allison and me—I took her up in the—

SID

Yeah. Right. O.K., gotta split now . . .

SIDNEY *starts across Fifth away from* GEORGIE, *they are small figures on
the deserted avenue.*

SID

quarter to four; got some quality Swedish merchandise
flyin' in.

GEORGIE

Stewardess?

SID

Air freight. Can't be beat for speed and reliability.

GEORGIE

Well, I won't keep you then . . .

SID

You bet you won't.

GEORGIE

O.K., so long . . .

On the other side of Fifth now, SID *pauses; speaks through megaphone.*

                              SID

Hey, friend . . .

                            GEORGIE

Yeah . . . ?

                              SID

Watch the skies. I repeat, watch the skies for low-flying
starlings. They ruin the motor.

                            GEORGIE

I'll watch out, Sid.

SIDNEY *disappears down the street, his megaphoned voice fading . . .*

                              SID

I tell you true, sir . . .

Sudden sound behind GEORGIE; *he quickly turns to:*
SILHOUETTE *of a little man against the glass of the G.M. building.*

                            GEORGIE

Who is that?

The little man freezes.

Who are you . . . ?

*The little man suddenly sprints, running out of sight around the corner of
the building,* georgie *racing after him.*

                            GEORGIE

Kellerman . . . !

ANGLE WIDENING *as he rounds corner of building quickly; stops short a few
yards from the* LITTLE MAN *who stands quite still with his back to us in the
middle of the street, his long coat flapping in the breeze.* georgie, *breathless,
whispers . . .*

                            GEORGIE

Kellerman . . .

The LITTLE MAN *turns to us.*
He is GEORGIE'*s ten-year-old son,* LEONARD. *He wears glasses, an under-
sized bathrobe, pajamas and furry red slippers with bells at the toes. The bells
jingle as he turns.*

                            GEORGIE

Leonard . . .

                            LEONARD

Hello, Georgie; how are ya?
        (*cleans glasses on lapel of bathrobe, puts them on, looks
        up at the sky*)
Rather pleasant evening.

GEORGIE

What . . . what are ya doing here?

LEONARD

If you will recall your divorce agreement; page
eighteen, paragraph six, it clearly states: "Visitation
Rights; it is agreed that said offspring, Leonard and
Paul, shall reside with their father for a time not more,
nor less, than fourteen days per year, per summer, per
child in one two-week or two one-week periods."

GEORGIE

Yes, I know, but—

LEONARD

So offspring Leonard is in the fourth day of his first
one-week period this year . . .
      (*crossing in front of* GEORGIE)
 . . . and I wish you'd can the noise and cut out the
broads so I can get some sleep.

LEONARD *starts briskly towards the building entrance, slippers jingling;*
GEORGIE *follows.*

GEORGIE

Leonard, I meant what're you doing out here in the—

LEONARD

Nobody calls me Leonard. Len or Lennie.

GEORGIE

O.K., Len; but what're ya—

LEONARD

Relax, Georgie; why don't you just admit you forgot
I was here?

GEORGIE

I didn't forget, I—

LEONARD

How about an honest relationship, Georgie? I'd
appreciate it. You forgot my visit again, right?

GEORGIE

I did not forget. Wasn't your room all ready for ya?

LEONARD

The air-conditioner's busted, the bathrobe's too small,
and how about these goddamn bells on my slippers?

GEORGIE

You've had the same slippers every summer for—

LEONARD

I'm ten years old and I don't jingle anymore, see. It's
embarrassing. Listen to them, will ya? Goddamn jingling.
(stops at entrance to GEORGIE's *building)*
Come on, the straight score, Georgie. You forgot
what I looked like again, right?

GEORGIE

Of course not, I—

LEONARD

Then why did you call me "Kellerman"?

GEORGIE

It was dark, and there's this guy I've been—

LEONARD

It's lucky for you I'm not a sensitive kid. Because, I tell ya,
this business of forgetting I'm here and buying me
baby-clothes and not remembering my face—if I was
one of those sensitive kids it could leave a scar.

FOLLOWING *them across lobby to elevator.*

LEONARD

Kid in my class, Jeffry; pull a thing like this on him,
he'd be wiped out, finished.

GEORGIE

I wasn't expecting you to be out in the street, that's all.

LEONARD

Let's just drop it, O.K.?

GEORGIE

What were you doin' out there at four in the morning?

LEONARD
(a rare inarticulate moment)
Well, there was . . . there was something I wanted to see.

GEORGIE

Why did you run away?

LEONARD

I got embarrassed and I ran away, O.K.?

GEORGIE

What did you want to see, Len?

The elevator doors open. LEONARD *walks briskly in, jingling.*

LEONARD

I'd rather not discuss it, Georgie.

GEORGIE *follows, punches button "50," the elevator hums, rising.*

GEORGIE

Whatever it is, you can tell me, Len. Don't worry.

LEONARD

I'd rather not discuss the matter.

Humming, rising elevator sound for a moment or two.

LEONARD

Actually, you might have some information on this. It might be worth mentioning, Georgie. There is something I wanted to see. That is, in the sky. Namely, God.

GEORGIE

God . . . ?

LEONARD
(looking away)

See, I told you it was embarrassing. But the fact is, I've been hearing a great deal of talk about God for a number of years without, y'know, ever actually, seeing him; and I figured if he's anywhere, he's well, in the sky, right? Right. And I figured he never shows himself when you're looking for him, but maybe, in the middle of the night when he thinks nobody's looking, I could sneak out real fast and catch a quick glimpse of—
    (quietly)
Oh, this is really embarrassing, I'm way past all this Santa Claus and Easter Bunny crap; but, the point is . . .
    (turns to GEORGIE*)*
 . . . there was nothing there. There was nobody there, Georgie. Nobody at all.
    (touches GEORGIE*'s arm)*
And if there's nobody there then what's all the talk about?
    (turns away again)
Anyway, I bring it up because I thought you might have some information on the subject.

GEORGIE
(kneeling next to him)

Listen, Len . . .

LEONARD

I wish you wouldn't crouch like that. It makes me feel short.

GEORGIE

About this God thing . . . here's how you should figure it; you look up at the sky and if what you see there is beautiful then you did see God. If you love somebody, your Mother or Paul or even me, there is God in that too . . . you buying any of this, Len?

LEONARD

No. And I'd appreciate your not mentioning this conversation to anyone.

The elevator doors roll open, revealing fiftieth floor hallway.

LEONARD

What's this?

GEORGIE
(stepping out of elevator)

My offices, the whole new layout, figured as long as we're up I'd show you around . . .

LEONARD *remains in elevator.*

GEORGIE

Come on, Len, I'll show you the new recording studios . . .
(no reply)
We'll record your voice . . . a great new song for ya—the "Ricky-Tick" song, it's—

LEONARD

I'd like to go to sleep, if you don't mind.

GEORGIE

Come on, Len—

LEONARD

And as long as I have to stay here another three days I hope you'll cut down on the noise and the broads.

GEORGIE

Hey, Len . . .

LEONARD

See you in the morning . . .
(he begins to cry quietly)

GEORGIE

Len, what's wrong?

LEONARD

It's these Goddamn slippers. Goddamn bells. They upset me, the jingling . . .

GEORGIE

Then why do you wear them?

LEONARD
(shouting, crying)

Because you gave them to me! Because they're from you. Don't you understand!? You dummy, don't you understand!? Oh, god, you're so dumb.
(he punches the "51" button)

GEORGIE *moves forward as the elevator doors close in his face. Cut to:*

VOICE FROM SPEAKERS
Hello. Good evening; you have called the Fifth Avenue
Church Dial-A-Prayer . . .

The desolately modern corridor leading to GEORGIE'S *Conference Room on
the fiftieth floor.*
TRAVELING WITH GEORGIE *down the corridor as a rich, intimate voice
echoes from all speakers.*

VOICE   *(cont)*
Let us pray . . .

GEORGIE
(snapping his fingers)
Go, baby, swing . . .

VOICE
Oh, God . . .

GEORGIE
I'm with ya, baby . . .

VOICE
. . . out of the silence of our souls we ask for thy solemn
word.   Out of the confusion of our lives we ask for a con-
crete word   which will guide us . . .

VOICE, *continuing as* GEORGIE *enters Conference Room; carved-oak pillars
rise to vaulted ceilings, tapestries, coats of arms, and gold records hang on the
walls, rococo beams support stalactited chandeliers; a seemingly endless conference table stretches away from us as we enter the room, Victorian high-
backed chairs, an infinite column of sentinels, line the table. It is a dream
born of Ocean Avenue, something between a very old bank and a very new
church.*

We are looking down at GEORGIE, *from speaker suspended on ceiling;*
GEORGIE, *at end of table, looking up at us . . .*

VOICE
. . . Speak to us today, oh God, out of thy great word
from the Bible . . . Oh, Lord, give us the word . . .

GEORGIE
Right, gimme the word . . .

VOICE
Amen . . .

GEORGIE
Wait a second, hey—

VOICE
Thanks for calling . . .

GEORGIE
Wait a second, you didn't gimme the word—

VOICE
I enjoyed praying with you . . .

GEORGIE
Gimme the goddamn word—

VOICE
Goodbye . . .

"Click" from speaker.

QUIET VOICE
O.K., O.K., Georgie . . . What is it . . . ?

Far at other end of table, in the open door, is IRWIN MARCY; *a harried, rumpled, middle-aged man, carrying a large file-folder and wearing a thrown-on suit over a pajama-shirt.*

IRWIN
. . . Georgie, what do you want . . . ?

GEORGIE *comes down the table toward him, arms extended with great affection.*

GEORGIE
Irwin, bunny, how are ya?

IRWIN
(sits, exhausted, at end of table)
Georgie, it's four-thirty in the morning, Georgie . . .

GEORGIE
(arm around him)
Irwin, my cuteness. How's the most adorable accountant
in the world?

IRWIN
Sleepy, very sleepy . . .

GEORGIE
Goodman and Marcy. Fine organization. Surely Goodman
and Marcy shall follow me all the days of my life . . .

IRWIN
Georgie, please, what do you—

GEORGIE
Irwin, you're losing weight, you don't look well—

IRWIN
I don't get any sleep—

GEORGIE
Sleep. Sleep is important. You must—

IRWIN

You keep waking me up, fourth time this week, emergency, crisis, come right over—

GEORGIE

I thought we should talk.

IRWIN

About what?

GEORGIE

Business. Let's talk business. Irwin, let's buy something.

IRWIN *nods forward, eyes closing.*

GEORGIE

Irwin, wake up. Let's make out a big check.
(*hand on his shoulder*)
Irwin, I'm concerned, you don't look well—

IRWIN

I'm sleepy, I—

GEORGIE

Are you my friend, Irwin?

IRWIN

Georgie, I'm your accountant . . .

GEORGIE

Irwin, my friend, let's buy this building.

IRWIN

Tonight? The whole building?

GEORGIE

Now; this week.

GEORGIE *goes to other end of table, sits; about a mile of table between them . . .*

IRWIN

Georgie, to plan such a venture . . . you'd have to reevaluate—

GEORGIE

What, what—?

IRWIN

Your expenses, Georgie . . . the planes, the incredible gifts . . . and, of course, the women . . .

GEORGIE

You know all about me . . .

IRWIN

I get the bills . . .

> **GEORGIE**
>
> The bills, the confessions, like a priest . . .

IRWIN *nods forward.*

> **GEORGIE**
>
> Please, Irwin, stay awake.

IRWIN *sits up.*

> **GEORGIE**
>
> Do you have any children?

> **IRWIN**
>
> Three.

> **GEORGIE**
>
> I didn't even know you were married. Sixteen years and I
> never asked you. You must hate me. What's your wife's name?

> **IRWIN**
>
> Marcia.

> **GEORGIE**
>
> Would you like a drink?

> **IRWIN**
>
> No thank you, I—

> **GEORGIE**
>
> Marcia. Do you love her?

> **IRWIN**
>
> Yes, of course, I—

> **GEORGIE**
>
> Do you love me?

> **IRWIN**
>
> Georgie, I'm your accountant . . . it's not a matter of love or
> hate . . .

GEORGIE *jumps up, goes down length of table to* IRWIN, *shouting urgently* .

> **GEORGIE**
>
> No. Wrong. Everything; it's all a matter of love and
> hate . . . What's wrong with you?! Don't you know
> about life?! Don't you listen to my songs?! I'm
> shouting. Forgive me. Irwin, have a drink. Irwin,
> wake up. Just stay awake. You know everything
> about me; what do you think about me?

> **IRWIN**
>
> Well, I . . . I don't really . . .

> **GEORGIE**
> *(grabs his arm)*
>
> Sixteen years—you must have some opinion—

IRWIN

Georgie, it's four-thirty in the morning, please—

GEORGIE

It's the longest continuous relationship I've got with *any*
body—

IRWIN

Georgie, please—

GEORGIE
(*holding his arms, shaking him*)
You've got to be my friend, after all this time—

IRWIN

Of course; yes, of course, Georgie . . .

GEORGIE *lets go of his arms; sits down on couch near conference table* . . .

GEORGIE

You don't approve of my women. You see, I'm still
relatively young, I—

IRWIN

There's no need to explain.

GEORGIE

As an older man, you don't realize . . .

IRWIN

I'm only ten months older than you, Georgie . . .

GEORGIE

Haven't slept for days . . .
(*lies back on couch*)
Did you bring the Quarterly Earnings Report?

IRWIN

Georgie, not again—

GEORGIE

Just read it to me, Irwin; only way I can sleep . . .

IRWIN

Fourth time this week—

GEORGIE

Just once more, bunny; those nice, warm numbers.

IRWIN

It's crazy, Georgie—

GEORGIE

Please, ten minutes.

IRWIN

All right, a few minutes . . .

(opens huge file envelope)
This is quite mad . . .
(clears his throat; reads)
"Horizons Unlimited; Quarterly Earnings Report;
including fees for individual assigned compositions,
air-play tabulations and mechanicals, per title . . . "

GEORGIE, *closes his eyes, smiles . . .*

GEORGIE
Beautiful, beautiful . . .

IRWIN
"Page one; installment payments accrued to total fees . . . "

GEORGIE
(softly)
Lovely, lovely . . . my Pop used to sing me to sleep . . .

IRWIN
"Third payment, U.S. Government for Coast
Guard National Anthem, 'Guardians of Our Shores';
eleven thousand, eight hundred…"

GEORGIE
(singing quietly)
"Georgie Porgie, puddin' 'n pie
Kissed the girls and made them cry . . . "

IRWIN
" . . . Final payment, including residuals, Gold Leaf Filter
jingle; twenty-two thousand, two hundred . . . "

GEORGIE
" . . . And when the boys came out to play,
Georgie Porgie ran, ran away . . . "

We begin to hear a distant, cheering crowd from the street below.

CHEERING CROWD
Jump, now! Jump, now! Jump, now! . . .

We travel with GEORGIE *to window as cheering builds louder; insistent, demanding.*

CHEERING CROWD
Jump, now! Jump, now! Jump, now! . . .

GEORGIE *reaches for drapes, pulls them back, cut to—*

Cheering crowd around Plaza fountain below; several hundred people gathered as though for a performance, some have binoculars, some wave banners, others are eating hot dogs and drinking sodas being sold by a vendor; the scene is quite orderly, they cheer happily, a suicide matinee . . .

CHEERING CROWD

Jump, now! Jump, now! . . .

Detail of crowd around fountain, a dozen chubby matinee ladies with shopping bags, applauding, chanting—

LADIES IN CROWD

Jump, now! Jump, now! . . .

GEORGIE, *on ledge outside window, leaning forward, about to oblige them . . .*

GEORGIE
(waving, smiling)

Hi, sports fans.

The attention of the matinee ladies is suddenly diverted away from him. The smile leaves his face . . .

GEORGIE

Hey . . . hey, you're not lookin' at me . . .

GEORGIE *carefully maneuvers on ledge, hugging wall to get a look around corner . . . We peek around corner with him and see—*GLORIA, *a few yards away on ledge, leaning forward and ready to jump; smiling, waving at crowd below, unaware of* GEORGIE; *crowd cheer of "Jump, now!" continues through scene . . .*

GEORGIE

Hey, Gloria, what's the trouble? . . . I been sending the checks regular . . .

GLORIA
(not turning; absorbed in her audience)

Who's that?

GEORGIE

It's me, pound-cake, your lovin'-ex.

GLORIA

Georgie; how are ya?

GEORGIE

I'm knockin' myself off.

GLORIA

Georgie, please, these are *my* people; *I'm* workin' this crowd.

GEORGIE

No, Gloria, I drew these fans. You're doin' *my* number, this is *my* material. I am going over very big here.

GLORIA

Oh, Georgie . . . you gonna ruin *this* for me like
everything else?

GEORGIE

Gloria . . . do you still love me?

GLORIA *moves her lips in reply but we cannot hear her . . .*
We move toward her, reaching our hand out toward her . . .

GEORGIE

Gloria . . . I can't hear you . . .

We move closer to her; she moves her lips again, backing away from us . . .
she steps backward off the ledge, losing her balance, a look of horror on her
face; she reaches out for us to help her as she falls backward, a siren
screams . . . we lunge forward with GEORGIE'S *hand, too late . . . sound of*
old guitar, soft but lively, playing "Goodbye" song . . .

GEORGIE *stretching out his hand toward us, "Goodbye" music building . . .*

He leans too far forward, losing his balance, failing forward toward us . . .

Cut to: the street below, the Calypso Band in full swing, smiling joyously up
at us . . . GEORGIE *amongst them, looking up at us, smiling cordially, beck-*
oning us down . . .

Cut to: GEORGIE *falling toward us, smiling back at his own image, peace-*
fully, relieved . . .

Cut to: DR. MOSES, *at desk in his office.*

GEORGIE

I don't know, Dr. Moses . . .

GEORGIE *is sitting on the edge of couch in* DR. MOSES' *office.*

GEORGIE

Worst night of my life and all I got was your goddamn
answering machine. Doc, what'll I do . . . this Kellerman
thing . . . whaddya think . . . ?

DR. MOSES *nods judiciously, leans forward in his chair, clasps his hands*
earnestly on top of his desk, and, his understanding eyes fixed on GEORGIE,
speaks in a rich, lilting, Jamaican accent.

DR. MOSES

I tink you got debbils in you head.

GEORGIE

Huh?

DR. MOSES

Yes, mon, you got de debbils in de head. De bad debbils come in de blood, and we got to get dem out. You go to lake, mon, get de codfish and put de fish on you forehead and it take out all de bad debbil out of you blood. Oh, yes, de fish, mon, de fish, take out all de bad debbil.

GEORGIE

Whaddya mean I—

DR. MOSES

Your hour is op now, mon.

GEORGIE

But, doctor—

DR. MOSES
(checking his watch)
Your hour is op now, mon; daylight come an' me wan' go home . . .
(clicks on intercom on desk)
Tally-mon!

SUSAN *enters through door behind desk, an efficient secretary, although she is naked except for a large lavender appointment book over her crotch.* MOSES *points to the appointment book.*

DR. MOSES

Tally-mon; tally me banana; daylight come and me wan' go—

An angry GEORGIE *suddenly wakes up on couch in Conference Room . . .* IRWIN *sound asleep in his chair, smiling, his file-folder held tight in his arms . . .* GEORGIE *takes tapestry off wall, drapes it around* IRWIN, *tucking him in.*

GEORGIE

Sleep, daddy-numbers, sleep...

Sudden sound of thwanging, pounding electric guitars, CAPTAIN LOVE *wailing offscreen . . .*

CAPTAIN LOVE

"Now Bunky told Lucille
Go walkin' out in the rain
And don't come back
Till you bring me somethin'
To put inside my vein,
One more ride . . .
Lucille, your man wants
One more ride
There's a worlda sunshine waitin' for me . . . "

GEORGIE *in back seat of limousine, East River lights receding in rear window; tape-deck speaker opposite, song continues from it . . .*

> " . . . on the other side . . .
> Hey, did this really happen
> Or was it all a dream
> Look down deep inside yourself
> You gonna hear somebody scream . . . "

Skyscrapers and bridge lights of lower Manhattan rushing toward us with the ribboning road . . .

> " . . . for one more ride
> Everybody wants
> Just one more, yeah,
> One more,
> One last one, one more . . . "

Back seat of limo, GEORGIE *tapping out beat on guitar wood . . .*

> " . . . one more, one more
> One more, ride, ride, ride . . . "

CHOMSKY, *the driver, rushing lights reflecting off windshield onto his face. Staccato, throbbing finish of song continues through scene—*

> **GEORGIE**
> We're gonna do it, Chomsky.

> **CHOMSKY**
> Yessir.

> **GEORGIE**
> We're gonna find him.

> **CHOMSKY**
> Yessir.

> **GEORGIE**
> Tonight.

> **CHOMSKY**
> Yessir.

> **GEORGIE**
> *(turns off tape deck)*
> You like that song, Chomsky?

> **CHOMSKY**
> Yessir.

> **GEORGIE**
> *(picks up guitar)*
> Any requests, Chomsky?

> **CHOMSKY**
> Nosir.

GEORGIE
Oh.

Turns, looks out of window, idly picking out melody on guitar . . .

We are traveling around a Fifth Avenue corner, brightly lit first floor of bank building, infinite row of desks, ALLISON *at desk near window, typing; she looks up at us, smiles as we pass her . . .*

GEORGIE
(whispering)
Allison . . .

We pass empty row of desks; she is gone . . .

GEORGIE
Chomsky, remember that girl, from the audition . . . ?

CHOMSKY
Sir?

GEORGIE
Ya drove us around last week, remember?

CHOMSKY
Many young ladies back there, sir.

GEORGIE
No, this one you would remember . . . she was quite
lovely, and . . . a little older than the others . . .

SID'S VOICE
Old chicks. Christ.

HALLORAN'S VOICE
Whaddya mean, Sid?

We see SID *standing in the dimly lit aisle of a huge empty theater. It is six days earlier. As* SID *joins* GEORGIE *and* HALLORAN *in row of seats lit only by a tiny clipboard light.*

SID
What the hell are we getting in here for these auditions?
The name of the show is "Now!" Now, you got it,
babies? I am not handing over "Now" music to
yesterday's chicks. Gentlemen, I tell you true.

HALLORAN
One more singer and we can go home.
(shouting)
Ronnie, who's next? Anybody out there?

We are watching the stage from the back of the theater; it is quite dark except for a small, standing work-lamp.

RONNIE'S VOICE
(echoing from backstage)

Linda Kaiser . . .

HALLORAN'S VOICE

Come on out, Miss Kaiser . . .

No reply; the white circle remains empty.

HALLORAN'S VOICE

Miss Kaiser?
(no reply)
Come on out where we can see you, darling . . .

The small figure of a GIRL *appears at the edge of the white circle, carrying a battered briefcase; at this distance we cannot see her face clearly. She moves nervously about the edges of the circle, a mosquito caught in a spotlight beam.*

LINDA

Hello. I'm sorry. I was late. I'm late. Hello.
(peers out into darkness)
Funny feeling. Can't see you. Dark.

HALLORAN'S VOICE

Darling, I'm Peter Halloran . . . and this is Sidney
Gill and Georgie Soloway, our composer and lyricist.

LINDA

Can't see you . . . but if you say you're there, I'll believe
you. In this light, either I'm auditioning for a part or
I'm a murder suspect.

SID'S VOICE
(whispering)

Old chick; old loony chick.

HALLORAN'S VOICE

Would you like to sing for us, Linda?

LINDA

Yes. Sing. Yes.

HALLORAN'S VOICE

Or we could just chat for a while if you'd like.

LINDA

Yes. Chat. Let's chat for a while. Great.

HALLORAN'S VOICE

Tell us what you've been up to lately.

LINDA

Up to . . .

HALLORAN'S VOICE

Tell us what you've been doing, dear.

> LINDA

Doing . . .

> HALLORAN'S VOICE

What do you consider yourself primarily, a singer, an actress, a . . .

> LINDA

An amnesia victim.
> *(sits on chair next to work lamp)*
Fellas, either you're in my nightmare, or I'm in yours.

> HALLORAN'S VOICE

Darling, what would you *like* to do?

> LINDA

Now? Right now? Leave.
> *(rises from chair, picks up briefcase)*
I can't do these auditions, I have to leave now . . .
> *(stops)*
"Filters Can Be Fun." I just remembered. That's the last thing I did. A commercial. I had fun with a filter. Green Mist cigarettes. Are we finished chatting? I think I'm finished chatting now, Mr. Halloran.

> HALLORAN'S VOICE

Would you like to sing for us now, darling?

> LINDA

Yes, darling.

> HALLORAN'S VOICE

Do you have an accompanist with you?

> LINDA

No. Nobody. Nothing. Nobody.

> HALLORAN'S VOICE

Do you have sheet music?

> LINDA

Got it. You bet. Got that.

> HALLORAN'S VOICE

If you'll just hand it over to Chuck, dear.

> LINDA

Chuck, dear. Where?

> HALLORAN'S VOICE

Right down in the pit there.

> LINDA

Oh . . .

Takes piece of sheet music from overstuffed briefcase, holds it out into the darkness below her; an unseen hand snatches it away.

LINDA

Ghosts. Place is fulla ghosts . . .

She is startled by a sudden piano-intro to "Painting the Clouds with Sunshine."

LINDA

Oh, a piano. There's a piano down there.
> *(sits on chair, holding briefcase tightly with one hand and work-lamp pole with the other)*

This is a very old . . . very old song. "Now" is not a good title for me. If your show was called "Last Tuesday" . . . or maybe "Nineteen Fifty-seven" . . . I had a very good summer in Nineteen Fifty-seven . . .

HALLORAN'S VOICE

Just relax and sing, Linda . . .

LINDA

What I'm going to do now is relax and sing, Pete.

She begins to sing; her voice is small and lovely and theatrically hopeless.

LINDA

"When I pretend I'm gay
Don't really feel that way
I'm only painting the clouds with sunshine . . .
Painting the blues
Beautiful hues
Painting with gold and old rose
Painting a frown
Trying to drown
All of my woes . . ."

Last row of theater; the three men partly lit by light on HALLORAN'S *clipboard, his pencil poised to cross name off; singing continues O.S.*

GEORGIE

Peter, let her sing a few more seconds . . .

SID

George, you wanna make a private score here, fine; but I can't hang in. Splittin'-time.
> *(rises, disappearing into darkness)*

Tomorrow, babies. Peace.

PETER

Georgie, she's—

GEORGIE

A few more seconds . . .

We are on stage with LINDA *again.*

> LINDA
> *(singing)*

" . . . though things may not look bright
 They'll all turn out all right
 If you'll keep painting
 The clouds with sunshine . . ."

> HALLORAN'S VOICE

Thank you very much, dear . . .

> LINDA
> *(singing)*

" . . . painting a frown, trying to drown . . ."

> HALLORAN'S VOICE

Linda, *thank* you . . .

> LINDA
> *(singing)*

" . . . all of my woes . . ."

> HALLORAN'S VOICE
> *(shouting)*

Miss Kaiser; thank you . . .

> LINDA

Oh.

> HALLORAN'S VOICE

A pleasure to meet you, Miss Kaiser; thank you.

> LINDA

The best part was just coming up.

> HALLORAN'S VOICE

That'll be fine for now; thank you.

> LINDA

I've got these three good notes and I never seem to
get to them.

> HALLORAN'S VOICE

Miss Kaiser, we—

> LINDA

I can't leave.

> HALLORAN'S VOICE

What?

> LINDA

I can't leave.
 (very quietly)
I'm sorry, but I can't leave.

She remains frozen on the chair; one hand gripping the briefcase, the other hand gripping the work-lamp pole; transfixed.

> LINDA *(cont)*
> I can't seem to let go of this lamp right now . . . Listen, you fellas go ahead, I'll be O.K. soon . . .

Last row of theater.

> HALLORAN
> Georgie, we got a crazy-lady here.

> GEORGIE
> Go ahead, Peter; I'll handle it.

As HALLORAN *exits into darkness.*

> GEORGIE
> Ronnie, give me the houselights and then you can go.

Houselights go on.
GEORGIE *and* LINDA *are alone in the vast, empty theater. The lights are mellow, but bright enough for us to see the red-plush boxes, ornate balconies, and the long shadowed folds of hanging drapes. She remains motionless on stage, frozen grip on briefcase and work-lamp pole; he starts toward her from the back of the theater.*

> GEORGIE
> Hello.

> LINDA
> Hello . . . I feel like I just auditioned for the part of human being, and I didn't get the job.

> GEORGIE
> Yeah, I know what you mean.

> LINDA
> See, it took me three weeks to get this audition and I bought a new dress and I worked on my song and now I can't just leave right away.

As GEORGIE *comes up on stage, kneels near her chair.*

> LINDA
> I just have to hang around here for a while, see.

> GEORGIE
> Fine; sit where you are.

> LINDA
> Thank you, but I can't move anyway; my hand is stuck on this lamp.

> GEORGIE
> Really, physically stuck . . . ?

LINDA

Oh yes. It happens all the time. I get stuck onto
things: chairs, coffee cups, doorknobs, people. I'll
be O.K. soon, just don't shake hands with me or
anything. You have kind eyes. Funny to see your face
after all that darkness. A nervous face, but very kind
eyes. God, I hate these auditions. I'm not what you're
looking for; I'm not even Linda Kaiser. She's my
roommate. My name is Allison Densly but I never
use it because it sounds so old, centuries old . . .

GEORGIE

It's a sweet name, graceful . . .

ALLISON

Sounds like a lot of doilies. It's very beautiful here now,
with the lights on. Great set for *Lucia di Lammermoor*.
Dawn on the moors. I study opera. Every day, an
hour. You like opera?
      (lifts her briefcase)
Got 'em all here. Opera is the best. People live at the
top of their lives and die very beautifully. Lucia and
Edgardo, they meet on this moor at dawn. He saves
her from this wild bull and she's crazy about him . . .
Oh, mister, listen to me, I'm still auditioning . . .
      (tears in her eyes)
 . . . all the time I think I'm auditioning. I get up in
the morning and the whole city says "Thank you
very much, Miss Densly, that'll be enough for
now . . . " Looka that, I cry odd; one eye at a time . . .

GEORGIE
      (gently, touching her arm)
Hey, you want some coffee, something you'd like . . .

ALLISON

Mostly I'd like to get my hand off this lamp. I've
gotta go back to work soon. I'm a Corporate
Librarian. That's a file clerk. With only three good
notes you gotta back yourself up with something.
      (turns to him)
You think I'll be able to get this lamp into a taxi?
      (blinking)
I'm crying from the left eye now . . .

GEORGIE

These auditions, I don't blame you, they . . .

ALLISON

Oh, mister, it's not that, it's not the audition . . .

GEORGIE

Then why are you crying?

ALLISON

It's my birthday.

GEORGIE

Oh.

ALLISON

I'm thirty-four years old today and I'm not prepared.
I'm prepared for twenty-two. Right now I could do
a great twenty-two. I got up this morning and I was
all of a sudden not young. Not old, but all of a
sudden not young.

GEORGIE

Sure you're young . . .

ALLISON

Not young enough for this dress. And not young
enough to be a Corporate Librarian with three
good notes and a briefcase fulla grand opera. Mister,
I don't understand what happened to the time. All
of a sudden I'm going into my tenth year of looking
for a new apartment. I'm not much of a singer and
I'm not a gifted file clerk either. The one thing I'm
good at is being married; but my husband wasn't. That
was ten years ago and I never learned another trade . . .
(gripping GEORGIE'S arm)
The time, mister . . . it's not a thief at all like they
say; it's something much sneakier . . . an embezzler; up
nights, juggling the books so you don't notice
anything's missing.
(suddenly smiles)
Hey, I let go of the lamp.

GEORGIE

Yeah...

ALLISON

Now I've got your arm . . .

GEORGIE

Yeah.

ALLISON

Looka that.

GEORGIE

Can you let go?

ALLISON

Yes, but I don't want to.

The glistening wing of GEORGIE'S *airplane. Plane banks sharply and dips away from us into an orange sun, five thousand feet above the city; sunset.*

ALLISON *turns toward the window as the plane banks . . .*

The earth rushes below us; a billow of clouds passes, uncovering a tiny city, New York slides by beneath us, lopsided and little.

GEORGIE *is strumming guitar; controls on automatic pilot.*

>   **ALLISON**
>   *(somewhat frightened, points to controls)*
>   Hey . . .

>   **GEORGIE**
>   Don't worry; Sam knows the way home . . .
>   *(sings, strums)*
>   "Now, I'm gonna teach you
>   A ricky-tick song . . .

She is still nervous.

>   **GEORGIE**   *(cont)*
>   "It's sorta silly
>   And it ain't too long
>   But you can't go wrong
>   Singin' a Ricky-Ticky song
>   You just go
>   Ricky-ticky, ticky, ticky, ticky,
>   A Rick-tick, ticky, ticky . . .

He continues the nonsense of the song. Still frightened, she joins him only hesitantly.

>   **GEORGIE**
>   "Oh, you can't go wrong
>   Singin' a Ricky-Ticky song . . . "
>   Now, I'm gonna teach you
>   A Scooba-Dooby song
>   It's equally silly
>   And equally long . . .

She smiles.

>   **GEORGIE**
>   "But you can't go wrong
>   Singin' a Scooba-Dooby song . . . "

She laughs, joining him.

BOTH
"You just go Scooba-dooby, doob, doob,
   Scooba, doob, doob . . . "

The song and their laughter continuing over a vast sky.

The plane ascending with their mood, rising through ribboning dream colors . . . until their voices grow softer, gentler, drifting with the grace of the plane, floating on whispers.

GEORGIE'S VOICE
Happy birthday, Allison . . .

Sound of match scratching in darkness.
A candle is lit, barely illuminating GEORGIE *and* ALLISON *at kitchen table in* ALLISON'S *tiny apartment.*

ALLISON
(blowing out match)
Candlelight is all this apartment can take.

GEORGIE
Can't see much, it's—

ALLISON
(flatly)
You want to sleep with me now?

GEORGIE
What about your roommate?

ALLISON
Linda Kaiser? I made her up. She protects me. Some
fellas, I have a roommate. Some I don't.
   (she looks directly at him)
The plane, mister . . . Is that your number, your
make-out routine?

GEORGIE
No. I usually go up by myself.

ALLISON
Sorry. Loneliness has made me a smart-ass.

GEORGIE
Yeah, when you're alone, it's—

ALLISON
I didn't say alone. I said lonely. There's a difference.
   (rises from table, picks up candle)
If we're going to bed, we better start now; it's a long trip . . .

We follow her through living room to bedroom.

ALLISON

It's dark, be careful not to step on my mother . . . She lives in the linoleum and moans all night.

GEORGIE

You make it all sound very attractive.

ALLISON

That's my routine. I make jokes.
(puts candle on side table, sits on bed)
I make jokes because you'll be gone before I wake up and I'm going to miss you.

GEORGIE

(sitting on edge of bed)

How do you know I—

ALLISON

Because that's the way it goes. One of the few things I know is the way it goes.

GEORGIE

Fact is, I will have to leave pretty early; my work—

ALLISON

I know your work; you're an escape artist. And if I tell you that I love you, you will leave my bed in a rocket. But I know all that, so don't worry, nothing dangerous will happen . . .
(she whispers, smiles)
There will be no loving . . . I promise you . . . you're safe.
(leans next to window)
Thank you for my birthday. I was sitting on my fire escape this morning with my imitation-citrus-flavored-dietary beverage thinking about dying. There's this man who types every morning and this lady who waters six geranium plants, they're right across the alley and they're there every morning like the sun; and I'm thinking isn't it amazing how we're all gonna die; isn't it amazing how we all keep typing and watering geraniums and buying new dishes and we're all gonna die anyway . . . But then you took me up and put the city in my hand. You're not gonna like this, but there was love in what you did. You will leave tomorrow but the feeling won't, and I thank you for it. This morning I was thinking about dying and tonight I think of living; that's a very snappy birthday present . . .
(she blows out the candle. They sit silently for a moment)
Pleasure to meet you, George.

GEORGIE

How-d'ya-do.

ALLISON

Funny; this is how I first saw you . . .

GEORGIE

Whaddya mean?

ALLISON

In the dark.

ALLISON'S *darkened room and pre-dawn window flash into the pre-dawn skyline rushing by* GEORGIE'S *limousine window; the present . . .*

GEORGIE
(whispering)
Hey . . . I love her . . .
(then, suddenly frightened)
Jesus . . . Kellerman, if he ruins *this* for me, I . . .
(leans forward urgently)
Chomsky . . . Chomsky, we gotta find him . . . *tonight.*

Shattering, clattering, echoing sound of running footfalls as—
We move back to reveal GEORGIE *running through the Lincoln Tunnel, sound of footfalls richocheting off the tiled walls of the deserted tunnel . . .*
Following GEORGIE *as he runs . . . We pass* DR. MOSES, *who stands on cat-walk just above us, dressed in tunnel-guard uniform . . .*

GEORGIE
(stops running, breathing hard)
Doc . . . this tunnel, I . . . it doesn't seem to have an end.

DR. MOSES *leans toward us on railing, smiles pleasantly, politely.*

DR. MOSES

That is correct.

GEORGIE

So, if it's all the same to you . . .

GEORGIE *turns, starts walking in opposite direction.*

DR. MOSES

I'm sorry, Mr. Soloway; it has no beginning either.

GEORGIE *suddenly stands still, turns toward us, terrified.*

DR. MOSES

That'll be twenty-five cents, please.

GEORGIE; *backseat of limo, his face covered with sweat, Lincoln Tunnel receding in rear window . . . the sound of several little kids singing—*

"Georgie Porgie, puddin' an' pie
Kissed the girls and made them cry . . . "

A faded sign over a darkened restaurant entrance: "LEON'S PORTS OF CALL—FOOD FROM FAR AND NEAR."

> " . . . and when the girls
> Came out to play
> Georgie Porgie ran, ran away . . . "

Ocean Avenue, Brooklyn, the present; as GEORGIE *leaves limousine for restaurant entrance. The limousine is out of place on this block of tenements and small, faded stores; the stubby buildings throwing long, dawn shadows on the old, crooked street.*

The door is open, we follow him inside; in the darkness we can just about see eight tables with chairs upended on them. At our right a long, wooden counter-bar runs to the back of the restaurant, and beyond the counter-bar an open doorway leads to the apartment upstairs. Far at the end of the counter bar we can barely see the small figure of LEON SOLOWAY. *He sits on a high wooden stool, his face in shadows; a bit of light glistening off his rimless glasses, his sparse, white hair and the telephone in his hand.*

GEORGIE

Hello, Pop . . . ?

LEON

Hello . . . ?

GEORGIE

Pop, it's me, Georgie.

LEON

Georgie . . . ?
  (puts down phone)
Georgie. Five A.M. Something wrong. What?

GEORGIE

No, Pop. Just wanted to talk.

LEON

To talk what? Five o'clock. What?

GEORGIE

How . . . how are ya, Pop?

LEON

Fine. Fine. Five o'clock.

GEORGIE

Uh . . . how's the restaurant?

LEON

Closed. It's five o' clock.

GEORGIE

How come you're up?

LEON

I don't sleep good. How come you?

GEORGIE

I don't sleep good either. You were on the phone . . .

LEON

The vegetable market, I call in the order. Georgie, I
don't see you now a long time . . . Georgie, I heard
your new tune. It's a crackerjack, believe me. Terrific.
Go home, go to sleep. Don't worry. A crackerjack.

GEORGIE

Thanks, Pop.

LEON

Listen, I got terrific news for you. Last week, I put you
in the menu. I got 'em all in there, the greats
from Show Business, sandwiches named after them.
And now you, Georgie.

GEORGIE

Thanks, Pop.

LEON

Yeah. Well . . . what's new with you? How's business?

GEORGIE

Business is good. Ya see "Time" magazine this week?

LEON

"Time" magazine . . . Yes. Terrific, Georgie. Except what
they did on the cover; they put gray in your hair . . .
    (leans close to GEORGIE; *touches his temple)*
Hey . . . you do got some gray in there . . .
    (looks at him a moment)
What else is new? How's Gloria?

GEORGIE

Whaddya mean how's Gloria? We were divorced
five years ago.

LEON

Yes, of course . . . for a second, I . . .

GEORGIE

Forget it. How's business with you, Pop?

LEON

New places opening in the neighborhood. Big places,
cheap food. They grab all the lunch business. Plastic
tables, plastic food, nobody cares. Across the street
now they got "Eat-O-Rama"; a monster; ninety-four

tables. Can you imagine, Georgie, what they take in there, one night, a place like that?

GEORGIE

Chrissakes, Pop, then why don't you move, expand, get a new restaurant? You keep sending back my checks, you—

LEON

I don't want them.

GEORGIE

What the hell's wrong, Pop? *Take* the goddamn money . . . please . . .

LEON

There's no point.

GEORGIE

Whaddya mean?

LEON

Because I'm dying.

GEORGIE

Huh . . . ?

LEON

I got something with the arteries. Arterial something. It makes me talk foolish. I forget things. Like about Gloria. My head gets silly. I get days mixed up. Sometimes years.

GEORGIE

Pop, I didn't know . . .

LEON

So there's no point in expanding at the present time.

GEORGIE

Pop, I'm sorry . . . how do ya feel?

LEON

Cheated. I had plans. Seems so fast. I'm very old, but it still seems fast. A finger snap. An appetizer.

GEORGIE

Is there . . . can I do anything?

LEON

Yeah. Queens Park Cemetery; remember the name. Terrific place. Right across the river. Terrific view.

GEORGIE

Pop, don't talk about—

LEON

I put your name in the menu. Got all the greats in

there, sandwiches named after them, the Jackie Gleason
Special, the Johnny Carson Salad, Sammy Davis,
Merv Griffin, alla them I got in there. And now you.

GEORGIE

Great. What am I?

LEON

You're a triple-decker sandwich.

GEORGIE

Beautiful.

LEON

The Georgie Soloway Triple-Decker. Fresh, thin-sliced
novie, golden lake sturgeon—

GEORGIE

Beautiful, beautiful . . .

LEON

—cream cheese, chives optional, sliced Bermuda onion—

GEORGIE

Wow.

LEON

—on toasted thick pumpernickel.

GEORGIE

With a side of coleslaw?

LEON

Of *course* with a side of coleslaw.

GEORGIE

Pop, I'm immortal.

LEON

Sure. Now go to sleep.

GEORGIE

Goodbye, Pop.

LEON

Goodbye, Georgie.

Roar of airplane motors.

Star-filled sky above jeweled skyline, red streaks of approaching dawn.
Sound of guitar-strum, GEORGIE'S *voice singing,* Country Western-*style.*

GEORGIE'S VOICE (O.S.)

"Oh, now, easy there, Sam
  Better take it slow
  'Cause the grub's run out
  An' the water's low

An' we still got miles and miles to go
Till we get to San Antonio . . . "

GEORGIE'S *plane, a silver and blue twin-engine Cessna, glides into view over skyline . . .*

GEORGIE'S VOICE
"Cactus cuts me, skeeters bite
Coyote laughin' out there in the night
Storm's comin' up
So we better make camp
Oh, life ain't simple
For a saddle tramp . . . "

Interior of plane, controls on automatic pilot; GEORGIE *relaxed, feet up on seat next to him, strumming guitar.*

GEORGIE
" . . . yeah, ol' Sam, he's a good ol' horse
Almost blind, he dunno we're lost,
When they find us
They won't give a damn,
They'll say, just an ol' horse
And a saddle tramp . . . "
    (hits final chords; smiles, whispers)
Number two on the Country Chart and
Climbing like a rocket.
    (turns to side window)
Jesus, Queens Park Cemetery . . . where the hell is that?

The East River slides by beneath us, and then a vast cemetery rises up toward us as the plane descends; the jagged outline of the tombstones and their long, dawn shadows form a skyline of their own.

GEORGIE'S VOICE
    (softly)
Found it, Pop . . . looks like a lot of little office
buildings . . . Big place, must be fifty acres . . .can you
imagine, Pop, can you imagine what they take in
there, one night, a place like that?

A mass of clouds rushes toward us; suddenly, brightly white, engulfing the plane. GEORGIE *grabs microphone from hook on control panel.*

GEORGIE
Hello; Sky-phone Operator Six; code four-seven-three;
Soloway.

OPERATOR'S VOICE
    (from speaker over front window)
Sky-phone Operator Six; Good morning.

GEORGIE *pulls throttle back sharply; motors moaning as plane suddenly climbs steeply.*

GEORGIE
Check Information; Mrs. Ruth Charleton, or a Dr. Charleton, in Queens.

GEORGIE'S *plane; climbing sharply, rapidly through clouds; motors roaring as voices continue.*

OPERATOR'S VOICE
Sir, I have an office and a residence for a Dr. Bernard L. Charleton.

GEORGIE
Yeah, sweetheart, gimme the residence.

Clouds and sky falling away below us as we continue to climb. A sleepy child's voice comes from speaker above window.

CHILD'S VOICE
Hello . . .

GEORGIE
Who is this, please?

CHILD'S VOICE
This is Danny Charleton. I waked up.

GEORGIE
Beautiful. Is your mother's name Ruthie? Ruth?

CHILD'S VOICE
Yes. I just now waked up.

GEORGIE
Great. May I speak to her, please?

CHILD'S VOICE
Okay.

Sky dropping away sharply at side window; motors whine as plane climbs more steeply.

RUTH'S VOICE
Hello? Hello?

GEORGIE
Hello, Ruthie? . . . Hey, Ruthie? . . .

RUTH'S VOICE
Now just *who* is this? *Who* is calling at this hour?

GEORGIE
Hey, Ruthie . . . it's me, Georgie . . .

> RUTH'S VOICE
>
> Who *is* this, for God's sake? I can't hear you.

> GEORGIE
> *(whispering)*
> I'm sorry, Ruthie . . . I'm sorry. . . .

> RUTH'S VOICE
>
> Hello! *Is anybody there*, for God's sake? It's six o'clock
> in the morning . . .

> GEORGIE
>
> Ruthie . . .

> RUTH'S VOICE
>
> Hello . . . who *is* this? . . . speak louder . . .

GEORGIE *turns to side window, clouds dropping away below frame as plane keeps climbing.*

> GEORGIE
>
> Ruthie . . . hey, Ruthie, the sky is falling . . .

> RUTHIE'S VOICE
>
> Hello . . . hello . . .

Sound of "click" on speaker as she hangs up.
We look out upon a vast field of billowing clouds.

> GEORGIE'S VOICE
>
> Level out . . . level out . . .

Sound of motors returning to normal humming tempo. Cloud field straightens out below us; endless, rolling white . . .

> GEORGIE'S VOICE
>
> . . . Automatic pilot . . . compass setting: fifteen,
> north-west . . . just close my eyes, just a little sleep . . .

As we skim across field of clouds . . .

> GEORGIE'S VOICE
>
> . . . like snow, like warm snow . . .

GEORGIE *sings in whispering, sleepy voice . . .*

> " . . . skipping o'er the keys,
> Lightly as a butterfly,
> Gentle as the breeze . . .
> One more time . . . "

The field of clouds rushing toward us, gliding, sailing, skimming through the endless white . . .

> GEORGIE'S VOICE
>
> "Let us do our lesson one more time,
> Music is a mountain,
> Let us see how far we all can climb . . ."

DR. MOSES' VOICE:

Hi-ya, crazy-head!

DR. MOSES, *in seat next to* GEORGIE, *dressed in ski-instructor's outfit, red turtleneck sweater, huge sunglasses, skis held over shoulder.*

DR. MOSES

You ready for your ski lesson, Georgie?

GEORGIE
(smiling)

Hi-ya, doc-baby . . .

DR. MOSES

Snow is perfect today . . .

We skim across an endless field of billowing clouds . . .

DR. MOSES' VOICE

Thought we'd work on your turns. Still haven't gotten the knack of the ol' turns, baby . . .

GEORGIE'S VOICE

Got to speak to Allison, first . . . tell her I love her.

Movement across clouds becomes movement across the dawn-lit sheets of ALLISON'S *bed; we move slowly to her sleeping face against the white pillow . . .*

GEORGIE'S VOICE

. . . I'm tired, doc, so tired . . . checked under the hood and I been driving a thousand miles without a motor . . .

Phone rings. ALLISON *sits up, dawn light falling in stripes across her face, picks up phone.*

ALLISON

Hello . . .

There is the filtered sound of a thick, deep male voice from phone.

MALE VOICE

Hello; is this Allison Densly?

ALLISON

Yes . . .

MALE VOICE

I'm a friend of Georgie Soloway's; I'm sorry to disturb you at this hour, but my conscience would not allow me to wait another moment . . .

ALLISON

Who is this . . . ?

MALE VOICE

I feel it is my duty to warn you—

ALLISON

Who is this, please?

Closeup; GEORGIE, *speaking into sky phone; he is whispering, his voice thick, sleepy.*

GEORGIE

My name is Harry Kellerman . . .

The bright sun flares out the front window of the plane; GEORGIE'S *reflection superimposed on the clouds outside.* GEORGIE *is seeing his own face. He speaks again, slowly . . .*

GEORGIE   *(cont)*

Harry . . . Kellerman.

DR. MOSES

Hey, Georgie . . . Today, we're gonna try the two-mile run, Georgie. Think you're ready, nutsy-person?

GEORGIE
(smiling)

Yeah, doc-baby . . .

ALLISON'S VOICE
(from speaker)

Hello . . . ? Hello . . . ?

GEORGIE *shoves the throttle forward; motors screaming as the plane goes into a dive . . .*

GEORGIE'S *plane diving steeply through clouds. Screaming motors cut to silence; we hear only a guitar-strum and* GEORGIE'S *lazy voice, singing softly . . .*

GEORGIE'S VOICE

"This is the last mornin'
    That I wake up in this dirty city . . .

A vast ski slope, GEORGIE *and* DR. MOSES, *skiing to rhythm of* GEORGIE'S *voice, the two skiers hurtling down at steep angle . . .*

GEORGIE'S VOICE

"Looking for the sunshine as
    The buildings black the skies
    This is the last mornin'
    That I wash in rusty water

And try to shave a face
    That I don't even recognize . . .
    I'm goin' home
    Home, goin' home
    I'm goin' home . . .

The city rushes up toward us faster and faster; we are hurtling past the City to the Coney Island shoreline, the ocean rising up towards us, suddenly filling the screen as we Cut to:

The two skiers sailing down the vast slope in slow motion, a wake of white snow rising up off their skis . . .

GEORGIE'S VOICE

" . . .This is a tough, cold city here
Guess I never cut it here
And I'm so tired
Of tryin' to stand against it all alone
This is the last mornin'
That I'm gonna try to fight it
'Cause I'm goin' home
Home, goin' home . . .

The two skiers hurtle forward down the vast, white slope . . .

GEORGIE'S VOICE

"Down below the subway's screamin'
As I lie here halfway dreamin'
Lookin' at the ceilin' wonderin' where
The dream went wrong . . .

END CREDITS *move up across the two tiny skiers as song continues to the end.*

GEORGIE'S VOICE

"This is the last mornin'
That I'm gonna have t'think about it
I'm goin' home . . .
I'm goin' home . . . home, goin' home . . . "

HERB GARDNER, recipient of The 2000 Lifetime Achievement Award from the Writers Guild of America began his artistic career as a sculptor of nativity scenes for the Bliss Display Company in 1953, but found greater success two years later when he was nineteen as a cartoonist of "The Nebbishes", a strip syndicated in more than forty newspapers including the Chicago Tribune, The San Francisco Chronicle, The Los Angeles Times, The Baltimore Sun, and the London Observer. The Nebbishes (or 'Lost Souls' in Yiddish) ran for six years becoming a national fad in the late 1950s. As the cartoon characters' speeches grew longer and the drawings of necessity smaller, Mr. Gardner turned to writing fiction. His novel **A Piece of the Action** was published in 1958. Simultaneously, Mr. Gardner wrote plays.

"*A Thousand Clowns*" (1962) was nominated for a Tony Award for Best Play and Mr. Gardner won the Variety Critics Poll as Outstanding New Playwright that year. The "*Goodbye People*" (1968), "*Thieves*" (1974). "*I'm Not Rappaport*" (1985). and "*Conversations with My Father*" (1991) followed. "*I'm Not Rappaport*" won the Outer Critics' Award, the John Gassner Award and the Tony Award for Best Play. "*Conversations with My Father*" was the runner-up for the Pulitzer Prize for Drama in 1992. Mr. Gardner's work has been performed by such actors as Jason Robards, Sandy Dennis, Yves Montand, Barbara Harris, Dustin Hoffman, Dom DeLuise, Charles Grodin, Marlo Thomas, Milton Berle, Sam Levine, F. Murray Abraham, Judd Hirsch, Cleavon Little, Paul Scofield, Walter Matthau and Ossie Davis.

Mr. Gardner also wrote the screenplays for "*Who is Harry Kellerman?*" (1971) and "*Thieves*" (1976). For his film adaptation of "*A Thousand Clowns*" (1965), Mr. Gardner won Best Screenplay Award from the Screenwriter's Guild and received Academy Award nominations for Best Screenplay and Best Picture of the Year. He also adapted and directed "The Goodbye People" (1983) and "I'm Not Rappaport" (1996) for the screen.

In recent years there have been very few times, if any, when a Herb Gardner play is not being performed somewhere in the United States or abroad.

CHEKHOV:
THE MAJOR PLAYS

English versions by
Jean-Claude van Itallie

The Cherry Orchard

"A CLASSIC RESTORED TO THE HAND, MIND AND BLOOD OF THE CREATOR."

—The New York Times

The Seagull

"SUBLIMELY UNDERSTOOD CHEKHOV ...ABSOLUTELY TRUE TO THE ORIGINAL"

—The New York Post

Three Sisters

"CAPTURES CHEKHOV'S EXUBERANCE, MUSIC AND COMPLEXITY"

—The Village Voice

Uncle Vanya

"THE CRISPEST AND MOST POWERFUL VERSION EXTANT."

—The New Republic

Paper•ISBN 1-55783-162-9 • $7.95

THIRTEEN BY SHANLEY

The Collected Plays, Vol. 1
by John Patrick Shanley
The Oscar–Winning author of
Moonstruck

In this Applause edition of John Patrick Shanley's complete plays, ther reader will intercept one of America's major dramatists in all his many expressive incarnations and moods. His restless poetic spirit takes refuge in a whole array of forms; he impatiently prowls the aisles of comedy, melodrama, tragedy, and farce as he forges an alloy all his own. Fanciful, surreal, disturbing, no other playwright of his generation has so captivated the imagination of the serious American play-going public. In addition to Shanley's sustained longer work, this volume also offers the six short plays wich appear under the title *Welcome to the Moon*.

Applause presents Volume One of Mr. Shanley's complete work as the inaugural volume of its Contemporary Masters series.

ISBN: 1–55783–099–1 $14.95 paper

WILLIAM GOLDMAN
FIVE SCREENPLAYS
WITH ESSAYS

ALL THE PRESIDENT'S MEN
Academy Award® Winner
"...**RIVETING SCREEN ADAPTATION** by William Goldman...a breathtaking adventure...an unequivocal smash-hit—the thinking man's *Jaws*."
—Vincent Canby, *THE NEW YORK TIMES*

HARPER
"**GOLDMAN'S SCRIPT CRACKLES, SNAPS AND POPS** with all sorts of familiar surprised and bubbles of biting dialogue." —*THE NEW YORK TIMES*

THE GREAT WALDO PEPPER
"Screenwriter William Goldman characteristically cooks up **ONE CLEVER REVERSAL OF EXPECTATIONS AFTER ANOTHER** to keep his lightweight vehicle airborne."
—*NEWSWEEK*

MAGIC
"AN ATMOSPHERIC THRILLER ... **AN ABSORBING CHARACTER STUDY.**" —*VARIETY*

MAVERICK
"Fast, funny and full of straight ahead action and tongue-in-cheek jokes...a smart, new-fangled Maverick."
—Caryn James, THE NEW YORK TIMES

CLOTH • ISBN 1-55783-266-8
PAPER • ISBN 1-55783-362-1

MASTERGATE
&
POWER FAILURE
2 Political Satires for the stage
by Larry Gelbart

REVIEWS OF *MASTERGATE*:

"IF GEORGE ORWELL WERE A GAG WRITER, HE COULD HAVE WRITTEN *MASTERGATE*. Larry Gelbart's scathingly funny takeoff on the Iran-Contra hearings [is] a spiky cactus flower in the desert of American political theatre."
—Jack Kroll, NEWSWEEK

"Larry Gelbart has written what may be the MOST PENETRATING, AND IS SURELY THE FUNNIEST, exegesis of the Iran-Contra fiasco to date."
—Frank Rick, THE NEW YORK TIMES

REVIEWS OF *POWER FAILURE*:

"There is in his broad etching ALL THE ETHICAL OUTRAGE OF AN ARTHUR MILLER KVETCHING. AND, OH, SO MUCH MORE FUN!"
—Carolyn Clay, THE BOSTON PHOENIX

Larry Gelbart, the creator of M*A*S*H, is also the author of *SLY FOX*, *A FUNNY THING HAPPENED ON THE WAY TO THE FORUM* and *CITY OF ANGELS*.

paper • 1-55783-177-7 • $10.95

A LITTLE NIGHT MUSIC

Music and Lyrics by Stephen Sondheim, Book by Hugh Wheeler

"Heady, civilized, sophisticated and enchanting. Good God! An adult musical."
—Clive Barnes, The New York Times

Cloth $19.95 ISBN: 1-55783-070-3 • Paper $12.95 ISBN: 1-55783-069-X

A FUNNY THING HAPPENED ON THE WAY TO THE FORUM

Music & Lyrics by Stephen Sondheim, Book by Burt Shevelove & Larry Gelbart

"A good, clean, dirty show! Bring back the belly laughs"   —Time
"It's funny, true nonsense! A merry good time!"   —Walter Kerr, Herald Tribune

Cloth $19.95 ISBN: 1-55783-064-9 • Paper $12.95 ISBN: 1-55783-063-0

SUNDAY IN THE PARK WITH GEORGE

Music and Lyrics by Stephen Sondheim, Book by James Lapine

"*Sunday* is itself a modernist creation, perhaps the first truly modernist work of musical theatre that Broadway has produced."

—Frank Rich, The New York Times

Cloth $19.95 ISBN: 1-55783-068-1 • Paper $12.95 ISBN: 1-55783-067-3

SWEENEY TODD

Music and Lyrics by Stephen Sondheim, Book by Hugh Wheeler

"There is more artistic energy, creative personality, and plain excitement than in a dozen average musicals."   —Richard Eder, The New York Times

Cloth $19.95 ISBN: 1-55783-066-5 • Paper $12.95 ISBN: 1-55783-065-7

Now also available all in one volume!

FOUR BY SONDHEIM

Cloth $35 ISBN: 1-55783-407-5